NIETZSCHE, GODFATHER OF FASCISM?

NIETZSCHE, GODFATHER OF FASCISM?

ON THE USES AND ABUSES OF A PHILOSOPHY

EDITED BY
JACOB GOLOMB AND ROBERT S. WISTRICH

PRINCETON UNIVERSITY PRESS
PRINCETON AND OXFORD

Published by
Princeton University Press,
41 William Street,
Princeton, New Jersey 08540

In the United Kingdom:
Princeton University Press,
3 Market Place,
Woodstock, Oxfordshire OX20 1SY

Library of Congress Cataloging-in-Publication Data
Nietzsche, godfather of fascism? : on the uses and abuses of a philosophy /
edited by Jacob Golomb and Robert S. Wistrich.
     p. cm.
  Includes bibliographical references and index.
  ISBN 0-691-00709-8 (alk. paper) — ISBN 0-691-00710-1 (pbk. : alk.
paper)
  1. Nietzsche, Friedrich Wilhelm, 1844–1900.   2. National socialism and
philosophy.   3. Fascism.   I. Golomb, Jacob.   II. Wistrich, Robert S.,
1945–
B3317 .N4939 2002
193 — dc21   2001055185

British Library Cataloging-in-Publication Data is available

This book has been composed in Sabon.

Printed on acid-free paper. ∞

www.puppress.princeton.edu

Printed in the United States of America

10 9 8 7 6 5 4 3 2 1

Power makes *stupid. . . . Deutschland, Deutschland über alles* —
I fear that was the end of German philosophy.
— Nietzsche, *Twilight of the Idols*

You say it is the good cause that hallows even war? I say unto you: it is
the good war that hallows any cause. War and courage have accomplished more great things than love of the neighbor.
— *Thus Spoke Zarathustra*

The secret for harvesting from existence the greatest fruitfulness and the
greatest enjoyment is — to *live dangerously*!
— *The Gay Science*

Vivi pericolosamente!
— Benito Mussolini, August 1924

CONTENTS

ACKNOWLEDGMENTS

The editors warmly thank Brigitta van Rheinberg for her invaluable encouragement, help, and advice over and above the call of duty, in seeing this project through from its beginnings. We are especially grateful to all the contributors for their cooperation and willingness to accept the many queries, requests, and occasional nagging demands of the editors. The observations and helpful suggestions of the two anonymous readers also proved useful.

Finally, we would like acknowledge the professionalism and acumen of the staff at Princeton University Press, especially Linda Truilo, who saw this volume through to its happy conclusion.

A NOTE ON SOURCES AND LIST OF ABBREVIATIONS

For the convenience of readers, most of the contributors have, wherever possible, followed the most accessible English-language translations and editions of Nietzsche's major works—those by Walter Kaufmann and R. J. Hollingdale (for details see the section "Works of Nietzsche Cited" at the end of this volume). All quotations from Nietzsche's writings are given within the text and identified by the use of the acronyms of their English titles, followed by Arabic numbers referring to the paragraphs or sections in which the passages appear. Where appropriate, Roman numerals are used to indicate the parts of the works in which they are to be found. Citations from his other works and letters are based on the texts as they appear in the Colli-Montinari *Kritische Gesamtausgabe* (*KGA*), or *Kritische Studienausgabe* (*KSA*), and *Sämtliche Briefe: Kritische Studienausgabe* (*KGB*) unless otherwise noted.

A	*The Antichrist*
BGE	*Beyond Good and Evil*
BT	*The Birth of Tragedy*
CW	*The Case of Wagner*
D	*Daybreak*
EH	*Ecce Homo*
GM	*On the Genealogy of Morals*
GS	*The Gay Science*
HH	*Human, All Too Human*
NCW	*Nietzsche contra Wagner*
TI	*Twilight of the Idols*
UM	*Untimely Meditations*
WP	*The Will to Power*
Z	*Thus Spoke Zarathustra*

CONTRIBUTORS

MENAHEM BRINKER is Professor of Hebrew Literature and Philosophy at the Hebrew University of Jerusalem and Henry B. Crown Professor of Modern Hebrew Studies at the University of Chicago. He is the author of five books in Hebrew on philosophy and literary theory, aesthetics, and modern Hebrew literature. His forthcoming book is *Last Jews or Modern Hebrews* (Yale UP).

DANIEL W. CONWAY is Professor of Philosophy and Director of Graduate Studies in Philosophy at The Pennsylvania State University. He has published widely on topics in political philosophy, contemporary European philosophy, and nineteenth-century philosophy. He is the author of *Nietzsche and the Political* (Routledge, 1997) and *Nietzsche's Dangerous Game* (Cambridge UP, 1997).

STANLEY CORNGOLD is Professor of German and Comparative Literature at Princeton University. He has written *Complex Pleasure: Forms of Feeling in German Literature* (Stanford UP, 1998), *The Fate of the Self: German Writers and French Theory* (Columbia UP, 1986; Duke UP, 1994), *Borrowed Lives* (SUNY Press, 1991), and *Franz Kafka: The Necessity of Form* (Cornell UP, 1988).

KURT RUDOLF FISCHER is Honorary Professor in the Institute für Philosophie, University of Vienna. He is the author of *Nietzsche und das 20. Jahrhundert*, *Philosophie aus Wien*, and *Aufsätze zur Anglo-Amerikanischen und Österreichischen Philosophie*, and the editor of *Österreichische Philosophie von Brentano bis Wittgenstein*.

JACOB GOLOMB teaches philosophy at the Hebrew University of Jerusalem and serves as the director of its Center for Austrian Studies. His books include *Nietzsche's Enticing Psychology of Power* (Hebrew University Magnes Press, 1989), *Introduction to Philosophies of Existence* (Ministry of Defence Press, 1990), and *In Search of Authenticity* (Routledge, 1995). Among his edited works is *Nietzsche and Jewish Culture* (Routledge, 1997). He is coeditor of *Nietzsche and Depth Psychology* (SUNY Press, 1999). His forthcoming book is *Nietzsche in Zion* (Cornell UP).

ROBERT C. HOLUB teaches German intellectual, cultural, and literary history in the German Department of the University of California, Berkeley. Among his numerous publications are *Reception Theory* (Routledge, 1984), *Reflections of Realism* (Wayne State UP, 1991), *Jürgen Habermas* (Routledge, 1991), and *Crossing Borders* (U of Wisconsin Press, 1991).

BEREL LANG is Professor of Humanities at Trinity College, Hartford Connecticut. His writings include *The Anatomy of Philosophical Style* (Blackwell, 1990), *Act and Idea in the Nazi Genocide* (U of Chicago Press, 1990), *The Future of the Holocaust* (Cornell UP, 1999), and *Holocaust Representation: Art within the Limits of History and Ethics* (Johns Hopkins UP, 2000).

The Late **WOLFGANG MÜLLER-LAUTER** was Professor Emeritus in the Department of Protestant Theology at Humboldt University in Berlin, was coeditor of *Nietzsche Studien* and of the de Gruyter critical edition of Nietzsche's complete works. His books include *Nietzsche: His Philosophy of Contradictions and the Contradictions of His Philosophy* (1971; Engl. ed., University of Illinois Press, 1999). His collected articles *Über Werden und Wille zur Macht* and *Über Freiheit und Chaos* were published by de Gruyter in 1999. He passed away on August 9, 2001.

ALEXANDER NEHAMAS is Edmund N. Carpenter II Professor in the Humanities and Professor of Philosophy at Princeton University. He is the author of *Nietzsche: Life as Literature* (Harvard UP, 1985) and *The Art of Living* (U of California Press, 1998). He is also the editor, with David J. Furley, of *Aristotle's Rhetoric: Philosophical Essays* (Princeton UP, 1994), and the author, with Paul Woodruff, of translations of and commentaries on Plato's *Phaedrus* (Hackett, 1995) and *Symposium* (Hackett, 1989).

DAVID OHANA is a historian of European Ideas and teaches at the Ben-Gurion University. He has written many articles on Nietzsche's reception in European and Zionist thought. Among his books in Hebrew are *The Order of the Nihilists* (1993), *The Promethean Passion* (2000), and *A Humanist in the Sun* (2000). Ohana is a coeditor with Robert S. Wistrich of *The Shaping of Israeli Identity* (Frank Cass, 1995) and the longer Hebrew version, *Myth and Memory* (Van Leer, 1996).

RODERICK STACKELBERG is the Robert K. and Ann J. Powers Professor of the Humanities at Gonzaga University in Spokane, Washington. He is the author of *Hitler's Germany: Origins, Interpretations, Legacies* (Routledge, 1999) and of several articles on Nietzsche, National Socialist ideology, and the *Historikerstreit.*

MARIO SZNAJDER, teaches in the Department of Political Sciences at the Hebrew University of Jerusalem. He is coauthor of *Naissance de l'idéologie fasciste* (Fayard, 1989), translated, into English as *The Birth of Fascist Ideology* (Princeton UP, 1994), and of *The Legacy of Human Rights Violations in the Southern Cone: Argentina, Chile and Uruguay* (Oxford UP, 1999).

GEOFFREY WAITE is Associate Professor of German Studies at Cornell University, teaching philosophy, literature, literary theory, and visual studies. His recent book is *Nietzsche's Corps/e: Aesthetics, Politics, Prophecy, Or, The Spectacular Technoculture of Everyday Life* (Duke UP, 2nd ed., 1999). He has also written on Althusser, Cassirer, Cronenberg, Feininger, Gramsci, Heidegger, Hölderlin, Lacan, Lenin, The Sex Pistols, Spinoza, and Velázquez.

ROBERT S. WISTRICH holds the Neuberger Chair of Modern European History at the Hebrew University of Jerusalem and is Academic Chairman of its Center for Austrian Studies. Among his many books are *Trotsky: Fate of a Revolutionary* (Stein and Day, 1979), *Who's Who in Nazi Germany* (Routledge, 1982, 1995), *Hitler's Apocalypse* (St. Martin's Press, 1986), *The Jews of Vienna in the Age of Franz Joseph* (Oxford UP, 1989), which won the Austrian state prize for history, and *Antisemitism: The Longest Hatred* (Patheon, 1991). His most recent book is *Hitler and the Holocaust* (Random House, 2001).

YIRMIYAHU YOVEL is Professor Emeritus in the Department of Philosophy of the Hebrew University of Jerusalem and Hans Jonas Professor at the Graduate Faculty, the New School for Social Research, New York. His publications include *Kant and the Philosophy of History* (Princeton UP, 1980, 1988) and *Spinoza and Other Heretics* (Princeton UP, 1989, 1992). Yovel is also the author of numerous essays and the editor of various volumes on philosophy. In 2000 he won the Israeli Prize for philosophy.

NIETZSCHE, GODFATHER OF FASCISM?

Introduction
Jacob Golomb and Robert S. Wistrich

Nietzsche and fascism? Is it not almost a contradiction in terms? What can Nietzsche have in common with this murderous ideology? The central ideal of Nietzsche's philosophy was the individual and his freedom to shape his own character and destiny. The German philosopher was frequently described as the "radical aristocrat" of the spirit because he abhorred mass culture and strove to cultivate a special kind of human being, the *Übermensch*, endowed with exceptional spiritual and mental qualities. What can such a thinker have in common with National Socialism's manipulation of the masses for chauvinistic goals that swallowed up the personalities, concerns, and life of the individual?

In 1934, Adolf Hitler paid a much publicized visit to the Nietzsche archives at Weimar. He had gone at the insistent request of its director, Elisabeth Förster-Nietzsche (sister of the long-deceased German philosopher), and he was accompanied by his personal photographer, Heinrich Hoffmann. The main purpose of the visit, it seems, was to enable Hoffmann to take a picture of Hitler contemplating the bust of Nietzsche, which stood in the reception room. Perhaps appropriately, only half of the philosopher's head was shown in the picture, which duly appeared in the German press with a caption that read, "The Führer before the bust of the German philosopher whose ideas have fertilized two great popular movements: the National Socialism of Germany and the Fascist movement of Italy."

Although Benito Mussolini was certainly familiar with Nietzsche's writings and was a long-time admirer of the philosopher, Hitler's own connection with Nietzsche remains uncertain. As a soldier during the First World War, he had carried the works of Schopenhauer and not those of Nietzsche in his backpack. There is no reference to Nietzsche in *Mein Kampf* (though there is to Schopenhauer), and in *Hitler's Table Talk*, he refers only indirectly to Nietzsche, saying: "In our part of the world, the Jews would have immediately eliminated Schopenhauer, Nietzsche, and Kant. If the Bolsheviks had dominion over us for two hundred years, what works of our past would be handed on to posterity? Our great men would fall into oblivion, or else they'd be presented to future generations as criminals and bandits."[1]

Thus the picture of Hitler gazing at Nietzsche's bust had more to do with a carefully orchestrated cult, one aspect of which was to connect National Socialism with the philosopher's legacy, at least by association. On October 1944, celebrating the hundredth anniversary of the birth of Nietzsche, Alfred Rosenberg, the leading Nazi party ideologist, delivered an official speech in Weimar, seeking to reinforce this impression: "In a truly historical sense, the National Socialist movement eclipses the rest of the world, much as Nietzsche, the individual, eclipsed the powers of his times."[2] Of course, Nietzsche was not the only German philosopher invoked as a spiritual guide and forerunner of the Nazi revolution, but his "Nazification" in the course of the Third Reich is a historical fact that cannot be denied, though it is more open to interpretation than is sometimes assumed.

The intriguing question that lies at the heart of this original collection of essays is how Nietzsche came to acquire the deadly "honor" of being considered the philosopher of the Third Reich and whether such claims have any justification. What was it in Nietzsche that attracted such a Nazi appropriation in the first place? To what extent is it legitimate to view Nietzsche as a protofascist thinker? Does it make any sense to hold him in some way responsible for the horrors of Auschwitz? These issues are not as clear-cut as they may seem, and though they have attracted much polemical heat, they have not received any truly systematic treatment. In this volume, we have attempted to fill that gap in as concise and comprehensive a way as possible by turning to a variety of distinguished historians, Nietzsche scholars, philosophers, and historians of ideas. It was clear from the outset that we could not expect, nor indeed did we strive for, unanimous conclusions on the thorny, complex, and emotionally charged question of Nietzsche and fascism. A whole range of views is presented here that attempts to do justice in different ways to the ambiguity and richness of Nietzsche's thought. Nietzsche encouraged his readers to shift their intellectual viewpoints and be willing to experience even radically incompatible perspectives. Thus by dealing with the subject matter of this collection from two different perspectives—that of philosophers and of historians—we hope that a Nietzschean spirit of intellectual tolerance will be reflected in this volume.

Nietzsche's life and thought will never be reducible to a single constituency or political ideology, as this volume makes plain. The ambiguities and contradictions in his work as well as his elusive, aphoristic style lend themselves to a wide range of meanings and a multiplicity of interpretations. Nevertheless, while acknowledging this diversity, the editors cannot in good conscience be exempted from the challenge of offering some guidelines regarding the central issues raised by a book about Nietzsche and fascism, even if the title (as seems appropriate in this case) ends with a question mark.

Nietzsche was clearly an elitist who believed in the right to rule of a "good and healthy aristocracy," one that would, if necessary, be ready to sacrifice untold numbers of human beings. He sometimes wrote as if nations primarily existed for the sake of producing a few "great men," who could not be expected to show consideration for "normal humanity." Not suprisingly, in the light of the cruel century that has just ended, one is bound to regard such statements with grave misgivings. From Mussolini and Hitler to Stalin, Mao, Pol Pot, and Saddam Hussein, the last eighty years have been riddled with so-called political geniuses imagining that they were "beyond good and evil" and free of any moral constraints. One has to ask if there is not something in Nietzsche's philosophy with its uninhibited cultivation of a heroic individualism and the will to power, which may have tended to favor the fascist ethos. Musssolini, for example, raised the Nietzschean formulation "live dangerously" (*vivi pericolosamente*) to the status of a fascist slogan. His reading of Nietzsche was one factor in converting him from Marxism to a philosophy of sacrifice and warlike deeds in defense of the fatherland. In this mutation, Mussolini was preceded by Gabriele d'Annunzio, whose passage from aestheticism to the political activism of a new, more virile and warlike age, was (as Mario Sznajder points out in his essay) greatly influenced by Nietzsche. Equally, there were other representatives of the First World War generation, like the radical German nationalist writer, Ernst Jünger, who would find in Nietzsche's writings a legitimization of the warrior ethos (as David Ohana makes clear).

There have also been Marxist critics like George Lukács, who saw in Nietzsche's philosophy nothing more than an ideological apologia for the rapacious plunder of German capitalist imperialism and a particularly destructive form of irrationalism. Lukács insisted both on the reactionary coherence of Nietzsche's "system" and on the "barren chaos" of his arbitrary language, singling him out as one of the most dangerous "intellectual class-enemies" of socialism. Lukács's own miserable record as an apologist (for the crimes of Stalinism), gave his one-sided reading of Nietzsche (which equated hostility to egalitarian socialism with fascist imperialism) transparently propagandist coloring, yet it is an interpretation that had considerable influence in its day.

Many commentators have raised the question as to whether the vulgar exploitation of Nietzsche by fascists, militarists, and Nazis could indeed be altogether arbitrary. While almost any philosophy can be propagandistically abused (as Hans Sluga has shown, Kant was a particular favorite among academic philosophers of the Third Reich!), Nietzsche's pathos, his imaginative excesses as well as his image as a prophet-seer and creator of myths, seems especially conducive to such abuse by fascists. The radical manner in which Nietzsche thrust himself against the boundaries of conventional (Judeo-Christian) morality and dramatically proclaimed that God (meaning the bourgeois Christian faith of the nineteenth century) was dead, undoubtedly appealed to something in Nazism that wished to transgress and transcend all existing taboos. The totalitarianism of the twentieth century (of both the Right and Left) presupposed a breakdown of all authority and moral norms, of which Nietzsche was indeed a clear-sighted prophet, precisely because he had diagnosed nihilism as the central problem of his society—that of fin de siècle Europe. For him there was no way back to the old moral certainties about "good" and "evil," no way to regain firm ground under one's feet. Humanity, long before 1914, had (spiritually speaking) already burned its bridges. Nietzsche was convinced that there was no escape from the "nihilism" of the age, except to go forward into a more "perfect nihilism," to use the term of Wolfgang Müller-Lauter in this volume. Nietzsche believed that only by honestly facing the stark truth that there is no truth, no goal, no value or meaning in itself, could one pave the way for a real intellectual liberation and a revaluation of all values. Nietzsche was more a herald and prophet of the crisis of values out of which Nazism emerged, rather than a godfather of the century's fascist movements per se.

Much of the confusion identifying Nietzsche with National Socialism can be traced back to the disastrous role of his sister Elisabeth Förster-Nietzsche (married to a prominent German anti-Semite) who took control of his manuscripts in the 1890s, when he was mentally and physically incapacitated. Already in the 1920s she promoted her brother as the philosopher of fascism, sending her warmest good wishes to Benito Mussolini as "the inspired reawakener of aristocratic values in Nietzsche's sense"; similarly, she invited Hitler several times to the archive in

Weimar, even giving him the symbolic gift of Nietzsche's walking stick in 1934. Nazi propaganda encouraged such (mis)appropriation, for example, by publishing popular and inexpensive anthologies and short collections of Nietzsche's sayings, which were then misused in their truncated form to promote militarism, toughness, and Germanic values. Alfred Bäumler, a professor of philosophy in Berlin after 1933, on seeing German youth march under the swastika banner could even write, "[A]nd when we call '*Heil* Hitler!' to this youth then we are greeting at the same time Friedrich Nietzsche with that call." Needless to say, Bäumler played a key role in the increasingly shameless appropriation of Nietzsche as a philosopher of the so-called Nordic race, a kind of intellectual Siegfried — anti-Roman, anti-Christian (which was true), and thoroughly in tune with the spirit of 1914. Aware that Nietzsche had no theory of *volk* or race, Bäumler nonetheless concocted a spurious link between the philosopher's individual struggle for integrity and Nazi collectivism. With the same sleight of hand, he could explain away Nietzsche's break with Wagner merely as a product of envy and dismiss his tirades against the Germans as expressing no more than his disapproval of certain non-Germanic elements in their character.

No less convoluted were the efforts of the Nazi commentator Heinrich Härtle in his 1937 book *Nietzsche und der Nationalsozialismus*, where he presented the philosopher "as a great ally in the present spiritual warfare." Härtle realized that Nietzsche's advocacy of European unity, his elitism and individualism, his critique of the state, his approval of race-mixing, and his anti-anti-Semitism were incompatible with Nazi ideology. By relativizing these shortcomings as minor issues (in the case of the Jews, he simply quoted those instances — comparatively few in number — where Nietzsche seemed to be attacking them) and as reflections of a different political environment in the nineteenth century, Härtle could present Nietzsche as a precursor of Hitler.

Sadly, such crude distortions were echoed in Allied war propaganda and in newspaper headlines in Britain and the United States, which (continuing the traditions of the First World War) sometimes depicted the "insane philosopher" as the source of a ruthless German barbarism and as Hitler's favorite author. Phrases torn out of their context such as the "superman," (or "Overman"), the "blond beast," "master morality," or the "will to power" were all too easily turned into slogans (even by distinguished philosophers like Sir Karl Popper[3]) to demonstrate Nietzsche's imagined identification with German militarism and imperialism, though nothing had been further from his mind.

Before 1939 not everyone shared this increasingly broad consensus, which saw Nietzsche as the spiritual godfather of fascism and Nazism. Opponents of Nazism like the German philosophers Karl Jaspers and

Karl Löwith sought to invalidate the official Nazi appropriation of Nietzsche in the 1930s. Together with a number of French intellectuals, they contributed to a special issue of *Acéphale* published in January 1937 and entitled *"Réparation à Nietzsche."* The most prominent of the French antifascist Nietzscheans was the left-wing existentialist thinker Georges Bataille, who sought to rescue Nietzsche by demonstrating the German philosopher's abhorrence of pan-Germanism, racism and the rabid anti-Semitism of Hitler's followers. In the United States, the most eminent postwar advocate of a "liberal" Nietzsche was Walter Kaufmann, an American scholar in Princeton who provided many of the most authoritative translations into English of Nietzsche's writings. His *Nietzsche: Philosopher, Psychologist, Antichrist* (1950) became a standard work in the critical rehabilitation of Nietzsche in the postwar English-speaking world, seeking to dissociate him from any connection with Social Darwinism and the intellectual origins of National Socialism.

One of Kaufmann's virtues was to document the scale of Nietzsche's contempt for the racist anti-Semites of his generation, such as the schoolteacher Bernhard Förster (his sister's husband), Theodor Fritsch, Paul de Lagarde, and Eugen Dühring. If Nazism conceived of Jewry as an inferior race of "subhumans" marked for annihilation, then Nietzsche's own writings show, as both Yirmiyahu Yovel and Robert Wistrich have argued, that the Jews represented for him a kind of spiritual crystallization of what he understood by the *Übermensch* (Overman) of the future.

At first sight, this sharp rejection of anti-Semitism might seem a good enough reason to answer negatively and decisively the question concerning Nietzsche's responsibility for Nazism. Certainly, a thinker who held a high opinion of Jewish qualities, looked to them as a spearhead for his own free-thinking Dionysian "revaluation of all values," and sought their full integration into European society could hardly be blamed for the Nazi Holocaust. On the other hand, in his sweeping rejection of Judeo-Christian values (as they were mirrored in German Protestantism) Nietzsche constantly referred to their origin in the sublime "vengefulness" of Israel and its alleged exploitation of so-called movements of "decadence" (like early Christianity, liberalism, and socialism) to ensure its own self-preservation and survival (Menahem Brinker). Even though Nietzsche's prime target was clearly Christianity—which he also blamed for the suffering of the Jews—the source of the infection ultimately lay in that fateful transvaluation of values initiated by priestly Judaism two millennia ago. It was a selective reading of this Nietzschean indictment of Judeo-Christianity that led the late Jacob Talmon, an Israeli historian, some forty years ago to see in Nietzsche a major intellectual signpost on the road to Auschwitz. Moreover, even when describing the "Judaization" of the world in terms that mixed admiration with disapprobation, Nietzsche seemed inadvertently to be feeding the myth of Jewish power, so beloved of Christian and racist anti-Semites. Though his intentions were profoundly hostile to anti-Semitism, this provocative technique was undoubtedly a dangerous game to play. While it would be senseless to hold Nietzsche responsible for such distortions, one can find troubling echoes of a vulgarized and debased Nietzscheanism in the later diatribes of Hitler, Himmler, Bormann, and Rosenberg against Judeo-Christianity.

The case of Nietzsche is a good illustration of the pitfalls in an overly schematic approach to intellectual history that takes particular strands in a thinker's oeuvre and seeks to fit them into more general constructs like fascism or National Socialism. On the basis of Nietzsche's declared hostility to Christianity, liberal democracy, and socialism, it is possible to see him as a precursor of the fascist synthesis. Some aspects of his admiration for ancient Greek culture and for "Romanitas" were used by both fascists and Nazis, who thoroughly distorted his philosophical intent. Though he took the ancient Greeks as cultural models, he did not subscribe to their self-conception as a "breed of masters," which prompted them to brand non-Greeks as "barbarians," fit only to be slaves. Indeed, all forms of xenophobia were profoundly alien to Nietzsche's outlook, none more so than the hot-headed nationalistic rivalries so typical of the European nation-state system into which he was born. This explains his revulsion from the German nationalism that had come into vogue in the 1880s following the unification of Germany and the success of Bismarckian power politics. In fact, Nietzsche was in many respects the least patriotic and least German of his philosophical contemporaries in the Second Reich.

This was one of the major reasons for his abandonment of Wagner and the Bayreuth Festival, which had degenerated into a chauvinist celebration of "German Art," "German virtues," and a so-called "Germanic essence," deeply contaminated by "the humbug of races" and anti-Semitism. The fact that the Wagnerites gave a romantic Christian veneer to their cult of "Germanism" further provoked his antagonism. Nietzsche reserved a special animus for the ways in which the Christian churches in Germany had allowed themselves to be swept along by the national intoxication after 1870. Above all he denounced the corruption of the German "spirit" by the new practitioners of power politics. Hence it was one of the worst Nazi distortions of Nietzsche's philosophy to claim that his notion of "the will to power" was consonant with what was being advocated in the Third Reich.

Far from relating to nationalist obsessions, Nietzsche had asserted a life-affirming outlook that sought to empower the individual to over-come his or her limitations by questioning all our assumptions concern-ing truth, logic, beliefs, culture, values, and history. As Jacob Golomb has shown, what Nietzsche prized above all was spiritual power (*Macht*) not the brute political force (*Kraft*) that he denounced with all the sarcasm at his command. This spiritual power of the sovereign, emancipated individual who is "master of a free will" involved a long and difficult process of sublimation, which would eventually culminate in self-mastery. It was a vision fundamentally antithetical to the totali-tarian collectivism of both the Right and the Left.

Nietzsche's indictment of the Christian and nationalist Right as well as of the official *Machtpolitik* and its consequences for German culture, was unequivocal. The break with Wagner is especially illuminating be-cause the Wagnerian ideology and the cult that developed in Bayreuth was a much more real precursor of *völkisch* and Hitlerian ideas. Once Nietzsche had thrown off the romantic nationalism of his early days, his devastating critique of Wagner — prophetic in many ways of what was to come — revealed his remarkably penetrating insight into its dangerous illusions. National Socialism could plausibly derive inspiration from Wagner but it could only use Nietzsche by fundamentally twisting his philosophy.

Nietzsche was undeniably mobilized by the Nazis as several historical essays in the present collection demonstrate. So what exactly was the role of Nietzsche and his writings in this process? Is Martin Jay right to claim in his *Fin-de-Siècle Socialism* (1988) that "while it may be ques-tionable to saddle Marx with responsibility for the Gulag archipelago or blame Nietzsche for Auschwitz, it is nevertheless true that their writ-ings could be misread as justifications for these horrors in a way that . . . John Stuart Mill or Alexis de Toqueville could not" (33). Even Jac-ques Derrida, despite insisting that "Nietzsche's utterances are not the same as those of the Nazi ideologists and not only because the latter grossly caricature the former to the point of apishness," cannot refrain from wondering, in reference to Nietzsche's case, "how and why what is so naively called a falsification was possible (one can't falsify anything)."[4]

Some of the essays in the present collection try to answer this intrigu-ing question. The enigma becomes even more perplexing in an argu-ment in which a distinguished scholar absolves Nietzsche from any re-sponsibility for the atrocities performed by the Nazis, yet holds him accountable for their misinterpretations. His claim is that Nietzsche had anticipated being misinterpreted as a fascist without doing enough to prevent these misinterpretations. Such a view is presented in Berel Lang's essay. Yet, in his 1990 book, Lang asserts that "to reconstruct in the imagination the events leading up to the Nazi genocide against the Jews without the name or presence of Nietzsche is to be compelled to change almost nothing else in that pattern."[5] So who is right? Lang ten years ago or the essay we have included? Can we, indeed ever reach a definite and sound judgment concerning Nietzsche's accountability, responsibility, or even culpability for Nazi misappropriations of his writings?

The essays below strive to provide us with some answers. But other, even more crucial questions hover over this issue. Was Nietzsche not trying to convince an entire culture and society to cultivate a new kind of man and mode of life (as the Nazis were also trying to do)? Has not the fact that he had no normative ethics, nor normative politics, facilitated his criminal misappropriation? Should we not consider his attempt to overthrow the values of the Enlightenment and eradicate the foundations of Christian morality an extremely dangerous maneuver, especially when he could clearly hear the loud strains of Wagnerian music and the nationalism of Bayreuth, which for many philosophers and historians already seems like a prefiguration of Nazism (see Yovel's essay in this volume)? Brinker and others in this book think that Nietzsche did have some responsibility for Nazi crimes—an argument that has also been made by Steven Aschheim in his study of the Nietzschean legacy in Germany. Many others, including both editors of this volume, think differently.

To tackle this question as soberly and objectively as possible requires going beyond a common defense of Nietzsche in the postwar scholarship. Walter Kaufmann and others were trying to sever Nietzsche altogether from Nazi ideology by stressing the fact that he was fundamentally an apolitical thinker who rejected pan-Germanism and anti-Semitism. But it does not necessarily follow that since Nietzsche detested German and other nationalistic attitudes, his teaching was essentially a nonpolitical one. Tempting as it may be to cleanse his thought from the taint of any political ideology, especially that of fascism, it is in fact a misguided strategy. For it is precisely by emphasizing the political import and content of Nietzsche's philosophy that one can put into a sharper relief his "antifascist" orientation.

The argument that presented Nietzsche as a staunch opponent of the nation-state was especially prevalent among his advocates during the first twenty years after the second World War. They wished to rehabilitate his reputation by denying any trace of resemblance between his writings and those who did almost everything to make them sound compatible with *Mein Kampf*. As a result, these apologists performed a sweeping depoliticization of Nietzsche's thought.[6] One of the most influential of these commentators was the previously mentioned Walter

Kaufmann. Against the generalizing accusations of Crane Brinton (1940, 1941) and others, that Nietzsche was the godfather of Nazism, Kaufmann presented the leitmotif of Nietzsche's life and thought as that of "the antipolitical individual who seeks self-perfection far from the modern world."[7]

It is noteworthy that much contemporary research — which has been less vulnerable to the atmosphere of suspicion that loomed over Nietzsche by the end of the Second World War — tended instead to emphasize the significance of politics in his philosophy. Such scholars sensibly conceded that even if one cannot find in Nietzsche's antisystematic writings any definite political thought, his radical discussions of morality and concept of the "modern man" had a far reaching political significance. It was within a definite cultural and political context that Nietzsche sought to attain his ideal of a unique and authentic individual cultivating Dionysian values.[8]

Nietzsche did, however, reject the view that one can justify or rationally derive a political order from certain universalistic principles. It is also true that during his life Nietzsche did not publish anything comparable to Spinoza's *Tractatus Politicus*, which was specifically dedicated to political issues. Of course, there were always political implications in writings like his *Genealogy of Morals*, which critically examined the moral values prevalent in modern society. Moreover, there was an early unpublished composition by Nietzsche (from 1872) that analyses the "Greek state," and we also have many long passages from his published works that squarely deal with politics.[9] We should not forget also that the last sentence Nietzsche had a chance to write before his final collapse did have a pronounced political connotation: "*Wilhelm, Bismarck und alle Antisemiten abgeschafft*" ("Wilhelm, Bismarck and all anti-Semites abolished").

It is worthwhile in this context to examine more closely Nietzsche's so-called confession that he was the "last *antipolitical* German". The German equivalent to this term is *antipolitisch* which is different from *unpolitisch* — referring to somebody who is utterly indifferent to politics. Indeed Nietzsche, in his *Twilight of the Idols*, in a section entitled "What the Germans Lack," distinguished between both of these attitudes to politics by contrasting the Bismarckian modern *Reich* that embodies a strong political power (*Grossmacht*) to a society that is essentially *antipolitisch*. The latter is a social framework that objects to using political force (*Kraft*) to promote its culture (and Nietzsche in this context gives as an example France, which he calls the "*Culturmacht*"). None of this made Nietzsche into an antipolitical person, let alone an anarchist. On the contrary, as a great advocate of human creativity, he could see the need for statehood and a civil society in whose framework creativity might take place and flourish. Nietzsche distinguished sharply between the more sublime spiritual and mental powers of individuals (or entire peoples) who generate and produce sublime cultures, and the physical or political force that found expression in overpowering *Kraft* or *Gewalt*. Possibly because Hegel, whom Nietzsche criticized in his writings, regarded the Prussian state of the nineteenth century as the highest rational manifestation of the Universal *Geist*, Nietzsche felt particularly driven to attack this idea of statehood that had attracted his contemporaries. In any case, it is noteworthy that Nietzsche wished his publisher to remove the passage from his *Ecce Homo* where he supposedly declared himself to be a nonpolitical thinker.

In this passage, Nietzsche actually tries to distance himself not from politics as such (a move that would indeed have made him a nonpolitical thinker) but from the nationalist German politics which at that time raised its ugly head to the ominous tunes of "*Deutschland, Deutschland über Alles.*" With this militaristic slogan, Nietzsche observes, came "the end of German philosophy." Thus his statement that he was the "last *antipolitical* German" could itself be seen as a political statement that strove to overcome nationalism and racism—the "anticultural sickness par excellence." At any rate, in that passage which, as mentioned above, was not intended for publication, Nietzsche states that due to him being "the last *antipolitical* German" he is "perhaps more German than present-day Germans, mere citizens of the German Reich, could possibly be." Nietzsche thereby admits to belonging to the German nation but clearly distances himself (at least in his main compositions during the middle period of his career) from the German Reich of Bismarck. One could almost say that Nietzsche was an antipolitical thinker for political reasons and a political thinker for philosophical reasons, among them his attempt to foster the existential ideal of personal authenticity. In other words, Nietzsche had adopted an antipolitical attitude for reasons that had to do with the future of human culture, an issue which he called "*grosse Politik.*" For Nietzsche, politics becomes "grand" when it sustains and assists in cultivating human greatness and cultural grandeur. This "great politics" is fundamentally a politics of culture. And if we broadly define politics as an organized and orchestrated mobilization of human resources for the sake of a group or nation, Nietzsche, was indeed deeply engrossed with a politics that would embark on the cultural engineering of the entire society. We ought also to recall that Nietzsche saw in the genuine philosopher the creator of values for future society. Like Plato, Nietzsche envisaged the philosopher as a legislator. Hence Nietzsche is no less political than he is "immoral"—in a very moral and political sense.

Nietzsche abhorred the state only insofar as it became a goal in itself and ceased to function as a means for the advancement and education of autonomous and creative human beings. His preferred and most admired models to achieve the latter ideal were the Greek *polis*, the *virtu* of ancient Rome, and the worldly individualism of the Italian Renaissance — cultural patterns that had never made national supremacy the cornerstone of their ideal or regarded the ethnic attributes of their citizens as a mark of creativity or superiority. But there was nothing in his writings to suggest that Nietzsche objected in principle to "the political organization" of statehood as long as it did not become a Leviathan repressing genuine culture and persons.

Nietzsche did not reject the state where it was conducive to authentic life aspirations — a vital element in his philosophy. But once this legitimate (and "natural") creation changed its nature and became a manifestation of extreme nationalism that hindered free and spontaneous creativity, Nietzsche vehemently opposed it and wished to curb its destructive effects. Perhaps under the influence of Hobbes, Nietzsche would call this kind of state "the coldest of all cold monsters."[10] However, where it encouraged individuals to shape and form their cultural identity in an authentic way, Nietzsche regarded the state as a "blessed means."

An illuminating case in point is Nietzsche's attitude toward the aspirations of the Jewish people to establish an independent state for themselves.

For Nietzsche, the history of the Jewish people was a great enigma. He was mesmerized by the example of the Jews in the Diaspora and their ability to establish an effective spiritual-cultural kingdom in Europe without any state or territorial basis. Despite their lack of such support and other adverse and taxing conditions, they had manifested a "plentitude of power *without equal* to which only the nobility had access" (*GS*, 136). Nietzsche's reference to the Jews as the most "powerful race," in spite of their obvious political and physical weakness, clearly showed that there was nothing physical in the sense of brute force (*Kraft*) in the Nietzschean concept of power (*Macht*). One might even assert that Nietzsche's vision of a "new Europe" devoid of national boundaries and united not by a common economic interest and financial policy but by the wish to foster a Dionysian, genuinely creative culture was partially inspired by the example of European Jewry. Moreover, Nietzsche stressed the fact that even in the most adverse circumstances, the Jewish people "have never ceased to believe in their calling to the highest things" (*D*, 205). This abundance of spiritual power could best function creatively without national institutions. Hence Nietzsche bestowed on them a vital role in the extraterritorial and supranational Europe of the future when their plentiful power will flow "into great spiritual men and works . . . into an eternal blessing for Europe" (ibid.).

Echoing the Old Testament prophecy about Israel's magnificent future and its spectacular salvation, Nietzsche claimed that the Jews would once again become the "founders and creators of values." The creation of values is the most significant task in Nietzsche's philosophy, which always returns to the "transfiguration of values" and the nature of Western culture, in which the Jews are destined to play the major role as well as to serve as catalysts. Nietzsche's hope of mobilizing European Jewry to assist him in this transfiguration of values is the background for his emotional exclamation: "What a blessing a Jew is among Germans!" Nietzsche speculated in this context about the possible intermarriage of Jews with Germans or with the best "European nobility" for the sake of enriching a renewed European culture. Nietzsche, in this regard, obviously underestimated the strong and persistent reluctance of many Jews to fully assimilate into their Gentile environment. His views on intermarriage may seem especially perplexing in light of his admiration for Jewish "purity of race," uniqueness, and pride.

Nietzsche's cosmopolitan notion of "Jewish calling" might also seem to contradict the national aspirations of the emerging Zionist political movement. But a closer look suggests otherwise. There exists a record of Nietzsche's conversations in the winter of 1883–34 in Nice with Joseph Paneth — an Austrian Jewish intellectual who was also a good friend of Freud. We know that Nietzsche and Paneth discussed the possibility of the revival of Jewish people in Palestine and their "regeneration" there.[11] Nietzsche was apparently not at all happy about the prospect that the Jews might estrange themselves from their Jewish tradition and history to become completely assimilated within the European nations, since such "free spirits (*freie Geister*) detached from anything are dangerous and destructive" (Elisabeth Förster-Nietzsche, 486). He added that one should not ignore the "impact of nationality" and, according to Paneth, he was "quite disappointed that I did not wish to hear anything about the restoration of a Palestinian state" (ibid.). It is certainly possible to imagine Nietzsche supporting the idea of a return of the Jews to the land of Israel and statehood, which, especially in the times of the ancient Hebrews — as he had strongly argued — provided the earthly sources for their spiritual power and legacy. This hypothesis is in a sense implied by Nietzsche's statement that "in the hands of the Jewish priests the great age in the history of Israel became an age of decay; the Exile" (*A*, 26). Logically, one way out of this state of "decadence" would be the reestablishment of a Jewish state that revived the secular kingdom of the ancient Hebrews in Zion.

Such a development could also serve Nietzsche's project of European cultural rejuvenation since it would be quite possible to enlist the "new Israel" and its revival for the sake of "new Europe." Hence Nietzsche did not see any tension or contradiction between his plan for enlisting Jews for the sake of his new Europe and the Zionist program. He had heard about and was quite aware of the Zionist sentiments awakening among the European Jewry in the last years of his lucidity, and had never given any sign of disapproval or indignation as he did so loudly and eloquently against many other nationalist trends and movements of his time, including the cult of Wagner in Bayreuth. On the contrary, he enthusiastically embraced the future prospects (without excluding the national option) of the Jewish people.[12]

But what of Nietzsche's famous immoralism and rejection of traditional Judeo-Christian values? What of his *Lebensphilosophie* and thoughts about regeneration that at times seemed to envisage the "breeding" of a new elite that would eliminate all the decadent elements within European culture? Did the Nazis not draw some inspiration from his shattering of all moral taboos, his radical, experimental style of thinking, and his apocalyptic visions of the future? Certainly, there were National Socialists who tried to integrate Nietzsche into the straitjacket of their ideology and exploited his dangerous notion of degeneration. But without its biological racism and anti-Semitism, the Nazi worldview had no real cohesion and Nietzsche was as fierce a critic of these aberrations as one can imagine. Moreover, his so-called immoralism, with its questioning of all dogmas and established values, was hardly the basis on which fascist, Nazi, or other totalitarian regimes consolidated their support. On the contrary, such regimes, however radical their intentions, were careful to appeal to conventional morality and nationalist feelings in order to broaden their following, just as they often paid lip service to democratic values in order better to destroy them. Nietzsche's skeptical outlook, with its love of ambivalence, ambiguity, and paradox, was far removed from such manipulations, which he could only have despised and abhorred. Certainly, Nietzsche was a disturbing thinker whose ideas will always remain open to a diversity of interpretations. He was no admirer of modernity or of the liberal vision of progress, nor was he a "humanist" in the conventional sense of that term. His work lacked a concrete social anchor and his solution to the problem of nihilism led to a cul-de-sac. But to hold Nietzsche responsible, even indirectly, for Auschwitz, is surely to turn things on their head.[13] No other thinker of his time saw as deeply into the pathologies of fin de siècle German and European culture, or grasped so acutely from within, the sickness at the heart of anti-Semitism in the Christian West. It would be more just to see in Nietzsche a tragic prophet of the spiritual vacuum that gave birth to the totalitarian abysses of the twentieth century. As such he remains profoundly relevant to our own time.

Jerusalem, January 2001

Notes

1. *Hitler's Table Talk*, trans. Norman Cameron and R. H. Stevens (London: Weidenfeld and Nicolson, 2nd ed., 1973), 89.

2. Quoted in the *Marbacher Katologe*: 'Das 20. Jahrhundert. Von Nietzsche bis zur Gruppe 47', ed. B. Zeller (Deutsche Schillergesellschaft Marbach a. N., 1980), 20 (our translation). Compare to A. Rosenberg, *Friedrich Nietzsche. Ansprache bei einer Gedenkstunde anlässlich des 100. Geburtstages Nietzsches am 15. Oktober 1944, in Weimar* (Munich: Zentralverlag der NSDAP, Franz Eher Nachfolger, 1944).

3. Karl Popper, *The Open Society and its Enemies* (London: Routledge and Kegan Paul, 1945), 1:230.

4. Jacques Derrida, "Otobiographies: The Teaching of Nietzsche and the Politics of the Proper Name," in *The Ear of the Other: Otobiography, Transference, Translation*, trans. Peggy Kamuf and Avital Ronell, ed. Christie V. McDonald (New York: Schocken, 1985), 30, 24.

5. Berel Lang, *Act and Idea in the Nazi Genocide* (Chicago: University of Chicago Press, 1990), 198.

6. For biographical details see Bruce Detwiler, *Nietzsche and the Politics of Aristocratic Radicalism* (Chicago: University of Chicago Press, 1990), 1–9.

7. Walter Kaufmann, *Nietzsche: Philosopher, Psychologist, Antichrist* (Princeton: Princeton University Press, 1950), 412, 418. This characterization of Nietzsche as an "antipolitical" thinker who is solely interested in cultivating the individual life does not prevent Kaufmann from dwelling at length on the bitter (mainly political) struggles in which Nietzsche was deeply involved with his ex-mentor Wagner and against German imperialism and anti-Semitism. These struggles placed Nietzsche well within the political framework of his times. However, one should not see here any contradiction on Kaufmann's part since Nietzsche's antipolitical attitude stemmed organically from his political and cultural interests and drives.

8. See, among many others, the following works: Daniel W. Conway, *Nietzsche and the Political* (London and New York: Routledge, 1997); Conway, *Nietzsche's Dangerous Game* (Cambridge: Cambridge University Press, 1997); Keith Ansell-Pearson, *An Introduction to Nietzsche as Political Thinker* (Cambridge: Cambridge University Press, 1994); Peter Pütz, "The Problem of Force in Nietzsche and His Critics," in *Nietzsche: Literature and Values*, eds. V. Dürr, R. Grimm, and K. Harms (Madison: University of Wisconsin Press, 1988), 14–28; Tracy B. Strong, "Nietzsche's Political Aesthetics," in *Nietzsche's New Seas: Explorations in Philosophy, Aesthetics, and Politics*, eds. Michael Allen Gillespie and Tracy B. Strong (Chicago: University of Chicago Press, 1988), 153–174; Geoffrey Waite, *Nietzsche's Corps/e: Aesthetics, Politics, or the Spectacular*

Technoculture of Everyday Life (Durham: Duke University Press 1996); and Peter Berkowitz, *Nietzsche: The Ethics of an Immoralist* (Cambridge: Harvard University Press, 1995). Berkowitz writes, "It is tempting to conclude that Nietzsche does not practice or contribute to political philosophy. . . . Yet Nietzsche moves within the domain of moral and political philosophy . . . [since] the question of human perfection lies at the heart of Nietzsche's inquiries" (1–2). See also Richard Rorty, *Contingency, Irony, and Solidarity* (Cambridge: Cambridge University Press, 1989), where Nietzsche is portrayed as an "ironic liberal" and serves Rorty as a heuristic means to promote his postmodern liberalism.

9. Nietzsche, "Der griechische Staat," *KSA*, vol. 1 (1988), 764–77. And see also part 8 of the first volume of *Menschliches, Allzumenschliches* (*KSA*) entitled "Ein Blick auf den Staat" ("A Glance at the State" in Hollingdale's translation).

10. Z, 160.

11. The letters of Paneth were first published in a biography of Nietzsche by his sister Elisabeth Förster-Nietzsche *Das Leben Friedrich Nietzsche*, (Leipzig, 1904), 2:474–475, 479–493. See also Richard Frank Krummel, "Joseph Paneth über seine Begegnung mit Nietzsche in der Zarathustra-Zeit," *Nietzsche Studien* 17 (1988): 478–95.

12. For elaboration of these points see Jacob Golomb, *Nietzsche in Zion* (Ithaca: Cornell University Press, forthcoming).

13. See Robert S. Wistrich, *Hitler and the Holocaust* (London: Weidenfeld and Nicolson, 2001).

PART ONE: IN THEORY

1

How to De-Nazify Nietzsche's Philosophical Anthropology?
Jacob Golomb

Most Nazi readings of Nietzsche's thought justify their acts of misappropriation by referring to his key notion of the will to power in terms of a violent, overpowering, and physical force, which, if used effectively and efficiently, will secure a convincing military victory and material conquest.[1]

Ironically, the first to interpret the will to power in terms of military imperialism was Max Nordau, a leading cultural critic and subsequently Herzl's most important convert to political Zionism, who passionately warned his readers against this "degenerate" thinker whose influence was likely to bring havoc to the cause of "enlightened" and progressive European culture.[2]

This essay, in tune with Nietzsche's philosophical anthropology as delineated in his *published writings*, will draw some fundamental distinctions between two of his central notions—those of *Kraft* against *Macht*. It will also introduce the main psychological typology delineated in his major writings between what I will henceforth refer to as "positive" versus "negative" power patterns. Consequently it will become clear that what Nazis referred to when using the so-called Nietzschean idea of a military and physical *Macht* was actually what Nietzsche understood to be *Kraft* and *Gewalt*. Moreover, even within the conceptual domain of *Macht*, it will become apparent that its violent and aggressive manifestations were confined by him, in most cases, to the behavioral patterns of persons who suffered from and expressed the psychological phenomenon of "negative" power. By the end of this essay it

ome clear that Nietzsche's notion of power and his typologies
ised on crude naturalism or on the biological and eugenic
s that were the *sine qua non* of Nazi racism.[3]

The key to the meaning of the will to power is Nietzsche's notion of
self-overcoming. *Selbstüberwindung* is a concept originating in Nietzsche's recognition of the role of sublimation. Sublimation, as the mental
mechanism that orders and subdues instinctual drives, is responsible for
the attainment of "self-mastery" (*D*, 109).[4]

As a *perpetual* willing, the will to power negates the already formulated (Apollonian) forms and replaces them with other creations. Dialectical self-overcoming is the clue, then, to Nietzsche's mature philosophizing.[5] It can be construed in part as an indirect "confession" of his
triumph over the negative (in his eyes) elements of his character and
culture.[6] Certain parts of Nietzsche's personal and intellectual biography are transformed by his mature philosophy, some are preserved intact, others are eliminated, while still others are elevated beyond the
merely biographical. Thus, Nietzsche's notion of self-overcoming also
contains the meaning of maturity and spiritual growth. In the later
stages of character development one must have vanquished whatever
elements are alien to the inner, organic personality — the elements pre-
cluding authentic creativity and freedom. If one were to ask Nietzsche,
"What is the purpose of this self-overcoming?" he could have succinctly
answered, "To achieve maturity and power." In this respect the will to
power is similar to the will to selfhood — namely to become an autonomous person capable of devising and effectuating values. The optimal
will to power is realized in the ideal *Übermensch*. On the other hand, if
this will is diminished in quality, one's tendency to escape from one's
individual self and to identify with the "herd" will intensify. Individuals
with a sound psychic make-up and personal authenticity are endowed
with a will to power of higher quality and greater vitality.[7] Their will
expresses the master morality, in contrast to the slave morality typical
of those possessing lesser power or *Macht*, although the latter may be
endowed with greater *physical* force or *Kraft*. The distinction between
Kraft and *Macht* is crucial to any understanding of Nietzsche's mature
doctrine of power: it represents his philosophical emphasis on the transition from physical force to mental and spiritual power.

Power (*Macht*) versus Force (*Kraft*) in Nietzsche

Nietzsche's notion of *Kraft* refers to a primitive energy, to a latent and
indefinite state that functions only when activated within a concrete
situation.[8] The transition from *Kraft* to *Macht* is thus a transition from

the potentiality of force to its actualization. Blind *Kraftquellen* are transmuted and become *mächtig* (powerful) through a concrete expression in a specific cultural and historical context. The transition from a primal, inchoate driving force into a rationally formulated power is essential to Nietzsche's original characterization of the process of sublimation. The Apollonian shapes and directs the "Dionysian-barbarian" drives and thereby achieves cultural value and esteem. The distinction between "force" and "power" is based on the assumption that that *power is a sublimated force*.[9] The *Naturtrieb* is simply the primordial, brute force; only its sublimated cultural manifestations are endowed with effective and actual power. Nietzsche later calls this sublimation "victory over strength [*Kraft*]."[10] Contrary to the brute force worshiped by slaves, only a force sublimated by rational Apollonian elements, and thereby elevated to a culturally valuable level, should merit our admiration. This is a qualitative power and its most intense expression can be found in the "genius,"[11] in whom this force is inwardly directed toward creating selfhood.[12]

Special mental resources are required to achieve "victory over strength" through this process of self-sublimation. But with this "triumph" we become a supreme work of art — an actualized *Macht*. The authentic selfhood of the *Übermensch*, like that of "the exceptional Greeks" (*HH*, II:1–221; *KSA*, 2:474), is achieved by one's ability to bring about a "transfiguration of nature," a purification of the primitive, coarse element of force into refined, creative power. Those who give vent to brute force or naked aggression do not belong within the category of the *Übermensch*, in spite of the desperate efforts of the Nazis to claim for Hitler precisely such a title.

Nietzsche valued the psychic and the spiritual more highly than the physical and the biological. This is evident even in those few passages that have sometimes been abused to give a distorted reading of Nietzsche's attitude toward physical strength, thereby suggesting that he worshipped pure violence:

> In the beginning, the noble caste was always the barbarian caste: their predominance did not lie mainly in physical strength [*Kraft*] but in the mental state [*in der seelischen*] — they were more *whole* human beings (which also means, at every level, 'more whole beasts').[13]

Triumph over blind nature and basic instincts, including the drive toward aggressive supremacy, is a sign of the powerful person. Nietzsche's discovery (in *Daybreak* and later works) that current morality was simply an artful disguise of the drive toward domination caused him to reject it, for it was not a genuine manifestation of power.

Macht, with its connotations of determination and freedom, is better

ιe notion of power as a sublimated and creative force than is
.h its implications of undefined potentiality. This point is fur-
plified in *Nachgelassene Fragmente*, part of which was post-
sly compiled and illegitimately published as *The Will to Power*.[14]
In . ny aphorisms Nietzsche rejects the "mechanistic" interpretation of
the world in favor of a dynamic one, and expresses dissatisfaction with
the concept of force, for it lacks the connotations of intentional, deliberate, creative direction.[15] Nietzsche is not satisfied with the notion of
"force" because it is a quantitative concept derived from descriptive
mechanistic physics, which fails to account for qualitative processes,
such as sublimation (see, for example, *WP*, 660).

A concept of force derived from the natural sciences is inappropriate
to philosophical anthropology. Nietzsche's notion of the will to power,
however, unifies under one heading a large number of psychological
observations. It is a term that grows out of many specifically psychological phenomena, such as sublimated creation, self-overcoming, will,
drives, intentional activity conscious of its own goals, moral praxis,
or ascetic religious patterns. This unifying notion became the core of
Nietzsche's mature psychology.[16] Another reason Nietzsche rejects the
concept of physical force (apart from its psychological inappropriate-
ness) is that it lacks intrinsic dynamic intensification. Force cannot be
used to explain the basic psychobiological phenomena of growth and
maturation by means of overcoming (*WP*, 643). Self-overcoming and
sublimation require an indefinite investment of energy for the cancellation, preservation, and elevation of a given activity. The concept of
force, however, is associated with the preservation of a certain amount
of energy within a closed system (*WP*, 1062, 1064). This renders it
unsuitable to a dynamic approach, one that generalizes the biological
notion of continuous growth into a comprehensive psychological theory. Put differently, the concept of force obeys the dictum *ex nihilo nihil
fit*, in that the effect contains nothing which did not already exist in the
cause. Sublimation, self-overcoming, and the effort of the psyche to intensify itself cannot be bound by such mechanistic principles. Causal
explanations do not apply in the mental domain of the human will, and
one is quite justified in speaking of the phenomenon of the dialectical
intensification of life, due to the operation of the will, which elevates it
to a qualitatively higher level and "degree" of power.[17] Mere preservation of Being leads to stagnation. The will to power strives to overcome
anything that curbs the Being's intensification or affirmation. Thus,
Nietzsche comes to realize that this dynamic growth is incompatible
with the laws of the conservation of energy of classical physics (*WP*,
689).

The aspects of force imbued with the element of power are manifest in the will to power. The substratum upon which the process of limitation operates is the force, and the element that forms and m this force is the will. Force is the necessary but not the sufficient con...tion for the display of power. The (Dionysian) force together with the (Apollonian) forms provide the essential conditions. This synthesis of Nietzsche's earlier dualistic principles into the monist will to power shapes his mature, "new psychology."[18]

According to various notes it appears that Nietzsche was not at all content with a psychology that had become "the morphology and *the doctrine of the development of the will to power*" (*BGE*, 23; *KSA*, 5:38) but wished to revise Schopenhauer's formula and generalize the psychological phenomenon of the will into a comprehensive metaphysical cosmology. This goal contrasted with his basic assumption that any metaphysical system was another redundant "shadow" of the dead God (*GS*, 108). It also contradicted other published writings in which he objected to Schopenhauer's cosmology of "the will in itself" as "a primeval mythology" (*GS*, 127; *KSA*, 3:483). This and other aphorisms indicate that Nietzsche could not subscribe to a cosmological and metaphysical doctrine of the will to power first, because he limits willing to "intellectual beings" only, and second, because he renders the concept of "substance" as an advantageous fiction (see, for instance, *GS*, 111). Hence, in contrast to Schopenhauer, Nietzsche does not identify "Being" with "willing." In his view, the latter is solely "a mechanism" (*GS* 127; *KSA*, 3:483), a functional psychological system, within which the will is not an entity but a function—merely another action. In Nietzsche's authorized writing, then, the will to power is based upon distinctly psychological and anthropological principles. For our purposes, this is what really matters since the Nazis did not deal professionally and theoretically (in opposition to Heidegger) with the metaphysics of the will to power or with its ontological ramifications. Nazism was mainly interested in the anthropological manifestations of this principle and with its derivative typological implications that were conductive to various distortions, biases, and falsifications. Hence the main thrust of this essay is directed toward the exposition of Nietzsche's psychological typology.[19]

The preeminence of psychology's role in Nietzsche's thought is exemplified even in his famous last entry, 1,067, of *The Will to Power*, an entry, so we are informed, that "Nietzsche jotted down in July 1885 but had set aside by February 1888 as material for which he had no further use."[20] The entry describes "this world" as "a monster of energy [*Kraft*]," in which every element consumes the other in a perpetual struggle for dominance and control. Just as the human "monster of energy" (*WP*, 995) sublimates tremendous force to create the *Über-*

mensch, so the entire "Dionysian world" creates itself "out of the play of contradictions back to the joy of concord" thereby becoming "*the will to power — and nothing besides!*" (*WP*, 1067).

This unofficial cosmology entails Nietzsche's view that the will to power also manifests itself in the wish to impose interpretative perspectives on nature in order to control it through a set of cognitive projections (*WP*, 643). The individual, capable of overcoming his or her surroundings, is not only conscious of that fact, but immediately attempts to project and generalize this insight (or self-interpretation) on the entire cosmos. This universal projection should be understood as a heuristic-didactic clarification of the fundamentally psychological consequences of the will to power that Nietzsche played with in his notebooks. Presumably, because such a clarification lends no philosophical legitimacy to Nietzsche's *Versuch* (experiment) and stands in opposition to some of his writings, he did not include such cosmological speculations in his published works.

Power (*Macht*) versus Violence (*Gewalt*)

The second volume of *Human, All Too Human* places even greater emphasis on the spiritual and qualitative characteristics of power, establishing more clearly the distinction between power and force. Nietzsche describes human beings in terms of Apollonian-Dionysian powers, organizing the world around them in their own image and in accordance with their own uniquely human categories. We are assisted in this project by an intellectual capacity to construct theoretical perspectives, which enable us to assimilate nature by anthropomorphizing it.[21] In this way intellectual activity, it is suggested, serves the psychological need for power. These needs are met even if we do not achieve victory in the practical arena of the history of force.[22] There is a growing tendency in Nietzsche's thought to spiritualize the notion of power as part of his attempt to distinguish power from the tangentially related concepts of *Kraft* and *Gewalt*. This movement serves to secure a central location for the concept of *Macht* in the context of his mature philosophy.

Nietzsche's first writings already portrayed humans as a complex of instinctual drives, each of which strives continually to dominate the others. Such a depiction naturally suggested acts of violence as inherent in all life activities — including those manifesting power. The internal logic of this early psychology required Nietzsche to distinguish acts of brute violence (*Gewalt*) from those elements of power included in the sublimated concept of *Macht*. The criterion of self-overcoming is crucial in this spiritualization of power.

> Writing ought always to advertise a victory—an overcoming of *oneself* which has to be communicated for the benefit of others; and there are dyspeptic authors who write only when they cannot digest something. . . . Through their anger they try unconsciously . . . to exercise violence (*Gewalt*) upon the reader—that is, they too desire victory but over others (*HH*, II 1:152; *KSA*, 2:441, my translation).

Here, as elsewhere (*BGE*, 259), Nietzsche identifies the use and exploitation of others with violence (*Gewalt*), contrasting this external manifestation of gross force with power that is directed toward an internal expression of self-overcoming. Internalized power must also be free of masochistic violence, since it seeks not the elimination of individual drives but rather their creative sublimation.

Nietzsche's emphasizes the development of selfhood and the intrinsic use of the energy provided by the will to power for creation of one's self.[23] While the process of self-overcoming is (by definition) free of violence directed at others, some processes of assimilation and internalization do manifest it to a degree, particularly those that employ force against an object external to the self. Recognizing this, Nietzsche imposes three important constraints on the violent ramifications of the will to power.

First, Nietzsche maintains that a genuine process of assimilation does not entail sheer negative destructiveness; the will is constrained in so far as the external object must not be entirely obliterated, but rather preserved in part by creative sublimation. For this reason, Nietzsche placed creativity in opposition to rejection and negation: "[A]ll rejection and negation . . . point to a lack of fruitfulness" (*HH*, II 1:332; *KSA*, 2:515). The violent implications of the creative assimilation of external entities only challenge their relative autonomy—but do not obliterate them.

A second constraint limiting the violence of assimilative acts follows from Nietzsche's insistence that these acts are not concerned with physical violence directed against concrete objects: what is used and assimilated is not the object as such, but one's own mental impression or experience of it. Consequently, power is not identified as the ability of an individual to master others by force in acts of confrontation (see, for instance, *HH*, II 1:228).

The third and most important constraint, however, derives from the purpose or goal of the affirmation of power. The point is not to change or reform the external object with the intent of destroying it, but ultimately to transfigure the agent of assimilation. Acts of violence may be typically instrumental in forcibly changing or transforming others but the instrumental use of others within a context of self-transformation and self-overcoming must be manifest in *sublimated* expressions of the will to power. These sublimated expressions are exactly what the "strong individual" lacks who treats "not only nature but societies and weaker individuals too as objects of plunder." Nietzsche continues,

> [H]e exploits them as much as he can and then goes on. . . . His demonstrations of power are at the same time demonstrations of revenge against the painful and fear-ridden state of his existence: then again, he wants through his actions to count as being more powerful than he is.[24]

The actions of one who is preoccupied with revenge cannot be properly motivated by the attitude of *amor fati*; he or she therefore lacks the truly positive power that Nietzsche's psychology extols. Positive power seeks an autonomous overcoming of the self, while revenge evades self-responsibility and only attempts to augment one's power by exploiting and mistreating external objects. The actual exploitation of others — or even the presence of a disposition to do so — signifies the absence of both autarky and authenticity attaching to a personal, positive power.[25] Moreover, "in every healthy aristocracy," consisting of equally powerful individuals, it is a sign of "good manners" to refrain "from injury, violence (*Gewalt*), and exploitation and placing one's will on a par with that of someone else" (*BGE*, 259; *KSA*, 5:207).

Powerful persons may at times spontaneously manifest the power at their disposal, but the *desire* for power is more clearly evidenced in the behavior of those in whom power is wanting and who require some kind of external affirmation. But where do such individuals find the power to exploit their weakness through such manipulative dynamics? It cannot be the case that the weak person starts without any power at all: the very need for power indicates the existence of some primary source of power. So conceived, "power" in Nietzschean psychology cannot be quantitatively variable from one person to another; the difference between the weak and the powerful (or the "slave" and "master") is not one of degree. Power is a feature of every individual's constitution, and the variations are to be accounted for in terms of *qualitatively* distinct ways in its expression. For Nietzsche, the main characteristic of power is its lack of susceptibility to any quantitative assessments in terms of force. The nature of the difference between the "man of power" (*HH*, I:44) and the "powerless" (*HH*, I:45) is a contrast in the *qualities* or forms through which a constant resource manifests itself.

Some interpreters have nonetheless suggested that relative, quantitatively variable assessment is appropriate to Nietzschean power, claiming that "the 'powerful' and the 'powerless' agree in desiring *more* power."[26] This characterization is clearly inappropriate. Nietzsche's powerful person makes no attempt to acquire *more* power, but wishes to be conscious of and to enjoy the free expression of that power through its spontaneous reactivation (*WP*, 661).

If the notion of "powerful master" and "powerful slave" had been quantitative and relative, Nietzsche would have been unable to explain how the historical domination of weak slave morality over the masters could have occurred.[27] Moreover, if the value of power depended on an estimation of quantitative degree, Nietzsche would clearly have committed a naturalistic fallacy, analyzing the specifically ethical value of a property (what ought to be) in terms of its natural characteristics (what naturally is). However, Nietzsche was conscious of such a fallacy and deliberately avoided it.

At this point one might pose the obvious question: why, after all, does Nietzsche disapprove of the weak who do their best (according to their inherent nature) to acquire power from others by means of their weakness, while approving of the powerful individuals who cannot help but manifest their power—even at the expense of others? This question can be answered if we look at Nietzsche's attitude toward the phenomenon of asceticism.

At the beginning, the ascetic-religious attitude as a complex expression of power had not been unequivocally rejected by Nietzsche. Indeed, when he speaks of the *Selbstüberwindung* of the Jesuits, one detects a note of admiration for their religious expression of self-overcoming (*HH*, I:55). As a direct manifestation of power, Nietzsche commends their example remarking that "no power could maintain itself if its advocates were nothing but hypocrites" (ibid., 74). This suggests one reason for Nietzsche's criticism of the pity evoked by the weak: the weak individuals may be hypocritically using their alleged powerlessness precisely as a vehicle for gaining power over others, for dominating the environment, and for escaping into neurosis. As a temporary means of gratification these manipulations may serve some point, but they must eventually be exposed as unreliable and ineffectual methods of self-affirmation. If it becomes apparent to others that the neurotic is exercising a tenacious control over them by exploiting his or her own illness, they will typically turn against the neurotic and refuse to console or pity this person. Whenever an individual's means of acquiring and sustaining power depend on the responses of his or her environment—rather than on inner resources—he or she cannot secure any long term satisfaction. If one were to redirect one's power, however, and successfully exercise authority over oneself rather than over one's environment, one would be far less vulnerable.

Nietzsche recommends a direct and independent struggle with external (social and economic) or internal (psychological) distress as the most reliable solution; in the long term it is the only way to ensure and affirm the *inherent* power of the individual personality. A character that develops exclusively through the formation of dependent relations with others can never become genuinely mature: it will not have developed its *own* power to its maximum potential. The affirmation of the self cannot be completed without the overcoming of its weak and regressive elements. Nietzsche emphasizes this point when remarking that the strength (*Kraft*) of the Catholic Church lies in the strength of its particular representatives who "continually establish further pillars of their power" (*HH*, I:55; *KSA*, 2:74) by using their inherent power in a life project of self-overcoming. Only such "servants" of the Church exemplify the truly powerful personality — and only such a personality can be sufficiently inspiring to exercise the requisite influence on the education of others. Here, as elsewhere in Nietzsche's writings, mental power emerges as primary. Nietzsche rejects the tendency to manipulate the external environment in an attempt to exploit and conquer it, and instead proposes a process that directs personal power toward the challenge of self-overcoming and "self-transfiguration."

Consequently, his positive attitude toward asceticism gradually underwent a change. He came to see asceticism as a defective method in so far as it failed to sublimate the instinctual drives; it is not a method capable of moving to creative assimilation, in which these drives are transformed and elevated. The ascetic saint does effect a kind of self-overcoming, and may possess an exceptional personal power. This power is misused, however, in one-sided repression and extirpation of other drives. The result is a perpetual cycle of self-abnegation that can never culminate in an act of affirmation. Nietzsche's distinction between repression and sublimation thus reemerges in the moral and religious contexts, both of which may allow the individual to treat "himself not as *individuum* but as *dividuum*" (*HH*, I:57; *KSA*, 2:76). The division of the personality and the repression of many essential elements characterizes the prevailing ethical norms, preventing human beings from achieving personal harmony and full expression. For these reasons, Nietzsche is compelled to reject any *repressive* morality.

However, the discussion of ascetic morality requires a third concept of force in addition to *Kraft* and *Macht* — the concept of *Gewalt* (violence):

> For certain men feel so great a need to exercise their strength [*ihre Gewalt*] and lust for power that, in default of other objects or because their efforts in other directions have always miscarried, they at last hit upon the idea of tyrannizing over certain parts of

PHILOSOPHICAL ANTHROPOLOGY

their own nature. . . . In every ascetic morality ma
part of himself as God and for that he needs to diabo
part (*HH*, I:137; *KSA*, 2:131).

The notion of power as *Macht* is thus located betwee
poles: quantitative, static *Kraft*, devoid of rational and creative sublimation, and the excessively dynamic and brutal *Gewalt*, suppressing and
annihilating all other vectors of force. *Macht*, however, contains the
meaning of cancellation as well as creative assimilation. Put differently,
creative power is a compromise between an unrestrained and destructive play of the instincts and their hostile repression. By describing ascetic attitudes in terms of violence, Nietzsche emphasizes that they actually constitute a violence performed on power itself. The ascetic does
finally achieve a kind of tranquillity by willing one drive to dominate
the others until they are all eradicated. However, this tranquillity is
achieved at the expense of annihilating the sublime creative energy. The
genuinely powerful individuals, by contrast, are continually readjusting
the forces of their personality, calling on different drives to motivate
positive action; using instinctual chaos as the material for a productive
life. The essential difference between the *Übermensch* and the ascetic
saint, then, may be formulated in terms of the distinction between
Macht and *Gewalt*, sublimation and repression. It should be noted,
however, that repression is also an operation requiring a kind of force in
the overcoming of drives, and so it is accompanied by a subjective experience similar to that characteristic of sublimation: "the saint practices
that defiance of oneself that is a close relation of lust for power and
bestows the feeling of power even upon the hermit" (*HH*, I:142; *KSA*,
2:138).

The similarity in one's subjective experiences of repression and of
sublimation can in large part account for Nietzsche's early enchantment
with the ascetic, and explain why he mistakenly identified it as an exemplar of personal power. It can also help to clarify why the image of the
saint typically produces responses of great respect and reverence from
others: they admire the heroic self-conquest, failing to distinguish the
kind of self-conquest achieved through violence (*Gewalt*), from the positive sublimation (*Macht*). Only the latter can culminate in genuine, personal power, and it comprises a distinct spiritual realm as well, rendering the personality more delicate and sublime. In practical contexts,
however, this personality may be less able to survive an environment
that exercises violent force (*Gewalt*) although it may possess an intrinsic
and genuine power, unlike the personality of those who wish to dominate and exploit others.

The portrait of the powerful personality that emerges depicts it as more vulnerable in direct confrontation with brute force, precisely because of its spiritual and rational elements. This feature clarifies an apparent paradox in Nietzsche's doctrine of the will to power: if Christianity (whose exemplar is the ascetic saint) represents a suppressed and declining will to power and a decadent system of instinctual drives, how did it defeat and overwhelm the elements that express an authentic will to power? If Nietzsche had been a pragmatist—the *successful* manifestation of power might have been his central criterion of power. But he is clearly not pragmatic in this way. A genuine power is not always obliged to show itself in terms of success in a world where force typically dominates spirit. Spiritual power, which is the only one that creates culture, is often vulnerable to the pressures of brute physical force. This is often the case on both the individual plane (the *Übermensch* versus the saint) and the historical-cultural plane (the ancient Greeks versus the barbarians; the superior "pagans," i.e., ancient Greeks, versus Christians). When the religious personality redirects its intense force outward, away from repressive self-tyranny and toward the domination of others, success is assured *a priori*. It intentionally sets out to suppress and destroy (*HH*, I:114) precisely those others engaged in self-formation, not self-denial. These others retain their superior power despite the fact that they exercise less force.[28]

Although the qualitative power of the individual or society is no guarantee of its material success and victory, it nonetheless ensures a spiritual and cultural superiority. For this reason Nietzsche is careful to distinguish between the history of power (spiritual and intellectual progress) and the history of force (physical and material domination). It is precisely those who have been in the weaker position relative to the history of force who are responsible for cultural advances relative to power: "It is the more unfettered, uncertain and morally weaker individuals upon whom *spiritual progress* depends."[29]

The strength of the powerful is not due to a greater degree of force, just as the weakness of the powerless is not simply represented in lower magnitudes of energy. Power and weakness do not signify different *quanta* but a different *direction* of the operation of power and distinct modes of derivation and intensification. It is useful here to recall the Kantian distinction between autonomy and heteronomy. Nietzsche himself uses this distinction implicitly in his analysis of those individuals who use their power hypocritically. He observes this same pattern in the wider historical-cultural context of religion and morality. A weak and persecuted social group or sect may attempt to subjugate the powerful by indirect means, just as the weak person extorts pity from the powerful as a means of absorbing some of their strength and undermining their autonomy. If religious and moral values emphasizing pity and justice are internalized by the powerful personality, they will inculcate feelings of guilt and humiliation. In this way the weaker obliquely draw the powerful "down" to their own level, and so avoid the challenge of elevating themselves through self-development. What authority the weak may obtain is not, then, internally located. The powerful personality, by contrast, autonomously legislates its own values and laws, becoming a model for others. If it prescribes laws to others as well, this is not because the powerful personality needs to dominate them to enhance its own authority, this is only the natural expression of its power. Thus Nietzsche says that "to be a lawgiver is a more sublimated form of tyranny" (*HH*, I:261; *KSA*, 2:215); that is, the law-giving of the powerful is a natural creative expression — not a direct act of violence (*Gewalt*) or an indirect, heteronomous tyranny.

The manipulative methods by which the weak press for domination always avoid any *direct* confrontation with the powerful. They do not engage in conflict as such, but move obliquely, attempt to penetrate the power structure from within. Thus, religious and moral norms based on the inculcation of guilt feelings provide them with an ideal vehicle with which to undermine that structure's foundations. The "slaves" employ "the instincts of cowardice, cunning and canaille" (*WP*, 864), inspired by their aspiration to gain domination over the genuinely powerful (*HH*, I:111; *KSA*, 2:114).

This exposition can, of course, also be applied to the anti-Semite, who is a weak and psychologically unstable individual, with the character of a "slave." The phenomenon of anti-Semitism, which was a "horror and an abomination" for Nietzsche, can be elucidated with reference to the psychological patterns of the weak and impoverished personality, described in Nietzsche's main writings. Lacking personal power, and as a result of ressentiment and mental impoverishment, the anti-Semite is dependent upon certain external surroundings for self-determination. He needs acts of violence and cruel exploitation of others (*Gewalt*) to enhance his feeble sense of power (*GS*, 359). He is a vengeful and reactive person who uses his hatred, a hatred in which "there is *fear*" (*GS*, 379), to attain some sort of security and self-identity. The Nazi paranoia toward the Jews is a case in point. Be it as it may, from the perspective of Nietzsche's anthropological typology it follows that the anti-Semite is actually the "slave" and not the "master."[30]

But why do strong autonomous agents internalize certain corrupting values and yield to the ressentiment of the weak? Why does their power not guarantee a self-legislating creativity that would be resistant to such internalizations?

Nietzsche recognized the seriousness of this question and tried hard to respond to it. In *Human, All Too Human* he suggests that the highly

piritual and intellectual component of power may in some
en even the most superior personality. Because such person-
genuinely free and independent, they are unlikely to adhere to
.....,   and inflexible complex of norms: the values they possess are
open to examination and susceptible to being "overcome." They will,
then, be more vulnerable to the surreptitious indoctrination that the
weak use against them. Their freedom from any given tradition induces
a kind of frailty, for it allows them to oscillate perpetually between
whatever possibilities they may encounter. In historical praxis, this dynamic may produce an impressionable personality, susceptible to manipulation and exploitation:

> Compared with him who has tradition on his side and requires no
> reasons for his actions, the free spirit is always weak, especially in
> actions; for he is aware of too many motives and points of view
> and therefore possesses an uncertain and unpracticed hand. What
> means are there of nonetheless rendering him *relatively strong*?
> How does the strong spirit come into being? (*HH*, I:230; *KSA*,
> 2:193).

The problem may be recast as that of turning spiritual power into a
concrete historical force: is it possible to preserve the spirit of a Hamlet
in the body of a Faust? Nietzsche's solution focuses on the social fabric
woven with religious and moral dogma that produce a psychological
pattern of guilt, vengeance, and bad conscience.[31] These are the weakest
threads of culture, responsible for the corruption of spiritual power and
intellectual progress. In emphasizing these elements, Nietzsche implicitly
admits that there can be no absolute psychological autonomy: even the
most powerful are not impervious to influence by the environment with
which they interact. The revaluation of prevalent cultural norms is essential to the evolution of the *Übermensch* psychology because even the
arena of the "authentic legislator" may be penetrated by environmental
values and forces. The absolutely autonomous will to power is, therefore, no more than a regulative idea — one that provides the model for
approximation, but which can in principle never be fully realized. Indeed, Nietzsche always refers to the will to power as something that is
never absolutely satisfied. It is a perpetual movement of the whole person in relation to everything he or she encounters, a movement to assimilate, overcome, and mature with it. By nature, this activity is incessant, for its range of operation is infinite and in principle inexhaustible.
Although Nietzsche wished to approximate the ideal will to power as
closely as possible by translating power into a concrete historical force,
he did not aim at exhausting or fully realizing its potential. There can
be no final conclusion to the Nietzschean dialectic of power.

The creative and spiritual dimensions of genuine power make it more vulnerable in the "battlefields" of life governed by the rules of crude force, and in which victory is conferred upon those who possess material strength. But for Nietzsche, for whom "life is no argument" (*GS*, 121), it is not paradoxical to consider *Macht* superior to *Kraft* and *Gewalt*. In his own way he aspires to the Socratic value of encouraging only the good life, rather than preserving life as such. This good life has nothing to do with the ideal of the Aryan race and the Third Reich, but actually it clearly negates them. This will become even further apparent once we explicate Nietzsche's basic anthropological typology between the negative versus the positive power patterns.

Nietzsche's Typology of the "Positive" versus the "Negative" Power Patterns

Nietzsche's distinctions (on the individual and historical levels) between power, force and violence are subsumed in Nietzsche's mature writings under what can be named here as his fundamental distinction between two patterns of behavior or two psychological types: one that expresses the existence of positive power and the other that indicates a lack of such a power, which I will call here the negative power.

Negative power is symptomatic of a weak personality, lacking in power but incessantly attempting to obtain it. In Nietzsche's view this pattern was characteristic of the early Christians, who formed their religion out of a desperate need for power:

> There are recipes for the feeling of power, firstly for those who can control themselves and who are thereby accustomed to a feeling of power; then for those in whom precisely this is lacking. Brahminism has catered for the men of the former sort, Christianity for men of the latter (*D*, 65; *KSA*, 3:63).

In a sense, Christianity reconstructed the concepts of sin, bad conscience, and guilt, and used them as instruments of cruelty and vengeance; these concepts have often justified the abuse, even the torture, of others, thereby intensifying the Christian's own feebleness:

> Oh, how much superfluous cruelty and vivisection have proceeded from those religions which invented sin! And from those people who desired by means of it to gain the highest enjoyment of their power! (*D*, 53; *KSA*, 3:57).

Clearly, no positive power is exhibited in the satisfaction derived from abusing and dominating one's fellow beings. Disguised cruelty and its attendant (perverse) pleasure are called upon only to reinforce an unstable character. Negative power does not express itself spontaneously, but derivatively: it is fundamentally deficient and defective, striving to encourage itself by enjoyment obtained from abuse and cruelty.

Nietzsche applies this anthropological typology for his moral considerations. He does not posit power against morality, but proposes an active morality of positive power against the traditional passive type, opting for courageous creativity and autonomy based on the acquired selfhood of the moral agent. He contrasts the characteristic features of these two moralities: "All actions may be traced back to evaluations, all evaluations are either *original* or *adopted*—the latter being by far the most common (*D*, 104; *KSA*, 3:92)."

The transmitted "morality of tradition," which mechanically and arbitrarily conditions us, is, in fact, anti-individualistic, repressing the genuine personality, making it into a "*dividuum*." Nietzsche proposes instead an egoistic morality that springs out of positive power and self-expression. The violence of the traditional morality against the individual explains its impoverishment, pessimism, and depression. As a result, vitality withers away, leaving a feeling of weakness, discontent and "the profoundest misery" (*D*, 106). This moral wretchedness, and other expressions of the traditionally accepted ethos, is a manifestation of the will to power. However, it is only the supreme expression of *negative* power, characterized by fear and weakness. The power impelling traditional morality is not sufficiently strong or independent, thus creating a perpetual anxiety that it may be undermined. This causes us to develop defense mechanisms against our doubts and instabilities that merely intensify them. Nietzsche therefore maintains that the supporters of official morality are directed by "an obscure anxiety and awe" (*D*, 107) of losing their influence and authority. In consequence, their "moral commands" attempt to enhance and reinforce power by exploiting other human beings.[32]

Nietzsche portrays in detail the cunning, devious, moral mechanisms that persons of negative power reinforce and use to affirm themselves. Their strategy is to establish the morality of duty, thus assuring (their own) "self-regard" (*D*, 112). They achieve this by shrewdly and insidiously assuming a sovereignty over individuals. Certain "rights" are granted that signify their recognition of others' powers, but in return others are required to comply with certain duties and to concede their rights to the "moralists." Thus all are trapped within a network of duties and rights, which eventually reinforces and reaffirms the defective power of the moralists of duty.

But why do those who supposedly possess positive power still fall into the circle of moral duty? Nietzsche says that persons who have "more than enough" power do not need to accept any rights—since these would be a superfluous token of recognition. Whoever accepts the concept of "rights" as externally conferred has only a "feeble sense of power" (D, 112). The willingness to accept certain rights indicates that one is not at the top of the power hierarchy. By granting rights and demanding certain duties in exchange, the "sovereign" of negative power succeeds in controlling others. It follows that a traditional morality based upon a system of duties and rights, is impelled by the "striving for distinction," especially pronounced in weak people moved by "the psychical extravagance of the lust for power!" (D, 113). In contrast to this morality of duty, through self-overcoming one can attain rights autonomously and freely; and generously confer them upon others—not as part of manipulative negotiation, but out of a *surplus* of personal power (D, 437, 449). In effect, Nietzsche claims that only the truly powerful person who experiences "the feeling of fullness, of power that seeks to overflow, the happiness of high tension, the consciousness of wealth that would give and bestow, the noble human being . . . helps the unfortunate, but not, or almost not, from pity, but prompted more by an urge begotten by excess of power" (BGE, 260). Persons who love and esteem their selves can unconditionally and spontaneously give love to others without being afraid that by this act they might weaken their own power and position. Similarly, genuine gifts generally come from persons who experience their own selves as gifts while genuinely altruistic acts are often performed by egoists endowed with a strong sense of positive power. Their inherent and abundant richness overflows and is offered *gratis* to others.

Nietzsche draws an ideal picture of an entire culture driven by powerful individuals—generous, independent, unprejudiced, endowed with the ability to perform a creative sublimation of instincts. Such persons have "the ability to accept contradictions," possess dynamic vitality and self-control, are devoid of bad conscience, have adopted the attitude of *amor fati*, and exhibit self-acceptance. These are the genuinely "free spirits" with the attitude of "*la gaya scienza*," people who embody intellectual tolerance and existential integrity. They are noble and courageous, rejecting the desire for expansion or domination as ultimate goals in themselves (D, 163; M, 164, 546). This picture could not be more opposed to that of the Nazi Aryan "Reich," which sought to suppress such positive power patterns and deliberately wiped out so many of its living models.

Nietzsche's Typology Is Beyond Eugenic and Racial Distinctions

Nietzsche's long list of predicates of persons endowed with positive power includes no biological values. His teaching is directed to help us activate or uncover the resources and origins of our ability to create and to manifest positive power patterns. Nietzsche supposes that these origins are rooted deeply within ourselves, but because of various psychological handicaps (cowardice, for example), we have repressed them and have prohibited their free operation. These handicaps have been projected as an ideological network with patterns of negative power, and Nietzsche uses his "hammering" method to shatter the prohibiting "idols" while freezing our faith in them. The very process of freezing our belief in most of the prevalent values of negative power is founded on the assumption that the "frozen" personality will reject certain values and accept other norms, which already exist both in our social surroundings and within ourselves.[33] The enticing psychological arguments for the morality of positive power, therefore, are not presented directly and prescriptively. Instead, the freezing process is employed indirectly by means of a *genealogy*, revealing the negative origins of prevalent norms, and arguing that the effects of our accepting these norms are psychologically and existentially destructive. However to evoke positive power one must first overcome the inhibiting forces. Both the positive enticement and the negative freezing assume that individuals possess an implicit set of values that drive them to reject negative patterns. Therefore, along with his enticing anthropology, Nietzsche must explicate these implicit norms and elaborate on them.

This explicatory feature of Nietzsche's discussion of power phenomena appears in a crucial passage in *Beyond Good and Evil*, where he says he has "finally discovered two basic types of morality and one basic difference":

> Wandering through the many subtler and coarser moralities which have so far been prevalent on earth, or still are prevalent, I found that certain features recurred regularly together and were closely associated — until I finally discovered two basic types and one basic difference.
>
> There are master morality and slave morality — I add immediately that in all the higher and more mixed cultures there also appear attempts at mediation between these two moralities, and yet more often the interpenetration and mutual misunderstanding of both, and at times they occur directly alongside each other — even in the same human being, within a *single* soul (*BGE*, 260; *KSA* 5:208).

Here, and in other related aphorisms (see, for example, *GM*, I:16, and *BGE*, 200, 260), several central and thematic ideas are expressed. Nietzsche describes his investigation of different moral patterns as a search for "certain features [that] recurred regularly together." This is obviously a description of the explicative method, which seeks to expose the definitive and essential features of certain phenomena. The two moral phenomena presented are actual cultural patterns, and are far from being a priori constructions of our "minds." "Master morality" and the pattern of the *Übermensch* are historical phenomena that Nietzsche defines more closely to avoid confusion with "slave morality."

Nietzsche, observing the cultural history of morality, discovers "the interpenetration and mutual misunderstanding of both." Moreover, history discloses the slow, gradual progression from the "morality of the herd" to a morality that increasingly stresses the value of the individual. According to Nietzsche, the gradual emergence of the morality of positive power is already taking place in the history of humankind (*GS*, 117–20). Thus the main goal of his explications is to speed up this process. It follows that we must understand his "transfiguration of all values" not as an abolition but as a transfiguration of negative power into positive morality. Of course, this is not a radical change ex nihilo; in order that significant change take place, the modifying element must already contain, at least implicitly, the seeds of this alteration. The process of "transfiguration," therefore, is well established both in our cultural history and also "within a single soul" — fluctuating between the opposing vectors of constructive and destructive powers. Nietzsche is describing here a more transitory, fluctuating emotional and mental state of the individual — "the true pathos of every period of our life" (*GS*, 317; *KSA*, 3:549).

We can now ask whether Nietzsche's moral commitment on the explicative level suffices to meet the charge of moral naturalism and complicity with the racial biologism so essential to Nazi ideology. Our argument shows that Nietzsche is clearly opposed to the naturalization of morality. Morality to him is not something given and delivered but something created and freely constructed. Most of Nietzsche's positive predicates have nothing to do with the given natural facts but have to be attained by the long and often arduous processes of self-education, self-overcoming, sublimation, and refinement. Thus, Nietzsche's philosophical anthropology does not seek to establish and to sanctify any "natural" laws. Nietzsche affirms psychological power not as it is actually given in nature, but only after it has passed through the sublimated process of transfiguration and self-overcoming. In short, the "is" properly becomes "ought" only if it undergoes an intensive elaboration and transformation.

Nevertheless, it still may be possible to insist that Nietzsche is not entirely free from naturalism in the sense of attempting to base his morality on certain natural phenomena. Nietzsche affirms that power is the basic drive of human nature. As such, "in itself it has, *like every drive,* neither this moral character nor any moral character at all" (D, 38). Therefore, if we keep in mind Nietzsche's statement that human beings themselves are a will to power (a monistic psychological principle), then any moral doctrine based upon it would necessarily be a naturalistic ethic, with the well-known attendant fallacies.[34] In my view, however, interpreting Nietzsche's moral attitude as purely naturalistic is quite inaccurate.

It is difficult to render this naturalistic interpretation compatible with the extensive normative and prescriptive passages of Nietzsche's writings, which unequivocally reject the negative "slave" morality and prefer the positive "master" morality. If Christianity is the "slave revolt" aiming to seize power from the masters, and if this rebellion has scored a decisive historical victory, it is hard to understand, on a naturalistic interpretation, why Nietzsche rejects this "natural" victory and strives to counteract it by reactivating, in a clearly normative manner, the defeated (positive) power morality. One of the basic tenets of naturalistic ethics is that whatever exists in nature (be it individual or historical and sociological) is desirable from the moral point of view. It is not clear how Nietzsche, if he were really the so-called "naturalist" that some have claimed, could reject the historical revolt of the slaves in his attempt to "reevaluate all values." The rejection of the historical "is" is viable if only some other set of norms is at work, invalidating the given moral patterns.

It might be argued that "naturalism" does not imply that everything that actually happens is justified, but that whatever is considered "natural" or "essential" ought to dominate, even if this is not so in reality. This reasoning, however, assumes universal agreement as to what is "natural" and "essential," and a general consent that this should be manifested in actual cultural "praxis." The fundamental gap between Nietzsche's moral attitude and that of the naturalistic argument appears precisely at this point. Nietzsche acknowledges that most persons do not wish to uncover their positive power and are afraid of reactivating it. On the contrary, they seek to repress it, to flee from it, or to rationalize it away by a network of opposing moral norms that inhibit its spontaneous expression. It follows that most persons do not participate in any general consent, and thus it is unreasonable to accuse Nietzsche of a naturalistic fallacy.[35] Moreover, if the patterns of positive power were generally accepted values — Nietzsche would not need his enticing philosophical anthropology to attract us to them. Furthermore, Nietzsche consistently resists turning the preservation of life into a supreme value, as most people commonly regard it. The very fact that Nietzsche is not interested in life as such, but in a certain type of life, places him far apart from the simple naturalistic attitude.

The normative network determining Nietzsche's rejection of traditionally accepted morality contains the key concept of power. Though this concept refers to certain psychological patterns, there is no power that is absolutely powerful, and the notions of the *Übermensch* or an entirely autonomous power represent rather a kind of regulative ideal. Yet once we delve into regulative ideals it clearly makes no sense to speak about naturalistic ethics, which are anchored in the given and the natural.

Further, a crude naturalistic interpretation of Nietzsche's morality is unjust to those aspects of his thought that emphasize art as the model of all moral patterns. Nietzsche stresses spontaneous creativity and a synthesis between the formal Apollonian principle and the Dionysian drives as vital aspects of human existence. He applies the model of art to moral considerations and pronounces the idea of creative formation — the "transfiguration of nature." A philosopher who talks about the improvement of human nature, the elevation of culture, and the transformation of mankind into "an *aesthetic phenomenon*" (BT, 5) is hardly — if at all — a moral naturalist or moral biologist. The ideal of a creative, unlimited and spontaneous activity would be seriously obstructed by grounding it in any natural phenomenon or principle, which is necessarily limited and bounded. The principle component of Nietzsche's morality is the element of selfhood and genuine freedom. This axiom would be greatly restricted had Nietzsche attempted to base the moral conduct on empirical, natural fact. The essence of naturalism allows very little room for spontaneous, creative, and autonomous freedom, which for Nietzsche is the alpha and omega of any potential morality.

Nietzsche's persistent attempt, by means of his philosophical psychology, to attain a "de-deification of nature" and to vanquish the remnants of God's "shadows," stands in opposition to the notion of rewrapping this "pure . . . newly redeemed nature" (GS, 109) in another web of values and concepts. To turn nature and race into a cradle of human and social morality is an illegitimate personification. Thus Nietzsche was bound to reject any naturalistic morality that endows a certain fragment of the entire universe with an ethical significance:

> Wise and noble men still believe in the "moral significance of existence." But one day this music of the spheres too will no longer be audible to them! They will awaken and perceive that their ears had been dreaming (GS, 109).

This remark also illuminates why Nietzsche consistently rejects "*[t]he delusion of a moral world-order*" and claims that in morality there is "*absolutely no eternal necessity*" (D, 563). It may be true that the concept of power around which Nietzsche designs his moral doctrine is composed of distinct psychological elements, but this does not justify the conclusion that the morality of power is simply a naturalistic ethics:

> Those moralists who perceive and exhibit the laws and habits of mankind . . . differ altogether from those who explain what has been observed. The latter have to be above all *inventive* and possess an imagination unchained by acuteness and knowledge (*M*, 428; cf. *M*, 248).

Here we must distinguish between two separate meanings of the term "naturalistic." First, we may speak of a naturalism based upon raw natural data. We confront these data, including the racial ones, within ourselves or our surroundings, and use them in establishing moral norms, without shaping or changing them. Such an ethics — of which Nazism is a historical example — directly transfers the empirical and natural data into the basis of evaluation. "Naturalism," however, has yet another connotation. Here, too, the raw material for morality is given and found in nature — but this in itself is *not* enough. Nature here is a necessary but *not sufficient* condition of morality. The natural given is only the raw material that, so to speak, stores up in itself the potential for moral realization. But the realization will occur if and only if the potential psychological factors are thoroughly elaborated, refined, and sublimated in a process of creative "invention." Thus we cannot speak here of a direct displacement from nature to morality, for Nietzsche offers a much more intricate and complex process of the "transfiguration" and *overcoming of nature*, within the context of aesthetic morality. The natural "is" will become the "ought" of positive morality not by a mechanistic, direct, and passive displacement, but by intentional and sublimated acts of transformation, by a prolonged period of education, and by the creation of "a new nature in us":

> So let us take care not to exchange the state of morality to which we are accustomed for a new evaluation of things head over heels and amid acts of violence (*Gewalt*) — no, let us continue to live in it for a long, long time yet — until . . . we become aware that *the new evaluation* has acquired predominance within us and the little doses of it to *which we must from now on accustom ourselves* have laid down a new nature in us (*D*, 534).

The transfiguration of our nature and the sublimation of our drives and psychological makeup, which provide the necessary and sufficient conditions of the morality of positive power, distance Nietzsche from Nazi eugenics or racism based on a given and preferred set of biological traits. This is evident even in those few passages mentioning the "blond beast" that were appropriated by the Nazis who strove to endow it with racial, i.e., Nordic and Aryan, connotations to give a distorted reading of Nietzsche.[36] As a matter of fact, it is quite ironic that the first appearance in Nietzsche's writings of this notorious concept of the "blond beast" (*GM*, I:11; *KSA*, 5:275) is far from denoting any specific racial notion but represents an amalgam of races and fictive mythological figures: "the Roman, Arabian, Germanic, Japanese nobility, the Homeric heroes, the Scandinavian Vikings."[37] Actually, the only idea of race that Nietzsche ever looked upon with favor was that of a *mixed* race (as mixed as possible)—a European race sprung from innumerable intermarriages between "the best aristocracy of Europe" and the Jews (*D*, 205; *HH*, I:475). This was his sarcastic attempt to counter the racial anti-Semitism that had begun to spread with Wagner and his zealous followers and a way to get even with the Germans, a nation he came to intensely dislike.

The fact is that Nietzsche was very far from delineating a racial typology. In this respect it is revealing that his own historical examples of societies that approximated "the essential characteristic of a good and healthy aristocracy" (*BGE*, 258) were the ancient Greek *polis* and the city government of Venice (*BGE*, 262)—in his view classic representations "of the morality of the powerful" (*BGE*, 262). He also refers in this context to the historical examples of ancient Rome and of the Italian Renaissance—namely to cultural patterns that never made racial supremacy the cornerstone of their non-nationalist ideals or never regarded the genetic features of particular person as an *a priori* mark of creativity or superiority.

One final remark concerns the notion of sublimation in Nietzsche's teaching, which always involves a rejection of the damaging processes of repression. According to Nietzsche, we must first restore to humankind its reservoir of repressed drives, unduly and harshly repressed by culture. But the choice is not simply between culture and raw barbarian nature. *The Birth of Tragedy* had already opposed the "Dionysian barbarian" (no less nihilistic than the excessively Apollonian or Christian antisensualism). The problem in Nietzsche's eyes was rather one of culture versus civilization—the former being based more on sublimation and vital creation than on repression and overspiritualization. Nietzsche never endorsed the prospect of chaotic turbulence and the uncontrolled release of the "blond beast" of prey in humankind. Thus, Thomas Mann was mistaken in accusing Nietzsche of calling for the massive and anarchic release of repressed instincts.[38] The "blond beast' was at best a stage but not the final aim of Nietzsche's thought. His philosophical anthropology—in sharp contrast to that of fascism or Nazism—never "heroized the instincts." The road to Nietzsche's *Übermensch* entailed, above all, the "heroization" of artistic sublimation.[39]

1. See the notorious Nazi interpretation of Nietzsche by Alfred Bäumler, the Nazi authority on Nietzsche who uncritically endorsed Elisabeth Förster-Nietzsche's edition of her brother's *Nachlass* and referred to the will to power as a political notion. (His most important work is *Nietzsche der Philosoph und Politiker* [Leipzig: Reclam, 1931]). Another example of misappropriation can be found in the *Reichsleiter*, Alfred Rosenberg's official speech delivered in Weimar on the occasion of the hundredth anniversary of Nietzsche's birth. See his *Friedrich Nietzsche: Ansprache bei einer Gedenkstunde anläßlich des 100. Geburtstages Friedrich Nietzsches am 15. October 1944 in Weimar* (Munich: Zentralverlag der NSDAP, Franz Eher Nachfolger, 1944).

2. Max Nordau, *Entartung*, 3rd ed. (Berlin: Carl Duncker, 1896), vol. 2, chap. 5; and the more accessible English edition *Degeneration* (Lincoln and London: University of Nebraska Press, 1993), 415–72. Nordau claims that the basic driving force in human beings (according to Nietzsche) is "cruelty" (424; 450). Consequently, the Nietzschean *Übermensch* is also presented by Nordau as lacking all Apollonian elements of sublimation and as externalizing, without any moral restraints, the cruelty of the Dionysian barbarian instincts by performing acts of crime and violence (431). For a more in-depth discussion see the second chapter of my forthcoming *Nietzsche in Zion* (Ithaca: Cornell University Press), "The Case of Max Nordau against Nietzsche: The Structure of Ambivalence" and my article by the same title (but in Hebrew) in, *Historia* 1, no.7 (February 2001): 51–77.

3. It would be cumbersome to adduce endless examples from Nazi works on Nietzsche, but see the bibliography for some references to the literature on Nietzsche during the Third Reich. This essay can also be seen as providing the textual evidence and arguments that will further strengthen Berel Lang's perceptive observation: "To reconstruct in the imagination the events leading up to the Nazi genocide against the Jews without the name or presence of Nietzsche is to be compelled to change almost nothing else in that pattern" (*Act and Idea in the Nazi Genocide* [Chicago: University of Chicago Press, 1990], 98).

4. For a fuller discussion of Nietzsche's notion of sublimation see my *Nietzsche's Enticing Psychology of Power* (Jerusalem and Ames: Hebrew University Magnes Press and Iowa State University Press, 1989), chap. 1.

5. Thus it is not a sheer coincidence that the first detailed discussion of this notion is found in a chapter in *Thus Spoke Zarathustra* entitled "On Self-Overcoming," where Nietzsche discusses it in terms of an unceasing will to overcome oneself: "[A]nd life itself confided this secret to me: I must be a struggle and a becoming and an end and an opposition to ends . . . Whatever I create and however much I love it—soon I must oppose it and my love; thus my will wills it" (*Z*, II:12). This essential relations between Nietzsche's concept of the "will to power" and his notions of *Selbstüberwindung* and "opposition" bring me to agree with the late Wolfgang Müller-Lauter's interpretation regarding "*Gegensätzlichkeit*" as a fundamental feature of the will to power. See his *Nietzsche:*

Seine Philosophie der Gegensätze und die Gegensätze seiner Philosophie (Berlin: de Gruyter, 1971), 10–33.

6. As Nietzsche admits, "[M]y writings speak only of overcomings: I am in them, together with everything that was inimical to me" (*HH*, II: Preface I). We may assume here that these "inimical" elements of his *Zeitgeist* include the strong religious sentiments that Nietzsche inherited from his Lutheran father and pious surroundings, his metaphysical-transcendental inclinations (Schopenhauer), his romantic predilections (Wagner), and the nihilist-pessimistic world outlook prevalent at that time in European culture, inspired by the "death of God" and Darwinian doctrine. We should add to these cultural trends, Nietzsche's own racial and nationalistic prejudices, so widely shared at the time of his youth. Nietzsche's basically positive views on Jews and his opposition to anti-Semitism are discussed in my "Nietzsche on Jews and Judaism," *Archiv für Geschichte der Philosophie* 67 (1985): 139–161, and in my "Nietzsche and the Marginal Jews" in, *Nietzsche and Jewish Culture*, ed. Jacob Golomb (London and New York: Routledge, 1997), 158–92.

7. On Nietzsche's ideal of authenticity (*Wahrhaftigkeit*), see my "Nietzsche on Authenticity," *Philosophy Today* 34 (1990): 243–58; and *In Search of Authenticity from Kierkegaard to Camus* (London: Routledge, 1995), 68–87.

8. See, e.g., *HH*, II:1–226; *KSA*, 2:481–82. This connotation of *Kraft* actually agrees with current everyday German usage, as in the expression "schlummernde *Kräfte im Menchen wecken*." And see "*Kraft*" in *Duden: Das grosse Wörterbuch der deutschen Sprache* (Menheim, 1978).

9. This connection between *Macht* and sublimation is offered as follows: "they [the Greeks] took this all-too-human to be inescapable and, instead of reviling it, preferred to accord it a kind of right of the second rank through regulating it within the usages of society and religion: indeed, everything in man possessing *power* they called divine and inscribed it on the walls of their Heaven" (*HH*, II:1–220; *KSA*, 2:473, 219).

10. This is also the title of the following aphorism: "We are still on our knees before strength — after the ancient custom of slaves — and yet when the degree of *worthiness to be revered* is fixed, only the *degree of rationality in strength* is decisive; we must assess to what extent precisely strength has been overcome by something higher, in the service of which it now stands as means and instrument!" (*D*, 548; *KSA* 3:318).

11. *D*, 548; *KSA* 3:318 and witness his claim in *Schopenhauer as Educator*, chap. 5, that "the saint," "the philosopher," and "the artist" best exemplify this self-control and overcoming.

12. This accomplished the "spectacle of that strength which employs genius *not for works* but for *itself as a work*" (*D*, 548; *KSA*, 3: 319; *D*, 548; *KSA*, 3: 318).

13. *BGE*, 257; *KSA*, 5: 206 (original italics). It is my slightly revised translation of Kaufmann's version: "their predominance did not lie mainly in physical strength but in strength of the soul" that does not contrast sharply enough (as does Nietzsche) between the physical *Kraft* and our mental, psychological qualities.

14. My occasional references to this unauthorized, and hence problematic,

collection do not imply that I accept Bäumler's description of this highly selective compilation of Nietzsche's notebooks of 1883–88 as his final "systematic work" (see Alfred Bäumler, "Nachwort" zur *Kröner Taschenausgabe* vol. 78, 1930). On the other hand, I do not fully agree with the view of Karl Schlechta who, trying to cleanse Nietzsche of the Nazi elements ascribed to him by Bäumler, maintains that "in *Der Wille zur Macht*, nicht Neues steht," (Karl Schlechta, "Philogischer Nachbericht," *Friedrich Nietzsche Werke* [Frankfurt am Main: Ullstein, 1977], 5:55), and thus suggests that the book is hardly worth reading. See also Tracy B. Strong's opinion that "at best, the book serves an indexing function", (*Friedrich Nietzsche and the Politics of Transfiguration* [Berkeley: University of California Press, 1975], 220). I am not using uncritically this collection of Nietzsche's notes as representative of his final or mature philosophy, but am rather referring to it to get a closer look at his process of thinking in the making, to see how various ideas and notions were tested, refined, or rejected. Hence I am referring to them more in the vein of what Walter Kaufmann suggested when publishing the English translation of *The Will to Power*, namely a "thought laboratory." And see the elaborated discussion of this whole issue by Bernd Magnus, "The Use and Abuse of *The Will to Power*" in *Reading Nietzsche*, ed. Robert C. Solomon and Kathleen M. Higgins (New York: Oxford University Press, 1988), 218–35.

15. See, *WP*, 619 where he states: "[T]he victorious concept force (*Kraft*), by means of which our physicists have created God and the world, still needs to be complete: an inner will must be ascribed to it, which I designate as 'will to power,' i.e., as an insatiable desire to manifest power; or as the employment and exercise of power, as a creative drive, etc."

16. Thus in his 1888 declaration of intentions — partly realized in his writings in this and the previous year — Nietzsche testifies to the centrality of the will to power in the "*Unitary conception of psychology*" (*WP*, 688). For a concise exposition of this psychology see my "Introductory Essay: Nietzsche's New Psychology," in *Nietzsche and Depth Psychology*, ed. Jacob Golomb, Weaver Santaniello, and Ronald Lehrer (Albany: State University of New York Press, 1999), 1–19.

17. "In our science, where the concept of cause and effect is reduced to the relationship of equivalence, with the object of proving that the same quantum of force (*Kraft*) is present on both sides, the *driving force is lacking*: we observe only results, and we consider them *equivalent* in content and force (*WP* 688, original italics).

18. And thus in many places Nietzsche referred to himself as the first great and "new psychologist" of the West. See *BGE*, 12, 45; *BT*, preface, 2; *HH*, preface, 8; *GS*, preface; *A*, 24, 28, 29. Most notable, see Nietzsche's remarks in *EH*, "Why I am a Destiny," sec. 6.

19. Nietzsche's attempt to locate humanity and culture within a metaphysics of the will to power is expressed mainly in the posthumous unauthorized collection, *The Will to Power* (especially in sections 618–715, "which has no parallels" — as Kaufmann rightly says in his translation — "in Nietzsche's books" *WP*, 332, fn. 53). Presumably, Nietzsche was not satisfied with these notes and ideas,

which stood in stark opposition to his published opinions. Aware of the contentiousness of such generalized speculations, he did not include them in any of his finished books with the possible exception of *BGE*, 36, where he conducts a speculative "experiment" (*den Versuch*, *KSA*, 5:54) regarding the entire world as the "will to power and nothing else" (*KSA*, 5:55).

20. Bernd Magnus, "The Use and Abuse of *The Will to Power*," 226.

21. Almost from the beginning of his treatment of power phenomena, Nietzsche identifies perspectivism with power (see *HH*, I: Preface, 6).

22. "Power *without* victories—The strongest knowledge (that of the total unfreedom of the human will) nonetheless is the poorest in successes, for it always has the strongest opponent, human vanity" (*HH*, II:1–50; *KSA*, 2:401).

23. " 'Will *a Self*'—Active, successful natures act, not according to the dictum 'know thyself,' but . . . '*will* a self and thou shalt *become* a self' " (*HH*, II:1–366; *KSA*, 2:524).

24. *HH*, II:2–181; *KSA*, 2:629–30. This passage represents one of the first portraits of the person of negative power.

25. Nietzsche's unequivocal rejection of human exploitation even causes him to qualify his known objection to socialism: "The *exploitation* of the worker was . . . a piece of stupidity, and exhausting of the soil at the expense of the future, an imperiling of society" (*HH*, II:2–286; 285).

26. See, for example, Walter Kaufmann, *Nietzsche: Philosopher, Psychologist, Antichrist* (Princeton: Princeton University Press, 1950), 185. This statement is rather surprising, since Kaufmann himself distinguishes between "force" and "power."

27. *GM*, III:13, and see chap. 7 of my *Nietzsche's Enticing Psychology of Power*.

28. See, for example, *HH*, I:68; *KSA*, 2:80–81.

29. *HH*, I:224; *KSA*, 2:188. This, of course, is not a renunciation of Darwinian theory, for the latter refers primarily to the material domination assured by the survival of the strongest (those possessing *Kraft*). Nietzsche rather offers a complementary perspective, treating "spiritual progress" as a function of agents who are wanting in force: "[T]o this extent the celebrated struggle for existence does not seem to me to be the only theory by which the progress or strengthening of a man or race can be explained" (*ibid.*).

30. This insight, of which the marginal German Jews were in tremendous need, clearly encouraged them to follow Nietzsche's attitude. For a fuller discussion see my "Nietzsche and the Marginal Jews."

31. Nietzsche's struggle with the phenomena of guilt feelings and bad conscience goes back to the beginning of his philosophizing. Already in *BT* (chap. 1) he criticized the mechanism of repression activated by guilt.

32. This view deviates from Kaufmann's interpretation to the effect that in *Daybreak* Nietzsche still attempts to explain psychological phenomena "in terms of two key concepts: fear and power" (*Nietzsche*, 188). However, my reading of this book suggests that fear and all the moral patterns founded upon it are to Nietzsche an epiphenomenon of negative power, occurring in all people who need morality as an efficient defensive system in overcoming the feeling of

impotence that besets them in their lack of positive, autonomous, and affirmative power. Moreover the concept of power had already become the exclusive monistic principle of Nietzsche's psychology in *Human, All Too Human*.

33. There is a striking similarity between the procedure of "coolly placing on ice" (*HH*, in *EH*, 1) and the aporetic tactics employed by Socrates, whom Nietzsche ambivalently admired. Socrates "froze" by logical means, whereas Nietzsche does so by means of genetic analyses. In his dialogues, Socrates seeks to freeze the listener's belief in X, for example, by showing that this logically entails a belief in Y. The listener is not ready to endorse belief in Y because of his or her belief in the set of values: p, s, t . . ., which the listener shares with Socrates. Nietzsche employs almost the same method. He shows his readers that their most "sacred" values have negative roots, and that the "effects" of their endorsement are stagnation, repression, inhibition of creativity, depression, regression, and so on. Most of us typically consider these effects undesirable, and wish to eliminate them.

34. See, for example, David Hume, *A Treatise of Human Nature* (Oxford, 1888, 1896), bk. III, pt. 2, sect. 1; G. E. Moore, *Principia Ethica* (Cambridge, 1903), chaps. 1–4; W. K. Frankena, "The Naturalistic Fallacy," *Mind* 48 (1939): 464–77.

35. At this point we may turn to Frankena's article (ibid.), where the naturalistic fallacy of Epicurean ethics is illuminated in the following argument: "(a) Pleasure is sought by all men; (b) What is sought by all men is good (by definition); (c) Therefore, pleasure is good."

36. Alfred Bäumler, for instance, in the second section of his *Nietzsche der Philosoph und Politiker*, tried to make Nietzsche into a philosopher of the Nordic race.

37. *GM*, I:11; *KSA*, 5:275. Peter Pütz is absolutely right in his observation about this passage: "[N]othing here indicates the privilege of a Nordic race; rather, what is meant — in this sarcastic analysis — is a group of aggressive warriors that emerge in all nations at times . . . who like Agamemnon and Achilles, accomplish both great and dreadful things, who, by giving free rein to their savagery, ensure that the poets will have something to sing about" (see Pütz, "The Problem of Force in Nietzsche and His Critics" in *Nietzsche: Literature and Values*, ed. Volker Dürr, Reinhold Grimm, and Kathy Harms [Madison: University of Wisconsin Press, 1988], 18 and also 14–28).

38. Thomas Mann, "Nietzsche's Philosophy in the Light of Recent History" in his, *Last Essays* (New York, 1959), 141–77.

39. This essay is dedicated to the memory of my dear colleague and renowned Nietzschean scholar Prof. Dr. Jörg Salaquarda from the University of Vienna.

2

Misinterpretation as the Author's Responsibility (Nietzsche's fascism, for instance)

Berel Lang

I am terrified by the thought of the sort of
people who may one day invoke my authority.
—Nietzsche, letter to Elisabeth Nietzsche, 1884

If . . . the only politics calling itself Nietzschean turned
out to be a Nazi one, then this is necessarily
significant. . . . One can't falsify just anything.
—Derrida, *The Ear of the Other*

At first glance, it would seem incongruous, perhaps even unjust to impose the concepts of misinterpretation and responsibility on an author who spent much of his life and work at war with both of them. It seems to me necessary, however, to view Nietzsche through those concepts before judging the charges that link (more pointedly, inculpate) him with fascism, if only because his views *on* writing and interpretation directly affect the way we read (or mis-read) his politics (if, of course, he has any).[1] Since, furthermore, Nietzsche himself created the genealogy as a genre of philosophical discourse, it is fitting on that ground as well to read genealogically what he himself wrote; that is, through the lineage—not the history, but the begetting—of his battle with the systematic concepts whose destruction he willed; that is, those concepts of which Nietzsche could well have said, in a gloss on the Greek, that it would have been better had they never been born.

I shall be moving back and forth, then, between several questions in the theory and practice of interpretation and the specific interpretive matter of Nietzsche's fascism. *If*, again, that's what it is. A framework for my inquiry emerges from a number of questions that are first asked and answered briefly and unequivocally (well, almost unequivocally)—

the answers then to be elaborated, although also, I admit, to some extent hedged or hemmed.

Question: Was Nietzsche a fascist or an advocate for fascism?
Answer: No.

Question: Has he been interpreted *as* a fascist?
Answer: Yes—by both fascists and anti-fascists (but not by all of either group; some of the dissenters—again on both sides—consider him an *anti*fascist, others as either so politically retrograde or advanced as to be *neither* pro- nor anti-).

Question: Did Nietzsche anticipate being misinterpreted?
Answer: Yes, often. Misinterpreted as a *fascist*? Also yes, that is, once we allow for the anachronism: if the doctrines of Mussolini's "*fascismo*" became fully actual only in his so-called "March on Rome," which was in 1922—twenty-two years after, not before, Nietzsche died. A second chronological datum makes the same point, albeit more eccentrically: Nietzsche's madness seized him early in 1889—a useful mnemonic reference for recalling the year of Hitler's birth. Understandably, the term "fascism" does not itself appear in Nietzsche's writing, but this does not mean that the term could not be rightly (and so also wrongly) applied to his views. Or that he could not himself have anticipated the weight of that charge.

Question: Did Nietzsche attempt in his writing to *prevent* the misinterpretations he foresaw?
Answer: Yes; that is, to some extent.

Question: Could he have done more than he did in those attempts?
Answer: Yes, demonstrably. As I shall show.

Question: Then is Nietzsche *responsible* for the misinterpretation?
Answer: Yes, of course, on the standard judicial model by which we hold people accountable for sins of omission or for acting negligently.

Question: If Nietzsche is responsible for, that is, contributed to such misinterpetation, and in some sense, then, chose to be misinterpreted as a fascist or advocate of fascism, would this imply that the charge is not a *mis*interpretation at all?
Answer: Maybe. Go back to the first question and start over.

Thus, to the sequence of argument underlying these responses as they revolve around the issues of whether, when, and how an author can be held responsible for his misinterpretation by others. To be sure, all the words in this phrase of my title beg certain current and well-known questions that I do not plan to "un-beg" here, offering instead only a brief apologia. So, "*mis*interpretation" implies that interpretation can go wrong—which in turn implies that it can also go right or at least righter than interpretations that don't. And these together imply that the focus of interpretation (also of misinterpretation) is a point or circle, perhaps only a penumbra, that serves the text as a center and its readers as a target. Call this center or target the/a "meaning" or "referent" or "*signifiée*" or even "thing-in-itself": without *some* one of these, neither interpretation nor misinterpretation would get very far; indeed, they would not move at all.

I realize that all the links in this chain of inference have recently come under attack by critics who dispute the very notion of "good" or "bad" interpretations—still more, of "right" and "wrong" or "true" and "false" ones. On these accounts, "*mis*interpretation" becomes only a misnomer for opinions with the bad taste to differ from our own—a conclusion that follows logically if we deny some objective status to the text and reject the author as irrelevant to its understanding. Both of which claims this oppositional view makes.[2] However else one judges this view of interpretation, its immediate advantage for my own project is that it leaves me free here to assume that *it is* contradictory. To suppose, that is, that interpretation and misinterpretation do intersect at a common object—that in this class at least, answering Stanley Fish's now perennial question, yes, there is a text; that the corpse named in the "death of the author" was evidently a case of mistaken identity. And then, too, that we have here recourse to the concept of responsibility, when the very category of moral categories (thanks, among others, to Nietzsche himself) has come under fire as tendentious—certainly as lacking the foundation traditionally claimed for them.

I shall be proceeding, then, as if writing were an act (that is, deliberate), with an at least one-time agent (that is, author), which at its conclusion produces a characteristic meaning or range of meaning. As the text's potential consequences for the reader are added to these, the process of interpretation meets the both necessary and sufficient conditions of ascribing responsibility to the author who did, after all, invite the reader in. Consider the transaction so described as just that: the author makes an offer, intending to win the reader over—at least to the extent of having the reader read; the reader, on the basis of that offer, then (becoming a reader) accepts. As in any other barter, the author also, sometimes, may thus be liable for misleading the reader (that is, for the reader's misreading of the offer or of the text)—an outcome that might or might not have been intended (it could have been accidental or, in some unusual cases, have occurred against the author's will). All this takes place as the text evokes and influences the reader's response. Arguably, authors also bear or share responsibility for consequences *out-*

side the text; consider, for example, the suicides that (allegedly) followed the publication and first readings of *Young Werther's Sorrows*. My interest here, however, is in the more immediate relation between text and reader as the former induces, invites, or even just allows the latter's misinterpretation.

These premises, in any event, converge as a single thesis on Nietzsche's "fascism" that summarizes the earlier sequence of questions and answers: namely, that Nietzsche is responsible — up to a point, of course — for the interpretation of his work as fascist, even if that reading is (as I also claim) a *mis*interpretation.

Several likely objections to this thesis warrant quick acknowledgment. The first balks at the blatant hedge behind which the thesis so quickly seeks shelter: ascribing to Nietzsche responsibility for his readers' misinterpretation of him *"up to a point"* — that phrase poised to take away with the other hand what the first hand had given only a moment before. And indeed, how we determine the "point" in "up to a point" without leaving the basic thesis vacuous, *is* an issue. But conceding this does not threaten the claims themselves, since certain other clear cases of misinterpretation (and still other clear cases of non-misinterpretation) can be demonstrated, with at least some of the former shown to be the author's responsibility. This is, in any event, what must (and I believe can) be demonstrated in order to locate the point referred in the expression "up to a point."

A second likely objection concerns my reference to the "work" of Nietzsche as if it constituted a single entity or system. And one "school" of Nietzsche interpretation has indeed read him this way, sometimes for only particular texts, but at times trans-textually as well — that is, finding unity in the whole of his oeuvre, even where contradictions appear (for philosophers, there's nothing novel in that, after all).[3] But there has been almost as much opinion directed *against* this unified field theory — as based on Nietzsche's own doctrine of "perspectivism" and his disparagement of "systematic" thinking ("I mistrust all systematizers and avoid them. The will to a system is a lack of integrity" *TI*, I:26). This skepticism reinforces the both literal and literary fragmentation widespread in his writing to such an extent that for many readers the aphorism remains his most characteristic genre. And when these features are added to his subversive views on truth and interpretation (truths: "a mobile army of metaphors, metonyms, and anthropomorphisms . . . which after long use seem firm, canonical. . . .";[4] interpretation: "Whatever exists . . . is again and again reinterpreted to new ends, taken over, transformed, and redirected by some power superior to it. . . . All subduing . . . involves a fresh interpretation, an adaptation through which any previous 'meaning' and 'purpose' are necessarily obscured or even obliterated" *GM*, II:12; "There are no facts, there are only interpretations"[5]), the problems facing any would-be interpreter of Nietzsche appear overwhelming. I do not even attempt here to judge this issue as a whole, but propose, more limitedly, that on *certain* questions, to read Nietzsche systematically and to read him antisystematically yield much the same conclusion (or, in a milder version, that on some issues those two modes of interpretation fit together consistently). On certain substantive questions at least—among them, the ones addressed here—there is only one Nietzsche, not several.

A third problem concerns the definition of fascism—since any charge of fascist allegiance presupposes a definition independent of a particular ascription. But disputes abound about any such definition—because of differences alleged between the Italian and Nazi versions of fascism, for instance, or because of *their* difference from the other totalitarian systems that multiplied so inventively during the twentieth century. The supposedly neutral dictionary definitions of the term are as ideologically complicit as many openly partisan statements—and indeed I turn for a working definition to the substantial agreement between an advocate and an opponent of fascism on its central features. So, on the one side, we find Mussolini, writing with Giovanni Gentile, in 1932:

> Against individualism, the Fascist conception is for the State . . . which is the conscience and universal will of man in his historical existence . . . [and which] interprets, develops and gives strength to the whole life of the people . . . It affirms the irremediable, fruitful and beneficent inequality of men, who cannot be leveled by such a mechanical and extrinsic fact as universal suffrage. . . . It thus [also] repudiates the doctrine of Pacifism. . . . War alone brings up to their highest tension all human energies. . . . All other trials are substitutes which never really put a man in front of himself in the alternative of life and death."[6]

And then, less dramatically but still, the historian Walter Z. Laqueur, wrote in 1996, with the experience of fascism behind him and so, as he hopefully expressed it, in the past tense:

> The interest of the state always took precedence over the right of the individual. State power was to be based on leadership, and the legitimacy of leadership was provided by the fact that the people followed the leader. Seen in this light, the leader embodied the will of the people, and fascism was the true democracy. . . . One nation is the others' natural enemy . . . and those with the greatest willpower will prevail.[7]

Two themes common to these compressed statements seem crucial: The first is the priority of the state over the individual. This priority is based not simply on the superiority of state power to individual power or the imbalance between state and individual rights (and, conversely, the imbalance between their respective obligations), but on the metaphysical character of the state as inspired by a common or general will. That collective impulse transcends the will and interests of individuals within the state, serving them in fact as a rule (inevitably, of course, in the form of a ruler). The second condition is the premise of natural (that is, innate or hard-wired) inequality among individuals and nations, an inequality demonstrated for both by the outcome of conflict among them, with such conflict — less nicely, war — thus becoming itself a constitutive value.

Certain aspects of fascism are quite untouched by these two conditions. Neither refers, for example, to the economic structure of the fascist state, as that typically inclines to state-sponsored privatization. But the two principles cited are more rudimentary for fascism in its theory and practice than that or any others; I will be treating them, at any rate, as necessary elements of fascist doctrine (Nietzsche's or anyone else's); taken together, they constitute a sufficient condition for that commitment as well.

Beyond this basic definition, I would also stipulate rather than attempt to prove two of the steps in the "question-answer" sequence first outlined above. The issue of Nietzsche's *actual* influence on twentieth century fascism — through whom and how — is interesting and perhaps important. But so far as it can be answered at all (not, I believe, very far), its analysis has led to divergent results, ranging from the claim that his voice was decisive in the rise of fascism (at least of Nazism) to much more modest estimates.[8] The issue of misinterpretation (and so also of his responsibility for it), however, turns not on Nietzsche's actual influence but on his invocation by fascists — that is, in their *professed* debt to him, as quite apart from the consequences that ensued from their understanding or misunderstanding of him. And about this invocation (both for and against it), the evidence is plentiful. To be sure, there is no positive evidence that Hitler himself ever read a word of Nietzsche; if he did read him, it was certainly not extensively. (When Hitler summons the authority of thinkers other than himself, which he doesn't do often, it is Schopenhauer whom he occasionally mentions, or, more frequently, when turning music into idea, Wagner). It is clear, however, that other figures committed to National Socialism did read Nietzsche as a herald of Nazi ideology, thus bringing Hitler to Nietzsche if not quite the other way round (this is epitomized in the well-known 1934 photograph of "Hitler contemplating the bust of Nietzsche" at the Weimar archive — a set-up contrived by Nietzsche's sister with whom he himself quarreled during his lifetime on almost every philosophical or political matter they discussed). Mussolini, even as a young man, not only read Nietz-

sche and contemporary commentators on him, but wrote a numbei
reviews and essays about him,[9] and certainly the intellectual figures
whom Mussolini attracted (like Gentile) claimed the affinity of Nietzsche for the tenets of the New Order of Italian fascism.

It might be objected that this stipulation "unfairly" ascribes to fascist
ideology a blanket acceptance of Nietzsche's doctrines. Even among the
staunchest fascists, after all, Nietzsche did not pass unchallenged. So,
for example, Ernst Krieck, among the most influential of "Hitler's Professors," could hardly have been more explicit in his bon mot, "Apart
from the fact that Nietzsche was not a socialist, not a nationalist, and
opposed to racial thinking, he could have been a leading National Socialist thinker."[10] But ideologies are typically indifferent to systematic
consistency; the more numerous claims for Nietzsche's fascism have
been quite willing to force consistency on his work even when they
recognize that aspects of it are not consonant with fascist ideology. This
is indeed part of the problem to which this essay is a response: the
misinterpretation of which Nietzsche has been the subject—but also for
which, beyond what his interpreters contribute, he too is responsible (at
least up to a point).

The second item I stipulate among the earlier set of questions and
answers concerns Nietzsche's assumption that he *would* be misinterpreted—for here again, the evidence (including the first epigraph at
the beginning of this chapter) seems unequivocal. To be sure, some of
his statements to this effect are largely self-serving. He evidently regarded his *neglect*, for example, as a form of misinterpretation—an understandable if not very compelling response by an author who found
himself, and the few friends he could impose on, obliged to pay the
costs of publishing every one of his books that appeared during his
lifetime (that is, when he was still in control of them).[11] But Nietzsche
relies on more than only an argument from silence in anticipating his
misinterpretation by others; he was aware even in his brief working life
(he was only forty-five, after all, when the curtain of madness fell) of
the inconsistent and often, for him, objectionable ideological partisans
who claimed his patronage. "I enjoy a strange and almost mysterious
respect among all radical parties (Socialists, Nihilists, anti-Semites, Orthodox Christians, Wagnerians)."[12] At the time, however, he viewed this
incongruous assortment as a "comic fact"—a judgment that would
later turn out not to be comic at all and one, again, that figures largely
in the record assessed here.

Let us turn at last then to Nietzsche on the two conditions of fascism
that have been stipulated. In respect to the first of these—the priority of
the state over the individual—there seems virtually no ground for attributing any such view to Nietzsche. The evidence for this denial in-

)sence of positive assertions and a bounty of negative
cluding his repeated condemnation not only of nation-
ı but also of the concept of the state as a primary factor
ıer culture or the individual.

statements against German nationalism, moreover, are
emphatic (e.g., *BGE*, 251). "[The Germans] have on
their consc... :e all that is with us today — this most *anti-cultural* sickness and unreason there is, nationalism, this national neurosis with
which Europe is sick, this perpetuation of European particularism, of
petty politics"(*EH*, "The Case of Wagner," 2). And then, with uncanny
prescience: "You [German intelligentsia] think that you seek the truth?
You seek a 'Führer' and would be glad to follow orders."[13]

To be sure, objections against nationalism are not necessarily objections to a role for the state as such — but also on that more general issue
his criticism is explicit and harsh: The state "is the coldest of all cold
monsters. Coldy it tells lies, too; and this lie crawls out of its mouth: 'I,
the state, am the people'"(*Z*, I "On The New Idol"). "Only where the
state ends, there begins the human being who is not superfluous: there
begins the song of necessity, the unique and inimitable manner"(ibid.).
"The state is always only the means of preserving many individuals:
How could it be the end! It is our hope that through the preservation of
so many inferior types a few individuals in whom humanity culminates
will be protected."[14] "Politics swallows up all serious concern for really
spiritual matters. 'Deutschland, Deutschland uber alles' — I fear that
was the end of German philosophy" (*TI*, "What the Germans Lack,"
1). And then, as if to put a final stop to any temptation: "Madness is
something rare in individuals — but in groups, parties, peoples, ages, it is
the rule" (*BGE*, 156).

When such statements are added to Nietzsche's insistence on the priority of the individual, the single person, in the repeated imperatives of
"*Werde wer du bist*" ["Become who you are"], and even in those passages where he extolls *the* "blond beast," or less pictorially but still, *the*
Übermensch, it seems unmistakably the individual about and to whom
Nietzsche is speaking: always in its ground the singular, always the particular — never as a social creature, never as part of a collective responsible for what the individual has been or may become. Admittedly, the
ideal of a *culture* is never far off, and it is not the isolate individual who
will constitute — or enjoy — that form of collectivity. But about the steps,
setting out from the individual that would lead to or shape a culture —
steps in respect to which a role for politics and the state would be
essential — Nietzsche is largely silent. The "will to power" that he affirms is basically at odds with anything like a collective will — not because a collective cannot have a will (the triumph of slave morality

clearly proved otherwise), but because the will to power acts collectively only when those making up the collective are too weak to exert themselves individually; it is a chorus of individual ressentiment that then culminates in the travesty (but nonetheless the power) of conventional morality. To this extent, the extreme view sometimes proposed, that Nietzsche does not *have* a politics, seems at least arguable (that is, putting aside the claim that to be a- or non-political is also a form of politics — which is in my view a historical or situational, not a theoretical argument).

What then, of the second condition of the Fascist Minimum: the natural hierarchy of values held by individuals and groups (nations, peoples, races), the specific order of which is determined by conflict among them, with such conflict itself then appearing as a value? Indisputably, Nietzsche adheres to *something* in each of the two parts of this claim — but in each part only with qualification. So, on the one hand, there is little question that for Nietzsche, a hierarchy of value distinguishes between individuals: few of either his advocates or critics dispute this. Indeed, the otherwise contradictory fascist and socialist readings of Nietzsche disclose a notable likeness on this one point; in common they depict a superior human being of the future — for the one, however, wearing the orderly face of fascism, for the other, introducing the many-sided selves of a socialist utopia. Even stopping short of these conflicting extrapolations, Nietzsche's attacks on democratic egalitarianism, which is for him epitomized in socialism, are as well known as his more positive claims for the significant differences — culturally, in ability, and finally in worth — that distinguish individuals. "Every superior human being will instinctively aspire after a secret citadel where he is *set free* from the crowd, the many, the majority, where as its exception, he may forget the rule 'man.' . . ."[15] Or again: "We to whom the democratic movement is not merely a form assumed by political organization in decay but also a form assumed by man in decay . . . in the process of becoming mediocre and losing his value, whither must we direct our hopes? Towards *new philosophers*, we have no other choice; towards spirits strong and original enough to make a start on antithetical evaluations."[16] "One speaks of 'equal rights' . . . as long as one has not gained the superiority one wants."[17] After the Danish critic, Georg Brandes (whose Jewish origin, incidentally, was known to Nietzsche) gave a series of lectures in Copenhagen representing and endorsing Nietzsche's view as "aristocratic radicalism," he wrote to Nietzsche describing the enthusiastic response of his audience; in his reply, Nietzsche cites the descriptive phrase used by Brandes as "the shrewdest remark that I have read about myself till now."[18] Admittedly, Nietzsche clearly relished Brandes's attention and regard; it is also true that "aristocracy" has historically served as a euphemism for varieties of oligarchy or tyranny. But once Nietzsche's claim for differences in individual worth is recognized, and the question of which qualities underlie that distinction becomes crucial, it is evident that whatever else the term may have meant for either Nietzsche or Brandes, "aristocratic" was not simply equated with the dominance of brute force.

We need recall again here that the inequality that Nietzsche identifies among individuals is not innate or fixed for them either as individuals or as members of groups. This does not mean that their constitution by nature is irrelevant, but that what is decisive is what the individual or the group strives for and achieves—a function of decision and action, not of "hard-wiring." As individuals create themselves, so do groups—nations, peoples, or what count for Nietzsche as "races." But for none of those levels is their character fixed or settled: group features change, and this explains how Nietzsche can reconcile his diatribes against "priestly" or rabbinic Judaism with his contrasting praise of both biblical and modern Judaism).[19] In genetic terms, in other words, Nietzsche is a Lamarckian, not a Mendelian—and if the former turns out to be faulty science in terms of contemporary biology, it makes for much more plausible social theory. (How *non*-biological—and vague—Nietzsche's conception of race was, becomes apparent in statements like this: "The industrious *races* [emphasis added] find leisure very hard to endure: It was a masterpiece of *English* instinct to make Sunday so extremely holy and boring that the English unconsciously long again for their week- and working-days."[20])

The second part of the second condition of fascism also has strong grounds in Nietzsche's writings: the contention that the natural inequality among individuals manifests itself through its *assertion*. This means in effect acting at someone else's expense—not simply in order to demonstrate the inequality between the actor and the acted upon, but as the expression of inequality in a situation where that expression shapes the outcome. In this sense, individuals will be constant warriors, and war itself a natural, hence desirable state: "You say it is the good cause that hallows even war? I say unto you: it is the good war that hallows any cause" (Z, I "On War and Warriors"). And then in still more graphic terms, "Life itself recognizes no solidarity, no 'equal rights,' between the healthy and the degenerate parts of an organism: one must excise the latter—or the whole will perish" (*WP*, 734). Even allowing for the typically high register of Nietzsche's rhetoric, statements like these cannot, as some commentators have proposed, be reduced to metaphors; here and elsewhere, Nietzsche extols war, combat, and the exercise of power; conflict, then, is one, if not the only, means for determining the composition of an "aristocracy." To this extent, a distinguishing feature of the rule of the "best" — and it is *to be* a rule — is linked, if not restricted the exercise of force. It is not only that Nietzsche's writing itself is o...en violent, but that it is often about and on the side of violence. And although the concept of violence encompasses a range of possible actions, attempts to interpret Nietzsche's advocacy of violence as *purely* symbolic (and nonviolent) seem to me to owe more to wishful thinking than to his texts.

Having said this, however, it bears repeating that the "will to power" motivating the violence that Nietzsche does endorse remains a function of the individual, not the group or the state. And once again, and still more emphatically, there is no reason for considering the ability or will to strive in war as a biological given, as hard-wired or genetic. Admittedly, Nietzsche directs harsh words against the "illusion" of free will, and he rehearses approvingly the Spinozistic conception of metaphysical determinism. But if the "will to power" were genetically transmissible, all his repeated exhortations (and anger against those who fail) would be foolishly, vacuously, beside the point; nobody would have to *become* what they were because they already *would be* what they were. The struggles or wars that determine the valuative hierarchy among individuals thus does not ratify an order fixed beforehand but creates one — a significant difference.

So far, then, an account of Nietzsche in relation to the Fascist Minimum — amounting to his rejection of its first necessary condition and his acceptance of the second one only with substantial qualification in each of its two parts. On these terms, any claim for Nietzsche's "fascism" will be severely — arguably fatally — limited. But that connection has nonetheless been commonly and repeatedly asserted, by both fascists and antifascists (although, again not by all of either) — an association that is, again, asserted for *him*, not for his contemporaries John Stuart Mill (whom Nietzsche himself called a "flathead") or Ralph Waldo Emerson (whom Nietzsche so admired) or Darwin (whose conception of natural conflict Nietzsche himself criticized). How did this association develop? And what makes it an instance of misinterpretation rather than a more straightforward case of assault and battery joined to an act of theft — the not uncommon act of partisans or ideologues searching for the sanction of authority and then finding a convenient and quotable formula, easily detached from its original context?

Misinterpretation as the *author's* responsibility, however, differs from readings of this sort that hardly qualify as interpretations at all — that pass the "point" where the reader rather than the author becomes responsible for what is "found" there. In some of its claims or versions, the fascist reading of Nietzsche may indeed come close to the latter, but a significant part of the burden of that misinterpretation remains Nietzsche's and not that of his readers. Admittedly, it has been argued that given the variety and extremity of Nietzsche's statements, virtually any philosophical (or political) position can be inferred—that *this* is the one and only constant in his thinking.[21] Even this exaggerated claim, however, would not explain why fascist commentators in particular have found in Nietzsche a special affinity. Is what I described above as his partial support of the one condition of the Fascist Minimum sufficient to explain this? But there seems more to it than that. Even making allowance for the Nazi effort to find authoritative figures in a historical past most of whose heroic intellectual figures (Goethe, Schiller, Kant) were unlikely allies (which does not mean, to be sure, that their names were not invoked) and making allowance also for the polemical clang— the *"Rausch"*—of Nietzsche's prose, which taken by itself (that is, minus its characteristic irony), fits the rhetorical mode of fascism, there *seems* something more substantive to the connection, and I offer two suggestions of what that "more" may be.

The first of these proposals is straightforwardly historical. This is Nietzsche's call for the "transvaluation" or overthrow of conventional values—the norms (religious, moral, social) governing the public domain and cultures of Europe. The two-fold Nietzschean project here of invoking a new mode of being, a new "man," and rejecting the old, that is, the current one, would indeed cohere with fascist ideology. But well before the advent of fascism, the same project had struck a chord in a multitude of other "radical" movements—many of them at odds with each other and most of them at odds with other sides of Nietzsche's thought. Steven Aschheim has enumerated the improbably large array of camp followers whose opposition to conventional norms led also to *their* regard for Nietzsche as a "godfather." These partisans, diverse and often in sharp disagreement among themselves, included socialists, Marxists, anti-Semites, Jungians (and Jung) and also Freudians (and Freud), anarchists, feminists, Zionists, futurists.[22] More recently, even with the benefit of hindsight that now includes the phenomenon of a substantial fascist past, claims have been entered on behalf of postmodernism and democratic liberalism as well.[23]

This widespread, superficially indiscriminate enthusiasm does not, however, answer the question of what *more specific* than Nietzsche's broadside attack on conventional norms explains the affinity for him of fascist advocates and apologists—an affinity that in the end was at least as sustained and consequential as that of any of the other groups mentioned. Here it seems to me that an explanation does emerge—from a connection that forcibly joined and so thought to co-opt the two conditions of the Fascist Minimum cited earlier. I refer in this to a conceptual sleight of hand termed in "informal" logic the "Fallacy of Composition": the attribution of a quality or qualities of individuals to the group of which the individuals are members. This logical misstep, in its political migration, turns out to fashion a harsh reality—and one can more readily see how that happens because its philosophical history extends at least as far back as Thrasymachus's appearance in Plato's *Republic*. Nietzsche's "aristocratic radicalism" was, I have argued, fundamentally individualistic: it is the power of the individual, in will and ability, that marks the basis of that principle. But power is itself a mass noun; and as the term evokes the association of collective or group power as superceding or "overpowering" the individual, it is an easy if unwarranted step to ascribe the individual predicate of power to the group—with *group power* (in the event, that of the state) then usurping the role of the individual. For surely, if power by itself is the issue, the cumulative strength of large numbers, even if those making up the numbers are individually less powerful, would indeed be significant—a transference that Nietzsche himself repeatedly cites and criticizes.

This scenario of a forced logical connection, I would emphasize, is more than only a "thought experiment" or an imaginary construct. Specific advocates of Nietzsche in the name of German nationalism, including figures early in the twentieth century like Werner Sombart and, during the Nazi regime, the philosopher Alfred Bäumler, openly described the deliberate effort required to force the interpretation of Nietzsche through this very transposition from the will to power in the individual to the authority of power on behalf of the state. (That transposition, Bäumler ingenuously notes, was "difficult but necessary.") The outcome of this process could not, in any event, be in doubt: the Nietzsche of fascism would *have* to accord significant authority to the state *and* have it appear consistent with whatever else he advocated. But, quite simply, this consistency is absent in Nietzsche himself.

I do not wish to claim too much for this interpretive reconstruction; it is itself perhaps a misinterpretation. That fascists saw in Nietzsche a kindred spirit, however, is beyond dispute; and if one asks how that association could be made, given Nietzsche's antagonism to so much required among the necessary conditions of fascism as stated above, then the argument presented here is the *kind* of explanation indicated by Nietzsche's writings, if not the one itself. To be sure, even acceptance of this contention does not solve a still more fundamental problem. For this historical reconstruction gives a still sharper point to the question of how *Nietzsche* can be held responsible for the "misinterpretation" described: Why should *he* be blamed for a logical blunder on the part of his readers? Surely their responsibility for such a mistake does not differ significantly from their accountability for many other missteps they might at other times be charged with.

But there is a gap between logic and rhetoric, and it is in this space that the charge of Nietzsche's responsibility for his "fascism" gains its purchase. It is not only that at the center of Nietzsche's social critique was a theory of how political power evolved (his genealogy) — but that he recognized that groups who thought in terms of collective rather than individual power, in the mystification of group will and spirit, would — in fact, they already *had* in his lifetime — see in the conception of power which he advanced a justification for their own collective, not individual, use of that predicate. He was as much aware of this as he was more generally of the easy — subtle, subterranean, glib — transition effected when individuals, failing to find sufficient capacity in themselves, join together to assert it: this is the basis of his critique of the bourgeois society in which he lived, a comfortably outfitted version of the slave-morality from which it emerged. (If you wish to know "which of them has won for the present, Rome or Judea," he asks, "there can be no doubt: "consider to whom one bows down in Rome itself today" (*GM*, I:16).

We find Nietzsche, then, in opposition to essential features of the fascism that purported to follow him historically, aware of elements in his own thought that might be appropriated by its advocates for their own purposes — and yet willing to accept the risk of such misrepresentation. Not, as I have emphasized, unknowingly, and not without remonstrating with those who did this (or might yet) without speaking out: Nietzsche's antinationalist statements, as I have indicated, are numerous and unequivocal, as are his many anti-anti-Semitic statements, which are themselves often related to his antinationalistic declarations. To defend the post-Enlightenment Jewish culture in Europe and specifically in Germany as Nietzsche did, in the face of then current anti-Semitism, was already to recognize and contest the protofascism best known to Nietzsche through his acquaintance with the Bayreuth circle around Wagner.

What more than this, one might ask, could or should Nietzsche have done? I have not yet even mentioned the defense on his behalf of the readerly equivalent of "caveat emptor" (I suppose it would be "caveat lector"), which absolves the seller (in the case of interpretation, the author) of any product liability. Is not reading, after all, even more than in the case of more ordinary "acquisitions," a *purely* voluntary act? And cannot the reader "see" more fully what he or she is "getting" than with most other "purchases"? To assign responsibility to the author in this transaction, even if only "up to a point," would argue for the founding of an agency to test books for their effects much as the Food and Drug Administration does in the United States when it assesses ingested products. But no. Only assume that words or books — ideas — do indeed have consequences (intellectual, moral, psychological, historical), *and* that those effects may be cloaked in the texts that provide a medium for them—and the question of the role and extent of the author's responsibility then becomes unavoidable.

What, however, does this mean in practice? Should Nietzsche be held responsible for not anticipating the rise of Mussolini and Hitler and their fascist states—or more modestly, for the use they or their supporters made of him? But already in his own lifetime, we saw, he was aware of the conflicting appropriations of his work, including the use made of him by partisans whom he *thought* he had been atttacking. Nietzsche himself labels *On the Genealogy of Morals* a *"Streitschrift"*—a polemic—thus a representation in his own hand of what he took to be a declaration of war against the world of known values. In choosing the means, we know (and he certainly knew) that we also choose the end. He was aware, then, of the risk, and yet he preferred the risk because of what it entailed: that is, the responsibility of each self, each reader, to create himself, to make of himself the individual of whom Nietzsche spoke. And then he accepted this risk even if it also nourished the possibility of abuse that later in fact ensued. His was not only a variation of a manufacturer whose product unexpectedly turns out to be dangerous (although even for that, the charge of negligence may at times be warranted), but knowing *something* of the potential danger and weighing it against the possible benefits of writing what he did, he held steady in his course. What more would be required than this to invite (and for Nietzsche to accept) a judgment of responsibility? Not (at least not directly) for what the fascists *did*, and not for their own contribution to the misinterpretation, by which they took the step from privileging the individual to privileging the group and then the state—but for *his* side of the misinterpretation which if it is not decisive is not negligible either. What this amounts to is failing to build a fence around what he did mean so as to separate it (and its consequences) from what he did not mean—and evidently failing (more precisely, refusing) to do this, because that would in his view have diminished the force of what he did mean for those who interpreted him correctly.

In sum: Nietzsche accepted the risk of misinterpretation, in sufficient if not (as it could not have been, then or ever) full knowledge—willing to chance misinterpretation (and so too, its consequences). He was willing, in other words, to have views ascribed to him that ran counter to those he held—willing to accept the risk because of the challenge he posed in doing so. It was for his audience to decide in the face of Nietzsche's attack on them how they would respond—with Nietzsche unwilling to hedge that attack by additional qualifications even if because of that refusal a certain unwanted outcome (i.e., misinterpretation) became more probable. Because the changes required to enter those would *also* have conduced to the weakening or diminution of what he wished, even more strongly, to affirm.

Would Nietzsche have persisted in this commitment if he had been able to survey the European landscape on May 8, 1945, at the end of the bitter Second World War in Europe — with the echo of his name sounding among fragments of the carnage? Nobody is in a position to answer this question, and speculation about it will almost certainly feed the impulse of interpretation to remake authors in their interpreters' image. We can, however, ask ourselves what *we* would have had Nietzsche do differently — asking this with the knowledge we have of those who, as I have claimed, misinterpreted his words. (This question would be pertinent even if the claim of his responsibility for the misinterpretation is rejected, but especially, of course, if one accepts it.)

Would we in our response to this question urge Nietzsche just to turn down the volume dial (the *Rausch*) of his writing? One notch? Two notches? Should he have left behind, instead of the quasi-posthumous *Will To Power*, a more sober "Last Will" in which he set everything straight — perhaps like Spinoza, whom he admired above all other philosophers, laid out in *more geometrico*? Should he have added disclaimers to his books — stating, for example, that he did not really mean to replace the political tyranny of a slavish majority with the tyranny of a violent minority? The more proposals of this sort that we make, the closer we come to asserting that it would have been better, quite simply, if Nietzsche had not been Nietzsche. Some readers of Nietzsche would undoubtedly be willing to say this — and Nietzsche or not, almost everybody could name *some* writer to fit the general form of this literary counterpart of capital punishment. But to assert this for (more accurately, against) Nietzsche? Even against the Nietzsche who, supposing that he was not a fascist or advocate, nonetheless and unapologetically extolled war and conflict and unequivocally rejected the Enlightenment ideals of human equality and universal rights?

We frequently hold people accountable for actions without willing them out of existence or even without willing them to be radically other than they are. Admittedly, the restraints on our judgment of such cases depend on mitigating factors in the actions considered or in their consequences (including here, I have claimed, writing and *its* consequences). A well-known essay on a topic related to the history of fascism was titled (and argued) "No Hitler, No Holocaust."[24] Nobody, to my knowledge, has gone so far as to assert, "No Nietzsche, No Fascism" or anything close to it, and presumably for good reason: the complex material and sociopsychological factors involved in the rise of twentieth-century totalitarianism (and fascism within that category) surely extend beyond the actions or will of any single individual. And even among single individuals who contributed to the rise of fascism, Nietzsche's name, however prominent, would hardly be foremost. Within the domain of likely contributory causes, furthermore, writings and their interpretation, even their *misinterpretation*, have earned a certain "benefit of clergy" because of the freedom that the most fanatical or dogmatic writing nonetheless leaves both in the text and the reader: coercive or even totalitarian prose still leaves gaps where physical force does not. But just as a pardon to Nietzsche should not be based on his status as a cultural monument, neither should (or need) it rely on a general amnesty extended to all writing. The moral criterion for ascribing responsibility in writing can hardly claim more (or less) than the assessment of responsibility is granted elsewhere: as for all acts, writings must be read—and judged—for themselves that is, individually. To decide to leave Nietzsche as Nietzsche thus does not nullify or even mitigate the judgment of his responsibility for his misinterpretation—any more than it absolves authors in general of responsibility for their misinterpretations (if only up to a point). The crux of my argument, set in general terms, has been that the responsibility of this author extends exactly as far as does the author's authority, and that this authority at times extends also to the reader's misinterpretation of what the author, aware of that possibility, says—including now, as an example of this, Nietzsche's fascism.

Notes

1. Always a possibility, once one discounts the a priori thesis that not to have a politics is already to have one (this claim, even if rejected as true a priori, might be warranted in particular historical circumstances). For the contention that Nietzsche *could not* have a politics, see Tracy B. Strong, "Nietzsche's Political Misappropriations," in Bernd Magnus and Kathleen M. Higgins, eds., *The Cambridge Companion to Nietzsche* (Cambridge: Cambridge University Press, 1996), 119–147.

2. Cited here for the purpose of flogging a by-no-means dead horse. So, says a serious literary critic writing recently in a serious literary journal, "I'm for getting rid of interpretation altogether. Banning it. Anyone caught interpreting will be made an associate dean. I'm also against texts. We would be better off without them. They simply are no fun. . . . They spoil the party. Like a cousin of mine who is ubiquitous and terrible at parties. . . . [A text] has no will, no power, no being beyond what we can make of it. And we can make of it what we will" (James Kincaid, "What Do We Owe Texts?" *Critical Inquiry* 25 [1999]: 762–63).

3. See, e.g., Arthur C. Danto, *Nietzsche as Philosopher* (New York: Macmillan, 1965), chap. 1.

4. "Truth and Lie in the Extra-Moral Sense," trans. Daniel Beazeale, in *Truth and Philosophy: Selections from Nietzsche's Notebooks of the 1870s* (Atlantic Highlands, N.J.: Humanities Press, 1979), 84.

5. Cited in Charles Larmore, *The Morals of Modernity* (Cambridge: Cambridge University Press, 1996), 80.

6. Benito Mussolini, "The Doctrine of Fascism," in *Italian Fascisms*, ed. Adrian Lyttelton (New York: Harper, 1973), 41–49.

7. Walter Z. Laqueur, *Fascism* (Oxford: Oxford University Press, 1996), 25.

8. This disagreement is obviously linked to the general question of how ideas or ideology affect any large-scale historical events. The lack of consensus on the latter question ensures that its particular instances will also be contested; I propose here only that such questions should be addressed in "triangulated" form, that is, in the context of alternatives—e.g., not to what extent Nietzsche was responsible for the rise of Nazism or fascism, but by comparing the putative consequences of his writings with the consequences of other acts or events, as for example (in this case) the Treaty of Versailles. Such speculative comparisons can hardly settle the historical issue, but they provide a more measured perspective.

9. See, e.g., Benito Mussolini, *La Filosofia della Forza* (1908), in *Omnia Opera*, vol. 1 (Florence: La Fenice, 1951), 174–84; see also Mussolini's analysis of "La Volontà di Potenza," (4 January 1930), in *Omnia Opera*, vol. 35 (Florence: La Fenice, 1962), 90–96.

10. Cited in Steven Aschheim, *The Nietzsche Legacy in Germany, 1890–1990* (Berkeley: University of California Press, 1992), 253.

11. To be sure, there is the oddity in this that for Nietzsche, *resistance* to his work, insofar as that manifested itself in public neglect, would also be evidence of a correct understanding: *of course*, the readers (and culture) he was so vehemently attacking would wish to bury him in silence and poverty—but only insofar as they correctly understood him to be attacking them.

12. Letter to Franz Overbeck, March 24, 1887, in *Selected Letters of Friedrich Nietzsche*, ed. and trans. Christopher Middleton (Cambridge, Mass.: Hackett, 1996), 264.

13. *Nachgelassene Fragmente* (Juli 1882–Winter 1883–84), (Berlin: Waltern de Gruyter, 1977), 61 (my translation).

14. Early draft of Nietzsche's "The Uses and Disadvantages of History for Life," cited in Geoffrey Hartman, *The Fateful Question of Culture* (New York: Columbia University Press, 1997), 6–7.

15. *Beyond Good and Evil*, trans. R. J. Hollingdale. (New York: Penguin, 1973), 57.

16. Ibid., 126.

17. *The Will to Power*, trans. Walter Kaufmann and R. J. Hollingdale (New York: Vintage, 1968), 86.

18. Letter to Georg Brandes, December 2, 1887, in *Selected Letters of Friedrich Nietzsche*, 279.

19. Yirmiyahu Yovel, *Dark Riddle: Hegel, Nietzsche, and the Jews* (University Park, Penn.: Penn State University Press, 1998), chaps. 7–10.

20. *Beyond Good and Evil*, 112.

21. See, e.g., Charles Larmore, "Nietzsche's Legacy," in his *The Morals of Modernity*, 79–88.

22. See, for example, Steven Aschheim, *The Nietzsche Legacy in Germany, 1890–1990*, 60–69.

23. See, for example, Richard Rorty, "Solidarity and Objectivity," in Richard Rorty, *Objectivity, Relativism, and Truth* (Cambridge: Cambridge University Press, 1991), 21–34; Lawrence Hatab, *A Nietzschean Defense of Democracy: An Experiment in Postmodern Politics* (Chicago: Open Court, 1995).

24. Milton Himmelfarb, "No Hitler, No Holocaust," *Commentary* 76 (March, 1984): 37–43.

3

Experiences with Nietzsche
Wolfgang Müller-Lauter

Nietzsche in the Service of National Socialist Propaganda

"Something said briefly can be the fruit of much long thought," Nietzsche wrote in his *Assorted Opinions and Maxims* (*HH*, II:127).[1] What is long thought, however, does not disappear into the brief remark as into a result. Rather, what is briefly said must always form the starting point of a long path of reflection. Nietzsche found ever more reason as he grew older to recommend that his texts be read "slowly, deeply, looking cautiously before and after, with reservations, with doors left open, with delicate eyes and fingers" (*D*, Preface, 5). Caution and precaution must (also) be understood literally: in his aphoristic books, the aphorisms refer to one another in more or less hidden ways. "One thing is necessary above all . . . , something that has been unlearned most thoroughly nowadays—and therefore it will be some time before my writings are 'readable'—something for which one has almost to be a cow and in any case not a 'modern man': *rumination*" (*GM*, Preface, 8).

One must, therefore, establish a critical distance between oneself and the seductive immediacy of the impression Nietzsche's aphorisms make; an effect that he intends as a means of temptation, particularly in the early books. To extract particular sentences or passages and then lash them superficially together in order to produce Nietzsche's *Weltan-*

schauung is only the most vulgar way in which he has been intellectually exploited. I first encountered the philosopher in this form—in sentences selected for popular nationalist consumption—as a schoolboy. It was in my home town of Weimar, more than sixty years ago, and in the years before the end of the war I encountered him again and again: at school appeals or in the University during recess, through the flag salutes of the Hitler Youth, later during community service, and at length in my military days, as well. The effect of Nietzsche's sentence, first heard when I was but a thirteen- or fourteen-year-old pupil at recess (and would afterward hear many more times) was unforgettable: "Praised be what makes hard!" That seemed an appropriate motto for what Adolf Hitler had announced to German youth as the "education of a new man": he must be "agile as a greyhound, rough like leather, hard as steel."[2] Over the next several years all young people would be bullied by this motto. And those among them who, for whatever reason, found the spirit of the times unsympathetic developed a variety of avoidance strategies, down to the most inconspicuous passive resistance. But the duties derived from that demand could only be imperfectly avoided. "Praise be what makes hard." The philosopher who wrote those words would have been seen by those outsiders, to whom I myself belonged, as allied with the hostile and threatening side of the propaganda of the day.

Two or three years later I attended the Zarathustra reading of a well-known Dresden actress in the Weimar auditorium, no doubt cosponsored by the Nietzsche archives. There I heard for the first time the passage from which the praise of hardness is taken. The sentence before runs, "Whoever has spared himself much, he is at length offended by his many reprieves." In this context, that praise makes a great deal of sense, as I thought at the time. When Zarathustra, in the course of his further travels, always must go higher, when he must along the way climb up upon his own head, or clamber out beyond his own heart, this clearly has nothing to do with the inert hardness of steel. The sentence following also shows clearly how the brown-shirted ideologues distorted the meaning of a Nietzsche quotation. It runs: "I do not praise the land where butter and honey—flow" (*Z*, III "The Wanderer"). The dash before the verb draws attention to Nietzsche's reservations about an all-too-comfortable life; perhaps one starts to recognize that too great prosperity has its troubling shadow side, as well. But one could ignore the dash, as many authors in those years did. Then the meaning of "flow" is obscured, milk and honey are no longer important, and more than their superfluity is negated. Then the philosopher could be enlisted in support of militaristic slogans of "cannon instead of butter." As I have also experienced.

My distaste for Nietzsche grew in the years that followed, even when it was clear to me that propaganda misused his aphorisms as catch-phrases, to which, at the same time, they were also suited.[3] Zarathustra crossed my path frequently; I found him an off-putting companion: "Oh my Brothers, am I cruel? But I say: what is falling, we should still push!" (Z, III "On Old and New Tablets"). I was also pushed away, as I fell out of the social vortex of the Zeitgeist. I got off easily. But I heard of many people who were tripped up and then pushed over. The camp in Buchenwald on the Ettersberg was nearby; and rumors of what went on there reached my ears. In any case, already by that time there was hardly anything I deemed the Nazis incapable of committing.

The Nietzsche reading in Weimar to which I alluded previously was not merely a piece of National Socialist propaganda. One must imagine a quite diverse audience in that Weimar auditorium. There were Nazis: I well remember the petit bourgeois in the Party uniforms, in whose faces one would recognize, as one circulated during the break, the disguised consternation brought about by an encounter with incomprehensible depth. There were also modest and educated older people, who quietly pointed this out to me with scorn and irony. There were enthusiasts, often gesturing in an esoteric manner, who had internalized Elisabeth Förster-Nietzsche's posthumous reconciliation of Richard Wagner and Friedrich Nietzsche. Wagnerian pathos, for its part, dominated the opera productions of the Weimar National Theater.[4]

My philosophical interests were awakened early; they replaced an initial religious orientation. (I had stumbled across the pre-Socratics, whom I read in translation. The "logical" derivation of world reality from a single "*Ur-ground*" fascinated me; the different interpretations of this by early philosophers and also by later metaphysical thinkers woke in me the question of the criterion for the truth of philosophical claims. The above-mentioned older and better educated companions gave me, as a fatherless youth, many suggestions for reading. At that time I ran aground on Kant's *Critique of Pure Reason*; however, the demand for an analytic return to the conditions of possibility of human knowledge and action has never left me since. The feeling of inner liberation called forth in me by the clarity of Lessing's polemical writings, and also of purgation from the intoxicating and obscurantist writings I had initially encountered, is unforgettable.)

I developed a particular interest in psychology. Here, in a way I found confusing, I was to encounter Nietzsche again. Not the psychologist Nietzsche, but the founder of experimental psychology, Wilhelm Wundt, threw a new light on the philosopher whom I had rejected. Wundt's claim to ground all the individual sciences in philosophy as general science had fascinated me. In 1941 a new edition of his book

Die Nationen und ihre Philosophie, which had been written during the First World War, was published. Here I found Nietzsche, to my surprise, situated in a tradition of idealistic philosophy.[5] Wundt managed this by presenting Nietzsche as a "poet-philosopher" who had earned a right to imaginative exaggeration by expressing a highest future ideal. The "Revaluation of all Values" was not to be a "total revaluation" but rather a modification of the moral, through which the Kantian imperative of duty and the philosophy of German idealism would both be deepened. Nietzsche's Overman is for Wundt only an idea pictured by his imagination, the "Eternal Return of the Same" an aesthetically effective image of eternity.

I knew little of German idealism; that Nietzsche's criticism of morality was directed against Kant's moral philosophy, though, and was no extension of it, was obvious. Moreover, Wundt's Nietzsche was thoroughly compatible with the Nietzsche favored during the Nazi period, the prophet and creator of myths. The psychologist did not open Nietzsche to me; rather, his voluntaristic idealism seemed to me questionable.

Of course it didn't take long for me to realize how poorly Nietzsche's thought did in fact fit into the National Socialist world view. More than his vitriolic words against the Germans, which might, as Alfred Bäumler showed, be attributed to Nietzsche's disappointment at his reception in the Fatherland, it was his massive attacks on anti-Semites that proved too much for the Nazis to swallow. In 1942 a friendly book-dealer steered me to a text just published by the Weimar Duncker press with the title *Nietzsche, Juden, Antijuden*. It was by the Wagnerian Curt von Westernhagen, who, to put it briefly, presented the philosopher as a friend of the Jews and his spirit as Jewish. But I could share only to a certain extent the book-dealer's malicious pleasure in having used this book to make a few Nazis unsure of themselves. My antipathy to Nietzsche was too great. Shortly before, a classmate had recommended to me *The Birth of Tragedy*. I had attempted it, but soon set it aside out of distaste: too much disorder, too much pathos, too much Wagner. The question whether the Nazis had more or less of a right to appropriate Nietzsche retreated behind more general reservations.

A copy of a 1942 review of Westernhagen's book in the *Völkischer Beobachter*, subsequently provided me with an impression of the intellectual debates of the time. *Sturmhauptführer* Heinrich Härtle signed the review. In his 1937 book *Nietzsche und der Nationalsozialismus*, Härtle had argued that only a self-conscious National Socialist could understand Nietzsche properly, though the philosopher himself had unfortunately misunderstood the concepts of People, State, and Race. Now this same Härtle, who had found Nietzsche's rejection of anti-Semitism particularly galling, took issue here with Westernhagen. The latter had, so Härtle maintained, dared "to collect *via* the detour through Nietzsche's attitude toward Judaism everything negative and assemble a caricature of Nietzsche's personality." The book "was born from hatred of Nietzsche"; "a Jew or a Jesuit might revenge himself on Nietzsche in this way." This technique of inverting a distortion can be found in the internal struggles of other ideologies. The opponent is characterized as that which he attacks. Here, the declared anti-Semite Westernhagen is reinterpreted as a sort of quasi-Jew himself. Also typical of debates on Nietzsche, Härtle accused Westernhagen of "arbitrarily selecting his quotations in accordance with his negative intention." And what does he offer by contrast? Quotations (though many fewer): "On the other hand, there are individual utterances that contain the sharpest attacks upon the Jews."[6]

In the ideological debates in Germany at that time, of which I then knew nothing, the National Socialist opponents of Nietzsche had a much easier polemical position to sustain those who claimed him as a precursor to the Nazi *Weltanschauung*. Let me recount two remarks that are typical of this ideological rejection of Nietzsche. Ernst Krieck, professor of philosophy and pedagogy in Heidelberg, summed up his view of the philosopher in two sentences: "All in all: Nietzsche was an opponent of Socialism, of Nationalism, and of Racial Thought." He adds ironically, "But for these three intellectual moments, he might perhaps have made an outstanding Nazi."[7] Similar remarks had been made, though independently of Krieck, already in 1934 by Arthur Drews, a professor of philosophy in Karlsruhe. One finds in Nietzsche neither national sympathy nor socialist awareness, he claimed. Nietzsche is, on the contrary, and particularly after his break with Richard Wagner, an enemy of everything German; he supports the creation of a "good European," and goes so far as to accord the Jews "a leading role in the dissolution of all nations." Finally, he is an individualist, with no notion of "the National Socialist *credo*: 'collective over individual utility.'" "After all this," Drews continued, "it must seem unbelievable that Nietzsche has been honored as the Philosopher of National Socialism, . . . for he preaches in all things the opposite of National Socialism," setting aside a few scattered utterances. The fact that such honors have repeatedly been bestowed on him has "as its main reason, that most people who talk about Nietzsche tend only to pick the 'raisins' from the cake of his 'philosophy,' and, because of his aphoristic style, lack any clear understanding of the way his entire thought coheres."[8] From the subordinating perspective of propaganda, it was finally a question of the "raisins." After the loss at Stalingrad, when anyone could have recognized that the Germans were defeated, Joseph Goebbels proclaimed "total war." On the tenth anniversary of the National Socialist seizure of power, he announced in the Berlin Sports Palace: "As we so often have in the past, so again now we shall bear the hardest burdens. And we shall once more justify the words of the philosopher: " 'What does not kill me makes me stronger!' "[9] Again, I found Nietzsche enlisted in the service of Nazi propaganda. Here, too.

Nietzsche had been simplified. The citation is from *Ecce Homo*, where Nietzsche describes himself as a decadent who has become, simultaneously, "hale." This haleness is manifested, for example, in that he can guess "remedies . . . against what is harmful"; that he "exploits bad accidents to his advantage": "what does not kill him makes him stronger" (*EH*, "Why I Am so Wise," 2). Nietzsche had to become such a hale person in order to endure suffering of various kinds, illnesses, and great personal injuries. There are more than a few remarks in which his astonishment that life was bearable at all is audible. This is the context as well for the posthumous note from 1887, where Nietzsche literally writes, in parentheses, the words that Goebbels quotes: "what does not kill me makes me stronger." Nietzsche invokes here "questions of force": "how far one can maintain oneself against the survival conditions of the society and its prejudices . . . how far against the truth, and accept in one's heart the questionable side of it? — how far against suffering, self-contempt, pity, illness, defilement, with the question mark whether or not one shall become master of it all?"[10] These are profound, existential questions, that have nothing to do with the demand that the Germans continue with a lost war. In the war I did not pursue the citation; I was not one of those German soldiers with Nietzsche's *Zarathustra* in his satchel. These fellows were anyway more prevalent in 1914–18 than in the Second World War.

Experiences with Nietzsche after the Second World War

In any case, my taste for Nietzsche had been so spoiled that during my philosophy studies after the war, I did not take part in any seminars or lectures on him. Only in 1962 as a university teacher, when I was preparing a lecture with the (for the time not very original) title "Nietzsche and the Consequences" did I begin to read Nietzsche carefully and rigorously. My subtitle was "On the Problematic of Nihilism." This was to show that I hoped to claim Nietzsche for the European developments in the twentieth century which he had prophesied or conjured up. I wanted to examine the thought-provoking remark of Albert Camus: "Nietzsche is actually what he took himself to be: the sharpest consciousness of nihilism. . . . [He announces, of] . . . the twentieth century." That he himself remains "entwined in the inner logic of nihilism" is perhaps unavoidable.[11] I wanted to talk in the lecture about the National Socialist Nietzscheans as well as their critics and penetrate to the nihilistic phenomena of the present. I never came to the "consequences" in the lecture, for I had entered into the subterranean realms and hidden backgrounds of Nietzsche's thought, which I had not suspected were there before.

In Germany in the 1950s, Georg Lukács's critique of Nietzsche held sway. But this Marxist demonization of the philosopher *is no less crude than his National Socialist* appropriation.[12] I was more impressed by Thomas Mann's Zurich lecture of 1947. Here he claims that one cannot by any means take Nietzsche "at his word." The novelist had gone so far as to call it "the ultimate inhumanity" to "meet the shrill and tormented challenges" of Nietzsche "with mockery and scolding — with simple stupidity and moral outrage."[13] Thomas Mann's lecture had a great influence on the Nietzsche reception of the postwar generation. Since it brought together various opposed tendencies of the philosopher's thought and impact, different strands could be taken up. Mazzino Montinari, for instance, was awakened by his reading of Thomas Mann from his "totally politicized" slumber after ten years of membership in the Italian Communist Party, and inspired to develop a new understanding of the relation between culture and politics. In Zürich, Thomas Mann had claimed that Nietzsche must put up with being called a humanist; he had emphasized the "socialist tenor of his [i.e., Nietzsche's] vision of a post-bourgeois life." Such remarks by Thomas Mann won Montinari over to the philosopher, while I found the novelist's critical comments on Nietzsche's "enthusiastic protection of life" against knowledge important. Like Mann, I took umbrage at the unconditional ranking of life above spirit, a ranking with whose dangerous implications I had become acquainted under the Nazis.

If, as early as my first Nietzsche lecture, I presented the philosopher as a profound enlightener, who, as an enlightener "of the Enlightenment" made a growing nihilism apparent, I did not disregard, nor have I at any time since, to what extreme exaggerations Nietzsche was misled in his quasi-Dionysian celebration of life, particularly in his last creative period. With his remarks on "great politics" and "breeding" above all, the Nazis could associate themselves at least verbally. In order to do this, they had to push the other, more penetrating, Nietzsche to one side, or to suppress him. I referred to Karl Jaspers, who wrote with regard to his great Nietzsche book of 1936 that he had tried there to protect the philosopher from such "derailments." For he had represented the essence of his thinking "as the space-creating, illuminating, dialectically daring, never fixed way of thinking."[14] To propound those "derailments" as the full and true Nietzsche was, and is, an abuse of the philosopher.

There I agree with Jaspers. A philosophically even stronger impression was made on me by Heidegger's Nietzsche lectures from the thirties and forties, first published in 1961. Here, Nietzsche is presented as the thinker who brings Western metaphysics to an end. According to Heidegger, Nietzsche had not, despite his own claims, overcome nihilism, but rather remains entwined within it. Admittedly I soon noticed that Heidegger had tweaked Nietzsche in a way that fit him into his own project of a history of being. To work out by contrast Nietzsche's own intentions is something that since the middle of the 1960s I have taken to be part of my own task.

As far as Nietzsche's direct political effectiveness is concerned, Jürgen Habermas's remark that he "is no longer contagious"[15] seems to have held true up to now. I also agree with Jacques Derrida, however, who has written that "the future of the Nietzsche text is not closed." Nietzsche's own understanding of "great politics" raises the question if it is "still to come in the wake of a seismic convulsion of which National Socialism or fascism will turn out to have been mere episodes?"[16] One can go so far as to see in Nietzsche's "complete nihilism" and the resulting unlimited emancipation of human possibilities in National Socialism one Nietzschean experiment[17] upon which other (quite different) ones might follow. The task of a "political reading" applies not only to Nietzsche, as Derrida adds in the quoted passage, but to "the Heideggerian, Marxian, or Freudian corpus, and for so many others as well."[18]

In any case, the "new Nietzsche" that emerged from France in the sixties and seventies and whose ever more dominant "representative" is Jacques Derrida, has nothing to do with Nietzsche's "great politics." In Germany this reading at first exercised only slight influence, though it triggered alarms among the ideologues in the GDR (and not only there). The debate made it sound as if, with the "French Nietzsche-Renaissance," 'fascism' itself stood at the door. The argument was no doubt premature. What unsettled the Marxist ideologues most was the rapprochement with Nietzsche "from the left" (already registered with disapproval by Ernst Bloch and Theodor W. Adorno). That, in the wake of an important lecture by Michel Foucault.[19] The fact that Nietzsche was viewed as one of the seminal thinkers of the century, alongside Marx (and Freud), and that he was discussed in this way in Western Europe and America was felt to be a dangerous challenge to Marxist orthodoxy, and combated accordingly. These impulses were absorbed by the freer spirits in Communist East Germany who, referring to the "many-sidedness of Nietzsche's thinking," demanded a more differentiated engagement with the "controversial philosopher." In particular one that would do justice to his "cultural and social criticism."[20]

The deconstructive Nietzsche interpretation that grew from "post-structuralism" emphasized as never before the linguistically polysemic and subterranean Nietzsche. The earlier search for Nietzsche's "system" has become obsolete here; with emphasis on the perspectival aspect of his thought, the fragmentary is granted decisive weight. Merely as an example one can recall Maurice Blanchot, who sees coherent discourse constantly knocked out of joint by Nietzsche's fragmentary text. By radicalizing his "pluralism," all "unity" is changed into discontinuity.[21] This point of view is truer to Nietzsche's philosophy than was the attempt to unify his thought metaphysically. Admittedly, I think Nietzsche's "coherent discourse" is not taken seriously enough by the so-called postmodernists. The dimension of the aesthetic, about whose high rank in Nietzsche's philosophy there can be no question, gains a stature for many of them that drains his philosophy of its more penetrating questions. So Gianni Vattimo praises Nietzsche as "the complete nihilist," for whom the "perfection of nihilism" exhausts "all that we can expect and hope for."[22] But Nietzsche did not try to make himself at home in nihilism but to overcome it. This overcoming is questionable, it is true, but this does not free us from the task of inquiring about it in the most accurate way we can. Since, as I have just related, my concern with Nietzsche has also centered on these questions, and still does, I will consider in what follows, four aspects of a thematic I can hardly hope to exhaust here.

On Nietzsche's Discussion of Nihilism

Nihilism as the Devaluation of All Prior Values

Nietzsche describes nihilism as the result of the *devaluation of the highest values*. "Values" are directing viewpoints through which human beings orient themselves and that determine their actions and thinking. The inner coherence of all social and cultural forms rests upon them. Western history represents a contextual tradition that is in large measure constituted by Christianity and Platonism, which are closely associated in Nietzsche. Its defining feature is the displacement of its highest values into a fictional Beyond. This fiction is more and more difficult to maintain in the modern era. Above all, the progressive development of the natural sciences hollows it out. The process of devaluation that is visible even here is what Nietzsche would like to make apparent, promote, accelerate. This is the sense in which the madman in *The Gay Science* must be understood, when he says that "we all" are the murderers of God. To conceive of this "deed" as an "event," and so to incorporate it into the continuity of the devaluing process — this is what must be done. "We," human beings, have killed God gradually. The sudden insight into the meaning of what has happened, that God is dead, is what drives that man "mad," while the thoughtless atheists he encounters fail to recognize that with the consciousness of this "deed," "a higher history than any history so far" has begun. The "event" that is God's death, however, is "still underway and wandering"; it will take time to "arrive" among humanity. Perhaps "for millennia" there will be caves in which one displays the "shadow" of the dead God (*GS*, 125; 180).

Among the shadows of God are the pseudo-authorities that humanity has made for itself: a conscience freed of theology in Kant, the authority of a transpersonal reason in the Hegelian sense, the social instinct in various versions, and history. Nietzsche had already combated the dominance of the latter, particularly in the Hegelian tradition, in his second *Untimely Meditation*. In these and other cases, "the nihilistic question 'what for?'" has been answered by finding an external goal to which one "can give oneself over."[23]

With the loss of those factors that provide a ground for meaning, the human being loses the ground beneath his feet. And once his or her earlier values have been recognized as deceptions, there is no going back to the earlier certainties and sureties. All "attempts to escape nihilism" by not drawing the ultimate consequences "bring forth the opposite, exacerbate the problem." One must progress from "incomplete" to "perfect nihilism."[24] Already in the "Words of consolation of a progress grown desperate," from *Human, All Too Human*, Nietzsche insists that "we cannot return to the old, we *have* burned our boats; all that remains is for us to be brave, come what may" (*HH*, I:248).

The Revaluation of Values as the Overcoming of Nihilism

Nietzsche followed his way bravely, at most suspecting, but not knowing, where it would lead. Only late in the day does "one muster the courage for what one really *knows*," Nietzsche noted in autumn of 1887. "That I have hitherto been a thorough-going nihilist, I have admitted to myself only recently: the energy, the nonchalance with which I advanced as a nihilist deceived me about this basic fact." His goal was insight into "'goal lessness' in itself."[25] This is the "*most extreme nihilism*," it claims that "the goal" is lacking, "that there is no truth; that there is no absolute way things are, no 'thing in itself.'" All "authorities" have collapsed. *Active nihilism* wants to destroy anything that would still invoke them. As a philosopher of *devaluation* Nietzsche himself was such an active nihilist (as an example of the unproductive counterpart to his own activism Nietzsche points to the Russian anarchists of his day, who want only to destroy). There is also a condition of *passive nihilism* (Nietzsche's most common example: Buddhism). Here, even when it has become impossible to ignore the erosion of all received values and goals in the collapsing culture, one seeks out what, in religious or aesthetic disguise, still "refreshes, heals, calms, numbs."

In this manifestation of an intrinsically ambiguous nihilism, one has been delivered over to *extremes*. Nietzsche, in penetrating the extreme, creates the premises for his own way beyond past nihilism. He asks what lurks in the recognition that there is no truth, no goal, no value, no meaning. For Nietzsche sees that this "judgment" still expresses an *evaluation*. In it, the "*value* of things" is placed "just there, in the fact that no reality corresponds or ever has corresponded to them."[26] Even if the "most extreme nihilism" is fixated on loss, it still derives its standard from the reality it has negated. True, it has discovered that the so-called "transcendent," "true world" is deception; it locates itself now on the basis of the apparently true "disparaged world" of "immanence," from whose stuff the Beyond had been constructed. But "the evaluative standards have been retained" from the "true world," through which the one remaining world is condemned. "That highest disappointment is held against the world, as well, and taken to show it as all the more contemptible." And thus one remains stuck in nihilism.

Whoever has the strength to overcome the judging values thereby overcomes the "most extreme nihilism."[27] For him "things" do not need to remain worthless, he can now rather bestow values upon them through his own efficacy. This requires a more radical understanding of the possibilities of human activity than is practiced in the familiar "*distinction between 'true' and 'false.'*" So, according to Nietzsche, the nihilistic determination of the "state of affairs," that there is no truth, no "being," no "meaning," etc., is "fundamentally different from the creative *positing*, from constructing, shaping, mastering, *willing*, as it exists in the essence of *philosophy*. To inscribe a meaning*—this task remains unconditionally in force, supposing no meaning is already there."

With this, Nietzsche has transcended his initial goal of insight into goallessness. He sees himself now as liberated for "*goal positing*" itself, through which "the factually real" can be fashioned.[28] Nietzsche, who predicted "*the advent of nihilism*" over the next two centuries, understands himself in the possibility of this creative positing "as the first perfect nihilist of Europe, who, however, has even now lived through the whole of nihilism, to the end, leaving it behind, outside himself." If the devaluation of received values leads to nihilism, the revaluation of all values that Nietzsche eventually makes the center of his thinking leads beyond it: to the necessity of positing new values.[29]

Such a transformed nihilism, Nietzsche writes, "as *the denial of a truthful world*, a *being*, might be *a divine way of thinking*."[30] Despite the subjunctive mode, this is not merely metaphoric. Already Zarathustra could not stand not being a god, if there were gods. His creative will finds a limit only in the Overman, he announces and hopes for, whose life after the death of all Gods is his ultimate will.[31] If Nietzsche here oversteps human finitude in the direction of a future superhumanity (however it is to be interpreted), he later absorbed the fashioning-creative into his "humanly possible," which was finally possible only in Nietzsche's own work. So *Thus Spoke Zarathustra* is celebrated in *Ecce Homo* as the book in which "man has been overcome at every moment; the concept of the 'Overman' has here become the greatest reality."[32] The subjunctive of the earlier passage has become indicative. The divine is here the Dionysian, expanded beyond its earlier presentation in *The Birth of Tragedy*.[33] Nietzsche understands himself and his creation as manifestations of a Dionysian superfluity of strength. This brings with it the final delimitation, to which *Ecce Homo* most clearly testifies. The boundaries of finitude are definitively transcended when Nietzsche, in his last writings, the so-called mad postcards, identifies with God the Creator, with Dionysus, etc. Even here the last consequence of a self-overcoming into transfinitude speaks to us. This is naturally not to claim that hubris drove Nietzsche to madness.[34] It is altogether too comfortable when reference to his personal "destiny" spares us having to confront his philosophy. As a philosopher, Nietzsche still belongs, quite clearly, to our "destiny." This, however, no longer in the sense in which he ends the section "Why I Am a Destiny" in *Ecce Homo*: " — have I been understood? — Dionysus versus the Crucified. . . ."[35] True, the "versus" in this formula has more than one meaning.[36] It at least also represents a declaration of war by the ancient-new god Dionysus against the Christian God and its "shadow."[37]

The Revaluation as Philosophical Task: The Philosopher as Free Spirit and Lawgiver

Nietzsche's experience of the devaluation of all values does not necessarily culminate in that radical form of revaluation we encounter in his late philosophy. Still in 1884 the revaluation of values serves Nietzsche as a "means" of enduring the thought of the eternal return. To it belongs "pleasure no longer in certainty but rather in uncertainty." This is the sound of the experimental thinking of the free spirit to which we will turn in a moment. "The constantly creative" in the human being should be given its due: "No longer the humble phrase 'it is all just subjective,' but instead 'it is also our *work*!' let us be proud of it!"[38] A year later, in 1885, the critical question still runs, "How must the human beings be constituted who undertake this revaluation."[39] It is as if another Nietzsche is speaking when we hear his claim in *Ecce Homo* that he alone is capable generally of "*reversing perspectives*: first reason why a 'revaluation of values' is perhaps possible for me alone." Nietzsche here claims to be able to decide for all. The "formula for an act of supreme self-examination on the part of humanity" has become in him "flesh and genius," he writes. He was the first to "discover the truth," because he "was the first to experience lies as lies."[40]

A more fitting distinction than that between a "tough" and a "gentle" Nietzsche[41] seems to me to be that between the questioning, searching, experimenting Nietzsche and the unconditionally judging (and simultaneously prejudging) Nietzsche, ready with a Yes or No to everything. His philosophy of Perhaps should be distinguished from his later philosophy of Legislation. In *Human, All Too Human* Nietzsche "experiments" with the possibility of a revaluation long before he understands himself as a nihilist. In those days, as he was writing this book, he tells us in the 1886 preface, he felt himself one of the free spirits, for he needed their company and conversation. Here he speaks of the "fears and frosts of the isolation" that result from the fact that no one "has ever before looked into the world with an equally profound degree of suspicion." As a free spirit, he describes himself as "restlessly and aimlessly on his way as if in a desert," driven by "a more and more perilous curiosity. 'Can all values not be turned around? And is good perhaps evil? And God only an invention and finesse of the Devil?"[42]

Nietzsche breaks off this sort of questioning and experimenting journey as a free spirit when, faced with a historically potent nihilism, he decides for a different kind of future philosophizing. In *Beyond Good and Evil* Nietzsche at first affiliates himself with the philosophy of the free spirits and their experimentation. In the preface to this book he sees their "task" as having grown from "a magnificent tension of the spirit" brought about by his struggle against Platonism and Christianity. We, so Nietzsche writes here, "we *good Europeans* and free, *very* free spirits," have "the whole need of the spirit and the whole tension of its bow." He sees "a new species of philosophers" arising, who could be called "Attempters" ("*Versucher*"); it is "probable enough" that these free spirits are "friends of truth," but it goes against "their taste" to identify a general truth. They say, "My judgment is *my* judgment: no one else is easily entitled to it." As friends of solitude they do not belong "among the *levelers*," who as "slaves of the democratic taste and its 'modern ideas'" wear the name free spirit impermissibly (*BGE*, 42–44). Gradually, Nietzsche sharpens the demands made upon the free spirit that its suspicion not pause before anything. This "cruelty to oneself" demanded by thought finally forces one to "sacrifice God for the nothing"; this "paradoxical mystery of the final cruelty was reserved for the generation that is now coming up: all of us already know something of this" (*BGE*, 55).

With the "Death of God," a legislating philosophy has become necessary. In *Beyond Good and Evil* the free spirits look forward to the philosopher of the future as "the man of the most comprehensive responsibility, who has the conscience for the over-all development of man." They themselves remain behind. That philosopher should be the strong man who not only will "make use of whatever political and economic states are at hand" to further his goals but also of religion as well. This is for "the strong and independent who are prepared and predestined to command . . . one more means for overcoming resistances, for the ability to rule" (*BGE*, 61). The search for "*new philosophers*," who could provide "the stimuli" for a total revaluation of all values in force until now gains particular urgency in light of Nietzsche's diagnosis of an "*over-all degeneration of man.*" He sees in the philosophers of the future, and therefore inflates their significance to the utmost, the "forerunners" of a will "that forces the will of millennia upon *new* tracks." (*BGE*, 203). One can detect in this will a reference to the Overman announced in *Thus Spoke Zarathustra*. In any case, "*genuine philosophers*, however, are *commanders and legislators*: they say, 'thus it shall be!' They first determine the Whither and What For of man."[43]

Nihilism as the Collapse of Meaning and the Search for New Authorities

With "What for?" nihilism asks for the meaning, with "Whither?" for the goal of human being. In a posthumously published fragment we have already considered, Nietzsche lists the instances of value that are expected to provide an "answer" to the question, "What for?" — "only in order not to have to *want* to posit the 'What for' oneself." His enumeration proceeds from the superhuman authorities (noted first) on up to an almost stereotypical attitude of fatalism: "'*there is no answer*' but 'it is on its way *somewhere*,' 'it is impossible to want a What For?' with *devotion* . . . or *revolt* . . . Agnosticism vis-à-vis. the goal" — and finally up to the "*negation* of the *What* For of life."[44] Fatalism and suicide are also answers to the questions of What For and Whither.

In *Beyond Good and Evil* the commanding and legislating authority of the future philosophers supplants the superhuman authorities that have been rejected in consequence of nihilism. Finally it is (as was discussed in the second section) Nietzsche's philosophy itself, rooted in Dionysus, that will undertake the revaluation of all values and the future establishment of human meaning and purpose. Man found his earlier "What For?" prepared for him. Shall he, nihilism having been overcome, once again, if in another way ("posited by human beings") find it prepared for him?

The insight into the devaluation of value should free the spirit for multifarious attempts and experiments of thinking. The revaluation, however, must determine the new paths of the will for millennia and therefore establish at least the frame for future evaluations. If we take that literally, then after the death of God (in the devaluation) the end of the free spirit (in the revaluation) is here announced. For a free spirit subject to "coercion" and "command" — whatever the evaluative system — is no longer a free spirit. It must be demonstrated, however, that Nietzsche wants to make room for experimental thinking under new conditions. Why, though, we must first ask, does the revaluation require a philosophical legislation? The essential reason for this can be found in Nietzsche's diagnosis (examined under the third heading) of the "degeneration" of (Western) man, discussed during his last two productive years under the rubric of decadence. Western man is in a condition in which collapse must proceed if no strong and powerful oppositional movement appears against it. In order to make this constellation clear, we must emphasis an aspect of Nietzsche's complex analyses of nihilism that is, in general, not recognized enough. The devaluation of all values in force until now is not constituted just by the cessation of a search for ersatz authorities for the dead God or by resignation and despair. The process of devaluation also does not occur as a sequence of attempts to find a new anchor. "Modern man believes provisionally first in this, then in that *value* only to drop them; the circle of outlived and disposed of values grows ever greater; the *emptiness* and *poverty of values* is ever more obvious; the movement is irresistible — although in a grand style delays are still attempted."[45] In order to delay the demise, one moves in a circle. What one leaves behind, one occasionally comes across again. Since until now no radical revaluation has set itself up, the earlier systems — if with less binding power — remain in force side by side. One rejects, but one does not reject totally; one leaves values in force, but with reservations. Here one can justify oneself with reference, for example, to Goethe's striving for a universal understanding, but "amenability to experience of whatever kind" has since led the Romantics to a "nihilistic sigh," a "not knowing which way to turn."[46] Nietzsche maintains that "a chaos of contradictory evaluations" rules over us: "from infinity one has made a kind of drunkenness."[47] A strength of willing must countervene such weakness. But "the authority is lacking," Nietzsche realizes. Even the "*reaction*" against romanticism ("disgust with the romantic ideals and lies") has not "*dared* the *reverse* evaluations!"[48] This is why the signs of cultural disintegration have multiplied in the course of the nineteenth century.[49] European nihilism remains caught within itself.[50]

If the forces pushing away from one another cannot be brought together under a single dominant perspective, the collapse and disintegration will continue. And what is valid at the general level, is as much the case in the details. Every individual, every community, every belief, every culture maintains itself by coordinating the many immanent perspectival aspirations. A merely "delaying" stability can be created by invoking "ersatz gods" to form contexts of meaning. But Nietzsche finds in the men of his time only a chaos of "contradictory estimations and *therefore contradictory impulses*."[51] The force of what has piled up from before can thus spur human beings against each other. Released from handed-down morality, "the 'individual' appears obliged to give himself laws." What is here at work is no active nihilism, rather a nihilistic activity. With its "all sorts of new what-fors and wherewithals," it does not get very far. "No shared formulas any longer" bind these questions. Rather, "misunderstandings" ally with "disrespect"; "decay, corruption, and the highest desires" become "gruesomely entangled." "The end is approaching fast," and "nothing will stand the day after tomorrow" (*BGE*, 262).

Both decay and corruption of the mere "individual legislation," as well as the disintegration of the impulses in the particular person and the cultural forms, indicate, as signs of weakness (of decadence), the necessity of a "philosophical legislation" by "the strong" assured of command. After the devaluation of all received values, this legislation can no longer invoke transcendent powers from the beyond. It has to be an expression of power that has its vanishing point entirely on "this side" (the earth). Accordingly, only those who have seen through the old "lies" and thought to the end the consequences of the old errors can represent this power.

In Nietzsche's typology of future human beings (in itself fraught with tension), when the ruling type moves into the foreground, it is not simply in order to rule per se. The strong ought rather to prepare a future life-affirming culture, in which oppositions are liberated and can intensify one another. This needs "a culture of exception . . . in consequence of a *richness of force*." A "superfluity of forces" shall even prepare "a greenhouse of luxury-culture."[52] When Nietzsche in this context thinks of a "race with its *own sphere of life*, with a superfluity of strength for beauty, courage, culture, manners to the most spiritual," we are quite likely reminded of the free spirits. At the same time, it seems that "the greenhouse for peculiar and select plants" to which the revaluation of values should give rise has no more room for Nietzsche's early free spiritedness with its perhaps even more radical question marks. For the coming race must be "an *affirming* race," "which can permit itself every luxury . . . , strong enough not to need the tyranny of the virtue-imperative."[53]

Even if it is not quite this tyranny that irritates the unlimited affirmation of life, with the intensification of the oppositions aimed at by strength, the danger of collapse, which seemed to have been overcome, rises again. In a note with the title "On Hierarchy" Nietzsche remarks that "the highest man, supposing that such a concept is permissible, would be the man who represents most strongly the *oppositional character of existence*." Here Nietzsche is considering an extension of humanity as embodied by the Renaissance and by pre-Socratic antiquity, whose overcoming in the end is what is at stake.[54] But to the extent that the "higher type" represents a great "sum of coordinated elements," it is endangered again by "disintegration." This arises once again behind the back of this type of overcoming of decadence: the higher types, as "the richest and most complex forms" of humanity not only "perish" more easily than mediocre people, "they are exposed to every kind of decadence."[55]

Does the possibility of descent belong to all ascents? Is nihilism the traveling companion of future humankind? Did Nietzsche show us new paths, or did he merely set milestones that we should pay attention to if we want to grope our way forward? In the sketch of a preface to the book *Will to Power*, Nietzsche writes with reference to the "emergence of nihilism," that it has "as a daring and tempting spirit . . . already wandered into every labyrinth of the future."[56] The "caves" in which the hermit-philosopher in *Beyond Good and Evil* is always digging deeper, "may be a labyrinth or a gold mine" (*BGE* 289). In Nietzsche's subterranean tunnels one can make many discoveries, one can go astray in them, or end up in a dead end. Whoever does not dare to enter them, does indeed escape this danger, but he or she remains, even at the dawn of the twenty-first century, on the surface of what humanity and things have to offer.

Excursus 1

Benito Mussolini made one of Nietzsche's formulations into his motto and raised it to a slogan of the fascist movement. It runs, "*Live dangerously*," and is embedded in Aphorism 283 of the *Gay Science*. Mus-

solini, who, after ten years of Marxist activity was by his own account'
"cured" of socialism through a reading of Nietzsche, happily and frequently changed Nietzsche's infinitive into an imperative. Live dangerously, *vivi pericolosamente*, which is supposed to mean, "Be prepared
for everything, for every sacrifice, for every danger, for every deed,
when it is a matter of defending the fatherland and fascism." In Nietzsche's text, there is nothing of all this. True, the philosopher welcomes
the fact that "a more virile, warlike age is about to begin, which will
restore honor to courage above all!" But he thereby anticipates a higher
age, one that "will carry heroism into the search for knowledge and
that will wage wars for the sake of ideas and their consequences"; he is
concerned here with "*preparatory human beings*," "human beings distinguished as much by . . . contempt for all great vanities as by magna-
nimity in victory and forbearance regarding the small vanities of the
vanquished."

Already in his socialist phase, Mussolini had viewed Karl Marx as
the "outstanding philosopher of worker-violence" (not only Nietzsche
can be misunderstood!), and he drew support from Nietzsche, as well,
for his political activism. Nietzsche's "live dangerously" was understood in German secondary literature of the thirties and forties, and
even more in tertiary literature (in teachers' union newsletters and the
like) as a slogan from the fascist Nietzsche reception. For the most part
without challenge, since Germany at the time maintained a definite, if
earnestly benevolent, distance from fascist ideology, it lacked "the racial
foundation of the concept of a people," as the National Socialist view
had it. I can still personally remember such remarks from a German-
Italian youth exchange in Weimar in the nineteen thirties.

Excursus 2

In 1938 Weimar, where, as a fourteen-year-old, I made my initial
acquaintance with Nietzsche, the leading editor of the first historical-
critical Nietzsche edition, Karl Schlechta, was confronted by serious
concerns, which now throw a revealing light on the position of Nietzsche under National Socialism. In February of 1938 the Office of Literature (*Amt für Schrifttumspflege*) in its *Journal of Opinions* (*Gutachte-
nanzeiger*) had reviewed the first volume of this edition under the rubric
"Unrecommended Editions of Selected, Complete, and New Writings."
An extended discussion, addressing all four volumes published until
that point, justified this placement. It expressed "mistrust" in the
"editor's posture toward the personality and work of the philoso-

pher," doubted whether "Nietzsche's spiritual inheritance in our time, which such an edition must alone serve" [!], could be properly tended by those here responsible; the office rejected, finally, this *Collected Works (Gesamtausgabe)*, as "a perfect example of the scientific reduction of great works and personalities." A lot could be concealed behind this. Nietzsche was attacked by more than a few influential representatives of the National Socialist *Weltanschauung* (a diffuse melange of "convictions," less coherent than is nowadays usually recognized). They would surely have had nothing against the propagandistic mobilization of the philosopher, but there were indeed convincing arguments from the National Socialist point of view that spoke against a scientific presentation of the "entire unabridged Nietzsche." The directors of the Nietzsche archives finally managed to defuse the official conflict, the background of which remains obscure, in September.[57] A ministerial appeal to Hitler was decisive for the unhindered continuation of the edition. He himself contributed his own discretionary funds to its financing—no doubt because of his good personal relations with Nietzsche's sister. But now the edition of the first volume of letters appeared in Weimar, which for the attentive reader would unmask Elisabeth Nietzsche as a forger. Schlechta recalls, "My colleagues and I demonstrably revealed the conscious forgeries in 1937—two years, that is, after the forger had been honored with a state funeral—in the forger's own house, through which the potentates of the day strode. When we published the first historical-critical volume of letters in 1938, we were anxious—let today's heroes know—about what might now come. Nothing happened. The heroes of the day did not read Nietzsche, they merely cited him."[58]

Excursus 3

Lukács aimed his polemic at Alfred Bäumler's version of Nietzsche.[59] What these two Nietzsche interpretations have in common and oppose can be discussed in terms of the differing systematizations of Nietzsche's philosophy.[60] According to Bäumler, the "unity" of Nietzsche's thought is not yet apparent in the texts he himself published. He achieved it only in the unpublished writings. Bäumler designated *The Will to Power* (a compilation put together by Nietzsche's sister and Peter Gast) explicitly as "a system."[61] Everyone who "wants to grasp the legend of the ever-changing [writer]" must "justify himself" before this "work."[62] Bäumler specifies the philosopher's "result" and assumes that he can systematically distinguish the "essential" from the "unessential" in Nietzsche on this basis. This homogenizes the philosophy in such a way that already at the start of the 1930s, Bäumler could claim that the "tense Nordic essence of Nietzsche" in his "doctrine of the will" could promote Germanism to its "most perfect expression."[63] "In place of a bourgeois moral philosophy" Bäumler posits a narrow *"philosophy of the will to power,"* which he sees as a "philosophy of *politics."*[64] What in Nietzsche occludes this political philosophy is discarded from his supposed "system." Thus it goes with the thought of the eternal return of the same, which Bäumler reduces to a purely personal and philosophically irrelevant "experience" of Nietzsche. By contrast, Lukács submits the "entire" Nietzsche corpus to his ideological regime. In so doing, he also speaks of Nietzsche's system. The fact that for Nietzsche, a will to system already represents a deficiency in intellectual integrity is something neither Bäumler nor Lukács takes seriously: they relativize such remarks in an inappropriate way.

In order to constitute a system, one needs a center, where all the strands converge. Bäumler speaks of the will to power as the "productive middle point that conditions and supports the particulars."[65] Lukács interprets this middle point as merely "the principle of methodological coherence" for Nietzsche's "structure of thought." He sees it as foreground, itself as only a 'product.'[66] He displaces Nietzsche's supposed system into the "return," which he calls "the genuine social middle point," and from which he aims to demonstrate the "ramifications" of Nietzsche's "intellectual coherence." In order to "determine" this, Lukács must admittedly ignore the actual intentions of this philosophy. Only thus can the systematic "unifying point" that "conditions and supports" his interpretation be "crystallized." This point consists in the fact that Nietzsche, in everything he writes, is fulfilling a "social assignment." In his "defense against socialism," he indirectly conducts an apology for capitalism that consists in a "struggle for the creation of an imperialistic Germany."[67] That Nietzsche knew little of socialism, and nothing of Marxism, and that he "didn't live to experience the imperialistic epoch," are facts Lukács nonchalantly dismisses.[68]

Lukács fulfills his own ideological "assignment" in a dual manner. By attributing a system to him, he can brand Nietzsche as the most dangerous class enemy of the present epoch. Simultaneously he presents his system as self-contradictory, in order to disavow him and to render him absurd. From a "logical-philosophical" perspective, Lukács finds in Nietzsche's writings nothing but "a barren chaos of the most vehement, mutually exclusive, arbitrary claims," nothing but "shreds of thought" that resist "formally every connection with one another."[69] This unsystematic, or antisystematic thinking is supposedly Nietzsche's system.

But such ideologically motivated assertions fail to take seriously the experimental, future-oriented character of Nietzsche's thinking, whose realization would point in many different directions.

Notes

This chapter was translated from German ("*Erfahrungen im Umgang mit Nietzsche*") by James McFarland. The translation was supervised by Professor Stanley Corngold from Princeton University. The editors of this volume would like to thank both of them for their efforts.

1. Compare here and in what follows aphorisms 128 and 129.
2. Quoted from *Meyers Lexicon*, 9th ed. (1939) article "*Jugend*," 6:619.
3. See Excursus 1, later in this chapter.
4. See Excursus 2, later in this chapter.
5. Wilhelm Wundt, Die Nationen und ihre Philosophie (Stuttgart, 1941), 113–18, 120–23.
6. "*Nietzsche — Judenfreund?*" *Völkischer Beobachter*, no. 332, November 27, 1936, p. 5 (GSA 72/ZA S 27.11.1936). I am grateful to Dr. Roswitha Wollkopf for the reference to this text and the copy from the Weimar archive.
7. Quoted in Georg Müller, *Nietzsche und die deutsche Katastrophe* (Gütersloh, 1946), 15.
8. Arthur Drews, "*Nietzsche als Philosoph des Nationalsozialismus?*" in *Nordische Stimmen* 4 (1934): 172–79.
9. Joseph Göbbels, *Reden*, no. 16 (30.1.1943), vol. 2: (1939–45), 168.
10. *Nachlaß* Autumn 1887 in *KGA* VIII 2, 10, p. 172.
11. Albert Camus, In *L'homme révolté* (Paris, 1951); *Der Mensch in der Revolte* (Hamburg, 1953), 84.
12. See Excursus 3 later in this chapter.
13. Thomas Mann, *Nietzsches Philosophie im Lichte unserer Erfahrung* (Berlin 1948), 47.
14. "Jaspers' Antwort," in *Philosophen des 20. Jahrhunderts, Karl Jaspers*, ed. P. A. Schilpp (Stuttgart 1957), 843.
15. Habermas, "Nachwort" to *Friedrich Nietzsche, Erkenntnistheoretische Schriften*,1968, 237. Compare with the exposition by Habermas in *"Die neue Unübersichtlichkeit," Kleine Politische Schriften* (Frankfurt am Main, 1985), 60.
16. Jacques Derrida, "Otobiographies: The Teaching of Nietzsche and the Politics of the Proper Name," in his *The Ear of the Other: Otobiography, Transference, Translation*, trans. Peggy Kauf and Avital Ronell, ed. Christie V. McDonald (New York: Schocken, 1985), 31.
17. Compare Kurt Rudolf Fischer, "Nazism as a Nietzschean 'Experiment,'" *Nietzsche-Studien* 6 (1977): 116–22, and see his chapter in the present volume.
18. Derrida, "Otobiographics," 31.
19. Michel Foucault, 'Nietzsche, Freud, Marx," *Cahiers de Royaumont* (Paris, 1967): 183–92.
20. Renate Reschke, "Kritische Aneignung und notwendige Auseinander-

setzung," *Weimarer Beiträge* 29 (1983): 1190–213 (here in particular pp. 1199, 1200, 1211, 1192.).

21. Maurice Blanchot, "Nietzsche et l'écriture fragmentaire," in: *L'entretien infini* (Paris, 1969), 227–55.

22. Gianni Vattimo, *La fina della modernità* (Milano: Garzanti, 1985). Compare Müller-Lauter, "Nietzsche und Heidegger als nihilistische Denker. Zu Gianni Vattimos 'postmodernistischer' Deutung," *Nietzsche-Studien* 27 (1998): 52–81.

23. *Nachlaß* Autumn 1887, 9 [43] in *KGA*, VIII 2:19. And see *WP*, 20.

24. *KGA*, VIII 2:14. *Nachlaß* Autumn 1887, 10 [47]. See *WP*, 21.

25. *Nachlaß*, 9 [123] in *KGA*, VIII 2:71. Schlechta sees in the fact that Nietzsche "continues down his fatal path, further than anyone else," his "intellectual character," and also sees in "his greatness" an "exemplary-deterrent greatnes," *Der Fall Nietzsche* (Munich, 1959), 2:98.

26. *Nachlaß* Autumn 1887, 9 [37] in *KGA*, VIII 2:15, 14.

27. Ibid., 61.

28. Ibid., 23.

29. *Nachlaß* November 1887–March 1888, 11 [411 (2–4)] in *KGA*, VIII 2:31. Occasionally Nietzsche's notion of the revaluation of values has the character of a restitution of original humanity. The earlier "leaders of humanity" have "only taught decadence-values as the highest values: therefore the revaluation of all values become nihilistic ('the Beyond')" (*Nachlaß* October 1888, 23 [3], 3 in *KGA*, VIII 3:414). Nietzsche wants to rectify this perversion through 'his' second revaluation, that can then be understood as the establishment of a "new innocence."

30. *Nachlaß* Autumn 1887, 9 [41] in *KGA* VIII 2:18.

31. *KGA*, VI 1:106 ; *Z*, II "Upon the Blessed Isles."

32. *KGA*, VI 3, 341–343; *EH*, "Thus Spoke Zarathustra," 6.

33. Nietzsche puts it well when, in *Twilight of the Idols*, he says of his late understanding of Dionysus: "And with that I again return to the place from which I set out" (*KGA*, VI 3:154; *Twilight of the Idols*, trans. R. J. Hollingdale (New York: Penguin, 1990), 121, indicating here *The Birth of Tragedy*. This book can also be understood as the "first revaluation of all values." At the same time, this is merely the first step in a long and ever deeper path of thinking toward his late revaluation.

34. On the history of Nietzsche's illness, see P. D. Volz, *Nietzsche im Labyrinth seiner Krankheit. Eine medizinische-biographische Untersuchung* (Würzburg, 1990).

35. *KGA*, VI 3:372; *EH*, "Why I Am a Destiny," 9.

36. S. G. Schank, *Dionysos gegen den Gekreuzigten. Eine philologische und philosophische Studie zu Nietzsches Ecce Homo* (Bern, 1993).

37. The "versus" also expresses an inner connection. Nietzsche's revaluation of all values reevaluates this, and is, therefore, orientated toward it. In its emphatic rhetoric, *Ecce Homo* states that it consists "in a liberation from all moral values, in saying Yes to and having confidence in all that has hitherto been forbidden, despised, and damned" (*KGA* VI 3:328; *EH*, "The Dawn" 1). It seems that in the end Nietzsche believed that he must battle against the primary representative of the old values, Christianity, demanding in a series of harsh

formulations that "the 'holy story'" be named the "cursed story" ("Law Against Christianity"; KGA, VI 3:252). See also on this text the discussion by M. Montinari in *KSA*, 14:450–53. (The final subtitle that Nietzsche gave to *The Antichrist* is "Malediction on Christianity." Nietzsche's decision in November 1888 focused the plan of his *Revaluation of All Values* on this book [see *KSA*, 14:434].)

38. *Nachlaß* Summer–Autumn 1884, 26 [284] in *KGA*, VII 2:223.

39. *Nachlaß* Autumn 1885–Autumn 1886, 2 [131] in *KGA*, VIII 1:130.

40. *KGA*, VI 3, 363f.; *EH*, "Why I am a Destiny," 1.

41. C. Brinton, *Nietzsche* (New York, 1965; first published, Cambridge: Harvard University Press, 1941).

42. *KGA*, IV 3:7–11; *HH* I, Preface, 3.

43. *KGA*, VI 2:149–53; *BGE*, 211. Compare also *BGE*, 213. In Nietzsche's "order of rank among philosophers" the commanding philosophers of the future are finally overcome through the consideration "that gods, too, philosophize, which has been suggested to me by many an inference" (*BGE*, 294). At the end of *Beyond Good and Evil* it is the philosophizing god Dionysus—and no longer a "free spirit"—with whom Nietzsche keeps company and has "conversations."

44. *Nachlaß* Autumn 1887, 9 [43] in *KGA*, VIII 2:20.

45. *Nachlaß* November 1887–March 1888, 11 [119] in *KGA*, VIII 2:198.

46. *KGA* VI 3:146; *Twilight of the Idols*, trans. R. J. Hollingdale (London: Penguin Books, 1968), "Expeditions of an Untimely Man," 50.

47. *Nachlaß* Autumn 1885, 44 [5] in *KGA*, VII 3:446.

48. *Nachlaß* Autumn 1885–Autumn 1886 2 [131] in *KGA*, VIII 1:128.

49. Already in his second *Untimely Meditation* Nietzsche had described how man is led by historicism into disorientation.

50. Later Nietzsche speaks of a *"desegregation of the will,"* when he describes the drifting apart of evaluations. In a note on the history of nihilism he explains: what no longer can constitute an intrinsic, articulated "unity," loses its powers of resistance against the stimuli it encounters. This desegregation is "Depersonalization": "A person is determined by accidents: he banalizes and banalizes experiences beyond all measure." "One avoids suffering and instinctively chooses as 'remedy' that which accelerates exhaustion." (*Nachlaß* May–June 1888, 17 [6]; *KGA*, VIII 3:325.) These and other symptoms of weakening and decline named by Nietzsche are even more evident at the end of this century; his analysis of nihilism has lost none of its actuality. One reads a note such as the following: "the dissolving of morality leads as a practical consequence to the atomistic individual and then to the division of individuals into pluralities. . . . Therefore now more than ever a goal is necessary and love, a new love." (*Nachlaß* November 1882–February 1883, 4 [83] in *KSA* VII 1:140).

51. *Nachlaß* Summer–Autumn 1884 in *KGA*, VII 2:179.

52. *Nachlaß* Autumn 1887, 9 [139] in *KGA*, VIII 2:78.

53. *Nachlaß* Autumn 1887, 9 [153] in *KGA*, VIII 2:89.

55. *Nachlaß* Spring 1888, 14 [133] in *KGA*, VIII 3:108. Compare also to *BGE*, 262.

56. *Nachlaß* November 1887–March 1888, 11 [413] in *KGA*, VIII 2:432.

57. Compare M. Zapata Galindo, *Triumph des Willens zur Macht. Zur Nietzsche-Rezeption im NS-Staat* (Hamburg, 1995), 198; M. Heinz and Th. Kisiel, "Heideggers Beziehungen zum Nietzsche-Archiv im Dritten Reich", in *Annäherungen an Martin Heidegger*, ed. FS Hugo Ott and v. H. Schäfer (Frankfurt and New York, 1996), 120.

58. Karl Schlechta, "Die Legende und ihre Freunde," in *Der Fall Nietzsche* (Munich, 1959), 94.

59. Eike Middell has determined that it is Bäumler's systematized Nietzsche against which Lukács polemicizes—the polemic is directed therefore against a fascist instrumentalizing of the philosopher by [his] interpreters" ("Totalität und Dekadenz. Zur Auseinandersetzung von Georg Lukács mit Friedrich Nietzsche," *Weimarer Beiträge* 31 (1985): 559–71; here, 561).

60. On the one-sidedness of the interpretations of Bäumler and Lukács, see M. Montinari, "Nietzsche zwischen Alfred Bäumler und Georg Lukács," in *Nietzsche lesen*, (Berlin and New York, 1982), 169–206. When Montinari remarks at the close of his discussion that both interpreters "underestimate the entire philological problematic" of the compilation of the *Will to Power* and Nietzsche's posthumous writings, he fundamentally underestimates the dishonesty of ideologies.

61. A. Bäumler, "Nachwort" to *Der Wille zur Macht. Versuch einer Umwertung aller Werte* (Leipzig, 1930), 699.

62. A. Bäumler, "Einführung" to *Die Unschuld des Werdens*, by Friedrich Nietzsche (1930), xxxvi.

63. A. Bäumler, *Nietzsche der Philosoph und Politiker* (Leipzig: Reclam, 1931), 49.

64. Bäumler, "Nietzsche und der Nationalsozialismus," in *Studien zur deutschen Geistesgeschichte*, (Berlin, 1937), 281–94; here, 292.

65. A. Bäumler, "Nachwort" to *Der Wille zur Macht. Versuch einer Umwertung aller Werte* (Leipzig, 1930), 699.

66. Georg Lukács, *Die Zerstörung der Vernunft* (Berlin, 1954), 316, 304. In the final analysis, according to Lukács, the will to power is only one of many "myths" of Nietzsche (253).

67. Ibid., 299, 250–56.

68. Ibid., 248.

69. Ibid., 317, 316. Lukács does not allow himself to be "held up" by the "crying contradictions" in Nietzsche's "mythical structures." Not only is the will to power a myth, but so are the "death of God" and the eternal return, which Bäumler excluded from his system of Nietzsche. According to Lukács, Nietzsche constructed this myth in order to eternalize capitalistic and imperialist domination. Compare Montinari, "Nietzsche zwischen Alfred Bäumler und Georg Lukács," 198.

4

Nietzsche and "Hitler"

Alexander Nehamas

When one is young, one venerates and despises without that
art of nuances which constitutes the best gain of life, and it is
only fair that one has to pay dearly for having assaulted men
and things in this manner with Yes and No. Everything is
arranged so that the worst of tastes, the taste for the
unconditional, should be cruelly fooled and abused until a man
learns to put a little art into his feelings and rather to risk
trying even what is artificial—as the real artists of life do.
—Nietzsche (*BGE*, 31)

The reason Hitler's name is in quotation marks in the title of this chapter is that I do not plan to discuss the historical connections between Nietzsche and National Socialism. I am concerned, instead, with a more abstract and, to me, more pressing problem. It concerns Nietzsche's attitude toward the evil hero—the great individual who still, by any reasonable standard, may be a completely unacceptable human being: the kind of person who provokes moral revulsion even in those of us who share, or perhaps (in light of having such a reaction) merely profess to share, Nietzsche's own revulsion at moral values and estimations. "Hitler" is supposed to stand for all such characters. But—that of course is why it is *his* name, and not, say, Genghis Khan's or Diocletian's, that I use in my title—Hitler is the most trenchant instance of such an evil hero. He is the one, we Nietzscheans, too, think of, inevitably, when we address—or when we skirt addressing—the issue of evil heroes and our reaction to them.

The question that keeps nagging, not only at the back of my mind, is "Does Nietzsche approve of 'Hitler'?" It is a question I, at least, have never faced squarely. Most of those who address it—unless they are willing to concede with J. P. Stern that "the pathos of personal authenticity . . . was the chief tenet of fascism and national socialism. No man came closer to the full realization of self-created 'values' than A. Hitler"[1]—

seem to me to skirt it, to avoid a direct confrontation with it. I will cite no authors because it would be absurd of me to *accuse* others of doing, at least in part, what I believe I have not done at all. The point is not to show that others have failed. The point is to confess that *I* have to begin, however inadequately, to confront the question directly. At this point, I don't know where such a direct confrontation will lead.

What, exactly, is the problem of the evil hero? Let me begin to approach it indirectly. In ancient Greek thought, there was universal agreement that what distinguishes human beings from one another is the quality called *arête*. Although we usually translate that word as "virtue," the fact that animals as well as inanimate objects exhibit it shows that a better rendering would be, precisely, "distinction," the quality that makes someone an outstanding member of some group. *Arête* is what makes anything justifiably notable. But this idea raises a serious problem, which we see addressed again and again in Greek philosophy.[2]

Being distinguished, outstanding, or justifiably notable involves three elements: the inner features that enable some people to be outstanding, the actual reputation such people enjoy, and the audience that is to appreciate them. In Homer, these three are harmonious: *arête* is therefore almost synonymous with "fame" (*kleos*). But what if they are not? What if someone had the right features but people failed to appreciate them, like Plato's Socrates, whom his contemporaries took to be the contrary of what he really was — a villain rather than (as Plato saw him) a noble human being? The psychological structure, the soul, that made Socrates a magnificent human being in Plato's eyes was invisible to his fellow citizens. The internal structure and the external face of *arête* came apart. In the *Republic*, Plato tried to put them together. He made those whose souls are truly outstanding — the philosophers — rulers, and therefore the most outstanding citizens, of a state whose population is educated so as to appreciate the coincidence of a harmonious soul and a position of public importance and accomplishment.

Even if we reject Plato's particular values, we can acknowledge the brilliance of his conception. But even if we accept them, we must acknowledge their impracticality, their ethereal purity that puts these values beyond the broadest reaches of the messy vicissitudes of history. Short of a solution that is both correct and practical, however, the ancient problem remains: What makes a human being outstanding? The right kind of soul, which no one perhaps may ever know or appreciate? Or the accomplishment of great deeds that make a difference, that make one stand apart, become a part of history and, in the greatest cases, become memorialized by the methods of a world that is, for better or worse, no longer that of Homer? As long as the two can diverge, a good person need not be great and a great person may not be at all good. That is how the problem of the evil hero arises.

This Greek conception of what distinguishes some human beings from others and the problems it generates are at the heart of Nietzsche's thought. The "tragic hero" of *The Birth of Tragedy*, the "exemplars" of *Schopenhauer as Educator*, the "free spirits" of *Human, All Too Human* and *The Gay Science*, the "*Übermensch*" of *Thus Spoke Zarathustra* (as well as, or ever more so, Zarathustra himself), the "nobles" of *Beyond Good and Evil*, the "masters" of *On the Genealogy of Morals*, the "individuals" of *Twilight of the Idols*, and finally his own figure in *Ecce Homo* are all different versions of Nietzsche's effort to articulate what makes some human beings remarkable, distinguished, different from the rest of the world. That is as central a philosophical concern of his as anything ever was. And it involves him in the very same difficulty with which Plato had fought in the *Republic*.

In *Beyond Good and Evil*, Nietzsche seems to advocate an aristocratic politics because he thinks, controversially, that only the existence of social distinctions can accomplish what he tends to consider the ultimate goal of politics:

> the craving for an ever new widening of distances within the soul itself, the development of ever higher, rarer, more remote, further-stretching, more comprehensive states — in brief, simply the enhancement of the type "man" (*BGE*, 257).

A little later, he writes that at certain great moments in history the "individual" appears, obliged to give himself laws and to develop his own arts and wiles for self-preservation, self-enhancement, self-redemption (*BGE*, 262).

"The noble soul," Nietzsche claims, "knows itself to be at a height" (*BGE*, 265). He continues,

> What is noble? What does the word "noble" still mean to us today? What betrays, what allows us to recognize the noble human being, under this heavy, overcast sky of the beginning rule of the plebs that makes everything opaque and leaden?
>
> It is not actions that prove him — actions are always open to many interpretations, always unfathomable — nor is it "works." . . . It is not the works, it is the *faith* that is decisive here, that determines the order of rank . . . some fundamental certainty that a noble soul has about itself, something that cannot be sought, nor found, nor perhaps lost.
>
> *The noble soul has reverence for itself* (*BGE*, 287).

When Nietzsche writes this way, it is tempting to think that nobility and heroism are simply states of the soul, internal dispositions independent of deeds and actions. Such a quietist conception seems to allow that a hermit, who withdraws completely from the world, lives in total isolation and dies forever unknown, can be as great an individual hero as one could possibly imagine. It is the right psychological structure that makes one the "enhanced type" of human being whom Nietzsche admires, whether or not anyone ever recognizes it. Socrates might have remained a statuary and never met Plato, Montaigne might have continued as mayor of Bordeaux and never have written the *Essays*, Napoleon might have preferred farming in Corsica instead of joining the French artillery: oblivion would not have deprived them of greatness.

> But that cannot be right. For, as every reader of *On the Genealogy of Morals* knows, to demand of strength that it should *not* express itself as strength . . . is just as absurd as to demand of weakness that it should express itself as strength . . . There is no "being" behind doing, effecting, becoming; "the doer" is merely a fiction added to the doing — the doing is everything (*GM*, I:13).[3]

The "inner," Nietzsche believes, cannot be separated from the "outer." His view is that the soul as an inner disposition that is quite independent of, even contrary to, an individual's behavior is an invention that allows those of no distinction to convince themselves that their ordinariness is not the inevitable consequence of their nature but the free product of their choice:

> The subject (or, to use a more popular expression, the *soul*) has perhaps been believed in hitherto more firmly than anything else on earth because it makes it possible to the majority of mortals, the weak and oppressed of every kind, the sublime self-deception that interprets weakness as freedom, and their being thus-and-so as a *merit* (*GM*, I:13).

The same principle applies to Nietzsche himself and to his work. In his study of what he calls Nietzsche's "heroic individualism," Leslie Thiele writes,

> The writings Nietzsche left behind are a testament to his understanding of art. They are, like all works of art, of secondary importance, being the relics of a spiritual struggle. The life that produced them remains the justification of their appearance; the works themselves are merely the excrement of digested experience.[4]

If that is right, Nietzsche would have been exactly what he is—whatever exactly that is—had he never written a word. But that is impossible. The "life" that produced those works was not lived independently of their being written. The writing was part and parcel of the life, not a "relic" of "a spiritual struggle" but the struggle itself. Nietzsche's "experience" does not precede his writings, it is *in* them. The works determine who Nietzsche is. Nietzsche's life is not a justification of his works but, in large part, their very product. Even in *Beyond Good and Evil*, Nietzsche is aware of this general connection. The same section that argues that "faith" and not works reveal nobility also contains this passage:

> Among artists and scholars today one finds enough of those who betray by their works how they are impelled by a profound desire for what is noble; but just this need *for* what is noble is fundamentally different from the needs of the noble soul itself and actually the eloquent and dangerous mark of its lack (*BGE*, 287).

And if that is so, all talk of "faith" aside, it *is* the nature of the works after all that reveals whether someone is or is not noble. If some works betray that those who produce them lack nobility, then those who possess it—given that they *must*, as the *Genealogy* claims, express their nobility in some way or other—must also produce works that reveal or perhaps even constitute it.

Nobility may well be a feature of the soul. But the soul, Nietzsche believes, is not a substance independent of the body. It is, perhaps, the "social structure of the drives and affects" (*BGE*, 12), but drives and affects are constituted in action. They are aspects of "the will," but the will is neither free nor unfree. Compulsion and total self-determination, Nietzsche famously writes, are both "mythological" ideas: "in real life it is only a matter of strong and weak wills" (*BGE*, 21). Nobility is therefore necessarily manifested in action: noble souls are those that act nobly. One could perhaps argue that the psychological state of nobility is the cause of the actions that manifest it, and that between cause and effect there can always intervene a series of accidents that prevents the realization of the effect. But Nietzsche cannot allow himself that view. The common notion of cause is derived, he writes, from the very "realm of the famous 'inner facts,' of which not a single one has so far proved to be factual" (*TI*, "The Four Great Errors," 3). "The popular mind," according to the passage of the *Genealogy* that says that the "doing" is everything, "in fact doubles the doing; when it sees the lightning flash, it is the doing of a doing: it posits the same event first as cause as then a second time as its effect" (*GM*, I:13).

Nobility of soul and nobility of action cannot therefore be separated from one another. Though it is very difficult to say what that is, noble actions must be of a certain kind: they are contrary to those that betray, as we have seen, its lack and they must be importantly different from the actions that are common in one's world. The individual, who constitutes "greater, more manifold, more comprehensive life transcends and *lives beyond* the old morality" (*BGE*, 262): that is part of what it is to "give laws to oneself," to create one's own values, which for Nietzsche is the hallmark of greatness. One is only an individual to the extent that one (to revert to the Greek notions with which we began) is different, stands out, is distinguished from the rest of one's world, from the crowd, which Nietzsche contemptuously dismisses as "the herd."

Can people really be different from the rest, can they really act in unprecedented ways, and not be known to have done so? Logically, of course, that possibility is quite real: Mendelssohn might never have come to appreciate Bach's then-neglected music; the burning of the Library at Alexandria may have deprived us of the works of the (now nameless) greatest Greek tragedian; I suppose the inventor of the wheel, if there was such a person, might qualify. But we, like Nietzsche, are interested in history. And I am not sure that within history it is possible to be different, which to say, to make a difference, and pass totally unnoticed. Bach did, after all, come to be recognized, while the hypothetical tragedian's influence (which is deeply connected with greatness) has now dissipated and pales before that of Aeschylus.

Let me use the old hackneyed philosophical example in order to illustrate this point. The tree that falls in the forest may well make a sound, but if no one hears it, its sound has not made a difference. But its fall, one may reply, may have the greatest consequences. By blocking a stream, the tree may have changed forever the shape of the forest, which may have caused a town to lose its livelihood, which may have brought some great empire down. I am sure that such things happen. But note that it is not clear that we can speak of the tree as having made a difference, since making a difference always requires a concrete alternative to which the difference is made. It might seem that a concrete alternative here is represented by the case where, the tree not having fallen, the empire in question was not brought down because the city did not lose its livelihood. But the fact is that there is no empire "in question": we simply don't know what empire, city, stream, or tree we are talking about. History is full of chance events of the sort the fallen tree represents, and some of those events may even be people's actions. But a difference is not made every time something happens, which is all the time, but only when history actually changes direction. And history changes direction only when it departs from a course on which it was already set. But history, as Nietzsche knew, has no direction in itself:

"We have invented the concept of 'end'; in reality there is no end" (*TI*, "The Four Great Errors," 8). History, then, changes direction only to the extent that we *discern* a change, since the direction *away from* which it changes is a direction *we* had found in it in the first place. To that extent, therefore, great individuals are those who make, and are known to make, a difference to history.

Making a difference is therefore necessary for being a hero. Is it also sufficient? What of those who make a *horrible* difference? In addition, we now face two related problems. The first is the problem of fame. Isn't being known the same as being famous? Isn't fame (*kleos*) just what the Homeric heroes pursue? Yet Nietzsche is disdainful of fame, both—he claims—in his own case ("That is how I have always lived. I had no wishes. A man over forty-four who can say that he never strove for *honors*" [*EH*, "Why I am So Clever," 9]) and more generally, praising that "*refined heroism* which disdains to offer itself for the veneration of the great masses, as its coarser brother does, and tends to go silently through the world and out of the world" (*HH*, I:291). "Fame (and the desire for it)," Leslie Thiele writes, "is the mark of a lower nature, of someone capable of being appreciated by . . . the 'herd'" (21). But being known is not equivalent to being famous, if that means being appreciated by the herd and venerated by the masses. One can also be known, for example, because of accomplishments that inspire the herd's fear and the masses' suspicion. Fame must in any case be kept distinct from admiration—one can well be famous because of something contemptible. Or perhaps one can be known to, and admired by, not all but only those who count, that is to say, other individuals who engage in the same type of noble activity.

This last point leads directly into our second problem. Does everyone who abhors "Hitler" necessarily belong to the masses? And how can we tell who the noble individuals are who will recognize the hero without already knowing what nobility is? For if we don't know what constitutes nobility, we will be unable to tell whether someone is taken to be noble by the right or the wrong sort of person and we will be unable to distinguish the noble from the ignoble at all. The problem of the hero's proper audience, which Plato once solved by imagining an impossibly perfect city, is Nietzsche's problem as well.[5]

To be noble, according to Nietzsche, is to have a certain kind of soul: "The noble human being," for example, "honors himself as one who is powerful, also as one who has power over himself, who knows how to speak and be silent, who delights in being severe and hard with himself and respects all severity and hardness" (*BGE*, 260). However hard that is to acknowledge, I must confess that Nietzsche's various descriptions of the noble soul are as weak, vague, and embarrassing as anything he ever wrote. They say little and the little they say is neither very interesting nor very useful. But even if we put that problem aside, another, more urgent problem confronts us.

Noble values, Nietzsche writes, depend on the principle — "most alien and embarrassing to the present taste" — that one has duties only to one's peers: that against beings of a lower rank, against everything alien, one may behave as one pleases or "as the heart" desires, and in any case "beyond good and evil." Although he goes on to write, as Walter Kaufmann delighted in pointing out, that "here pity and like feelings may find their place" (*BGE*, 260), the fact remains that a "good and healthy aristocracy . . . accepts with a good conscience the sacrifice of untold human beings who, *for its sake*, must be reduced and lowered to incomplete human beings, to slaves, to instruments" (*BGE*, 258). This is not just a point about a social class: "Egoism belongs to the nature of a noble soul — I mean that unshakable faith that to a being such as 'we are' other beings must be subordinate by nature and have to sacrifice themselves" (*BGE*, 265).

That faith in the dispensability and merely instrumental value of others is the feature of nobility that produces the problem that makes me so uneasy, the problem of the evil hero. Joachim Fest may well be right when he portrays Adolf Hitler as someone who, despite his occasional appeals to Nietzsche, did not satisfy his criteria of nobility.[6] Keith Ansell-Pearson may be correct when he claims that resentment is totally incompatible with a noble soul and that "Hitler was a man whose whole being was pervaded by feelings of deep-seated resentment and poisonous revenge, and he can hardly be held up as an example of Nietzsche's model of the noble individual."[7] Nevertheless, though Hitler may have had the wrong kind of soul — whatever exactly that is — "Hitler" need not. Nobility and cruelty are not just compatible: they seem to go hand-in-hand in Nietzsche, and that gives his views their most disturbing ethical and political consequences. Politics, Nietzsche seems to believe, should aim at producing noble individuals, and noble individuals are not only not to be criticized because of their cruelty; on the contrary, they are often to be praised and admired for it.

So, then, what are we to make of a philosophy that seems to say that we should value cruelty, "appropriation, injury, overpowering of what is alien and weaker; suppression, hardness, imposition of one's own forms, incorporation and at least, at its mildest, exploitation" because "exploitation . . . belongs to the *essence* of what lives, as a basic organic function; it is a consequence of the will to power, which is after all the will to life" (*BGE*, 259)? What is the proper reaction to such a view of life and the world?

We can of course criticize cruelty, appropriation, injury, and the rest, but only when they spring from ignoble natures and serve ignoble purposes. Like everything else, according to Nietzsche, they are not wrong in themselves, but only in relation to their origins and ends. There is no point, it seems, where, as with the historical Hitler, or Stalin, cruelty reaches a level of magnitude that renders its purpose irrelevant, where revulsion at the deeds that spring from it *themselves*, independently of any other consideration, becomes appropriate. Quite apart, of course, from the fact that those who engage in such deeds are not immoral—since nothing is immoral according to Nietzsche—it is not even the case that we could describe them as inhuman, since all are features of the will to life itself and therefore manifestations, however disturbing of what, precisely, lies *within* human powers.

One might think, and I have thought so at times, that this concern with criticism, with judging, is itself a sign of an ignoble nature—something we had better leave behind and not concern ourselves with. Nietzsche, after all, writes that he "demands" that philosophers "take their stand *beyond* good and evil and leave the illusion of moral judgment *beneath* themselves" (*TI*, "The 'Improvers' of Mankind," 1). But moral judgment, as Nietzsche is well aware, is only one species of judgment. In his discussion of Sainte-Beuve, he virtually defines philosophy as "the task of judging in all significant matters" (*TI*, "Skirmishes of an Untimely Man," 3). Nietzsche was an inveterate judge of everything around him. He also admired self-reference. He might therefore have appreciated what I now propose to do, which is to apply what he considers to be the task of philosophy to his own philosophy. How are we to judge—not of course from a moral point of view—a philosophy that refuses to condemn in absolute terms any manifestation of cruelty or injustice? Is that a noble philosophy, a philosophy we can admire?

I am in deep sympathy with Nietzsche's immoralism, his idea that good and evil qualities are closely interconnected. Sometimes he seems to believe that whoever has a great virtue will also have to have a great vice. More often, he claims that the very same psychological quality that constitutes a vice in one context constitutes a virtue in another. Every belligerent urge that is essential to establishing a new state, for example, becomes dangerous once that state is in place; it is renamed, reconceived as a vice, and repressed (*BGE*, 201). Honesty is an intellectual, sublimated expression of the same drive that in other contexts manifests itself as cruelty (*BGE*, 230)—and so indeed, Nietzsche argues consistently, is high culture in general (*BGE*, 229).[8]

If Nietzsche is right that good and evil qualities are connected in that way, the right way to treat the drives that produce immorality is not to try to eliminate or repress them but to sublimate and spiritualize them, to use them for producing admirable goals. Nietzsche is clear:

The spiritualization of sensuality is called *love* . . . the spiritualization of hostility . . . consists in a profound appreciation of the
value of having enemies [including internal ones: "the price of
fruitfulness is to be rich in internal oppositions] . . . in the political
realm, too, [he writes naively] hostility has become more spiritual
(*TI*, "Morality as Anti-Nature," 3).

To try instead to destroy "the passions and cravings, merely as a pre-
ventive measure against their stupidity and the unpleasant consequences
of this stupidity—today this itself strikes us as merely another acute
form of stupidity" (*TI*, "Morality as Anti-Nature," 1). Yet that is just
what he claims "the church," which he identifies with morality, does:

The church fights passion with excision in every sense: its practice,
its "cure," is *castratism*. It never asks: "How can one spiritualize,
beautify, deify a craving?" It has always laid the stress of discipline
on extirpation (of sensuality, of pride, of the lust to rule, of avarice, of vengefulness). But an attack on the roots of passion means
an attack on the roots of life: the practice of the church is *hostile
to life* (*TI*, "Morality as Anti-Nature," 1)

Nietzsche sometimes writes, in an almost moralistic vein, that to
"deny" or to be "hostile" to life, is simply wrong (*WP*, 351). More
often, he argues that it is self-defeating, because, with his uncanny psychological sense, he sees that the effort to extirpate the passions requires
the very same passions that are being extirpated. The effort to eliminate
a passion requires its exercise: if cruelty, for example, is a natural passion, we can suppress it only by treating ourselves cruelly. Nietzsche, in
contrast to morality as he understands it, does not mind: such behavior
is cruelty made sublime. But he also accepts the consequence of his
view: sublimated cruelty, in particular situations, may well erupt in its
crudest, most horrifying forms. In a related context, he writes,

One may be quite justified in continuing to fear the blond beast at
the core of all noble races and in being on one's guard against it:
but who would not a hundred times sooner fear when one can
also admire than *not* fear but be permanently condemned to the
repellent sight of the ill-constituted, dwarfed, atrophied, and poisoned? (*GM*, I:11; cf. I:12).

But that is just our problem. Can we admire a philosophy that does
not put *anything* beyond the pale? Let us revert to Hitler (no quotation
marks). Can we admire a philosophy that may imply that what was
wrong with Hitler's methodical, cold-blooded extermination of six million people was the fact that it was motivated by resentment and the
absurd belief that they constituted a danger to his race? Isn't it horribly

obvious that such an action would have been wrong whatever the motives and beliefs on which it was based? We must be careful here. Nietzsche writes, "Restoration of 'nature': an action in itself is perfectly devoid of value: it all depends on *who* performs it. One and the same 'crime' can be in one case the greatest privilege, in another a stigma" (*WP*, 292; cf. *BGE*, 30). We might try to imagine that six million people were in fact a danger to us, that it was a question of either us or them, and that we engaged in a war against them that resulted in their extermination. Such an action might seem justifiable, and that in might appear to argue in favor of Nietzsche's claim: the same action—the destruction of six million people can be accepted in one case and condemned in another. But the situation is more complicated. The issue is how we are to describe an action once we abstract from the agent who performed it (and therefore from its original motives and ends). In the present case, I believe, if the alternative we are imagining is to be "the same action" as the Nazis' attempt to exterminate the Jews, it must be at least as methodical and cold-blooded as theirs. That seems to me to exclude the case of war as we generally understand it. It also suggests that it is very unlikely that the people in question could be a danger to us in any real sense, since our ability to exterminate them in the manner in which the Jews were exterminated suggests precisely that we have immense power over them.

Must a Nietzschean refuse to condemn any manifestation of cruelty "in itself"? Can't I believe that some of its instances are such that they are categorically different from the rest, and that they cannot ever, in whatever context, be praiseworthy? Nietzsche seems to say I can't: "The concept 'reprehensible action' presents us with difficulties. Nothing that happened at all can be reprehensible in itself: for one should not want to eliminate it: for everything is so bound up with everything else, that to want to exclude something means to exclude everything. A reprehensible action means: a reprehended world" (*WP*, 293).[9]

Perhaps changing the scale of the example may allow the point to emerge more clearly. Suppose I live under a brutally oppressive regime. An official has been assassinated. The police grab a completely innocent woman at random in the street. They torture her in the square and will eventually kill her in retaliation. I watch, with the mixture of fascination and horror that always attends such sights. I am tempted to try to save her. I know I can't, and that any effort will cause us both to die in the same way—perhaps provoke the murder of others as well. I hold back. What I do is reasonable—but not right. Perhaps I have no obligation to try to save that woman: it is not obvious that we have a duty to be moral saints. And yet I feel both guilty and ashamed.

Is it wrong to feel that way? I believe not. I believe that in such situations one can never be sure that it is right not to intervene, even if we can easily understand why almost no one ever does. I believe that utilitarian calculations about endangering greater numbers are beside the point, manifestations of bad faith. Why? Because, I think, it is a complete accident that the police chose that woman and not me for their purposes. Nothing relevant distinguishes me from the woman: they just happened to pick her, not me. I am not even sure that, had I been in her place, I would have thought that someone should try to save me. But I am sure I would have thought that they should feel guilty and ashamed if they didn't. Of course, there is here and in countless other situations in life an element of what Bernard Williams has called "moral luck": perhaps my life unfolds in such a way that one way, retrospectively, I may be able to justify my not having acted to save that unknown woman's life.[10] But to the extent that I can't, I must regret and, in Nietzsche's sense, "reprehend" my having acted as I did.

The same is true of the Jews. Their extermination had something essentially fortuitous about it. Since they were innocent, what happened to them could have happened to *anyone*: their being Jewish was not, in that context, a relevant consideration; in that context, we are all Jews — or blacks or Kossovars. But the enormity of the Jews' extermination, by changing the scale, introduces a radically different factor into the situation: it is difficult to imagine what possible development in *anyone's* life could possibly allow one to justify a harm of such magnitude. And without such justification, the action becomes reprehensible "in itself" — an action that should never occur.

Just as actions we have a duty to stop must never occur and are reprehensible in themselves, so actions we have a duty to perform are admirable, however foolish and ineffectual they turn out to be and however seldom we can perform them. Now Nietzsche writes, as we have seen, that it is in "the nature of the noble soul" to have "that unshakable faith that to a being such as 'we are' other beings must be subordinate by nature and have to sacrifice themselves" (*BGE*, 265), that "one has duties only to one's peers" (*BGE*, 260). But when what separates us from others is totally fortuitous, as in the situations we have discussed, there are no grounds for thinking that "we" are different from those others, that they are not our peers. Who counts as our peer can vary with the context.

What does it mean that differences between people are fortuitous or accidental, if Nietzsche seems to believe that there is no difference between essential and accidental properties, that "a thing is the sum of its effects"?[11] The distinction, as I am using it here, does not characterize the metaphysical status of properties; rather, it applies to those properties that I can claim as accomplishments, as features that I have made *mine*, on the basis of which I have constructed myself and which are therefore, to whatever extent, my merits, and to those which have not functioned in that manner and which I merely possess.[12] My being six steps away from the woman the police arrested is a fortuitous difference between us, unless my life turns out to be such that that event itself becomes a reason why it is admirable and worthwhile. It is not clear that any accomplishment can turn the fact that I was not eliminated by the Nazis into an irrelevant difference between me and those who were. I can never, at least, be sure that they were not my peers.

To believe that our peers are a fixed single group is to think that we have a special status that gives our actions a special value, whatever our actions might be. The ancien régime may have thought so. Nietzsche's "healthy" aristocrats, whether social or spiritual, may have agreed. But this attitude — that is my central claim in this essay — is inconsistent with his view that the "subject" does not precede, determine, or cause its actions, but is actually constituted by them: "the popular mind in fact doubles the doing; when it sees the lightning flash, it is the doing of a doing: it posits the same event first as cause and then a second time as its effect" (*GM*, I:13; *WP*, 531). Actions confer status, and not, as Nietzsche sometimes thinks when he is concerned with nobility, the other way around: that is exactly what makes his account of nobility so unsatisfying. The Homeric heroes of the *Genealogy* may well have believed that they were capable of deeds to which they, and only they, had a right. But if Achilles had remained hiding in women's clothes to avoid the war in Troy, he would have proved that he was not a hero and that he had no right to the deeds he actually performed (and which, of course, had he stayed at home, he would not have performed). We can think that we are different from people whose circumstances differ from ours because of the sheer accident only if we separate our own selves from our action, thinking that who we are is something over and above what we do and can determine independently the character and value of our deeds. Who "we" are, who our "peers" can be, is also, as Nietzsche failed to see, a matter of perspective and can change as our circumstances themselves change. "The order of rank" is compatible with many circles of duties, and there may be duties that we owe, in some extreme circumstances, to absolutely everyone. Such duties may govern a small part of our interactions with others: what is considered moral action, I believe, is a limited element in human ethical life and has little to do with our "rational essence." It governs those situations in which there is no reason to think that we are different from the rest of the world. But such differences are contextual, and the situations to which they give rise don't exhaust the range of our interactions as, under the influence of Kantian reflection, we are tempted to believe.

Nietzsche considered morality dangerous because it attempts to impose the same code of behavior on everyone, making it difficult for his *immoralist* heroes to function, and he claimed that as "a fundamental principle of society . . . it immediately proves to be what it really is—a will to the *denial* of life, a principle of disintegration and decay" (*BGE*, 259). I believe, with him, that moral principles do not, cannot, and should not, govern all our relationships with one another, and that they are not generally a sound basis for the practice of politics. But I also believe, against him, that Kant's insight into our sense of solidarity with other members of our species needs to keep a place within the economy of our life, even if not for Kant's own reasons.

Objectivity, Nietzsche famously said, is not "contemplation without interest" but the ability to see each thing from many points of view, the ability "to employ a *variety* of perspectives and affective interpretations in the service of knowledge" (*GM*, III:12; TI, "What the Germans Lack," 6). He applied his idea to his own examination of Christian morality, to which he said both Yes—for the many who need it—and No—for the few who do not. He did not go far enough, and he never saw that there may be particular, specific, perhaps even extraordinary situations in which moral considerations might be appropriate even for the few who manage to live beyond good and evil. He did not see that the error of morality, which

> takes good and evil for realities that contradict one another (not as complementary value concepts, which would be the truth), . . . advises taking the side of the good, . . . desires that the good should renounce and oppose the evil down to its ultimate roots [and] therewith denies life which has in all its instincts both Yes and No (*WP*, 351),

is an error he may have made himself when he insisted that there are absolutely no situations in which moral principles could ever constrain his own heroes. He did not see that by restricting the area of life to which morality is relevant, he could see it from yet another perspective, increase his objectivity toward it, become able to say another Yes and No to it.

Both "Yes" and "No" are essential to Nietzsche's thought about values: "Every naturalism in morality," he writes,"—that is, every healthy morality—is dominated by an instinct of life; some commandment of life is fulfilled by a determinate canon of 'shalt' and 'shalt not'" (*TI*, "Morality as Anti-Nature," 4). In *The Gay Science* 344, he famously denies the unconditional value of truth on the grounds that in life "both truth and untruth constantly prove to be useful" (344). His absolute rejection of moral considerations on behalf of his noble heroes may not fit so well with his general approach. And if I am right that Nietzsche depends, and must depend, on a separation of the doer from the deed when he completely rejects moral considerations, the deliciously ironic point emerges that in order to deny morality unconditionally (which is, on his own grounds, the manner of the moralist), he needs to appeal exactly to the distinction that he believes is the great invention of morality itself! For it is only by distinguishing between the doer and the deed, he argues, that morality could demand, absurdly, that strength express itself as weakness and reinterpret weakness as the product of choice:

> The weakness of the weak — that is to say, their *essence*, their effects, their ineluctable, irremovable reality — [came to be seen as] a voluntary achievement, willed, chosen, a *deed*, a *meritorious* act. This type of man *needs* to believe in a neutral independent "subject." . . . The subject (or, to use a more popular expression, the *soul*) has perhaps been believed in hitherto more firmly than anything else on earth because it makes possible to the majority of mortals, the weak and oppressed of every kind, the sublime self-deception that interprets weakness a freedom, and their being thus-and-thus as a *merit* (*GM*, I:13).

But that way of thinking can also proceed, in certain circumstances, from the opposite direction. When, for example, I feel justified in discriminating against you because my skin is white while yours is not, I focus on a feature that is simply part of my "being thus-and-thus" and consider it a merit, an accomplishment, the sort of thing that is the result of strength and choice, independently of anything I have in fact accomplished. I therefore say that who I am — in this case, white — confers on me and others like me a value that is separate from whatever it is that we do, that it confers value on whatever we do, and the absence of which prevents your deeds, whatever they are, to have a value that can ever equal mine. But unlike, say, talent, which is both individual and exhausted in accomplishment, skin color does not in itself underwrite achievement, and is therefore not a merit. If it is not a merit, it does not distinguish us from one another: in that context, we are both white, we are both black. We are peers. And I have duties toward you as I have duties toward all my peers, in the various contexts in which I find myself. Nobility, whatever else it is, is many-dimensional. One of its aspects is the ability to realize that not everything about a noble person is itself noble, except perhaps for that ability itself. That is not an argument that is intended to convince a racist or a Hitler. But it is designed to convince a Nietzschean, perhaps even a "Hitler," who wants to remain consistent in refusing to separate the doer from the deed.

And so, I don't need to make a moral judgment of Nietzsche's philosophy in order to disagree with him: "Hitler" may create values, he may meet Nietzsche's (vague) psychological criteria for nobility, but can still be horribly immoral, acting in a way no one ever should act, whoever it is, whatever the circumstances. Nietzsche famously declared that morality has an immoral basis: "*All* the means by which one has so far attempted to make humanity moral were through and through *immoral*" (*TI*, "The 'Improvers' of Mankind," 5); "morality is a special case of immorality" (*WP*, 308; cf. 401, 461). I have argued against him that his own absolute rejection of morality itself has a moral basis. His desire to abandon moral considerations completely, a dogmatism of Nietzsche's own, requires him to appeal to the same means he believes all *dogmatisms*, particularly morality itself, are obliged to use in order to justify their absolute prescriptions and prohibitions.

Is Nietzsche's philosophy, then, admirable? No, to the extent that it refuses to reject the evil hero unconditionally. Yes, because it gives us itself the nonmoral means to reject its refusal. It therefore prompts, like everything in life, including morality, a No and a Yes. In refuting it, we affirm it. Its error is a testament to its truth.[13]

Notes

1. J. P. Stern, *A Study of Nietzsche* (Cambridge: Cambridge University Press, 1979), 117.

2. I offer an extended discussion of that issue *in The Art of Living: Socratic Reflections from Plato to Foucault* (Berkeley: University of California Press, 1998), chap. 3.

3. Translation by Walter Kaufmann in *The Basic Writings of Nietzsche*, slightly modified.

4. Leslie Paul Thiele, *Friedrich Nietzsche and the Politics of the Soul: A Study of Heroic Individualism* (Princeton: Princeton University Press, 1990), 131.

5. A further parallel suggests that Nietzsche's relation to Plato is much more complex than we generally believe: Plato's Socratic dialogues imply that only one good person can recognize another, and that to approach someone who professes to teach what *arête* is may cause the greatest harm unless one already knows what *arête* is and can defend oneself against wrong conceptions of it. But if one already knows what *arête* is, one will not need to approach its professor! See *Protagoras* 313a1–314c2 with *Laches* 189d3–190c6 and, for discussion, Alexander Nehamas, *The Art of Living*, 79–82.

6. Joachim C. Fest, *Hitler* (San Diego: Harcourt Brace, 1974). Fest does not discuss the question of Hitler and Nietzsche in great detail, especially since he believes that, intellectually, Wagner was much more important to Hitler than Nietzsche, although he remarks at one point—closely connected to our present discussion—that Hitler "concurred with Nietzsche's saying that a nation was nothing but nature's byway for producing a few important men. 'Geniuses of the extraordinary type,' [Hitler] remarked, with a side glance at himself, 'can show no consideration for normal humanity.' Their superior insight, their higher mission, justified any harshness" (531). But the portrait of Hitler that emerges from his detailed study is not congruent with Nietzsche's (admittedly vague) image of nobility. Fest's Prologue, "Hitler and Historical Greatness," is also relevant to our concerns.

7. Keith Ansell-Pearson, *An Introduction to Nietzsche as Political Thinker* (Cambridge: Cambridge University Press, 1994), 33.

8. On the essential identity of the moral and the immoral, of good and evil, see also *BGE*, 2:295; *WP*, 272.

9. The passage continues, adding a complicated twist to this line of thought: "And then further: in a reprehended world reprehending would also be reprehensible—And the consequence of a way of thinking that reprehended everything would be a way of living that affirmed everything—If becoming is a great ring, then everything is equally valuable, eternal, necessary.—In all correlation of Yes and No, of preference and rejection, love and hate, all that is expressed is a perspective, an interest of certain types of life: in itself, everything that is says Yes." The last part of this statement should be contrasted with passages like *WP*, 351 and *GS*, 344, discussed later in this chapter.

10. See the title essay in Bernard Williams's collection, *Moral Luck* (Cambridge: Cambridge University Press, 1981), 20–39.

11. I have discussed Nietzsche's view in chapter 3 of *Nietzsche: Life as Literature* (Cambridge: Harvard University Press, 1985).

12. We shall see in the closing paragraphs of this essay that this is a distinction on which Nietzsche depends crucially for his attack on "slave" morality in *On the Genealogy of Morals*, although, I must admit, his vocabulary there is the opposite of mine: he writes that the "weak" misinterpret their weakness, "that is to say, their *essence* . . . [as] a *deed*, a *meritorious* act" (1:13), whereas I want to claim that "deeds" are what finally constitute the essence of a person. I believe the difference is simply terminological.

13. I am grateful to the audience at the Spindel Conference and to my students in a graduate seminar at Princeton University for their generous reaction to this problematic essay. I am particularly indebted to Florian Becker, Akeel Bilgrami, Maudemarie Clark, Keith Donoghue, Mathias Risse, and Robert Gooding-Williams, whose comments led me to a number of corrections, and to Jacqueline Scott, who organized the conference.

5

Nietzsche and the Jews
Menahem Brinker

There is a considerable literature on the Nazi use, appropriation, and manipulation of Nietzsche's name, philosophy, and writings. Debates focused around this issue started even before the Nazis rose to power and are still continuing today. The Jewish theme as it figures in Nietzsche's thought is also mentioned in a large part of these discussions, yet in most cases it is marginalized by more dominant themes. Among them one can find Nietzsche's scorn for the idea of equality, his contempt for democracy, and his critique of the idea of progress and the Nazi slogans about a "degenerate" culture, the concepts of the "Overman," and *amor fati*. After all, these were motifs that were central to the Nazis. The reason that the Jewish theme was relatively marginal in these discussions was that even those who looked for the links connecting Nietzsche to Nazi mentality knew very well that they could not be found in Nietzsche's utterances on the Jews. Even people who were almost completely ignorant of the true content of Nietzsche's philosophy had heard about his quarrel with Wagner and the Wagnerians. Nevertheless through the years of the Third Reich, echoes of Nietzsche's vocabulary could often be heard in Nazi attacks on the Jewish origins of all decadent "modern" ideologies such as liberalism, democracy, socialism, anarchism, and communism. This fact raises the question as to whether a writer who sees all modern political movements as the last masks of an intrinsic nihilism can truly be deemed an "apolitical thinker." At any rate, the use that the Nazis made of Nietzsche did include his treatment of the Jews. Hence an elucidation of Nietzsche's views on the subject is necessary for understanding both his own thought and the nature and extent of the Nazi tamperings.[1]

1.

Already in earlier studies of Nietzsche, his approach to historical Judaism had been distinguished from the attitude he adapted to contemporary Jews. In the last decade, however, a threefold distinction was introduced into discussions of the subject. Scholars have separated Nietzsche's admiration for the Hebrew Bible and for early Israel from his hostile and highly critical appraisal of Rabbinic post-exilic Judaism, and both of these from his appreciation of the postemancipation modern Jew. One of the aims of this essay is to demonstrate that, despite the validity of this distinction, Nietzsche also had a more general perception of the "Jewish race" in the specific sense that he attached to this term. A race is for him primarily a group of people united by their common life-experience which is interiorized and passed on from one generation to the next as a cultural heritage and as inherited traits of character.[2] Hence the analytic approach should be supplemented by a consideration of the philosopher's global conception of the Jews.

Two authors, Michael Duffy and Willard Mittelman have presented a short description of the evolution of Nietzsche's views on the Jews, offering a biographical explanation of each twist in this development.[3] First came Nietzsche's gradual liberation from the anti-Semitic prejudices of the cultural milieu in which he grew up. The last remnants of this conventional anti-Semitism disappeared when he befriended Paul Rée and decided to cling to the relationship with this Jewish intellectual despite the urgings of his mentors at that time, Richard and Cosima Wagner. The rift with the Wagners and the Wagner circle that ensued brought forth the first expressions of Nietzsche's hostility toward the anti-Semites of his time. It was at this stage that Nietzsche recommended (in *Human, All Too Human*) the expulsion of the anti-Semites from Europe and in *Daybreak* spoke of the need to fuse the Jewish race with the other races of Europe for the advancement and betterment of European culture.[4]

His position becomes much more complex with *Zarathustra* and in particular with the two books that succeeded it, *Beyond Good and Evil* and *On the Genealogy of Morals*. In these two books Nietzsche for the first time pinpointed the Jews of the period that followed the destruction of the Second Temple as the initiators of the "slave revolution in morality."⁵ He conceives their belief in a moral world-order (imbued in them by the prophets) and in particular the otherworldly connotations added to it in this period as a compensation for their political and military impotence. At the same time, the new, revolutionary moral values that they introduced to the ancient world ("blessed are the meek") were derived from the hatred they bore toward those who destroyed them, which later developed into a more general *ressentiment* toward any happy and successful human being or group. Through Christianity, which in Nietzsche's eyes was but a baser form of the new Judaic values, the Jews achieved their revenge. All Europe came to despise the body, physical beauty, health, and other instinctive values. The success of "Jewish revenge" lay in making the spirit of *decadence* dominant in Europe.

Nietzsche repeated this description in one of his last books *The Antichrist*. But in this book, which was meant to be the first part of a comprehensive work on the history of European nihilism, Nietzsche also expressed his admiration for the strength of the Jewish people, which applied to the entire history of this nation. In sharp contrast to what was implicitly assumed in the early work, the Jews were presented as not really believing in the new valuation that they had proclaimed. Being a strong and a healthy "race," there was no place in their existence for decadent feelings. They had never truly despised earthly life-enhancing values and were never really resigned to their defeat. On the contrary, the new valuation itself was a powerful act of revenge that they wreaked on their enemies. Although the content of the new Judeo-Christian values was decadent, the very ability to bring about such a revolutionary revaluation pointed to the great strength of the Jews as a people. They were able to create a new form of life in a situation that would have caused normal and weaker peoples to disappear. The success of this revenge showed that Jewish hatred was far from being impotent. The spirituality of the Jews was not something other worldly but had much to do with the wisdom and cunning with which they executed their plan of revenge. Duffy and Mittelman take these compliments at face value, and, according to them, Nietzsche reverted in *The Antichrist* to his former positive appreciation of the Jews. This was in contrast to his pronouncements in *On the Genealogy of Morals*, which stressed the impotence of the weak and miserable Jews and their *ressentiment* as the sole cause of the revolution that they had effected in morality.

Duffy and Mittelman find the sharp language Nietzsche uses in this book, in describing the Jewish "revolution," as an exception to the tone that he adopts in his other writings and explain it by the deterioration of his former good relations with Paul Rée. Nietzsche wrote *On the*

Genealogy of Morals after realizing that Rée had won Lou Andreas-Salomé's heart, which he attributed to his friend's treachery and cunning. The harsh things that he now said about the Jews are reminiscent of the raging expressions the philosopher used in his private correspondence to describe Rée's "betrayal." Much like the two other authors whose views shall be considered below, Duffy and Mittelman sought to make it clear that Nietzsche's hostile attitude to Jewish values related to only one specific epoch in Jewish history, and even then he never failed to bring out the strength and creativity of the Jews that were essential for "the revolution in morality."

To my mind, Nietzsche's philosophical development cannot be fully explained by biographical events because it has a kind of intrinsic "logic" of its own. Admittedly, Nietzsche's gradual liberation from the fashionable anti-Semitism of his milieu — in his own terms a process of self-overcoming — was publicly and dramatically acted out in his quarrel with Wagner and the Wagnerians. This was perhaps accelerated by their own racist response to the presence of Rée. Yet the harshness of the *Genealogy* cannot be primarily explained by the conflict with Rée and Lou. First, it is clearly the culmination of certain earlier motifs. The history of Judeo-Christian decadence shares several important features with the history of that other "decadent" revolution — the one that happened in Athens. Second, Nietzsche now explains the developments in Judaism in terms of the psychology of impotence and compensation rather than in terms of betrayal and deceit. Therefore, there is really no strict parallel between the rhetoric that Nietzsche uses in the *Genealogy* and the language he used in referring to Rée's betrayal. True, in *Antichrist* Nietzsche praised the Jews for not being themselves decadents. From a purely Nietzschean point of view this was indeed a compliment. Yet from a more conventional moral point of view this praise only added to their "guilt." By inventing the "day of judgment" and the "other world" they do not really compensate themselves for their political and military defeat in "this world" since they do not themselves believe in these new myths. Therefore only the others, their conquerors, imbibe the decadent poison they have concocted. Being racially strong and remote from any decadent feelings, the Jews do not need any transcendent therapy. What they required was a palpable revenge for their humiliation. By using their intellectual superiority they achieved victory over their enemies, a triumph that had been denied them because of their military weakness. Therefore, according to *Antichrist*, the Jews found a real remedy for their sickness in this world by poisoning their enemies. Actually an old anti-Semitic dormant stereotype is grafted here in new philosophical soil. Protected by their racial purity and inner strength and by the walls of a hermetic geographical separation, the cunning Jews were not exposed themselves to the disease they were spreading within the camp of their enemies.

2.

The two books I shall discuss in the following pages differ from Duffy and Mittelman's assessment of the different attitudes to the Jews displayed respectively in *On the Genealogy of Morals* and *The Antichrist*. Yovel perceives that the compliments the Jews are paid in *Antichrist* are quite ambiguous and Santaniello thinks that the text of the earlier book is more favorable to the Jews since it places more stress on Judeo-Christian continuity. It therefore expresses more clearly the fact that Nietzsche is attacking Rabbinic Judaism only because its culture and values inspired the emergence of the Christian Church. In her view, *The Antichrist*, mars the generally favorable picture Nietzsche usually paints of Jewish culture, as opposed to his total disparagement of Christianity.

Santaniello's book holds the record in recent attempts to reconstruct Nietzsche's thought in a way that stresses the depth of his admiration for the Jewish people. We are presented with a systematic interpretation of Nietzsche's conception of European decadence and nihilism from a perspective that places his diametrically opposed valuations of Judaism and Christianity at the core of the discussion. Nietzsche's thought, especially in the first part of the book, is conducted in a biographical register that emphasizes the centrality of the anti-anti-Semitic motif in Nietzsche's life with regard to the Wagners, to Paul Rée, his own fervently anti-Semitic sister Elisabeth, and her racist husband, Bernhard Förster. The unique contribution of this book lies in the identification of some public figures who served Nietzsche as models for several fictional characters in *Thus Spoke Zarathustra*.[6] These were also the arch-anti-Semites of the time. There is also a discussion of the theological controversies of the age that were relevant to the rise of anti-Semitic waves to which (as the book persuasively argues) Nietzsche indirectly responded in his writings.

Beside his brother-in-law Förster and the preacher Adolf Stöcker, Nietzsche constantly had in mind (in all his attacks on the anti-Semites) the figure of Eugen Dühring, a founding father of both national socialist ideology and virulent secular anti-Semitism. Santaniello singles him out as the model for "The Last Man" in *Thus Spoke Zarathustra*. Indeed it seems very plausible that it is Dühring who is in the back of Nietzsche's mind when he indicates the similarity between the anti-Semitic and Socialist agitators. After all, according to a Nietzschean "genealogy," both of these modern popular movements stem from the *ressentiment* felt by the unfortunate and by inferiors toward those who surpass them in fortune or natural endowments. Clearly, for Nietzsche, Dühring represents a modern embodiment of the vengeful spirit of slave morality. As a socialist, he desires revenge upon those who were fortunate enough to inherit a lot of money, and, as a German, he begrudges the Jews for their being intellectually superior to ordinary Germans. As a secularized Christian, Dühring insists that a combination of nationalism and socialism is the modern heir of the Christian ethics of love. Yet his message is one of envy and hate, which is the source of his popularity with the vulgar masses. Other insights in Santaniello relate to Nietzsche's identification of anti-Semitism with the Protestant German Church. He was keenly aware of the theological literature that sought to deny the Jewishness of Jesus and that tried to cut all ties between Christianity and Judaism. In her view, it was Nietzsche's wish to undermine the theology of his time that led him to condemn Rabbinical Judaism. The denunciation of priestly Judaism derived from his desire to ridicule nineteenth-century Christian anti-Semitic theology. He wished to point out to those anti-Semitic theologians that the Judaism that they despised above anything else was actually the genealogical-historical origin of their most cherished values. To her mind, it was neither Judaism, nor Christianity as such, but rather Christian and secular modern anti-Semitism that worried him. Her thesis even goes so far as to claim that it was anti-Semitism that drew Nietzsche into what he called "the history of European nihilism."

This seems largely exaggerated since both nihilism and the need to overcome it were already present in Nietzsche's thought when he wrote his earliest philosophical compositions, *The Birth of Tragedy* and *Schopenhauer as Educator*. Santaniello, however, believes that his six-year membership in Wagner's circle gave Nietzsche access to their secret aims, which included the destruction of the Jews. Alarmed by what he found, Nietzsche tried with the last remnants of his health and sanity to appeal to world public opinion to prevent the impending disaster before it was too late. Santaniello's explanation of the Nazi appropriation of Nietzsche's name and writings is not that there was some spiritual affinity or a scheme to benefit from his fame and influence for the sake of their cause. They "co-opted" him in order to silence him. They wanted to get Nietzsche out of their way because he was a witness who saw through them, understood their evil plans, and had warned his listeners against them.

One can hardly go much further in transforming Nietzsche's disgust with the anti-Semites into his central concern in life and thought. Yet this approach, which was already anticipated by earlier publications,[7] suffers from a major flaw: there is no corpse. Every single fact in the conspiracy theory Santaniello puts together is there. Nietzsche was obviously not only disgusted but also horrified by anti-Semites like his brother-in-law and clearly saw in Dühring a kind of prototypical "Nazi." One can indeed quote him on the possible disasters that will befall Europe from that corner. Yet the main link in the chain is missing: no protocols of the Wagners' circle have been found, and, like other prophecies of Nietzsche that came true, one can explain his clairvoyance by his extraordinary sensitivity to the cultural-political moods of his time rather than by his access to any secret knowledge.

Viewing anti-Semitism as the impetus for Nietzsche's interest in the Jewish origins of Christianity causes Santaniello to assume total continuity between the two versions of the story that Nietzsche tells in the *Genealogy* and in *Antichrist*. In contrast to Duffy and Mittelman, she finds the *Genealogy* to be both more important philosophically and more sympathetic to the Jews. In the earlier book Nietzsche pointed to a very specific group of Jews, at a definite time and place as the initiators of "the slave-revolt in morality." His severe criticism of these Jews did not derive from anti-Semitic prejudice but on the contrary, it was entailed by the hostility he felt to his own Protestant anti-Semitic milieu. His research led him to the discovery that the ultimate origin of the *ressentiment* that the majority of contemporary Christians directed at the Jews was to be found precisely in the response of the Jews to the destruction of their original state. The discovery of the true meaning of slave morality and the role of the Jews in conceiving it, is in itself a result of Nietzsche's reaction to the semiofficial anti-Semitism of the Second Reich. Nietzsche insisted that this revolution represented before anything else a sea-change in the culture of the Jews themselves. It did not qualify either his admiration for ancient Israel or the high esteem in which he held postemancipatory modern Jews. Clearly, one can agree with Santaniello and Yovel, who both stress the implicit sting directed against Christian anti-Semites: Nietzsche compels them to grasp that the source of all their sacred values resides in the people whom they despise so much. Still, I do not share these writers' conviction that this sting captures the motive and the meaning of Nietzsche's genealogy.

Santaniello thinks that the same polemical motive that gave rise to the discussion of the Jewish origins of Christianity in the *Genealogy* is at work also in *Antichrist*. The main innovation of the later book, the "physiological portrait" of Jesus that stresses how special his personality must have been and how atypical it was for both the Jewish rabbis and for the founders of the Church, does not impress her as a considerable change in the basic Nietzschean outlook. For her the main thrust of this conception is the polemical insistence (as against Ernest Renan and other anti-Jewish theologians) that the rise of Christianity cannot be comprehended without taking into account the Jewish background of Jesus. Nietzsche takes pleasure in reminding all those who seek to "liberate" Christianity from its Semitic vestiges that Jesus lived and died as a Jew. Against Renan, Nietzsche claims that nothing was farther from Jesus' mind than founding a new religion or a new church; and that the first Christian, who was also the last one, was the product essentially of Jewish values. Again, she quotes Nietzsche's praise of the strength of the Jewish people that cannot be compared to any other in its ability to preserve itself against all decadent temptations. For her these words prove that the "constants" in Nietzsche's attitude toward the Jews were respect and high esteem to the point of admiration. Nietzsche's portrait of Jesus and his emphasis of how far he was from both typical normative Jewishness and from the characteristic Church mentality is not even mentioned in her book. Of the three publications I have discussed in this essay, only that of Yovel mentions and discusses Nietzsche's portrait of Jesus. It seems to me, however, that his discussion may have missed a few crucial points in Nietzsche's analysis, out of the desire to clear him of all charges in relation to anti-Semitism.

3.

Santaniello's book is the most extreme publication in a line of publications that have rediscovered, as if for the first time, that far from being anti-Semitic himself, Nietzsche actually admired "the Jewish race" and was of the opinion that other European peoples might learn from his experience. Indeed, with regard to the Jews of his time or the Germans or nationalism in general, one cannot imagine a greater abyss than the one that separates the spirit of Nietzsche from the Nazi *Weltanschauung*.

Nevertheless there is a conspicuous limitation on all attempts to disconnect completely Nietzsche's writings on Judaism from traditional anti-Semitic motifs. All of these attempts try to confine the harsh language that Nietzsche uses in referring to the "priestly revengeful people" to the Rabbinical period alone and to ignore a very fundamental ambivalence that accompanies Nietzsche's declared admiration for people (like Socrates or the Jews) who succeeded in bringing about moral (unhealthy) revolutions. Only Yovel's book actually recognizes Nietzsche's ambivalence but tries to dissolve it into the distinction between separate periods in the history of the Jews.

I see this as a misleading simplification of Nietzsche's more comprehensive view of "the Jewish race," which included more permanent features that manifest themselves throughout all the periods and the various stages of religious and cultural evolution within Judaism. These traits are highly ambivalent in Nietzsche's eyes. I shall now try to show that a similar ambivalence occurs in regard to all great or creative moral revolutionaries or innovators of values in history.

For example, Socrates responds to ancient Greek despair by inventing a new value (or deity) called Reason for the young Athenian aristocrats who were his interlocutors. They knew reason only as the faculty of moderating and restraining passions. Suddenly they have to encounter a new and "unclassified monster" who awaits them at every corner and challenges them to explain the motives of their actions "according to Reason." They learn of the existence of a new creature—Socrates—for whom pure Rationality is the motive for action, while the irrational domain (the *daemonion*) acts as restraint. Nietzsche shares their astonishment and contempt for the impolite, awkward pressure that the ugly dialectician imposes on them. Yet he is compelled also to admire the endurance, persistence, and, above all, the inventiveness of this moral revolutionary from classical Greece, the godfather of Western philosophy. He is amazed by this performance though it is this ancient Greek philosopher who brings about the death of Tragedy, the most sublime and unique fruit of classical Antiquity.

The same ambivalence is felt by Nietzsche toward the personality of Jesus. Nietzsche does not ascribe to Jesus (as he does to Socrates) a new interpretation of existence. Moreover, he feels contempt for Jesus' faith. This Jew of lowly origins shares Plato's myth of "the other world" on a much more primitive intellectual level. He really believes in his "father in heaven," to whom he has direct access. His faith accompanies him wherever he goes, immersing his soul in its own internal symbolism, preventing his senses from noticing external danger, and making him lose all natural instincts of self-preservation and self-defense. In all these respects, Jesus is a special phenomenon but his uniqueness is at the same time the most perfect incarnation of the new spirituality, invented by the Jews. This spirituality fills the soul with "a new mysterious passion," and causes both its adherents and victims to pass through a process of denaturalization, in which the most basic and natural instincts are castrated and one becomes "purified" of all earthly desire—in other words—a complete decadent! Nietzsche was of course sharply critical of all decadence. Still, he is driven to admire Jesus in the same way as one admires an artistic masterpiece. In his eyes Jesus is the "most perfect decadent" ever seen on earth, and and his indifference to all natural forceful instincts bring Nietzsche both to admire him and to treat him with a certain contempt.

The same intense ambivalence also exists in Nietzsche toward "the Jewish race" as a whole. Judaism was the spiritual laboratory that shaped Jesus, but it was also the Halachic-Rabbinical establishment against which he had directed his anarchistic revolt. In opposition to Renan and all his German followers who saw Jesus as representing "Aryan" values, Nietzsche insisted that Jesus could not be conceived without his Jewish background. Yet, he also stressed the fact that, in his view, Jesus was a very atypical Jew (precisely as Socrates was an atypical Greek). The Jews had invented "a moral God," i.e., a God who rewarded the just and punished the wicked, an avenger God. Revenge against those hostile to them (and to their God) was an essential motif in the Jewish eschatological vision. It was usually disguised as Law and Justice, for the last day *is* the day of judgment. However, Jesus' God was very distinct from the Judaic tradition of the judging and punishing God of the last day. He was the "Father in heaven" who redeems immediately, here and now, anyone whose heart is pure, and who does not harbor in his soul any grudge, envy, or hatred toward other human beings. According to Nietzsche, Jesus' otherworldliness reflected a certain mood and way of life in *this* world. Santaniello is therefore wrong in claiming that the discussion in *The Antichrist* does not add anything essential to the discussion in the *Genealogy*. It is only in the later book that we understand the reasons why Nietzsche found Jesus to be so different from both the Rabbinical culture that preceded him and the Christian Church that succeeded him.

It is also only in *The Antichrist* that Nietzsche makes it clear that it is not Jesus but Paul who really represents the continuity of spirit that exists between Judaism and the Christian Church. Anti-Semitic theologians attempt to make us forget that Jesus was a Jew but Santaniello succeeds in forgetting that for Nietzsche the most typical Jew (at least in the time of Jesus) was Paul. Paul is the characteristic product of the Jewish spirit of *ressentiment*, typical of slave-morality in general, and it is he who deliberately falsified the mystical message of Jesus and conquered the spirit of Europe, poisoning it with decadence. Paul and the Church convinced people that they can be redeemed by faith alone, without making any other effort. In this endeavor they followed the example of sectarian Jews. Yet the Jewish priests merely pretended to have faith and to believe in the new values while hoping that others (their enemies) would accept them. The only Jew that fully believed and felt himself redeemed by his faith was Jesus. Faith made him (in relation to the Christians that come after him) the most atypical of Jews. Paul, on the other hand, acted out of a physiological-psychological "Jewish" motivation, characteristic of people driven by *ressentiment*.

The wish to deny any anti-Jewish attitude on Nietzsche's part dictates a very specific selection of his words and thoughts. Santaniello remembers Jesus but forgets Paul while Yovel gives a strange, even twisted, interpretation to the Judeo-Christian typological and psychological continuities, the existence of which he acknowledges. For example, Yovel writes that "in the continuum leading from priestly Judaism to the Christian Church Jesus is not only a link but also a break. This is a 'pure moment' that transcends decadence. It is only used by others to enforce it."

It is hard to see how Jesus, who is described by Nietzsche as "the most perfect decadent ever seen on earth," can be construed by Yovel as a breach in the continuum of decadent culture extending from priestly Judaism to the Christian Church. Yet when we realize that, at least in the *The Antichrist*, *ressentiment* and decadence are not one and the same thing, but almost antipodal psychological phenomena, we can understand what has misled Yovel. In Nietzsche's theory, the *ressentiment* of the Jewish priests and later on that of Paul and the Church is presented as a cause of European decadence without necessarily being an inherent component of it. There is here a continuum of people full of impotent envy and hatred that induce decadent feelings in both themselves and others. Precisely because he is a perfect decadent, Jesus transcends the (theological) spirit of revenge that is typical of vanquished Judaism and of the Christian Church, which holds itself to be the heir to Israel. Nietzsche's pivotal psychological and genealogical insight is that entirely natural cravings and passions for revenge that are continuously denied external outlet, are bound to turn inward and give rise to the psychic phenomenon of *ressentiment*. This interiorised aggression is "a hatred that creates ideals . . . a power which changes values and create values." At a given moment in history it created the faith in the "backward world" of a rewarding and punishing God. A whole-hearted straightforward acceptance of this new faith could calm and soothe the interiorized aggression that had causally shaped the new faith. Thus, hatred and vengefulness would be sublimated and people might put their trust in God and his inexorable justice, thereby obviating earthly revenge. Yet of all the participants in this moral drama, Jesus is the only one in whose soul the spiritualization of all earthly desires is so complete that it leaves no room for hostility, even toward his torturers. The Jewish teachers and priests that preceded him as well as the founders of the Christian Church that succeeded him never underwent this change of heart. Either they did not succeed in maintaining their faith in the supernatural or else they never had it in the first place and were just cheating (it seems to me that Nietzsche wavers between these two possibilities). In any case, precisely because of this lack of perfect faith, their decadence is never as perfect as that of Jesus. They are simply Jewish priests or Christian clerics whose souls are full of hatred and envy of anything successful as they spread the decadence that infects others.

In the *Genealogy*, there was still room for a certain ambiguity: Did the preachers who spoke of the Day of Judgment and of the other world actually believe in what they were preaching? Were they decadent themselves or only messengers of decadent ideas? It seemed that at least the prophets believed in the new values that they had brought to the world. One thing, however, was unequivocal: whether they believed it or not, the preachers were driven by *ressentiment* and they helped to instill and cultivate this psychic disposition in all their listeners. Nietzsche's speculative analysis of the true personality of Jesus, with its emphasis on his remoteness from his Jewish teachers no less than his Christian disciples, together with Nietzsche's praise of the Jews for being averse to all kinds of decadence, implies a basic distinction between *ressentiment* and decadence. These are two distinct mental dispositions that breed two different interpretations of the human condition. They do not necessarily inhere in the same human subject, and sometimes it is even impossible for them to coexist in the same human being.

In the *Genealogy* Nietzsche discusses only the psychological-existential Jewish origin of slave morality and the way in which it became dominant in Europe through the lure of the crucified Son of God. Jesus was only mentioned there as a stage in the process through which the values of oppressed slaves came to prevail over the ancient values of the Greek and Roman aristocracies. Hence one could have thought that Nietzsche equated *ressentiment* with decadence. On the other hand, however, in *The Antichrist*, Nietzsche carried out a detailed analysis of the personality of Jesus. He wishes to redeem Jesus' real personality from its distortion by Paul and the Christian Church. Jesus was seen as a man unable to hate anyone. A person who was condemned to live (by "a physiological necessity," to use a Nietzschean idiom) with a heart full of love toward anything that exists. For that very reason Jesus could not transcend decadence but his life was its most perfect incarnation. We cannot grasp Nietzsche's description unless we understand that by adding new insights to those included in the *Genealogy*, Nietzsche views *ressentiment* as an external cause of decadence rather than as one of its internal components.

That is why it is practically impossible to grant to the text of *The Antichrist* a full acquittal from the charge of using traditional anti-Semitic imagery. A deeply entrenched anti-Semitic concept infiltrates Nietzsche's attempt to effect a moral counterrevolution (reverting from the Judeo-Christian slave revolt back to the aristocratic values of classical Europe). Protected by their lack of faith and by the ghetto walls, the Jews were sending a paralyzing new faith to the Gentiles to avenge the wrongs done to them by their conquerors. This poisonous potion was conveyed to their enemies by its first victim: Jesus Christ. Jesus was a victim of the Jews not because he was offered to the Roman rulers as a rebel but because the new Jewish doctrines made him unable to defend himself against his enemies. Jesus is really the sacrificial lamb of the Jews. Drunk with the new mystic faith to the point of losing all contact with reality, he brings the same decadent affliction upon any place in which he is celebrated as an exemplary human being and "Son of God." The assumption that the Jews are incapable of simple faith in God is not an invention of Nietzsche. It is the anti-Semitic consensus of nearly all of the German philosophers who preceded him. In his provocative way, Nietzsche turns it into a compliment: the Jews are incapable of decadence. Yet despite the changed evaluation, an ancient anti-Semitic image of the Jews persists and appears in Nietzsche in a new cloak.

Once again we encounter a fundamental Nietzschean ambivalence. The weak bring about harmful revolutions in the domain of values. Yet if they succeed in establishing a new interpretation of existence and make it last for a long period, they cannot really be regarded as impotent. Both the Jewish and the Socratic revolutions succeeded. This in itself made Nietzsche ambivalent toward the "perpetrators." The victory of "the (Jewish) slave revolt in the domain of Morality" is effected through the strong instincts of a people that wishes to exist "at any price" and proves capable of existing under the "most adverse conditions." True, their political and military weakness—to the point of impotence—makes the Jews incapable of direct and "honest" acts of revenge. They are driven to give their horrible revenge a cunningly theological twist. Yet the very impulse for revenge is fully natural and attests to their firm character. Only in this way can Nietzsche disdain Jewish "priestly" *ressentiment* and at the same time display respectful understanding of the Jews that borders sometimes on an astonished admiration.

All the four authors I have discussed are right in claiming that Nietzsche's hostility to the Christian Church is more intense than his antipathy toward Rabbinical Judaism. This is certainly true, and the reason is that according to the crude conception of Jewish "revenge" introduced in *The Antichrist*, Nietzsche allows the Jews to abide by their earthly values—their deceitful act of revenge having been accomplished. According to this work, one should not take too seriously Jewish declarations of transcendental faith. The Jews did not really need for long a theology as compensation for their miseries. While they adhered to their earthly ethics—their tribal way of life that made them such a powerful people—the Christian Church institutionalized *ressentiment* in the form of permanent theological *Weltanschauung*. The true Christian believers were the genuine decadents while the preachers and priests merely took advantage of the ignorance and weakness of ordinary folk for their own gain.

This assessment is obviously imbued with ambivalence. Nietzsche admired the traits that made both Socrates and the Jews creators of a new tables of values. Yet he also regarded them as responsible for European nihilism and decadence. He admired their creative powers but profoundly detested their creation, while realizing that it did not occur in a spiritual vacuum. The set of values created, in both cases, was successful because of the terrible conditions of the times, which had made the victims of these alternative interpretations of the world (the Greek pessimists and the slaves and other oppressed people in the Roman Empire) seize upon the new doctrines as a therapy. Nietzsche is equally ambivalent toward these victims. When he considers them as helpless victims of a metaphysical fraud, brought about through a historical "accident," he pities them. When he contemplates their need for metaphysical "crutches" or consolation, and their gullibility in the face of Socratic sophistries or the egregious absurdities of the Church, he despises them.

On the face of it, one could ascribe a certain kind of healthy will to power even to the extreme case of Jesus with his complete denial of the external world and intense focus on the psychic life with its internal, almost autistic, symbolism. Had Nietzsche thought of the will to power in purely psychological terms, there could have been a case for such an assessment. But the text of *The Antichrist* makes it clear that Nietzsche cannot ascribe power to an extreme introversion that derives from an acute vulnerability to any encounter with the real world. Nietzsche's conception of "positive" versus "negative" feelings of power is never purely psychological.[8] It has cognitive and social dimensions. Only one who squares up to reality without illusion and is able to work one's way through it — always competing with the will to power of others has positive power. Having this ability is conditional upon the general situation of the individual in the world. Nietzsche insists on the term "physiology" when evoking the totality of one's situation in the world, including one's interpretative response to it. A new valuation of existence indicates a certain amount of positive power even when it covers up some physiological weakness. When there is no innovation of values one cannot really speak of power. That is why Nietzsche does not ascribe power to Jesus but only a "mystifying charm" derived from absolute weakness. Yet besides his admiration for the creators of new values (including unwholesome values), Nietzsche can also appreciate aesthetically perfect embodiments of a value scheme — such as Jesus — that he sharply negates.

Ambivalence and ambiguity seem intrinsic to Nietzsche's genealogical philosophizing. *Ressentiment* is to be equated with decadence in some contexts while in others it is only an external cause of decadence. Moral revolutionaries will at times be acknowledged as powerful people (regardless of the content of their innovations) while in other texts and contexts, positive power will be ascribed only to acts that stem from an instinctive assurance that does not question entrenched traditional values — such is the cases of ancient Israel and classical, pre-Socratic Athens.

4.

I have discussed the ambivalence in Nietzsche's thought on the origins of decadence in some detail because it helps us understand how his writings could be easily manipulated by the Nazis. It is not enough to point out the chasm separating Nietzsche's views on the Jewish "race" from all kinds of racist anti-Semitism beginning with that of Wagner. According to Nietzsche, the narcotic of transcendental faith that had poisoned Europe had its origins in the moral pathos of Judeo-Christianity. Other "races" had absorbed this "poison" more comprehensively, hence their decadence was more far reaching. But decadence and nihilism encompassed much more than the original Judeo-Christian system of beliefs. Among the negative consequences of the moral revolution "that is hidden only because it succeeded" was the idea of equality in all its abstract philosophical or theological forms (equality before God, Nature, or History). Superficially, one could exclude any political implications from Nietzsche's critique of equality and pretend that its aim was simply to protest the idea that geniuses like Leonardo da Vinci or Mozart be regarded as inherently equal in value to any unproductive simpleton of the herd.

Yet Nietzsche continually stressed that it was the political implications of the idea of equality, as found in democracy and socialism, that he found catastrophic. To his mind these abominable "modern ideas" like all feelings of "neighborly love" or social and class solidarity were nothing but remote echoes of slave morality. For Nietzsche, the idea of equality was both a denial of the real state of affairs of the hierarchy (aristocrats and slaves) that exists "in the nature of things" and also the ideological result of the "natural order" or rather "disorder" for those romantic souls that cannot bear too much reality. Democracy and socialism were an integral part of the sickness of decadence or nihilism that romantic souls had already begun to construct for themselves in ancient times, and now, with the loss of faith, these ideas become more influential. All this is part of continuous sickness — and from all this one has to recover.

No doubt, one can find in Nietzsche's writings other assessments of liberalism and of democratic ideals, but these belong to the period preceding *Thus Spoke Zarathustra*. When he wrote *Human, All Too Human* and *Daybreak*, Nietzsche still looked favorably on the dissemination and advance of liberal and democratic trends in Europe. Far from being an "a political thinker," he changed his views in accordance with evolving philosophical convictions. In contrast to the early positivism of his philological writings, Nietzsche was already an anti-Platonist and sought to replace the value of truth ("*Wahrheit*") as the full correspondence of "knowledge" with independent reality, with the existentialist value of truthfulness ("*Wahrhaftigkeit*"). Yet in the spirit of Comte, he still remained an admirer of the sciences. At that time he believed that the scientific spirit spread healthy skepticism and a much needed critical attitude to all dogmatic doctrines (and superstitions). Giving up absolute truth seemed to him necessary for better relations among people, social classes, and nations. Democracy seemed to encourage this undogmatic, critical, and skeptical pursuit of truth that never ends in absolute certainties. According to his essays of that period, this modern ideal of the scientific spirit supports democratic aspirations and is also supported by them, and he welcomed this interaction and identified it with the idea of human progress in which he then ardently believed.

All of this changed utterly during the few years of the writing of *Thus Spoke Zarathustra* when a new, more "tragic" Nietzschean philosophy was born. Science and the positivistic admiration of scientific facts were now deemed "new idols" that did not serve authenticity and truthfulness but rather blocked and oppressed it. Democracy was depicted as a superstition based on the modern (thus decadent) idea of the equal value of all human actions, all human creations, and all human beings — another mask for the intrinsic nihilism of modernity. Because democracy renounces the value hierarchies necessary for a non-nihilistic culture, it was seen by Nietzsche as one of the "idols of the herd." It was henceforth to be resisted along with the other political currents of the age — including liberalism, nationalism, socialism, anarchism, and anti-Semitism. Nietzsche had to create his personal hierarchy of values, leaving politics to demagogues and leaders of the herd.

Unlike Walter Kaufmann and an entire generation of Nietzsche scholars that followed him, I do not think that the Nietzschean freethinker who frees himself from the "new idols" can completely isolate himself from politics. Indeed, even after exposing the inner emptiness of all the political aspirations of his time, Nietzsche himself continued to be intensely interested in politics — awaiting the emergence of a new Napoleon who could unite Europe, transcending parochial nationalism, eradicating racism and anti-Semitism, but also blocking the influence of "modern ideas" like democracy and socialism. Nietzsche could support

the assimilation of the Jews (and the improvement of workers conditions in his "democratic" period), yet increasingly he began to favor
political and militaristic restraints to discipline the herd. It is easy to
dismiss Nietzsche's contradictions as indicative of his approaching madness, to view them as the hallucinations of a philosophical revolutionary
who was also a political conservative, lacking any sense of the political
realities of his time: a lonely thinker who secretly believed that he lived
in Athens or in Sparta. There may be a grain of truth in this assessment.
Yet one should not forget the inner connection of these "mad expectations" to some of the fundamentals of Nietzsche's thought. In his view,
politics had no value other than the service it could render to culture.
Culture was created by the few, and high culture was also needed by
"the happy few." Not all kinds of politics were of service to culture.
Democracy, for example, might subvert cultural values by teaching the
equal value of everything and by tempting people to prefer comfort and
security to the creative greatness that may require danger and risk.

Thus the claim that Nietzsche's philosophy was "a political" does
not necessarily entail indifference to political developments and events.
Even after finding all existing political trends equally empty, Nietzsche
anticipated with a mixture of horror and joy the catastrophes of "great
politics." These cataclysms would demonstrate to Nietzsche's "new philosophers," the emptiness of modern mass democracy. They would bring
European nihilism to the surface and force free Dionysian thinkers to
mark themselves off from the politics of the herd. They might well
be followed by a veritable cultural renaissance and the advent of the
Overman.

Nietzsche's liberal admirers remained tone-deaf to these strands in
Nietzsche's later writings. It is precisely this deafness and willful ignorance that makes it so difficult to understand the fate of Nietzsche's
ideas in the Third Reich. No doubt when the Nazis presented themselves as the masters of Europe, as the new aristocrats who would put
an end to decadent culture, they were committing a fraud, one more
intellectual atrocity to be placed alongside other, far more monstrous,
crimes. Nietzsche would surely have been one of the first thinkers to see
them as the most terrible outgrowth of European nihilism and he would
have torn to pieces their "aristocratic" pretensions just as he had already done with some of their predecessors. Yet the Nazis could also
take advantage of Nietzsche's contempt for democracy and his equation
of the principle of equality with decadence. Moreover, it was easy to
connect the fact that Jews were prominent in liberal and radical movements with an attack on their role as source of egalitarian ideas, and to
exploit Nietzsche's admiration for authoritarian hierarchical societies
along with his rejection of the existing status quo. Without acknowledg-

ing these connections, we would be limiting ourselves to the examination of forgeries, omissions, and falsifications. But the problem is far broader than simply measuring the distance between Nietzsche and the Nazis. One must try to understand how the Nazi appropriation of Nietzsche was possible. By dwelling excessively on the "falsification theme" the writings of philosophical interpreters of Nietzsche can teach us very little. The historians can do much better.

Notes

1. On this topic, see Steven E. Aschheim, *The Nietzsche Legacy in Germany, 1890–1990* (Berkeley: University of California Press, 1992), 272–84, and Hans Sluga, *Heidegger's Crisis: Philosophy and Politics in Nazi Germany* (Cambridge: Harvard University Press, 1993).

2. One result of the prevalent association of Nietzsche with Nazism is that there has been no research of Nietzsche's use of the term "race." The issue was utterly daunting to the many authors who strove to disentangle him from his Nazi falsifiers. I have found some important relevant remarks in Yirmiyahu Yovel's *Darl Riddle: Hegel, Nietzsche, and the Jews* (Cambridge: Polity Press, 1998), 176–80. From *Beyond Good and Evil* onward, Nietzsche talks often about "races," e.g., the Jewish "race" praised as "the purest of European races." Yovel notes correctly that almost all Nietzsche's statements about "race" could be made even more appositely about "people" — for example, that the English "race" is not "philosophical." Nietzsche recommends cross-breeding of races in Europe, although with reference to ancient times it is the races that remained pure that he lauds. Strangely, he regards this as indicative of their vigor. Still, it is never quite clear whether this vigor is attributed to a uniform heritage (a set of values passed on through the generations) or whether it is also a continuity of "blood." Undoubtedly his notion of "race" and the purity of race that he mentions (not only regarding the Jews) is not purely biological. It is a concept combining physiological-hereditary factors alongside shared experiences of the forefathers instilled in their issue. Such traumas left their imprint in the form of cultural internalization (heritage) and perhaps genetically as well. Although Nietzsche was often compared to Darwin in the nineteenth century, it is evident that, as Yovel remarks, he is more of a Lamarckian in so far as accumulated cultural impressions are considered as capable of being "genetically" transmitted. The Nazi racists who suspected that Nietzsche was very remote from their materialist, biological determinist conception were quite right. For Nietzsche "race" connotes a combination of spiritual internalizations of historical experience, with the biological mechanism securing their transmission.

3. I shall, in what follows, be reviewing three invaluable publications that are representative of the new approach to our topic: Michael Duffy and Willard Mittelman, "Nietzsche's Attitude towards the Jews," *Journal of the History of Ideas* (1988): 301–17; Weaver Santaniello, *Nietzsche, God and the Jews: His*

Critique of Judea-Christianity in Relation to the Nazi Myth (Albany: State University of New York Press, 1994); Yovel, *A Dark Riddle*.

4. The expulsion of the anti-Semites is discussed in section 251 of *Beyond Good and Evil*. The famous passage welcoming the entry of the Jews into European culture is section 205 in *Daybreak*.

5. There is a great deal of vagueness in Nietzsche's various texts about the "slave revolt in morality" as a historical event. On the one hand there is the theory—mainly in *Beyond Good and Evil* and in *The Antichrist*—viewing this revolt as the "revenge of Judea on Rome," hence the slave rebellion develops during the political and military decline of the Jews after the destruction of the temple, or even later, following the failure of the Bar Kochba rebellion. On the other hand, the content of this revolt is a revaluation related to the Jewish theological shift from the earthly tribal deity—a symbolic epitome of a collective will to power—to the consoling fiction of a cosmic deity, the God of justice and right who rewards and punishes at the end of days. Nietzsche was well aware that this shift had occurred much earlier, in the days of the prophets, perhaps prior to the destruction of the First Temple. Thus, in *On the Genealogy of Morals*, the event appears unhitched to Rome and is rather associated with the priest typology of resentment and with the priestly "vengeful and grudge-bearing" nation. The very use of the term 'priests' in this book indicates total severance from historical reality, for it is patently the Christian priest that Nietzsche has in mind here as the prototype of his Jewish counterparts and anticipators (prophets, pharisees, Rabbis).

6. See Santaniello, *Nietzsche, God and the Jews*, esp. 132–45, including notes.

7. See, for example, by Peter Viereck, *Metapolitics: The Roots of the Nazi Mind* (New York: Capricorn Books, 1941).

8. Compare with Jacob Golomb, *Nietzsche's Enticing Psychology of Power* (Ames: Iowa State University Press, 1987), pt. 3.

6

Nietzsche contra Wagner on the Jews
Yirmiyahu Yovel

"Wagner's Antipode"

The mature Nietzsche once described himself as "Wagner's antipode."
In his own view, he was as opposed to Wagner as the North Pole is to
the South. Moreover, it was his break with Wagner in the mid 1870s
that finally allowed Nietzsche to find his own identity, to develop his
own intellectual personality and mission. In the 1880s Nietzsche continued to take Wagner seriously even as a fierce opponent. He looked upon
Wagner as a temptation he had to overcome, as a servitude and even as
an "infection" or "disease" he had to experience before liberating himself and coming into his own. Under the heading of "Wagner," Nietzsche did not only mean the music dramas, but a whole complex of
attitudes and a worldview, which included romanticism, Schopenhauer's
negation of the will, German nationalism, and anti-Semitism, among
others. Similarly, in calling Wagner his "antipode" Nietzsche intended
to dissipate all these intertwined shadows—including anti-Semitism—
which Wagner's domineering figure had cast in his way. For Nietzsche, his overcoming of Wagner was at the same time a powerful self-
overcoming for Nietzsche—so deep had Wagner penetrated his own
self, albeit as an alien and self-alienating force.

Nietzsche was Wagner's junior by thirty-one years. When he first met the Master, Wagner was nearing the height of his creative career, while Nietzsche was still a student in Leipzig. A few years later Nietzsche became a young professor in Basel and used to visit the Wagner's home and stay at their Tribschen villa in Switzerland. In those years Nietzsche developed a strong affective link to both Wagner and Cosima, though in different ways. In Wagner he saw not only a great artistic innovator, the most exciting in Europe, and a personal patron, but also, in a certain sense, elements of a substitute father; while Cosima (whom Nietzsche secretly dubbed "Ariadne") seems to have taken for him the role of an idealized, imaginary lover. Even in later years, when he fiercely opposed Wagner, Nietzsche remembered those Tribschen days with warmth and nostalgia, saying he "should not want to give them away out of his life at any price," because his first contact with Wagner "was also the first deep breath of my life" (*EH*, "Why I Am So Clever?" 5).

Another person who commanded Nietzsche's mixed veneration was the eminent Basel historian Jakob Burckhardt, who remained an ambivalent Master-figure in Nietzsche's life until his last lucid hours; yet unlike Wagner, Burckhardt did not let his relationship with the younger man become too intimate. Burckhardt severely criticized the Jews and was chillingly indifferent to their historical plight; whether or not he was anti-Semitic, there is no doubt that Nietzsche perceived him as such.[1] And, of course, in Wagner and Cosima, Nietzsche met passionate anti-Semites, as virulent as Bernhard Förster, his future brother-in-law, who, to Nietzsche's great distress, struck a deep chord in his ambivalently beloved sister Elisabeth. Thus, in those important and problematic years — which later Nietzsche described as his "residence in the zone of the disease"[2] — some of the persons most intimately related to him were fiercely anti-Semitic: this fact is significant if we are to realize how momentous — and painfully liberating — was Nietzsche's subsequent overcoming of Wagner's influence several years later.

Even during his years "in the zone of the disease," Nietzsche's negative feelings against the Jews were relatively mild and conventional, the result of a Christian upbringing and prevailing prejudices against emancipated Jews. He lacked the hatred, the ideological anger, and the bite of professed anti-Semites such as Wagner. Still, he often willingly expressed his anti-Jewish bias, especially when talking or writing to more assertively anti-Semitic friends like the Wagners, or like Carl Von Gersdorf, his old, not-too-bright buddy from their student days in Leipzig. The latter had praised Wagner's pamphlet on the Jews as brilliant after reading only a few pages. In one letter Nietzsche told Gersdorf that he was going to decline an attractive offer — travel to Greece as companion to one Professor Mendelssohn of Freiburg — who was no other than the son of the composer, Felix Mendelssohn-Bartholdy. As Ronald Hayman points out, Nietzsche could not have accepted the invitation without deeply offending the author of *Das Judentum in der Musik* and his no less anti-Semitic wife.[3]

The young Nietzsche's adulation of Wagner reached a famous climax in the second part of *The Birth of Tragedy* (published in 1872), which in maturity Nietzsche repudiated and disavowed. Wagner, through his music, was to become the cultural savior of Europe—his work capable of reviving the Dionysian spirit that had made a tragic world-experience possible in ancient Greece. It would redeem Europe from the centuries-old decadence inspired by the Platonic Socrates and his ideal of the rational, "theoretical man." The irony is that after his break with Wagner, Nietzsche, as we shall see, assigned a similar role—to serve as catalyst in Europe's revival from decadence—to the modernizing Jews whom Wagner abominated so much and whose self-destruction he demanded as a condition for such revival. Replacing Wagner with the modern secular Jew cast in the role of creating the new Dionysian Europe was to be the harshest blow that the later Nietzsche would deal to his older, bigoted, and hate-inspired former friend and mentor.

With Wagner, Nietzsche also overcame several positions manifest in *The Birth of Tragedy*, which later were banned from his thinking. These included his early romanticism and echoes of a nationalistic tendency; the extravagant belief in aesthetics as the true metaphysical domain and in art as the sole redeemer; the quest for boundless, infinite, obscure emotion and the tendency toward false depth and humorless heaviness, which Nietzsche, in a polemical generalization, attributed not to Wagner alone but to the self-aggrandizing spirit of *Deutschtum* in his time. No less important, Nietzsche overcame the Schopenhauerian disdain for the individual and the advocacy of self-negation—the submersion of the individual will and life in some common mystical substance (which many in Bismark's Reich interpreted as the German *Vaterland*). No less importantly, he denounced the back-door Christianity that, he felt, hovered over Wagner's pretended revolutionary atheism and the fervent German nationalism that he served—offering another way of turning the individual into "an animal of the herd." And last but not least—the plebeian anti-Semitism of which Wagner became a popular apostle, together with Eugen Dühring, Paul de Lagarde, and the obsessive Förster, Nietzsche's despised brother-in-law.

It should by now be clear that Wagner's anti-Semitism did not appear to Nietzsche as a marginal caprice, a mere affectation of a great and somewhat erratic artist, but as part of his overall cultural significance. The mature Nietzsche even referred to Wagner's anti-Semitism as epitomizing all his other faults. Explaining his break with Wagner in *Nietzsche contra Wagner*, Nietzsche says, "Since Wagner had moved to Germany, he had condescended step by step to everything I despise — even to anti-Semitism."[4] And in *Ecce Homo* he adds, "What did I never forgive Wagner? That he *condescended* to the Germans — that he became *reichsdeutsch* [i.e., a German political nationalist]."[5] It is significant that the verb "to condescend" occurs in both quotations: to Nietzsche, a true thinker or artist can become anti-Semitic or a German nationalist only by stooping down, by lowering himself to the level of the vulgar — as Wagner had done not only in his politics, but even in his music, and especially in creating Bayreuth. Here one must remember that Bayreuth, alongside Wagner's anti-Semitism and *Reichsdeutschtum*, figured as both a reason for Nietzsche's break with Wagner and as the location where it first happened. As he reports in the same passage of his *Nietzsche contra Wagner*, "By the summer of 1876, during the time of the first *Festspiele*, I said farewell to Wagner in my heart" (*NCW*, "How I broke away from Wagner," 1). Bayreuth played this crucial role because, to Nietzsche, it manifested Wagner's catering to the vulgar both institutionally and in his very music. "In Bayreuth — he says — one is honest only in the mass; as an individual one lies, one lies to oneself. One leaves oneself at home when one goes to Bayreuth; one renounces the right to one's own tongue and choice, to one's taste, even to one's courage . . . against both God and world." Nietzsche goes on to attack the theatricality of the Bayreuth cult and identifies its core defect: "solitude is lacking." Music is by nature the most inward of the arts, and therefore the most personal; yet in Wagner, "Even the most personal conscience is vanquished by the leveling magic of the great number; the neighbor reigns, one becomes a mere neighbor."[6]

This is the anti-Schopenhauerian, anti-romantic Nietzsche speaking. In his former phase, he would not have had such praise for the individual, nor such scorn for the attempt to sweep him into some ecstatic collective experience. But Nietzsche had by now come into his own. He valued the cultivation of the high-grade individual, and of a cheerful, courageous pessimism in a world free of Christianity, of God, and above all — of God's shadows. He equally abhorred the vulgarity of the multitude, pettiness, moral bickering, the negation of life, and especially the false self-affirmation that does not flow spontaneously of itself but depends on the vengeful negation of someone else in order to exist. This is *ressentiment*, the ultimate defect according to Nietzsche's ethical psychology and the common genealogical source of such apparently distant phenomena as Christianity, anti-Semitism, socialism, nationalism, as well as much of Wagner's work.

There is no doubt that Nietzsche drew an analogy between Bayreuth and the mass movements of nationalism and anti-Semitism. Wagner's music, and its public consecration in a ritual shrine, express the same

"leveling magic of the great number" as did the political mass movements of his time (*NCW*, "How I broke away," 1). Nietzsche argues
that Bayreuth brings into the open the fact that Wagner is external and
mass-oriented in his very music. His true goal lies in neither the music
as such, nor in the words, but in the external effect they produce. Wagner is thus "a first-rate actor" in whatever he does or writes (*CW*, 8);
and he uses his actor's gifts for domination; he became a musical dra-
matist in order to satisfy a deeper drive—that of an autocrat, a tyrant
(ibid.). Nietzsche presumably wished to say that Wagner used music,
and its ritual institutionalization, as a form of modern politics—
perhaps as political aesthetics—an Ersatz to political theology.

One can debate whether Nietzsche's description is fair to Wagner
personally, but there can be no doubt that Nietzsche's foresaw the future career of Bayreuth as a politico musical shrine, one that culminated
in the marriage not only of art and nationalistic politics but of Wagner
and Hitler. Of course, this outcome was not Wagner's own doing and
cannot be laid at his feet; yet there was something in the composer's
linkage of music, myth, Germanism, and anti-Semitism that made this
perverse evolution possible.

Nietzsche also denounced the emotions Wagner's music often con-
veys—"the convulsive nature of his affects, his overexcited sensibility,
his taste that requires ever stronger spices."[7] In the better part of his
audience Wagner invokes a romantic aspiration "to the sublime, the
profound, the overwhelming" but responds to it with heavy, obscure,
shapeless music that creates a false semblance of its object and "puts on
the lie of the great style." This makes Wagner the "heir of Hegel,"
whose Idea Wagner put to music (*CW*, 10). They both shared a nebu-
lous quality, a tendency of "shaping clouds," of "whirling, hurling, and
twirling," by which Hegel had lured his adepts and which Wagner continued through his musical works.

In more formal terms, Nietzsche criticized Wagner's use of an "infinite melody," which other critics had praised as an innovation. But
Nietzsche associated it with shamelessness and a failed imitation of the
sublime. Such music, he claimed, produces "chaos in place of rhythm,"
and makes one "swim and float" instead of "walking and dancing"
(*NCW*, "Wagner as a Danger," 1). By contrast, Nietzsche praised Bizet's
Carmen (another intended affront to the anti-French Wagner) because
its "evil, subtly fatalistic" nature is masterfully conveyed by its lightness
and precision. Bizet's music "does not *sweat*" (like that of Wagner); it
has shape and clarity ("it builds, organizes, finishes"), and moves with
a light, supple step. And Nietzsche, thoroughly cured of his youthful
romanticism, now added with a grain of merry, anti-Wagnerian spite,
"What is [aesthetically] good is light; whatever is divine moves on ten-

der feet—[this is the] first principle of my aesthetics"(CW, 1). Hence, he looked to Mozart's "golden seriousness" which contrasted with the grim, philistine "German" seriousness he heard in Wagner.

Wagner's true genius lies elsewhere—in depicting the subtle moments of life, the minute detail, the nuances of the world—he is a great miniaturist. Here Nietzsche's earlier admiration remains intact. Wagner is unequaled in putting into sound the feeling of brief joys, the "quiet, disquieting midnight of the soul," those moments in which a passing deep happiness is exhausted, leaving bitter drops of sadness in the drained goblet: Wagner is "the master of the very minute" (NCW, "Where I Admire"); yet he refuses to accept his true calling and instead constructs those heroic panoramas in which he poses and therefore fails.

Nietzsche's famous complaint—that Wagner had started as a revolutionary atheist and ended (in *Parsifal*) as an obedient Christian—finds a parallel in his account of the *Ring* (CW, 4). In Nietzsche's interpretation, Wotan's web of treaties signifies the old social order that Siegfried sets out to uproot. Wagner had started as a social revolutionary, projecting the typically modern outlook of optimism, humanism, progress, and social utopia, including even women's emancipation, represented by Brünhilde's rebellion against Wotan and becoming human through Siegfried. But once Wagner was imbued with Schopenhauer's pessimistic philosophy, he became ashamed of his erstwhile optimism. Thus the project of the *Ring* was seemingly shipwrecked. Finally, Wagner solved the impasse by "translating the *Ring* into Schopenhauer's terms," that is, by having everything go wrong: the new world is no better than the old, so everything perishes and nothingness prevails.

Nietzsche and the Jews

The Jewish question was more central to Nietzsche than meets the eye, and his view of it remained ambivalent though by no means confused or incoherent. On the contrary, the basic trends in his attitude to the Jews were compatible with each other and with the basic ideas of his philosophy. My aim is to bring to light the clear structure of this ambivalence. First, two preliminary remarks:

(1) I am dealing with Nietzsche as philosopher, not with the popular uses and abuses of his thought or with what is vaguely called "Nietzscheanism," despite the interest this may have for the historian or sociologist.

(2) When Nietzsche attacks the anti-Semites or defends the Jews, he was aiming at real people—the actual community of the Jews, and anti-

Semitism as a contemporary movement. By contrast, when dealing with ancient priestly Judaism, Nietzsche treated it as a psycho-cultural category latent in the Protestant Christian Church of his day, which Nietzsche, as a "genealogist" of this culture, wished to expose. Contrary to many anti-Semites—and also to the trend of Jewish apologetics—Nietzsche did not project his critique of ancient Judaism into a political attitude against the Jews of his day. This break allowed him to be at the same time—and with intense passion—both an anti-anti-Semite and a critic of ancient priestly Judaism, the fountain of Christianity.

The Anti-Anti-Semite

A selection of four kinds of text allowed me to recognize Nietzsche's fierce and univocal opposition to contemporary anti-Semitism. These texts are taken from (1) his published writings; (2) his intimate letters—to his sister, his mother, and his close friends; (3) his "twilight letters" written on the verge of madness; (4) a correspondence with the anti-Semitic agitator Fritsch, who tried to recruit Nietzsche—(and "Zarathustra," too, as Nietzsche says with disgust)[8] into his camp.

I shall quote some illustrations of the first two categories:

> They [the anti-Semites] are all men of ressentiment, physiologically unfortunate and worm-eaten, a whole tremulous realm of subterranean revenge, inexhaustible and insatiable in outbursts against the fortunate and happy (*GM*, III:14).

> It is certain that the Jews, if they desired—or if they were driven to it, as the anti-Semites seem to wish—could now have . . . literally the supremacy over Europe, that is certain; that they are not working and planning for that end is equally certain. Meanwhile, they rather wish and desire, even somewhat importantly, to be insorbed and absorbed by Europe; they long to be finally settled, authorized and respected somewhere and wish to put an end to the nomadic life, to the "Wandering Jew"; and one should certainly take account of this impulse and tendency . . ., for which purpose it would perhaps be useful and fair to banish the anti-Semitic bawlers out of the country (*BGE*, 251).

Letter to Franz Overbeck:

> This accursed anti-Semitism . . . is the reason for the great rift between myself and my sister (*BW*, III:503).

To his sister, Elisabeth Nietzsche (upon her engagement to the virulent anti-Semite Förster):

> You have gone over my antipodes. . . . I will not conceal that I consider this engagement an insult—or a stupidity that will harm you as much as me (*BW*, V:377).

To his mother:

> Because of people of these species [anti-Semites], I couldn't go to Paraguay [where members of Förster's anti-Semitic circle had set up an experimental colony]. I am so happy that they voluntarily exile themselves from Europe. For even if I shall be a bad German—I am in any event a very good European (*BW*, V:443).

Again to his sister, Elisabeth Förster-Nietzsche, several years later:

> Your association with an anti-Semite expresses a foreignness to my whole way of life which fills me ever again and again with ire or melancholy. . . . It is a matter of honor to me to be absolutely clean and unequivocal in relation to anti-Semitism, namely opposed as I am in my writings. . . . My disgust with this party (which would like all too well the advantage of my name!) is as outspoken as possible. And that I am unable to do anything against it, that in every Anti-Semitic Correspondence Sheet the name of Zarathustra is used, has already made me almost sick several times (*BW*,V:479).

The intimate texts carry special weight, because they prove that Nietzsche's opposition to anti-Semitism was not merely external or "politically correct" (as with many liberals) but penetrated into the deep recesses of his being. I think that this outcome was reinforced by Nietzsche's intense relations with anti-Semites like his sister, Richard and Cosima Wagner, and perhaps also Jacob Burckhardt. Such intense psychological tensions may have served as a lever in providing heightened energy for Nietzsche's overcoming his earlier anti-Semitism not as a liberal rationalist but in a "Nietzschean" way—namely with all the passion of his being.

The Philosophical Context of Nietzsche's Anti-Anti-Semitism

But even without considering psychology, there are sufficient philosophical grounds for Nietzsche's active adoption of anti-anti-Semitism. The anti-Semitic movement contained and heightened most of the decadent elements in modern culture that Nietzsche's philosophy set out to combat:

1. Anti-Semitism as a mass movement was seen by Nietzsche as vulgar, ideological, a new form of "slave morality" representative of the herd.
2. Anti-Semitism was a popular neurosis, affecting weak people who lacked existential power and self-confidence.
3. Anti-Semitism, especially in Germany, served to reinforce the Second Reich and the cult of the state, which Nietzsche, "the last Unpolitical German," had denounced as "the New Idol."
4. Anti-Semitism was also a lubricant of German nationalism, which the mature Nietzsche opposed most insistently (though he did so "from the right").
5. Anti-Semitism also depended on racism, which Nietzsche's philosophy rejected as a value distinction among groups, though he did use race as a descriptive category. Nietzsche favored the mixing of races within the new Europe he envisaged.
6. At the root of anti-Semitism lay a common genealogical structure of fear, insecurity, existential weakness, and, above all, *ressentiment* — the malignant rancor against the mentally powerful and self-affirming, as well as the hatred toward the other as a precondition for self-esteem. The ardor of the anti-Semite conceals his or her deep insecurity: he does not start with the celebratory affirmation of his own being, but with the negation of the other by which alone the anti-Semite proves able to reaffirm his own self — which he does in an overblown, empty, and arrogant manner.

Nietzsche's four negations — those of nationalism, racism, anti-Semitism, and the cult of the state — also explain why he was bound to have opposed fascism and Nazism, although these ideologies successfully manipulated his philosophy for their devious purposes.

Ancient "Priestly" Judaism

Nietzsche's attack on ancient "priestly" Judaism is as fierce and uncompromising as his assault on anti-Semitism. The Jewish priests, so he claimed, excelled in *ressentiment* and falsified all natural values. They spread the spurious ideas of a "moral world order," sin, guilt, punishment, repentance, pity, and the love of the neighbor. The meek and the weak are the good who deserve salvation; all men are equal in their duties toward a transcendent God and the values of love and mercy he demands. Thereby Nietzsche attributes to the Jewish priests a direct Christian content, and often describes them as Christian from the start. Yet beneath his doctrine of mercy, the priest's soul was full of malice and *ressentiment*, the rancor of the mentally weak whose will to power turns into hostility and revenge against the other, who becomes the only way to affirm himself. Thereby the Jewish priests, pictured as early Christians, have created the "slave morality" that official Christianity then propagated throughout the world. Whereas the anti-Semite accuses the Jews of having killed Jesus Christ, Nietzsche accuses them of having begotten him.

Priestly morality is the morality of the existentially impotent, in whom *ressentiment* against the powerful and the self-assured has become a value-creating force. The existential "slaves" take vengeance on their "masters" upon an ideal plane, in that they succeed to impose their own values on the masters, and even cause them to interiorize those new values, and thereby subjugate them. Henceforth the powerful person sees himself/herself as sinner not only in the eyes of others but in his/her self-perception as well, which is the ultimate form of subordination (and also mental corruption).

Nietzsche placed the critique of ancient Judaism at a crucial junction of his philosophy. It is grounded in *ressentiment* (a key Nietzschean category), and is responsible for the corruption of Europe through Christianity. However, his critique does not serve Nietzsche in the fight against contemporary Jews, but rather against contemporary Christianity, and the "modern Ideas" he sees as its secular offshoots (liberalism, nationalism, socialism, etc.). And the modern anti-Semite is analyzed as the genealogical cousin of the ancient Jewish priest.

Nietzsche's analysis, like Socrates' dialectic, ends in an ironic reversal. While the anti-Semite in his psychology resembles the ancient Jewish priests, the modern Jew is their complete opposite (or "antipode"). As such, modern Jews, once they have become secularized, are candidates for helping create a new Dionysian culture, and redeeming Europe from the decadence instilled by their forefathers.

It follows that Nietzsche holds two rather clear positions — one against modern anti-Semitism and the other against ancient priestly Judaism — both of them linked by the same genealogical root, *ressentiment*. Nietzsche's ambivalence derives mainly from combining these two positions, which look contradictory but are not so in effect. This analysis also explains (in part) why Nietzsche's position has so frequently been abused. For the intellectual revolution he was seeking did not actually take place, while his ideas were generalized, vulgarized, and delivered to a public in which the old psychology still prevailed.

The Three Phases of Judaism

To understand this better we must realize that Nietzsche does not attribute a constant essence or genealogical pattern to Judaism. Indeed, he distinguished three periods or phases within it.

1. In biblical times (the Old Testament) Nietzsche perceived a Dionysian greatness and natural sublimity that aroused his reverence. He did not accept the content of their religious belief, but he admired the attitude to life and religion of biblical personalities because it was vital, natural, this-worldly, and built on self-affirmation rather than self-recrimination.

2. The Second Temple and its priests were the object of Nietzsche's harsh and merciless attack. Here was the origin of the "slave morality" revolution, of the major denaturation and reversal of values that led to Christianity.

3. Diaspora Jews also aroused Nietzsche's admiration, because they had demonstrated the power of affirming life in the face of suffering and drawing power from it. Moreover, Diaspora Jews had the merit of having rejected Christ and of having served as constant critics and as a counterbalance to Christianity.

Contemporary Jews and the Closing of the Circle

As a result of their hard schooling and invigorating experience, the Jews reached the modern era as the strongest and most stable race in Europe, and could have dominated it, though they did not wish to do so.[9] However, once they had decided to mingle with the other European nations, then because of their greater existential power they would naturally, without intending so, reach a dominant position, in the sense of determining the norms and the new values in Europe. If, however, the Jews continued their seclusion, Nietzsche grimly predicted that they would "lose Europe" (that is, emigrate or be driven of it) just as their ancestors had left or been driven from Egypt. Nietzsche advocated the first alternative. The Jews were to pour their gifts and power into a new Europe that would be freed of the Christian heritage: the forebears of Christ must work today in the service of the modern anti-Christ (i.e., Nietzsche-Dionysus), and thereby pay their debt to Europe for what their priestly ancestors had done to it.

For this to happen, European society would have had to open up to the Jews and welcome them; and the Jews would have needed to end their voluntary seclusion and involve themselves with all European matters much as their own affairs: in this way they would, undoubtedly, have attained excellence and end up determining the shape of a new Europe. Nietzsche welcomed this prospect with enthusiasm, because he saw the Jews as allies and as levers in the transition to a higher human psychology and culture. If the Nazis considered the Jews as *Untermenschen*, to Nietzsche they were a possible catalyst of the *Übermensch*.

I must emphasize that Nietzsche's pro-Jewish attitude did not derive from liberalism. Just as his attack on nationalism and racism came "from the right,"[10] so did his defense of the Jews derive — for good or bad — from Nietzsche's own Dionysian and antiliberal sources. The Jews were expected to enhance Nietzsche's illiberal philosophy of life — a task that many Jews, who were and are liberals, could hardly welcome.

It should be noted that Nietzsche's admiration for Diaspora Jews was not in praise of them as bearers of a religious culture, but rather for displaying the human, existential qualities he desired for his revolution. Nietzsche expected them to secularize and practice creative assimilation in the framework of an atheistic Europe.[11]

In a way, the Jews in Nietzsche's later thought assumed the role that their archenemy, Wagner, had formerly fulfilled. In the first edition of *The Birth of Tragedy*, Wagner, through his music, was presented as the redeemer of European culture, but now, most scandalously, he lost this role to none other than the Jews whom he hated and despised so much. (Perhaps unconsciously, Nietzsche thus gets even with his former anti-Semitic friend and master).

It was indeed Nietzsche's break with Wagner that opened the way to assigning a fully fledged redemptive role to his Jewish opponents. Both stories — the Jewish story and the one told in *The Birth of Tragedy* — have striking structural similarities, since both are stories of ancient corruption and modern redemption; but there is also a difference: Wagner was supposed to redeem Europe of a corruption perpetrated by others (Socratic Hellenism, Euripides), whereas the Jews, are expected to redeem the evil they themselves (through their ancestors) had done.

Judaism in Music—Argument or Invective?

I turn now to Wagner's 1850 treatise *Das Judentum in der Musik*. What is its main claim and typical mode of discourse, especially in comparison with Nietzsche? It is characteristic that Wagner and Nietzsche both denounce a "politically correct" way of talking about the Jews, but do so from opposite directions. Nietzsche chides the "merely political" liberals who conceal their antipathy for the Jews under a cloak of polite jargon, while making no effort to overcome their actual anti-Jewish prejudice. He wants to see committed, passionate, "Dionysian" opponents of anti-Semitism, of which he himself is an exemplar. Wagner, too, begins *Judaism in Music* with a similar point, that liberal humanists (as he himself once had been) conceal their aversion for the Jews under a false barrier of verbal restraint—though this is unnatural and hypocritical. Anti-Jewish passions must neither be concealed nor overcome, but unleashed in a candid, overt, and unbridled manner. We loathe the Jews, says Wagner, they provoke disgust and abhorrence in us—so let us express our feelings overtly and in public. This is legitimate, the way that sincere people should behave. Restraint, on the other hand, is bad and hypocritical.[12]

This is Wagner's main message in *Judaism in Music*: legitimizing the public use of hate speech against the Jews. This also determines the mode of discourse of *Judaism in Music*: Wagner does not argue, but makes a pulpit pronouncement, designed to remove in other people the same restraints that he has broken down himself. His work is self-referential, in that it fulfills its own recommendation—to publicly express disgust toward the Jews and present them as the corrupters of German culture—and hails what it does as being proper and correct, even moral. This made Wagner (especially with the republication of *Judaism in Music* in 1869, when he already was famous and influential) a founding father of the anti-Semitic modern movement, which spread hatred and fear against the Jews in the public German arena, catering to the same prejudices and passions that he had vented and helped to legitimize.

The *laisser-aller* advocated by Wagner appealed to common persons who, carried away by negative passions, hailed their lack of self-mastery as if it were a virtue ("sincerity"). However, the claim that "sincerity" is moral and restraint is merely hypocritical is the antithesis of civilized life. Moreover, civilization cannot forgo a certain duality arising from the gap between one's raw, "sincere" passions and a justified social taboo, which harnesses their public outburst. Like shame, a measure of social hypocrisy / duality is often inevitable as a barrier against the volcano of aggression and barbarism. Even decent people may be divided between their self-imposed moral restraint and their inability to interiorize it fully. Yet there is a world of difference between admitting that one has not fully overcome an ugly passion and removing the moral restraint against it—legitimizing the Devil because he is in all of us. This is what Wagner had done. His primitive political psychology suited the vulgar masses that nourished the anti-Semitic movements and later the Nazi political orgies.

However, in giving an apostolic legitimization to this kind of political psychology, Wagner the social propagandist stood in opposition to

Wagner the artist. For (to give an artistic parallel), had Wagner held the same view about music drama — that unshaped, vulgar emotions must be expressed unbridled in it — we would have had Wotan mostly cursing Brünhilde, Hunding assaulting Siegmund on the spot, Alberich wildly screaming and squeaking, Siegfried babbling like a half-wit, while the orchestra produces a cacophony of formless emotions, and the famous Wagnerian "leitmotifs" degenerate into simplistic clichés. Happily, Wagner as artist was not a pupil of Wagner the pamphletist.

As to the mode of discourse of *Judaism in Music*, it is neither analytic nor argumentative, but essentially invective. The work is a discharge of aversion, which calls itself legitimate and appeals to others to follow its example. In this sense, it is not a theoretical discussion, but an outburst, a lengthy vituperation.

Judaism in Music contains no theory worthy of the name, let alone a philosophy. With a single exception, its mode of writing is exclamatory, not theoretical. The only argument we do find in it is based on the romantic belief, current then in Germany, that peoples are organic entities, each revolving around a unique essence or spirit that others cannot share. Because the Jews are alien to the German organic essence — and already severed from their own origins — they cannot join the German nation and culture except by grotesquely aping from without — or desecrating and corrupting it. Although this view was not specifically Wagnerian, but borrowed from nineteenth-century romantic nationalism, Wagner helped shape a more chauvinistic version of it: not only defending "pure" Germanism as one culture among several, but Germanizing culture in general. The human spirit, he claimed, found a privileged, authentic, superior embodiment in the German language and in German music, drama, poetry, and philosophy. When, after Hitler, people ask, "How could Nazism arise in the nation of philosophers and musicians?" the answer is, because philosophy and music had been Germanized a long time before. They were no longer understood as universal (as the query presupposes) but as specific products of the organic German *Volk* and essence. Wagner was a major voice for that view, not only in his essays but in his art as well. If music were universal, then Jews could authentically join it. But if music, like thought itself, is Germanized, nobody else has a true part in it, least of all the Jews.

There is a contemporary debate on whether Wagner's anti-Semitism is expressed in his music, or in certain characters in his operas (Kundry, Mime, etc.) This debate is hard to resolve, for two reasons. First, much of the answer lies in the eye of the beholder. And second, even where Wagner himself might have expressed an anti-Jewish feeling, he did it in the subtext and through various allusions, and not by direct references. (Still, in Mime's case, the allusions are quite blatant). An alternative method, I suggest, is to examine not the characters' description but the attitude toward them that the text of a Wagner drama presents as natural and correct. Following this method, we observe a striking analogy between *Judaism in Music* and a central scene in *Siegfried*, where Siegfried pours his loathing on Mime without yet having a reason to do so. He is still ignorant of Mime's true intention; all he knows is that Mime, whom he considers his father, has raised, fed, and educated him—and yet Siegfried cannot stand the dwarf and, following Wagner's advice in *Judaism in Music*, voices his "natural" loathing in the open:

> *Siegfried*:
> Much you've taught me, Mime
> and much I've learnt from you.
> But what you most have sought to teach me
> I never succeeded in learning:
> how to tolerate you [or: stand, suffer you : *dich leiden*].
> Though you bring me food and drink,
> loathing alone feeds me.
> Though you make me a soft couch to sleep on,
> slumber is hard to come by—
> As soon as I set eyes on you
> I see that all you are is evil.
> When I watch you standing, shuffling and shambling,
> servilely stooping, squinting and blinking,
> I long to seize you by your blinking neck
> and make an end of your obscene blinking.

Siegfried at this point knows nothing of Mime's schemes. In his subjective state of knowledge, his words clearly express ingratitude, and his loathing of Mime is gratuitous. Yet Siegfried is a natural hero, the spontaneous voice of nature and innocence, so he cannot be wrong. What he loathes must be judged vile, and what he does—openly expressing his disgust—must be justified. Thus Siegfried is both taking Wagner's advice in *Judaism in Music* and repeating it under his own authority to the audience. This throws Mime into an analogous role to the Jews. Siegfried, indeed, shows the German masses who "spontaneously" loathe the Jews the way to express their feelings just as eir mythological hero has done.

It should be noticed that Wagner's anti-Semitism is of the modern type, which sees its prime enemy in the secularizing, emancipated Jew aspiring to be assimilated into German culture and society. Wagner's attack on Felix Mendelssohn-Bartholdy is aimed no less at his grandfather, Moses Mendelssohn, who devoted his life to showing that Jews can excel in European and German cultural matters. This is a new anti-

Semitism, aimed especially against the Jews who had come out of the ghetto. The traditional orthodox Jews, who prefer seclusion, do not pose the same threat to Wagner, except as a pool from which secular modern Jews have issued.

Nietzsche opposes *Judaism in Music* on all these points. He viewed modern secular Jews as a promise of redemption for Europe; suspects any kind of mass political psychology, and stresses self-overcoming as a sign of human worth. There is nothing more detestable to him than *laisser-aller* — letting oneself be swept along by crude, unshaped passions. Nietzsche opposes this vulgarity no less than Kantian moralism, and aspires (somewhat like Spinoza) to a new order of the passions, in which the instincts reshape themselves into a higher human quality.[13]

Nietzsche equally opposed Wagner in denouncing the politicization of culture. Politics is the enemy of culture (*TI*, VIII:1,4); therefore he, Nietzsche, is "the last Unpolitical German." Wagner, on the contrary, saw culture itself as politics; it ought to energize great audiences around a primordial nationalist experience, with aesthetics functioning as a substitute, secular religion. Art and culture thereby replace a political theology for him — or rather, they are supposed to create a new, semi-theological aesthetics, serving modern politics by mobilizing the masses and making the work of a secular "redemptor" possible.

That Hitler saw himself in this Wagnerian role is fairly clear. But we should not therefore rush to say that Wagner is thereby reflected in Hitler and can be understood through him.[14] Nor can Wagner be simply and directly considered as a harbinger of Nazism. The Nazis used and abused Wagner as they did Nietzsche. Yet their cases are only superficially parallel. The long history of Nietzsche's manipulation starts with his own sister Elisabeth, who falsified his work and enlisted her insane (and later dead) brother into her anti-Semitic camp, while building (in the Nietzsche archives in Weimar) a perverse shrine to his name and a power base for herself (as Winifred Wagner later did in Bayreuth). These two "women-priests" can therefore symbolize the broader abuse that both Nietzsche and Wagner suffered in Germany. Yet there was a major difference between both cases. The abuse of Nietzsche was often deliberate, and knowingly deceitful; and even when it was not deliberate, it resulted from a simplistic reading and outright misunderstanding of his complex position. Wagner's abuse was a tendentious, perhaps manipulative development of positions he actually held (and which Nietzsche noticed and criticized), and so he provided a basis that the Nazi movement could later simplify and amplify in its own service; whereas linking Nietzsche's ideas with Nazism is both absurd and contradictory. Referring again to the two "women-priests" as symbols, we can perhaps say that Elisabeth Förster-Nietzsche manipulated her brother's views and traded in a counterfeit Nietzsche, while Winifred Wagner "Nazified" Bayreuth and thus linked Wagner and Hitler in a common shrine.

Notes

1. See discussion in my *Dark Riddle: Hegel, Nietzsche and the Jews* (Cambridge: Polity Press, 1998), 212–13, n. 130.

2. See ibid., 119–22.

3. Ronald Hayman, *Nietzsche, A Critical Life* (New York: Oxford, 1980), 189.

4. In "How I broke away from Wagner," a section of *Nietzsche contra Wagner* that is drawn from a new preface (1886) he wrote to *Human, All too Human*, vol. II.

5. *EH*, "Why I Am So Clever," 5 (italics in original).

6. *NCW*, "Where I Offer Objections" (drawn from *The Gay Science*).

7. *The Case of Wagner*, 5. Notice that these descriptions usually define kitsch, though Nietzsche does not use this word (but he uses the words "hysterical" and "sick" instead): "Wagner's art is sick" (ibid.).

8. This indicates, by the way, that Nietzsche was aware of being abused already in his lifetime.

9. This is asserted particularly in *Daybreak* (205), the text Nietzsche considered his most distinctive comment on the Jews. A highly dramatic and rhetorical text, it sets out in prophetic tones the dilemma that modern Jews would be facing in the twentieth century: either to lose Europe (e.g., to emigrate or be expelled from it) or to integrate into it and dominate its values. The anti-Semite would have expected Nietzsche to prefer the first option—yet he preferred the second!

10. From an aristocratic ethics of virtue and excellence and a Dionysian ethics of power.

11. In any case, my study shows that the Jewish issue was far more central to Nietzsche's thought and project than is usually recognized. The former corrupters of European culture and its designated redeemers, the Jews, are placed by Nietzsche at two of the critical historical junctures in his philosophy and, ironically, continue to play the negative and positive role of a world-historical people, perhaps even a "chosen" people in a new, heretical Nietzschean sense.

12. To which Nietzsche seems to have responded indirectly in the following aphorism: "Long ago I posed the problem whether convictions are not more dangerous than lies as enemies of truth. . . . 'Respect for all who have convictions!' I have heard that sort of thing even out of the mouth of anti-Semites" (*A*, 55).

13. Thereby he does not mean a Kantian sense of duty, that represses the instincts, but rather a sublimation of the instincts themselves, reshaping them into a higher, aristocratic human quality.

14. As Joachim Köhler seems to suggest in *Wagners Hitler: Der Prophet und sein Vollstrecker* (Karl Blessing Verlag, 1997), a book that is based on Hartmut Zelinski's work, but apparently stretches its conclusions. Without going into detail, let me remark that even if Hitler saw himself in the role of a Wagnerian redeemer who realized the composer's prophecies and worldview, it does not follow that Wagner was replicated in Hitler or would have recognized himself in the hysterical, mass-murdering Nazi Führer. The Nazis abused everything they touched, even their intellectual kin.

7

Between the Cross and the Swastika: A Nietzschean Perspective

Robert S. Wistrich

Friedrich Nietzsche was one of the great intellectual iconoclasts of the nineteenth century. In some respects more radical than even Marx or Freud, this descendant of generations of German Protestant pastors became perhaps the most implacable foe of Christianity in modern times. Hence a full reckoning with his thought would ultimately involve a serious examination of the entire Christian heritage of the West. Our purpose is, however, more limited — it is to focus on Nietzsche's attitude toward Jews, Judaism, and anti-Semitism in the light of the Holocaust and the often repeated charge that he was one of the philosophical godfathers of fascism. This accusation has been made even by those who may sometimes concede that he anticipated with the clarity of a prophet the morality of the new age ahead.[1] Nonetheless, they insist on a causal connection between his visionary thought and the genocidal project of the Third Reich. While I believe that this guilt by association involves a serious, not to say scandalous, injustice to Nietzsche's work and intentions, it cannot be dismissed out of hand. To answer the charge we need to analyze aspects of Nietzsche's biography, including his views about the historical relationship between Judaism and Christianity and his attitude toward contemporary Germans and Jews and toward the rise of anti-Semitism in his own lifetime — as well as to consider those elements in his philosophy that were compatible (or otherwise) with fascism and Nazism. We must remember, too, that Nietzsche's voice was often deliberately prophetic in tone, his writings were at times even apocalyptic in their resonance (e.g., *The Twilight of the Idols* and *The Antichrist*), with all of the puzzling strands of obscurity, enigma, and paradox that frequently accompany such dramatic modes of utterance. In *Ecce Homo* — written in 1888, the last and the most productive year of his intellectual life (shortly before the onset of insanity) — it seemed as if he had a frantic premonition of his fate: "The memory of something dreadful will be linked with my name, of an unparalleled crisis. . . . I am no man; I am dynamite." In the same text, Nietzsche envisages terrible political convulsions and disasters, cryptically warning his readers, "There will be wars such as never were on earth. Only after me will there be high politics on earth."

On 18 October 1888 he writes to his friend Franz Overbeck from Turin that he was now "moving against the Germans on all fronts; you'll have no cause to complain about ambiguity. This irresponsible race, which has on its conscience all of our civilization's great disasters, and which at every decisive moment of history had 'something else in mind' — today has in mind 'The Reich.' . . . [T]here has never been a more crucial moment in history — but who'd be expected to know that?"[2]

Yet despite Nietzsche's palpable revulsion from the national vanities and bombastic pomposity of the new united Germany, after his death in 1900 he was to be rapidly converted by some of his right-wing *völkisch* disciples into an advocate of German imperialism, militarism, and great power politics.[3] To some extent, as we shall see, this was a shameless manipulation of his legacy. At the same time, there was also something elusive in Nietzsche's fragmented, diffuse, and lyrical oeuvre — experimental in method, aphoristic in style, and anti-systematic in nature — that laid itself open to such uses and abuses, to multiple and opposed interpretations, not to say misappropriations; so much so, that it often seems difficult to ascertain who the "real" Nietzsche was or if such a person actually existed. His life and work appears in retrospect like a battlefield of contending polarities — suspended between the Apollonian and Dionysian impulses, between and beyond good and evil, or the "master" and "slave" moralities — those antitheses he harbored within his soul until the twilight of madness descended upon him in 1889, leaving the final verdict to the care of posterity. For some, he will be primarily remembered as the atheistic philosopher of nihilism, who first pronounced that "God is dead" (by which he meant the nineteenth-century "Christian God"); as the Antichrist who came to reevaluate all values (the notorious *Umwertung aller Werte*) — the first moralist of what has been called a post-God society. For others, including some postmodernists, this lyrical apostle of existentialism, who helped undermine the bases of Western metaphysics with his relativistic, perspectival

.ruth, was a great liberator; a truly "free spirit" who loos-
.l from the yoke of sham certainties, moral absolutes, and
.ıs, teaching humankind the harder, more courageous path of
:oming. The Nietzschean message of *Thus Spoke Zarathustra*,
"ı a. hat which must always overcome itself," certainly breathed a
fresh new music into European philosophy — that of Dionysian laughter,
the will to power and a pagan affirmation of life in all its suffering and
tragedy. Yet the individualistic philosopher of the *Übermensch* who passionately strove for self-transcendence and appealed to human beings to
rise above their mundane limitations, was to be grotesquely misinterpreted, as if he were actually the prophet of a Germanic *Herrenvolk* —
the Nordic master race understood as a collective "Overman." Little
did it matter that Zarathustra had boldly proclaimed that "what is
great in man is that he is a bridge not an end"; for the "terrible sim-
plifiers" of the twentieth century, his existentialist, freedom-oriented
will to power was no more than a means to their very prosaic but sinister political end — that of total domination over others. This process of
creeping annexation was begun shortly after Nietzsche's mental collapse, by his own sister Elisabeth Förster-Nietzsche — who by 1896 had
already gained full control of his archives and writings and, until her
death in 1934, would play havoc with his reputation by eagerly foster-
ing an image of her brother's work as being "proto-Nazi" in spirit.[4]

It is interesting to recall that at the age of twenty, in 1864, the young
Friedrich had written the following revealing words to Elisabeth: "If
you want to find peace of mind and happiness, then believe. If you want
to be a disciple of truth, then search."[5] By then, he had already abandoned the Protestant Christian faith that had been bequeathed to him
by his country clergyman father from Saxony (who died of brain disease
when Friedrich was only five) and a fanatically pious mother. But his
sister would subsequently combine her strict allegiance to Christianity
with a belief in Aryan racial supremacy and eventually with loyalty to
Hitler and National Socialism. As director of the Nietzsche archives in
Weimar, she began to turn it into a propaganda center for Nazism. This
development was to a large extent already prefigured by her marriage in
May 1885 to a leading Berlin anti-Semitic agitator and high school
teacher Bernhard Förster, who had instigated the notorious 1881 national petition to limit Jewish immigration and participation in German
public life. (Later, Förster insulted and manhandled Jewish streetcar
passengers in Berlin — the ensuing scandal helped to precipitate his departure for Paraguay). Elisabeth's marriage to Förster outraged Nietzsche, leading to a break with his sister, with whom he had earlier enjoyed a rather close relationship.[6] Now, as he confided to a friend, there
could be no question of reconciliation "with a vengeful anti-Semitic
goose."

To make matters worse, the Förster couple had deliberately married on Wagner's birthday—seven years after Nietzsche's definitive break with the illustrious German composer. A year later, in 1886, the Försters embarked on an extraordinary utopian settlement project—bringing blond-haired, blue-eyed German families to the jungles of Paraguay to establish Nueva Germania—a breeding colony devoted to the ideals of Aryan racial purity, free of Jewish capitalist influence.[7] Shortly after Förster's suicide in 1890, Elisabeth returned to Germany to take care of her mentally paralyzed brother, until his death in 1900. She would be responsible for compiling Nietzsche's *The Will to Power* (1901) presenting her own tendentious editing of this unfinished work as his last great "synthesis." From 1892 onward, she controlled and censored Nietzsche's unpublished works, forging, altering, or destroying documents, especially those concerning herself, their split over Christianity and anti-Semitism, or negative remarks about Wagner. Elisabeth's school of falsification was to be continued by the Nazis when they decided thirty-five years later to place Nietzsche in the service of their own racist ideology. Indeed, the official philosopher of National Socialism, Alfred Rosenberg, did not hesitate to mendaciously distort citations and alter Nietzsche's remarks, especially on Judaism and the Jews, even inventing quotes when it suited his purpose.[8] More sophisticated Nazi philosophers like Alfred Bäumler took greater care to qualify their statements by phrases suggesting that certain words "could have been spoken by Nietzsche" or alleging that they sounded as if they came from one of his works.[9]

In any event, this tradition of historical falsification went back to Elisabeth Förster-Nietzsche, and even in its infancy her brother had cause to deplore the consequences. In a letter to his close friend, Franz Overbeck (Professor of Church History at the University of Basel) in 1886, he could still note with some detached amusement that his *Zarathustra* book "has charmed the anti-Semites." Nietzsche observed that in the *Antisemitic Correspondence* published by the insatiable racist demagogue Theodor Fritsch, his name was "mentioned almost in every issue." He added that "there is a special anti-Semitic interpretation of it which made me laugh very much."[10] Writing to his sister, during Christmas 1887, he was, however, no longer laughing—having established beyond doubt the essentially anti-Semitic character of the Försters' German colony in Paraguay. He reproached Elisabeth with some bitterness:

> One of the greatest stupidities you have committed—for yourself and for me! Your association with an anti-Semitic chief expresses a foreignness to my whole way of life which fills me ever again with ire or melancholy. If is a matter of honour to me to be abso-

lutely clean and unequivocal regarding anti-Semitism, namely *opposed*, as I am in my writings. I have been persecuted in recent times with letters and *Anti-Semitic Correspondence* sheets; my disgust with this party (which would like all too well the advantage of my name!) is as *outspoken* as possible, but the relation to Förster, as well as the after-effect of my former anti-Semitic publisher Schmeitzner, always brings the adherents of this disagreeable party back to the idea that I must after all belong to them.[11]

Nietzsche had already been warned some time earlier by an Austrian Jewish admirer, Dr. Josef Paneth, that such associations could only damage his credibility:[12] now he informed his sister that every time *Zarathustra* was mentioned in Fritsch's anti-Semitic rag sheet, he had become almost physically sick.[13] A year later, in his last book, *Ecce Homo*, Nietzsche expressed his unqualified horror that the right-wing, anti-Semitic Junker newspaper, *Kreuzzeitung* had cited him with approval as if he embraced its own blinkered nationalist philosophy. Before he finally descended into the black hole of insanity, Nietzsche became literally obsessed with the need to "expel the anti-Semitic screamers out of the country."[14] In the margin of his last letter (January 1889) to his colleague, the great Swiss historian of the Italian Renaissance, Jacob Burckhardt, Nietzsche scrawled, "Abolished [Kaiser] Wilhelm, Bismarck, and all anti-Semites" — while a final note to Overbeck concludes, "Just now I am having all anti-Semites shot."[15] Nietzsche's last words to Fräulein von Salis, are no less graphic: "I have just taken possession of my kingdom, am casting the Pope into prison, and am having Wilhelm, Bismarck, and Stöcker shot." Adolf Stöcker, as the Protestant *Hofprediger* (court-preacher) and founder of the Christian Social party, (who had in 1888 been Germany's leading Christian anti-Semite for almost a decade), along with the Prussian nationalist historian Von Treitschke, symbolized in Nietzsche's eyes much of what he hated about the new German Reich.[16]

Nietzsche's antipathy to German nationalism and to overblown Teutonic rhetoric comes out clearly in many other texts and in itself already stands as an important argument against tainting him with the stigma of the swastika. In *Ecce Homo* he notes disapprovingly that "Germany" has become an argument, "*Deutschland, Deutschland über alles*," a principle: the Teutons supposedly represent the " 'moral world-order.' . . . There is now a historiography that is *reichsdeutsch*; there is, even I fear, an anti-Semitic one . . . and Herr von Treitschke is not ashamed."[17]

Nietzsche had even less time for the new myths of Aryan racial superiority (though he did on occasions use terms like "Aryan" humanity somewhat loosely) and rejected the increasingly popular concepts of "pure blood." These categories, which he examined critically in his "Law of Manu" observations dealing with outcasts, struck him as far from harmless. He feared that they might someday be invoked to justify the oppression of non-Aryans. He also observed in the notes of *The Will to Power* that *"the Aryan influence has corrupted all the world"* — a characteristic Nietzschean way of counteracting the arguments of contemporary German racists against so-called "Semites." Significantly, too, in a passage of *On the Genealogy of Morals* that discusses the "blond beast," Nietzsche carefully insists that "between the old Germanic tribes and the Germans there exists scarcely a conceptual relation, not to speak of a blood relation."

Moreover, Nietzsche manifestly did not share Richard Wagner's enthusiasm either for primordial Germanic myths or for contemporary German culture. This was noted by at least one rabidly Nazi writer, Curt von Westernhagen, who announced in his book *Nietzsche, Juden, Antijuden* (1936) that the time had come to expose the "defective personality of Nietzsche whose inordinate tributes for, and espousal of, Jews had caused him to depart from the Germanic principles enunciated by Meister Richard Wagner."[18]

Nietzsche's complex relationship with Wagner, which began in 1868, when at the age of twenty-four he first came under the maestro's spell in Tribschen (Switzerland), is clearly critical to any assessment of his attitude to Jews, Judaism, Germanism, and Christianity. In 1869 Richard Wagner had just republished his earlier notoriously malevolent work of anti-Semitic incitement *Das Judentum in der Musik*, which had denounced and indeed demonised the "Judaization" of German art. Nietzsche did not comment directly on this inflammatory work but his correspondence with Richard and Cosima Wagner (and others) between 1868 and 1878 betrays a tendency to slide on occasions into mundane and stereotypical anti-Jewish remarks. However, in a notebook entry of January 1874, Nietzsche somewhat critically remarked that Wagner "insults Jews who in present-day Germany possess the most money and own the press. At first, he had no vocational reasons, later his insults were acts of revenge."[19]

The young Nietzsche had initially been bowled over by the "fabulously lively and fiery" Wagner. Not only was the composer witty, entertaining, and a musical genius but also a father figure to venerate and to fear. No doubt, when he aped the anti-Jewish slurs of the Wagners (Cosima was at times even more virulent than her husband), he may have genuinely believed that the "Jewish press" had been persecuting his much idolised mentor. But by the time of their break, Nietzsche would better understand the raw emotions (especially the psychology of envy) behind Wagner's anti-Semitism. Nietzsche shrewdly remarks that "Wagner is Schopenhauerian in his hatred of the Jews to whose greatest deed he is not able to do justice: Christianity! After all, the Jews are the inventors of Christianity."[20] Increasingly, he saw Wagner as an arch-anti-Semite to be vigorously opposed. Nor could he stomach Wagner's growing German chauvinism, his Francophobe abusiveness, and evolution toward Christian religious piety in his final opera, *Parsifal*. Later, Nietzsche would positively invoke those very Jews like Jacques Offenbach and Heinrich Heine (with his "divine sarcasm") whom the Wagnerian anti-Semites constantly vilified as destroyers of "German values." Already in 1884, Nietzsche had observed, "Offenbach has even more right to the title of 'genius' than Wagner. Wagner is heavy, ponderous: nothing is more alien to him than moments of exuberant perfection achieved by this buffoon [*Hanswurst*] Offenbach."[21] ("Buffoon" in this context is a complement, which denotes a natural and playful naïveté). In 1887 he would call Offenbach "that most sophisticated and exuberant satyr, who keeps to the great tradition as a musician"—a real relief from the sentimental and "at bottom the *degenerate* [*entarteten*] composers of German romanticism." Nietzsche, here, exploits Richard Wagner's own term of "degenerate" (used in polemics against his musical opponents), like a boomerang to strike out against its originator; to execrate the man whom he had once hailed in his first book, *The Birth of Tragedy* (1872), as the redeemer—prophet who would lead the way forward to a Germanic rebirth of the Hellenic world.[22] But ever since seeing the *Ring* at Bayreuth in 1874, Nietzsche had become more allergic to the "brutal Teutonisms" of Wagner's operas and to the mean-spirited anti-Semitism and the xenophobic Germanity of the master's propaganda organ, the *Bayreuther Blätter*.[23] His unrestrained admiration for Bizet's *Carmen*—given the Spanish-Jewish ancestry of the composer—was a further turning of his back on the Wagnerian "sickness."[24] Bizet better exemplified the *revised* Dionysian principle of Nietzschean aesthetics—that whatever is divine "moves on light dancing feet."

By the time Nietzsche published his *Human, All Too Human* (1878), he had come to the conclusion that Wagner—the extroverted, conquering all-Germanic hero—was nothing but a lamentable *decadent* ready to crawl on his knees before the Cross, while still clinging to his dark Teutonic gods. It was the beginning of a long gruelling vendetta that would culminate in 1888, five years after the composer's death, with *Nietzsche contra Wagner*. But already in 1878, much to the Wagner's fury, Nietzsche had referred admiringly to the accumulation of capital, spirit, and will by the European Jews—while chillingly observing that this was an acquisition "so huge that it had to incur envy and hate-filled measures in the form of literary indecencies in almost all our nations . . . making Jews scapegoats for all conceivable public and private misfortunes and leading them to the slaughter house."[25] Nietzsche deplored the narrow nationalism that was already then seeking to exclude the Jews—an outlook that stood in sharp conflict with his militantly assertive "good Europeanism." The Germans, he insisted, must accept the Jews (as the English and French had already done), thereby also benefiting from their high intelligence and economic abilities.

It was at this time (in 1876) that Nietzsche told his Austro-Polish Jewish admirer Siegfried Lipiner of his "very great expectations" concerning young people of Jewish origin.[26] For almost a decade he would also nurture an intimate friendship with a highly assimilated, self-effacing, and alienated Jewish intellectual, Dr. Paul Rée, whom he valued highly for his psychological insights into human behavior. Both his sister and the Wagnerians in Bayreuth would predictably blame this cool, cerebral "Israelite" for the rift between Nietzsche and Wagner.[27] In fact, it would be far more accurate to say that it was Nietzsche's emancipation from Wagner's influence that opened the door to his new insights into Judaism, Christianity, anti-Semitism, and the state of German culture.

By the late 1870s, Nietzsche had increasingly and voluntarily exiled himself from the new German Reich in favor of constant wandering in Southern France, Italy, and the Swiss Engadine Mountains in search of more conducive climes for his mental and physical health. He had little regard for the Prusso-German cult of the authoritarian state (that "coldest of all cold monsters")[28] and openly despised the benighted obscurantism that he came to detect in German Christian anti-Semitism. In *Beyond Good and Evil*, he commented (disapprovingly) that he had not met a German "who was favourably disposed toward Jews" (251). His remarks about Germans as a national group, throughout the 1880s, became more and more acerbic, at times even openly offensive. He deplored their obtuseness, "the blond head, the blue eye, the lack of 'esprit' on their faces, language and bearing," above all "the hideous excitation brought on by alcoholism"; the endemic German cultural and political provincialism; and especially the Förster-Wagner-Dühring morass of racist anti-Semitism. Here is Nietzsche in *Genealogy* on that "apostle of revenge in Berlin, Eugen Dühring, who in the Germany of today employs the most indecent and repulsive moralistic trash; he is the prime moral big mouth in existence, even among like-minded anti-Semites. All of them are people of *ressentiment*" (II:11).[29] Nietzsche's contempt for these "latest speculators in idealism—the anti-Semites," rolling their eyes heavenward in the "Christian-Aryan petty-bourgeois mode" can hardly be exaggerated or easily matched. Behind the gathering drumbeat of a poisonously anti-Semitic German nationalism, he detected "worm-eaten physiological mishaps" and pathological self-haters infecting the happiness of the healthy with their own sense of misery. As Nietzsche put it in 1888, anti-Semite was another name for the "socially lowest people," the losers, the misfits, the bungled, botched, and so-called underprivileged — the *Schlechtweggekommene*.[30] Moreover, the comparison between Germans and Jews in Nietzsche's writings of this period invariably rebounds to the detriment of the former. Thus in *The Gay Science*, the Germans are described as a lamentable, unreasoning race into whose thick heads sense literally needs to be knocked.[31] Jews, on the other hand, have always had to rely on logic and persuasion: "Everywhere that Jews have come into prominence, they have taught more keen decision-making, sharper analysing, and more precise writing: it was always their task to bring reason [*raison*] to a nation."[32] Yet these and many other Nietzschean statements — some of them amounting to hyperbolic praise of Jews, did not stop Nazi academic propagandists like Heinrich Härtle from claiming that "never has anyone attacked Jews more sharply than Nietzsche" — a comment whose cynicism it would be difficult to equal.[33]

Nietzsche's confessional "autobiography," *Ecce Homo*, gives the lie to such assertions, reminding his readers that to be "a good German" one must first "de-Germanize" oneself (*entdeutschen*), unless one is of Jewish descent: "Jews among Germans are always the higher race — more refined, spiritual, kind. '*L'adorable Heine*,' they say in Paris."[34]

It was the Danish literary critic Georg Brandes (Morris Cohen), an exemplar of Jewish *délicatesse* and a model "good European," who had "discovered" Nietzsche for the world of academia in 1887, giving him hope that his message of "aristocratic radicalism" might yet be understood in his own lifetime.[35] There were, however, no Germans of whom he could say as much — indeed, apart from a few artists (Wagner above all), he claimed that he had never enjoyed "a single good hour with Germans."[36] On October 15, 1888, his forty-fourth birthday, he summed it all up by declaring, "What a blessing it is to find a Jew among the German horned cattle!" At least they (the Jews), unlike the typical German professors (by definition they were hopeless cases), understood him. In a letter to Theodor Fritsch of March 23, 1887, he scolded the anti-Semitic propagandist (a true "proto-Nazi"), telling him that the most valuable contribution he could make to the history of German culture would be to publish a lengthy list of German scholars, artists, poets, writers, actors, and virtuosos of Jewish descent! Jews, he told Fritsch, were much more interesting than Germans.[37] Furthermore, anti-Semitism had become a contributing factor to his great estrangement from the prevailing German spirit; though he admitted that he had derived some entertainment from recently reading "the books of the puffed-up and sentimental blockhead named Paul de Lagarde!" (De

Lagarde was a leading German academic orientalist and a rabid anti-Semite, highly appreciated by the Nazis).[38] At this same time, in his unpublished notes of 1887, we find Nietzsche raging against the "damnable Germans' anti-Semitism, this poisonous *névrose nationale*"[39] that had so ruinously intruded into his own personal life. He was, for example, aghast at the thought that his epic *Zarathustra* had entered the world as "*indecent* literature" since its publisher, Ernst Schmeitzner, was an anti-Semite.[40] And then, there were the ubiquitous Wagnerians—"a hair-raising company!" "Not a single abortion is missing among them, not even the anti-Semite. Poor Wagner! Where had he landed!—If he had at least entered into swine! But to descend among Germans!"[41]

In *The Case of Wagner* (1888), Nietzsche definitively closed the account: "Wagner's stage requires but one thing: Germans! The definition of a German: an obedient person with long legs. . . . There is a deep significance in the fact that the rise of Wagner should have coincided with the rise of the 'Empire': both phenomena are proof of one and the same thing—obedience and long legs—never have people been more obedient, never have they been so well ordered about."[42]

"*Wagner est une névrose*"—this Nietzschean denunciation exposed his narcotic art as diseased, morbid, hysterical, and brutal. Wagner was "a great corrupter of music"—the opiate of the Second German Reich—a master of hypnotic trickery, an incomparable histrionic personality, a tyrant with an actor's genius. To me, this reads like an uncanny anticipatory description of Wagner's political alter ego, Adolf Hitler. Can we really doubt, then, where Nietzsche would have stood with regard to the politics of the Nazis? Could the man who saw with such clairvoyance through the original Bayreuth circle (a key link in the German ideology that led to National Socialism) have been taken in by its plebeian offspring? This is hardly likely. Yet through the efforts of his sister, Elisabeth, and the German *völkisch* Right, before and after 1914, Nietzsche—the great antidogmatist, anti-anti-Semite, and unmasker of Wagnerian *Kitsch*—could still be mythified into a war-mongering Jew-baiter and ultimately into a philosophical alibi for Adolf Hitler.

Clearly, there must have been some intellectual ingredients—however secondary they might be in the overall Nietzschean perspective—that made such a distortion possible. For instance, Nietzsche does at times seem to accept the biological discourse of his contemporaries depicting the battle of races and castes as the verifiable stuff of history. He also appears to condone the aesthetic justification for elitist rule and even for slavery, as in the case of classical antiquity. Moreover, he did envisage a new "master race" for Europe (though one of mixed blood, which would include the Jews)—a ruling caste whose model was ultimately taken from the ancient Greeks.[43] Similarly, Nietzsche did accept a La-

marckian view about the inheritance of acquired characteristics, he believed in the degeneracy of half-breeds and consistently abhorred the
"herd mentality" as well as the egalitarian doctrines of democrats, anarchists, and socialists. Above all, he declared a war to the death against
Christianity — one that had important implications for his view of Judaism, since the two were, as he put it, "racially related."[44] Nietzsche insisted that Christianity was "to be understood entirely in terms of the
soil from which it grew — it is *not* a countermovement to the Jewish
instinct; it is the successor itself, a further step in its frightening logic."[45]
At the same time, Nietzsche denounced "the attempt to pull away the
Old Testament from under the feet of the Jews — with the claim that it
. . . *belongs* to the Christians as the *true* Israel, while the Jews had
merely usurped it." This, he vehemently rejected as a philological farce
fraudulently practiced by Christian theology through the ages (*D*, 84).

Although he was strongly opposed to Christian anti-Semitism, Nietzsche nonetheless blamed the Jews for the "denaturalisation [*Entnatur-
lichung*] of natural values" implemented by Christianity. The Jews had
"made humanity into something so false that, still today, a Christian
can feel anti-Semitic without understanding himself as the last stage of
Judaism" (*A*, 24, my translation). Nietzsche's unfavorable contrast of
the "holy unnaturalness" of the Judaic features in Christianity with
Greek *naturalness* and pagan nature-worship is a recurring and significant refrain. So, too, is his hatred of "the Jewish fanaticism of a St.
Paul" — the "greatest of all apostles of revenge" — responsible in his eyes
for the most fateful and catastrophic revaluation (*Umwertung*) of values
in world-history.[46] Paul had brought with him from Judaism an enmity
to everything noble, proud, and privileged — in short precisely that disastrous subversion of the reigning order that had allegedly produced
the downfall of the Roman Empire and destroyed the values of the classical world. Against this background there can be no doubt that Nietzsche despised and condemned the "priestly" Judaism of the Second
Temple period for being the parent of Christianity — which he furiously
execrated as "the one immortal blemish of mankind." The Jewish
priests had spread spurious ideas of a "moral world order," sin, guilt,
punishment, repentance, pity, and the love of neighbor. According to
this debasing Judeo-Christianity, the wretched, the poor, the lowly, the
humble, the meek, the sick, and the weak are those who truly deserve
salvation — not the strong, the healthy, the brave, and the beautiful
(*GM*, I:7). But according to *The Antichrist*, Judeo-Christian doctrines of
mercy were in reality full of malice and *ressentiment* against the powerful and self-assured; they were nothing but the vengeance of "slaves"
against their "masters." The so-called "slave revolt in morals," — an
event of world historical importance — had been invented by priestly

Judaism (synonymous for Nietzsche with the early Christians) as a form of self-affirmation and ascetic will to power.[47] It had then been propagated and expanded by official Christianity throughout the world. In its modern secularized forms such as liberalism, scientific rationalism, or socialism, the "slave revolt" had emerged as the prime source of the Western decadence against which Nietzsche was strenuously fighting.

Ressentiment, according to Nietzsche, had first succeeded in becoming a revolutionary force in ancient priestly Judaism, an agent of change that had indeed created *new values* (abhorrent though they might be) that were then transformed by Christianity into a powerful universal religion. His attack on this value system is, of course, uncompromisingly fierce, branding it as a negation of what is "outside," what is "different," what is "not itself" (*GM*, I:7). It is the petty, rancorous gaze of the slave at what *he is not*—the very opposite of a noble, life-affirming ethic. According to Nietzsche, the Jewish revolution in ethics that had triumphed in Pauline Christianity was therefore a victory of *ressentiment*, one through which the Jews took vengeance on a hostile Gentile world.[48] "Jewish hatred" was the trunk of that tree of vengefulness that had created new ideals and values, beginning with Christian love, which was not the antithesis of its parent but rather its fulfillment. (*GM*, I:8).[49] Thus Nietzsche writes that it was "the Jews who with awe-inspiring consistency dared to invert the aristocratic value equation (good = noble = powerful = beautiful = happy = beloved of God) and to hang on to this 'inversion' with all their strength" (*GM*, I:7).[50]

In these and other texts Nietzsche interprets priestly Judaism as being identical with early Christianity itself. Thus, when he refers to the Apocalypse of John (a quintessentially Christian book), he treats it as a purely Jewish text that expresses Jewish hatred of Rome (*GM*, I:16).[51] In the deadly confrontation between two opposing value systems, aristocratic Roman values had been totally vanquished by Judeo-Christianity. Under the sign of the Cross, Israel had in fact achieved the ultimate "revaluation of all values." Perhaps to provoke the Christian anti-Semites of his own day as well as to illustrate the historical triumph of Judea over Rome (ibid.), Nietzsche wrote, "Consider to whom one bows down in Rome itself today, as if they were the epitome of all the highest values—and not only in Rome but over almost half the earth [. . .]: *three Jews*, as is known, and *one* Jewess" (*GM* I:16). Who are the members of this Christian holy quartet? Jesus of Nazareth, the fisherman Peter, the rug weaver Paul, and Mary, the mother of the aforementioned Jesus—all of them Jews! This was a useful rhetorical device against Christians, but also one with a nasty sting against the Jews. For if anti-Semites traditionally indict the Jews as Christ-killers, Nietzsche finds them guilty for having begotten him! This Jesus of Nazareth, this

"Redeemer," whose birth 2000 years ago Christians have recently celebrated, was he not a "seduction and a by-path to precisely those *Jewish*
values" (i.e. victory of the poor, the sick, and the sinners!)? "Did Israel
not attain the ultimate goal of its sublime vengefulness through the by-
path of this 'Redeemer', this ostensible opponent and disintegrator of
Israel?" (ibid.) All of this sounds like an extraordinary Machiavellian
scenario. The Jews crucified the man Jesus as an enticing bait for the
world to swallow — for he would be that ghastly paradox of a "God on
the Cross," the awesome image of "an unimaginable ultimate cruelty
and self-crucifixion of God for the salvation of man." (In *The Antichrist*, Nietzsche coins the epigram, "In truth, there was only *one* Christian, and he died on the cross," to highlight the gulf between what Jesus
had personally lived and the religion founded in his name.) Through the
"Redeemer," and the intoxicating power of the symbol of the "Holy
Cross," Jewish ideals triumphed over Rome. The Jews had created
Christianity — a religion in which they did not themselves believe — in
order to sap and weaken their Roman conquerors.

After all, Nietzsche tells us that the Jews had always known how "to
place themselves at the head of all movements of decadence." Yet, they
themselves were "the antithesis of all decadents," a people who used the
power of these instincts of decadence as a strategy for their own survival and self-preservation.[52] Nietzsche thoroughly detested the content
of Judeo-Christianity for its alleged denigration of the world, its unnatural anti-aesthetic and anti-life character — yet he nevertheless admired
the tough vital energy that the Jews had retained throughout their history. This was especially visible in the "heroic" early biblical period,
before the fall of the First Temple and the Babylonian exile. The Isra-
elites of that era are very positively seen by Nietzsche as a proud, sovereign people of high spirit, courage, and unconquerable will.

> At the time of the kings, Israel also stood in the right, that is, the
> natural, relationship to all things. Its Yahweh was the expression
> of a consciousness of power, of joy in oneself, of hope for oneself:
> through him victory and welfare were expected; through him na-
> ture was trusted to give what the people needed — above all, rain.
> Yahweh is the god of Israel and therefore the god of justice (*A*,
> 25).[53]

This biblical Judaism — so natural, vital, and sublime — recounted in the
stories of the Patriarchs and of Moses, Joshua, Samson, Samuel, David,
and Solomon — expresses the people's own self-affirmation and flowing
power. In *Beyond Good and Evil* Nietzsche glowingly contrasts it with
the "rococo taste" of the New Testament. "In the Jewish 'Old Testament,' the book of divine justice, there are human beings, things, and

speeches in so grand a style that Greek and Indian literature have nothing to compare with it. With terror and reverence one stands before these tremendous remnants of what man once was" (*BGE*, 52, revised translation). There is here, perhaps an echo of Heine's confession: "I see now that the Greeks were only beautiful youths; the Jews, however, were always men . . . martyrs who gave the world a god and a morality and fought and suffered on all the battlefields of thought."

To have glued Old and New Testament together as *one* book, as the "Bible" — the book *par excellence* — was for Nietzsche a "sin against the spirit" (*BGE*, 52).[54] In the *Genealogy of Morals* the dichotomy is even more graphic. In the Old Testament one finds

> great human beings, a heroic landscape, and something of the very rarest quality in the world, the incomparable *naiveté* of the *strong heart*; what is more, I find people. In the new one, on the other hand, I find nothing but petty sectarianism, mere rococo of the soul, mere involution, nooks, queer things . . . a garrulous swell of feeling that almost stupefies; impassioned vehemence, not passion; embarrassing gesticulation (*GM*, III:22).

Nietzsche, in one stroke, reverses almost two millennia of Christian dogma — Catholic, Protestant, and Eastern Orthodox. The movement from biblical Judaism to Christianity is *not* a progress but a *regression*; a path from grandeur, nobility, and sublimity ("Dionysian" values to use his Greek analogy) to decline, degeneration, and enfeeblement. In *The Antichrist* he specifically mocks "the simplicity of Christian theologians" who insist on the positive development from the "God of Israel," the god of the people, to the Christian God" — supposedly "the quintessence of everything good." On the contrary, the priestly culture of Judaism that had produced Christianity had "accomplished a miracle of falsification" and "denaturation" of natural values (*A*, 26). Happiness was now a reward, unhappiness a "punishment for disobeying God" — all the "natural concepts of cause and effect were turned upside down once and for all. The history of Israel itself was reinterpreted as "a stupid salvation mechanism before Yahweh," in which the priest and "the Law" alone can redeem men from their sins (ibid.). It was on this false soil that Christianity had grown up as a revolt against the natural instincts, expressing a disgust for reality and fabricating the illusions of the kingdom of Heaven. In Nietzsche's feverish indictment, culminating in the finale of *The Antichrist*, no prisoners are taken: "The Christian church has left nothing untouched by its corruption; it has turned every value into an unvalue, every truth into a lie, every integrity into a vileness of the soul. . . . This eternal indictment I will write on all walls . . . , I call Christianity the one great curse, the one great innermost corruption, the one great instinct of revenge. . . . I call it the one immortal blemish of mankind" (A, 62).

It has often been suggested that Nietzsche's demonization of Christianity was in essence *anti-Semitic*, since the Jews were its originators and therefore they bore ultimate responsibility for this supreme evil. But this is, I believe, a profound misreading of Nietzsche's view of Judaism and the Jews against which he never directed language of comparable harshness. Nietzsche laid the axe to the (Judeo-) Christian branches but did not seek to cut off the ancient Jewish roots of the tree, since he hoped to integrate the descendants of the Jews into a new society. Nietzsche consistently distinguished between the grandeur and decadence of Judaism—something he did not allow for Christianity. Even priestly Judaism, in its perversity, was regarded as superior to Christianity, since it had at least created new values. Moreover, as we shall see, Nietzsche, despite his hostility to rabbinical Judaism, expressed a complex admiration for Diaspora Jews (especially for his contemporaries)—convinced, as he was, that they were specially suited to promote his Dionysian revolution of values and to act as a catalyst in delivering Europe from the culture of decadence. He genuinely hoped that he would now find in Jewry allies for his war against a bankrupt, life-negating Christian morality and the detested imagery of a "God on the Cross," which they had done so much to forge almost two millennia earlier.

Through their long history of suffering (*Leidensschule*) Jews had acquired unique mental qualities of intelligence and shrewdness, wit (*Geist*) and intellect (*Geistigkeit*), and adaptability (*Anpassungskunst*) to add to their "moral genius" (*Genialität*), their money, and their patience.[55] Adversity and profound suffering had turned them into the strongest, toughest, purest race in Europe ("*stärkste, zäheste und reinste Rasse*")—not in the sense of brute force (*Kraft*) but of positive spiritual power (*Macht*).[56] Hence he saw the Jews as very much a part of the new elite of the future that would rule over the West—an "aristocracy of the spirit," whose creative assimilation would help revive modern post-Christian Europe by giving it new norms and values. This does not mean that Nietzsche was an unqualified philo-Semite. He recognized that every nation possessed "unpleasant, indeed dangerous qualities" and in *Human, All Too Human* he had summarily referred to the youthful stock-exchange Jews as perhaps "the most repulsive invention of the entire human race."(HH, I:475, my translation). But in the same text he also blamed Christian Europe for the grief-laden history of the Jews, who had given humanity "the noblest human being (Christ), the purest sage (Spinoza), the mightiest book and the most efficacious moral code in the world."

If that were not enough, Nietzsche even asserted that in the darkest periods of the Middle Ages, Jewish freethinkers, scholars, and physicians had held the banner of intellectual independence aloft and encouraged the humanist enlightenment that derived from Graeco-Roman antiquity (*HH*, I:475). In a remarkable reversal of conventional Western Christian opinion, he added, "If Christianity has done everything to orientalize the occident, Judaism has always played an essential part in occidentalizing it again."[57]

Nietzsche evidently also had in mind the skeptical, critical role of Jewish thinkers from Spinoza to Heine, the German-Jewish poet and social outsider with whom he felt such a strong affinity: "I seek in vain in all the realms of thousands of years for an equally sweet and passionate music. He possessed that divine sarcasm (*Bosheit*) without which I cannot imagine perfection. . . . And how he handles his German! It will be said one day that Heine and I have been by far the foremost artists of the German language—at an incalculable distance from everything mere Germans have done with it."[58]

Nietzsche admired the resilience and affirmation of life, (despite their semitragic circumstances), that writers like Heine had exhibited. The Jewish ability to survive as Christianity's "Other" in the harsh discipline of the Diaspora, fortified by the hatred of the Gentiles, was a strong point in their favor. In *Daybreak* (205), Nietzsche's evaluation of Jewish "psychological and spiritual resources" attains to a crescendo of praise. They were the "least liable to resort to drink or suicide in order to escape from some profound dilemma"; they possessed in their history "a great fund of examples of the coldest self-possession and endurance in fearful situations . . . their courage beneath the cloak of miserable submissions, their heroism . . . surpasses the virtues of all the saints" (*D*, 205).

The Jews had successfully overcome two millennia of the Christian "teaching of contempt" and "never ceased to believe themselves called to the highest things" (*D* 205). Barred from all honors, they had put to effective use the occupations left to them but still retained a "liberality of soul" as a result of their extraordinarily diverse experiences of human society. Nietzsche also praised the way in which "they honour their fathers and their children, the rationality of their marriages and marriage customs" which "distinguished them among all Europeans" (ibid.). True, they had not yet developed chivalrous or noble sentiments, but Nietzsche predicted that within a hundred years as a result of intermarriage "with the best aristocracy of Europe" they would acquire these virtues, too, and be willingly accepted as "masters." Hence, the coming twentieth century would mark the fateful decision concerning the destiny of European Jewry—whether they would become "the masters of Europe' or "lose Europe as they once a long time ago lost Egypt,

where they placed themselves before a similar either-or" (ibid.). Nietz-
sche did not, however, mention that in Jewish tradition the "loss" of
Egypt was in fact an exodus from servitude that led to the Promised
Land of Israel. Nor did he take a clearly identifiable position on the
Zionist movement that was just beginning at this time.

According to Nietzsche, the Jews themselves knew that a physical
conquest of Europe was unthinkable but that the old continent might
fall into their hands like a ripe fruit, once they had achieved the first
rank in every domain of European distinction. Indeed, he appeared to
welcome the prospect of a future Jewish leadership in which they would
become "the inventors and signposts of the nations of Europe," producing great men and great works that would make the ancient Jewish God
"*rejoice* in himself, his creation and his chosen people — and let us all,
all of us, rejoice with him!"[59]

We should try to avoid reading this prophecy in the light of the Holocaust, despite the grim, rather startling warning that the Jews must
either master or "lose" Europe (*D* 205).[60] By mastery, Nietzsche probably meant that Jews had the power to transform European values in
depth, as they had already done before, through the medium of Christianity. "Losing" Europe may have been a pointer to the anti-Semitic
stormclouds on the horizon, suggesting the deeply unpleasant possibilities of emigration or expulsion. In *Beyond Good and Evil*, Nietzsche
tries to clarify the point that

> the Jews, if they wanted it — or if they were forced into it, which
> seems to be what the anti-Semites want — *could* even *now* have
> preponderance, indeed quite literally mastery over Europe, that is
> certain. Meanwhile they want and wish rather, even with some
> importunity, to be absorbed and assimilated by Europe; they long
> to be fixed, permitted, respected somewhere at long last, putting
> an end to the nomad's life, to the "Wandering Jew"; and this bent
> and impulse (which may even express an attenuation of the Jewish
> instincts) should be noted well and *accommodated*" (*BGE*, 251,
> revised translation).[61]

Certainly, in these and other passages it is apparent that Nietzsche
grants a remarkable centrality and potency to the Jews as a people with
a world historical mission. But it would be misleading to see in this
belief an equivalent or a mirror-image of the paranoid concept of the
Jews as a world power developed by anti-Semites and Nazis. Hyam
Maccoby has gone so far as to suggest that Nietzsche was an unconscious believer in the Christian myth of the Jews as dangerously powerful and secretly striving for domination — despite the admiring tone with
which the philosopher invested such statements.[62] While one might

agree that Nietzsche is playing a somewhat dangerous, dialectical game with anti-Semitism by invoking the Jews' ability to become Europe's masters, his intentions are clearly very different to those of the anti-Semites. He wants to see the Jews fully integrated into modern society, so that they can be a blessing for it. To that end, he favors the seculari-zation and creative assimilation of Jews *as Jews* into the new Europe.[63] To that purpose, he also adds, that "it might be useful and fair to expel the anti-Semitic screamers from the country." Nothing, I would have thought, could be more remote from the Nazi vision of a regenerated *Judenrein* Europe based on Aryan-German racial supremacy! Indeed, as Yirimayahu Yovel has tellingly formulated it, "If the Nazis considered the Jews as *Untermenschen*, for Nietzsche they were a possible catalyst of the *Übermensch*."[64]

No doubt his exceptionally positive evaluation of their historic role was one reason for the attraction of Jewish intellectuals to Nietzsche's work.[65] His influence on young Zionists like Martin Buber, who warmly responded around 1900 to the Nietzschean call for a "transvaluation of all aspects of the life of the people," is well known. So, too is Nietz-sche's impact on Micha Josef Berdyczewski and the East European Zion-ists who sought to radically reconstitute a Jewish national secular cul-ture from the very foundations.[66] It was indeed this radicalism that prompted Ahad Ha'am's fear that Nietzscheanism might dangerously threaten the ethical and spiritual continuity of Jewish values. But its influence was strong, precisely because it coincided with a Jewish artis-tic and national renaissance that was already seeking a new vision of what it meant to be a human being and desired a liberation from the spiritual desiccation of the Diaspora.[67] Nietzsche's assault on conven-tional morality and the spiritual discontents of bourgeois civilization appealed to many Zionists of this new generation looking for an au-thentically life-affirming philosophy and an aesthetically oriented na-tional rebirth. It also had an attraction for a broad array of "marginal Jews" — artists and intellectuals in Central Europe who had already lost their moorings in Jewish tradition without being fully absorbed by Ger-man or Austrian society. They included such diverse personalities as Arthur Schnitzler, Sigmund Freud, Stefan Zweig, Franz Kafka, Franz Werfel, Karl Kraus, Kurt Tucholsky, Walter Benjamin, and Theodor Lessing.[68] To this galaxy of talents one could also add a long list of prominent non-Jewish authors from Rilke and Thomas Mann to Stefan George, Gottfried Benn, and George Bernard Shaw, not to mention phi-losophers, historians, and military men such as Max Scheler, Ludwig Klages, Oswald Spengler, or Count von Stauffenberg, who planted the bomb that nearly killed Hitler in 1944. Gottfried Benn, the leading Ger-man expressionist poet of the 1920s, looking back fifty years after the philosopher's death, was not exaggerating greatly when he recalled that Nietzsche had found and *exhausted* all the definitive formulations for the next generation— "the rest was exegesis."[69]

Nietzsche's hybrid status as a philosopher-artist, his critique of all established thinking, his creative use of the dynamic of incessant self-contradiction, and his refusal of the closure entailed by an internally consistent systematic worldview, help to account for the diversity and range of his influence. Nazi and fascist readings of his work were indeed only one among many examples of the possible outcomes of his philosophy, though they proved the most disastrous of all for his subsequent reputation. The "fascist" Nietzsche was above all considered to be a heroic irrationalist and vitalist who had glorified war and violence, inspiring the anti-Marxist revolutions of the interwar period.[70] According to the French fascist Pierre Drieu la Rochelle, it was the Nietzschean emphasis on the Will that inspired the voluntarism and political activism of his comrades.[71] Such one-dimensional readings were vehemently rejected by another French writer, the anarchist Georges Bataille, who in the 1930s sought to establish the "radical incompatibility" between Nietzsche (as a thinker who abhorred mass politics) and "the Fascist reactionaries." He argued that nothing was more alien to Nietzsche than the pan-Germanism, racism, militarism, and anti-Semitism of the Nazis, into whose service the German philosopher had been posthumously pressed.[72] Bataille was one of the few intellectuals (one might add the names of Thomas Mann, Jaspers, and Camus) who in the 1930s and 1940s tried to rescue Nietzsche's reputation from the rising fascist tide.[73] In Nazi Germany, at that time, pamphlets of Nazified Nietzschean *dicta*, were being produced, presenting him as an Aryan racial supremacist and ferocious anti-Semite.[74] What did it matter that in his own lifetime he had sharply opposed virtually every prominent anti-Semite including the Wagners, Dühring, de Lagarde, Stöcker, Förster, Gobineau, Renan, Wellhausen, and his own sister? What counted for the Nazis was their desire to politicize and militarize the Nietzschean concept of the will to power and to manipulate Nietzsche's onslaught against Judeo-Christianity for the benefit of the new Germanic *Herrenvolk*.

Nietzsche's diatribes against the evil genius of "rabbi" Paul and the New Testament (which represented the depraved "priestly" element in Judaism) were naturally grist to the Nazi mill. So, too, were ranting passages like the following, in *The Antichrist*:

> One does well to put on gloves when reading the New Testament. One is almost forced to do so by the proximity of so much uncleanness. We would no more choose to associate with the "first Christians" than we would with Polish Jews: not that one would

need raise a single objection [*Einwand*] to them. . . . They both do not smell good (*A*, 46).

Having abjectly yielded to classic German prejudices against Polish Jews, Nietzsche aggravated this lapse by depicting Pontius Pilate approvingly as a ""noble Roman" who could not persuade himself "to take Jew-dealings (*Judenhandel*) seriously" (*A*, 46).

It is also true that the Nietzschean image of Judeo-Christianity as "the vampire of the *Imperium Romanum*," was a stereotype that found more than an echo in the Christophobia of leading Nazis like Hitler, Bormann, Rosenberg, Ley, and Himmler. Though there is no evidence that Hitler ever seriously read Nietzsche, in his wartime *Table Talk* there are references to Rome, Judea, and early Christianity that do sound like a crude and vulgarized version of Nietzschean ideas.[75] For instance, on July 11–12, 1941, shortly after the invasion of the USSR, Hitler called the coming of Christianity "the heaviest blow that had ever struck humanity," since it had destroyed the Roman Empire and 1500 years of civilization. Like Bolshevism, Christianity had been invented by the Jews — so he asserted — to subvert and destroy the foundations of culture. Hitler, like Nietzsche, was obsessed with the apostle Paul, whom he crassly described as the "first man to take advantage of using a religion as a means of propaganda." In decadent Rome, Paul had found the ideal terrain for his egalitarianism, his "crypto-Marxist" theories, and the "insane idea" of a universal god, who stood above the state. For Hitler, this wicked Judeo-Christian monotheistic creed was part of a conspiracy to undermine the natural order, where the strong must always prevail over the weak and power alone can guarantee right. When Hitler further denounced Judeo-Christian morality as antithetical to the life-force and the instinct for self-preservation or when he praised the healthy pagan values of classical antiquity, he seemed to come uncomfortably close to echoing Nietzsche without ever quoting him.[76]

By the same token, Hitler's diatribes against the barbarism, credulity, ignorance, and "poverty of spirit" encouraged by the Christian churches also contain crude echoes of eighteenth-century rationalists like Gibbon and Voltaire — whom nobody has ever suspected of proto-Nazism. Even if Nietzsche's anti-Christian virulence could be shown to have inadvertently paved the way for some of the Christophobic *Judenhass* exhibited by the Nazi leaders, he can hardly be said to have caused it. Similarly, to radically question such sacred taboos of Western culture as Democracy or Christianity does not automatically make one into a fascist anti-Semite.

In fact, Nietzsche sharply condemned anti-Christian anti-Semites like

Eugen Dühring in his own day, no less fiercely than he mocked the attitudes of Christian anti-Judaism. He ridiculed Dühring's stance that the Germans should turn their backs on the Old Testament for racial reasons or the fantastic notion that Christ was an "Aryan" and anti-Semite—positions that were close to official policy under the Third Reich. Similarly we have already shown how strongly Nietzsche reacted against the German-Christian-Aryan anti-Semitism of the Wagnerites, whose input into Nazi ideology and myth-making was much greater than his own. Above all, his loathing of the German nationalists and his growing empathy for, even identification with, contemporary Jews, suggests how little Nietzsche and his philosophy were ultimately compatible with Nazism. He was after all a "good European," who believed in the value of "mixed races" and "mixed cultures." He was genuinely convinced that the Jews were destined by their unique historical experience to play an especially beneficial role in the post-Christian future.

Friedrich Nietzsche was both fascinated and horrified by the symbolism of the Cross. I venture to add that he would have been even more appalled by the anti-Semitic German ideology of Death embodied in the Nazi Swastika, whose forerunners he denounced without compromise during his own lifetime. I believe that he would have been repelled by the fanatically racist and *anti-Jewish* side of National Socialism, which led to the Holocaust—the ultimate expression of that demonic European nihilism whose symptoms he had so acutely diagnosed. One hundred years after his death, his prophetic utterances still challenge us to critically reexamine the emotionally charged relationship between Jews, Christianity, and the Nazi genocide.

Notes

1. See, for example, Max I. Dimont, *Jews, God and History* (New York, 1994). The revised and updated edition presents Nietzsche's philosophy as laying the "cornerstone for the Nazi state" and as "a complete reversal of the teachings of Gospel and Decalogue" (329). For all his brilliant prose, Dimont tells us, Nietzsche was the "father" of Nazism. A more sophisticated version of this notion can be found in S. Giora Shoham, *Valhalla, Calvary and Auschwitz* (Cincinnati: Bowman and Cody, 1995), 228–29, 266–67, where Nietzsche's role in shattering the moral inhibitions created by Christianity is seen as paving the way for Nazi neo-paganism.

2. Quoted in Weaver Santaniello, *Nietzsche, God and the Jews: His critique of Judeo-Christianity in Relation to the Nazi Myth* (Albany: State University of New York Press, 1994), 115.

3. Steven E. Aschheim, "Nietzsche and the German Radical Right 1914–1933," in *The Intellectual Revolt against Liberal Democracy 1870–1945*, ed.

Zeev Sternhell (Jerusalem: Israel Academy of Sciences and Humanities, 1996), 159–76.

4. On these falsifications, see H. F. Peters, *Zarathustra's Sister: The Case of Elisabeth and Friedrich Nietzsche* (New York: Markus Wiener, 1985).

5. In Walter Kaufmann, ed., *The Portable Nietzsche* (New York: Viking, 1976), 30. This is a reprint of the 1954 edition. Here, as in other places, I have somewhat modified the translation in accordance with my reading of the complete critical German edition of Nietzsche's *KSA*.

6. Walter Kaufmann, *Nietzsche: Philosopher, Psychologist, Antichrist*, 4th ed. (Princeton: Princeton University Press, 1974), 42–45. On anti-Semitism as "the cause of the break between myself and my sister . . ." and his alienation from Wagner, see Nietzsche's letter to Franz Overbeck (April 2, 1884) quoted in Peter Bergmann, *Nietzsche: The "Last Anti-Political German"* (Bloomington: Indiana University Press 1987), 157. Also Weaver Santaniello, "A Post-Holocaust Re-examination of Nietzsche and the Jews: *Vis-à-vis* Christendom and Nazism," in, *Nietzsche and Jewish Culture*, ed. Jacob Golomb (London and New York: Routledge, 1997), 22–25.

7. See Ben MacIntyre, *Beyond the Fatherland: The Search for Elisabeth Nietzsche* (New York: Farrar, Straus, Giroux, 1992).

8. See Alfred Rosenberg, *Friedrich Nietzsche* (Munich: Zentralverlag der NSDAP, 1944) and Hans Sluga, *Heidegger's Crisis: Philosophy and Politics in Nazi Germany* (Cambridge: Harvard University Press, 1993), 232–33. Santaniello ("A Post-Holocaust Re-examination," 42) suggests that when Rosenberg placed a wreath on Nietzsche's grave, dedicated "To the great fighter," it was a sinister way of silencing his true views rather than a genuine tribute from the leading ideologue of Nazism. This strikes me as farfetched.

9. See Alfred Bäumler, *Nietzsche als Philosoph and Politiker* (Leipzig: Reklam, 1931), 157, which claims that Nietzsche's philo-Semitic comments were simply an attention-seeking device to get Germans to listen to him. For Nazi interpretations of Nietzsche, see Sluga, *Heidegger's Crisis*, 179–89 and Rudolf E. Kuenzli, "The Nazi Appropriation of Nietzsche, *Nietzsche Studien* 12 (1983): 428–35.

10. See Yirmiyahu Yovel, *Dark Riddle: Hegel, Nietzsche and the Jews* (Cambridge: Polity Press, 1998), 127–29 for Nietzsche's responses to the anti-Semitic material sent to him by Fritsch. In a letter of March 29, 1887 he made known his abhorrence of the anti-Semitic views of Dühring, Wagner, Drumont and de Lagarde. Caustically, he asked Fritsch, "Finally, what do you think I feel when Zarathustra's name is borne in the mouths of anti-Semites?"

11. Letter to Elisabeth Förster-Nietzsche, in *The Portable Nietzsche*, 456–7.

12. See Siegfried Mandel, *Nietzsche and the Jews. Exaltation and Denigration* (New York, 1998), 188f.

13. *The Portable Nietzsche*, pp.456–57.

14. Friedrich Nietzsche, *Beyond Good and Evil*, trans. Marianne Cowan (Chicago: Gateway Edition, 1965), sec. 251, p.187. I have modified the translation.

15. Letters to Burckhardt and Overbeck, in *The Portable Nietzsche*, 687. I have slightly changed the translation.

16. For Nietzsche's view of Stöcker, see Kaufmann, *Nietzsche*, 172–73.

17. Quoted in ibid, 163; from *EH*, The Case of Wagner, 2.

18. Von Westernhagen, (whose book was published by Alexander Duncker in Weimar, 1936) was a convinced Nazi but one who could see the difference between Nietzsche and Gobineau. See Mandel, *Nietzsche and the Jews*, 13; Kaufmann, *Nietzsche*, 267, n.6.

19. Mandel, *Nietzsche and the Jews*, 288, deals at some length with the more offensive earlier characterisations of "Judaization," "Jewish money-bags," etc., in Nietzsche's work.

20. Santaniello, *Nietzsche, God, and the Jews*, 163, n.78. This is, of course, a double-edged tribute.

21. See *Die Nachgelassenen Fragmente. Eine Auswahl* (Stuttgart, 1996), 277.

22. Sebastian Hausmann ("Eine Erinnerung an Nietzsche" [1922]) believed that the deepest reason for his break with Wagner was personal rather than an issue of their respective worldviews. Nietzsche was "far too conscious of his own intellectual importance to submit to being used as a mere instrument in the hands of a supposedly greater genius." Quoted in Sander L. Gilman, ed., *Conversations with Nietzsche. A Life in the Words of His Contemporaries* (New York: Oxford University Press, 1991), 138.

23. On the rupture between Wagner and Nietzsche, see also Robert Gutman, *Richard Wagner* (1968, San Diego: Harvest, 1990), 358–60; David Large, "Wagner's Bayreuth Disciples," in *Wagnerism in European Culture and Politics*, ed. David C. Large and William Weber (Ithaca, Cornell University Press, 1984); Mandel, *Nietzsche and the Jews*, 112.

24. For the electrifying effect of Bizet's music on Nietzsche, see the remarks of Resa von Schirnhofer, in Gilman, ed., *Conversations with Nietzsche*, 150.

25. From *Human, All Too Human*, in *The Portable Nietzsche*, 62. Here, as elsewhere, I have modified some of Kaufmann's translation.

26. On Lipiner, see William J. McGrath, *Dionysian Art and Populist Politics in Austria* (New Haven and London: Yale University Press, 1974).

27. Cosima Wagner wrote to a friend that in the end "Israel took over in the shape of a Dr. Rée, very slick, very cool . . . representing the relationship of Judea and Germania. . . . It is the victory of evil over good." See Erich Heller's introduction to *Human, All Too Human*, translated by R. J. Hollingdale (Cambridge: Cambridge University Press, 1986).

28. See *The Portable Nietzsche*, 160. The expression comes from *Z*, I, "On the New Idol."

29. Compare also Ernst Nolte, *Nietzsche und der Nietzscheanismus* (Frankfurt am Main: Propylaen, 1990), 104–6.

30. Nietzsche made it plain that he regarded anti-Semitism as a deliberate effort to try and "rouse up all the horned-beast elements in the people by a brazen abuse of the cheapest of all agitators' tricks, moral attitudinizing. "That such a "swindle" could succeed in Germany was "connected with the undeniable stagnation of the German spirit" — the exclusive diet of "newspapers, politics, beer, and Wagnerian music" and the "strong but narrow principle "'Deutschland, Deutschland über alles.'" I consider this to be a prescient, not to say, prophetic insight.

31. Mandel, *Nietzsche and the Jews*, 226.

32. Ibid., 228.

33. Heinrich Härtle, *Nietzsche und der Nationalsozialismus* (Munich: Zentralverlag der NSDAP, 1939). Härtle was nonetheless aware that there were discrepancies between Nietzsche's thought and National Socialism—especially in his "inadequate" attention to biological facts and belief in the virtues of racial mixing. See Sluga, *Heidegger's Crisis*, 84–85.

34. Kaufmann, *Nietzsche*, 376–8. see Sander Gilman, "Nietzsche, Heine and the Idea of the Jew," in *Nietzsche and Jewish Culture*, ed. Jacob Golomb (London and New York: Routledge, 1997), 76–100, for the Heine connection.

35. For the Brandes-Nietzsche correspondence, see Georg Brandes, *Friedrich Nietzsche: An Essay on Aristocratic Radicalism* (1889; London: William Heinemann, 1914).

36. In, "Why I am So Clever," 5, he emphasized that his relation with Wagner had been the most intimate and profound of his whole life but that he felt only contempt for the Wagnerians.

37. Quoted in Yovel, *Dark Riddle*, 127.

38. With regard to de Lagarde, it is interesting to read Richard Reuter's testimony, first published in 1895, which states that de Lagarde's *Deutsche Schriften* had a considerable impact on Nietzsche in the summer of 1876. De Lagarde's critique of conditions in the German Empire, his devastating judgment on Protestant Christianity, and his sharply polemical style impressed the younger Nietzsche—though he was later led to diametrically opposite conclusions. See Gilman, ed., *Conversations with Nietzsche*, 81–82.

39. *Basic Writings of Nietzsche*, trans. Walter Kaufmann (New York: Random House, 1968), Appendix, 798.

40. Ibid.

41. From *EH*, "Human, All Too Human," 2, cited in Mandel, *Nietzsche and the Jews*, 245.

42. For other polemics in this vein, see Friedrich Nietzsche, "What the Germans Lack," in *Twilight of the Idols*, trans. and ed. R. J. Hollingdale (London: Penguin Books, 1968), 60–66.

43. See Hubert Cancik, "Mongols, Semites and the Pure-Bred Greeks: Nietzsche's Handling of the Racial Doctrines of His Time," in *Nietzsche and Jewish Culture*, ed. Jacob Golomb, 55–75.

44. Friedrich Nietzsche, *The Anti-Christ*, trans. and ed. R. J. Hollingdale (London: Penguin Books, 1968), 44, 157–59. In this section, Nietzsche wildly fulminates against Judeo-Christian megalomania and the "*arrogance of the elect.*"

45. Ibid., 134. My translation differs slightly.

46. Ibid. The Jews are even described by Nietzsche as the "*most catastrophic people of world history,*" for having radically falsified natural values—a process that reached its culmination in Paul.

47. Ibid. Nietzsche recalls here his arguments in *Beyond Good and Evil* (195), where the historic significance of the Jewish people is identified with "the beginning of the *slave revolt in morality.*"

48. *The Anti-Christ*, trans, and ed. Hollingdale (1968). For Nietzsche, this was the "*most fundamental of all declarations of war,*" but in the course of two millennia, it had proven victorious.

49. Jesus, with his gospel of love, was in Nietzsche's eyes the ultimate consummation and triumph of Jewish hatred and *"sublime vengefulness"* — the victory of the grand politics of revenge.

50. This inversion was for Nietzsche, the demonstration that the Jews embodied "the most deeply repressed priestly vengefulness." This was perhaps the most flawed and potentially pernicious of his claims about Judaism.

51. Nietzsche presents ancient Judea as an "antipodal monstrosity," a symbol of "anti-nature itself" in Roman eyes, while the Jewish hostility to Rome is misleadingly represented as a wanton hatred — a notion that all too easily provided grist to the anti-Semitic will. Ironically, the Gospel of John is the most *anti-Jewish* book of the New Testament!

52. *The Anti-Christ* (1968), 135.

53. *A*, 25 in *The Portable Nietzsche*, 594.

54. Indeed, for Nietzsche, this was "possibly the greatest recklessness . . . that literary Europe has on its conscience."

55. These positive characterisations are taken mainly from *Daybreak*, *Beyond Good and Evil*, and *The Gay Science*. See, for example, *Daybreak*, sect. 205, p. 206.

56. For a detailed distinction between *Kraft* and *Macht*, see Jacob Golomb, *Nietzsche's Enticing Psychology of Power* (Ames: Iowa State University Press, 1989), 179–221 and his chapter in this book.

57. Ibid. Nietzsche credits the Jews with enabling Europe to reconnect to its Greek heritage and embrace a "more rational and certainly unmythical explanation of the world."

58. *Ecce Homo*, "How One Becomes What One Is" in *The Portable Nietzsche*, 660, my revised translation.

59. Ibid. See also Yovel, *Dark Riddle*, 176 for an interesting discussion of this text.

60. See also Yovel, *Dark Riddle*, 172–77.

61. In this same passage, Nietzsche observes that "a thinker with the future of Europe on his conscience, will count on the Jews" (and the Russians) and he advises a policy similar to that of the British aristocracy — to meet the Jews halfway, though with caution and selectivity.

62. Hyam Maccoby, "Nietzsche's love-hate affair. Are life-affirming Jews nearer to Superman than decadent Christians?" *The Times Literary Supplement*, June 25, 1999, pp.14–15.

63. Yirmiyahu Yovel, "Nietzsche and the Jews. The structure of an Ambivalence," in *Nietzsche and Jewish Culture*, ed. Golomb, 129.

64. Yovel, *The Dark Riddle*, 176.

65. Jacob Golomb, "Nietzsche and the Marginal Jews," in *Nietzsche and Jewish Culture*, ed. Golomb, 158–92.

66. See David Ohana, "Zarathustra in Jerusalem: Nietzsche and the 'New Hebrews,'" in *The Shaping of Israeli Identity: Myth, Memory and Trauma*, ed. Robert Wistrich and David Ohana (London: Frank Cass, 1995), 38–60.

67. Paul Mendes-Flohr, "Zarathustra's Apostle: Martin Buber and the Jewish Renaissance," in *Nietzsche and Jewish Culture*, ed. Golomb, 233–43.

68. Jacob Golomb, "Nietzsche and the Marginal Jews," 162–73. Golomb

emphasizes the attraction that Nietzschean concepts of personal authenticity, self-overcoming, and the "transfiguration of all values" exercised on the fin-de-siècle generation of secular, marginalised Jewish intellectuals.

69. Quoted in Kaufmann, *Nietzsche*, 412.

70. See, e.g., Gilbert Merlio ("The Critique of Liberal Democracy in the Works of Oswald Spengler," in, *The Intellectual Revolt*, ed. Sternhell, 177–89), who points to the "vulgarized Nietzscheanism" that became common ground between the conservative *völkisch* and fascist Right. Left-wing critics like George Lukács (*The Destruction of Reason* [London, 1962]), fully embraced the Nazi and fascist appropriation of Nietzsche as a *true* reflection of his thought. For Lukács, Hitler was "the executor of Nietzsche's spiritual testament"—the link being the philosopher's "irrationalism," his hatred of egalitarian doctrines and of socialism, and his alleged justification of warlike, imperialist barbarism. Most extreme of all is George Lichtheim's claim that Nietzsche provided inspiration for the SS program of mass murder in Eastern Europe. See his *Europe in the Twentieth Century* (New York, 1972), 186.

71. Drieu La Rochelle was a convinced Nietzschean and "socialist" fascist opposed to the historical materialism and determinism of the Marxists. In his *Journal 1939–1945* (Paris: Gallimard, 1992), 417, there is, however, a most perceptive remark, dated August, 7 1944: "*Nietzsche aurait vomi le Nazisme comme Weimar et Guillaume II. Mais n'empêche que le monde du XXe siècle ressemble à son ombre, qu'il en est le prophète. D'ailleurs, avec beaucoup de finesse il en a prévu toutes les rudesses et les grossièretés.*"

72. See Georges Bataille, *On Nietzsche* (London, 1992), 169–73 (the French edition appeared in 1945). See "Sur Nietzsche," *Oeuvres Complètes*, vol. 4, (Paris: Gallimard, 1970). In the second issue of *Acéphale* (January 1937), Bataille had already sought to rescue Nietzsche from the fascists in the name of a left-wing existentialist interpretation. See Elisabeth Roudinesco's biography *Jacques Lacan* (New York: Columbia University Press, 1997), 131–33 for the details.

73. The most ambivalent and interesting of Nietzsche's defenders was Thomas Mann, who in the 1930s had been upset by Nazi efforts to mobilize the philosopher for their own goals. In 1947, Mann suggested that it was fascism that created Nietzsche, rather than the reverse. Yet his philosophy had "presaged the dawning imperialism and as a quivering floatstick indicated the fascist era of the West." See Steven E. Aschheim, *The Nietzsche Legacy in Germany, 1890–1990* (Berkeley: University of California Press, 1992), 319.

74. Ibid., 232–71 for ways in which Nietzsche was incorporated into the Nazi pantheon. I believe that Aschheim underestimates the grave distortions of Nietzsche's thought that were required to give some plausibility to this operation. But he does succeed in highlighting those aspects of Nietzsche that could also appeal to German *völkisch* radicals and Nazis.

75. See Hitler's *Table Talk 1941–1944* (London: Weidenfeld & Nicolson, 1953), 720–22.

76. Robert Wistrich, *Hitler's Apocalypse* (London: Weidenfeld and Nicolson, 1985), 145–53.

PART TWO: IN PRACTICE

8

Ecce Caesar:
Nietzsche's Imperial Aspirations
Daniel W. Conway

It is only beginning with me that the earth knows *great politics.*
—Nietzsche, *Ecce Homo*

It is a historical fact that Nietzsche was widely admired by twentieth-century fascists. Mussolini was an avid disciple of Nietzsche's teachings and often acknowledged his influence on the development of the fascist philosophy. Hitler, too, was eager to associate his regime with Nietzsche's name and reputation. Responding in part to the cloying advances of Nietzsche's sister Elisabeth, Hitler became a patron of the Nietzsche archives and an occasional visitor to Weimar.[1]

The case for Nietzsche's direct contributions to the rise and development of European fascism nevertheless remains inconclusive. First of all, he was read neither carefully nor well by Mussolini, and not at all by Hitler.[2] Nor was his philosophy studied carefully by the ideologues who supported these leaders and helped formulate their official positions.[3] A direct link between Nietzsche and fascism is therefore difficult to establish with certainty. Indeed, the Nietzsche who was enshrined in Fascist Italy and Nazi Germany bears only a crude resemblance to the author of the books from which the fascists claimed to derive philosophical inspiration. Second, Nietzsche was openly contemptuous of several elements of fascism that constitute its ideological basis—such as nationalism, tribalism, anti-Semitism, militarism, anti-intellectualism, xenophobia, and isolationism. He explicitly stated on a number of occasions that the future of Europe lay not in the decadent "particularism" favored by the protofascists of his day, but in a pan-Europeanism that would collect all races, peoples, and nations within a single, unifying culture. He furthermore complained that the rise of nationalism in Germany would make it nearly impossible for him to cultivate a sympathetic readership in his fatherland for centuries to come (*EH*, "The Case of Wagner," 2–4).

Finally, the question of direct influence is difficult in general to settle with respect to issues of moral responsibility. Even if we are willing to apportion some measure of blame to a philosopher whose ideas are supposedly enacted by avowed disciples, are we equally willing to do so in the case of his more careless and uninformed followers? Would it not be unfair to assign Nietzsche greater responsibility for what he is said to have claimed than for what his writings in fact support? He was, after all, a prescient critic of the primal animosities that coalesced beneath the thunderhead of fascism. In this light, it is somewhat ironic that he has so often been vilified as the spiritual father of fascism.

At the same time, however, it would be wrong to ignore the profound impact of Nietzsche's philosophy on the rise of fascism.[4] He may not have been the father of fascism, but he certainly was in and of the family. As the editors have suggested in their title for this book, Nietzsche might be described more accurately as a *godfather* of fascism. Although sharply critical of the protofascist movements of his day, he also expressed in his writings a deeper sympathy with a number of their signature dissatisfactions. He is a predecessor whose unreflective prejudices and political naïveté meshed neatly with the dark furies that would later breathe life into European fascism. In the indirect expression of these prejudices, Nietzsche's affinities with fascism became most readily apparent. This means that his influence on the development of fascism in the twentieth century was far more affective than intellectual in nature. Owing to the strength of this prereflective, emotional bond, his readers among the fascists were able to set aside his overt political teachings and identify themselves with the more primal impulses at work in his thought.

But there is another, previously overlooked dimension—namely, the imperial aspirations that inform his political thinking—that may help us to chart the continuity of his philosophy with the primal impulses that also gave rise to fascism. Although his imperial aspirations were based on little more than fantasies—he commanded neither the power nor the opportunity to implement his imperial designs—they nevertheless afford us an insight into the prephilosophical prejudices that informed his thinking. I am particularly interested in this chapter to trace Nietzsche's imperial aspirations to his unabashed admiration for the amoral, self-perpetuating structure of the Roman Empire. This admiration in turn fed his animosity toward the Jews, whom he regarded as the nemeses par excellence of imperial rule. His ostensibly political opposition to the Jews thus grants us an opportunity to survey his prereflective, prephilosophical attitudes. As we will see, these prejudices were neither novel nor benign, and they belie the free-thinking cosmopolitanism that he claimed for himself and his fellow "good Europeans."

Against the backdrop of his imperial aspirations, his peculiar ambivalence toward the Jews emerges in sharper relief. Although his enmity for the anti-Semites occasionally eclipsed his suspicions of the Jews, his Judeophobia was deeper and more complex. Because he regarded the Jews as the greatest enemies of empire, he was obliged to pursue his imperial aspirations under the considerable burden of his suspicions of the Jews. This burden not only produced various smudges on his blueprint for empire, but also exposed the limits of his commitment to an imperial renewal of European culture.

Nietzsche's Empire

It should come as no great surprise that Nietzsche had empire on his mind in the late 1880s. The "scramble for Africa" was well underway, as the recently emergent nation-states of Europe contended for colonial possessions on the dark continent. Closer to home, Bismarck's volteface in the mid-1880s on the question of Africa had not only furnished Germany with a colonial empire of her own, but also provoked Nietzsche's attacks on the petty ambitions and nationalistic myopia of the Reich.[5] Closer still to home, he protested in vain as his beloved sister and her new husband, Bernhard Förster, set sail for Paraguay in 1886. There they presided over the colony of Nueva Germania, which was devoted to protecting the purity of the Aryan race.[6]

By the late 1880s, Nietzsche had become extremely critical of European imperialism. Whereas Bismarck and his supporters welcomed the opportunity to display the military might of the Reich in far-flung colonies, Nietzsche viewed imperial expansion as the natural progression of the decadence that had seized Europe in the nineteenth century. Much to his dismay, in fact, Europe was disintegrating before his very eyes. Whereas "progressive" political thinkers celebrated the emergence of the modern nation-state, Nietzsche bemoaned the loss of the integrated, unified Europe to which his eighteenth-century heroes, Goethe and Napoleon, had pledged their estimable allegiance. He consequently diagnosed the widespread fascination with empire as symptomatic of the most recent advance of European decadence. Under the deranging influence of this disease, he opined, the Germans in particular "take pleasure in the national scabies of the heart and blood poisoning that now leads the nations of Europe to delimit and barricade themselves against each other as if it were a matter of quarantine" (*GS*, 377).[7]

Nietzsche thus believed that Europe, like all things decadent, was dying from the inside. European culture was now so thoroughly impoverished that it could no longer collect its constituent peoples and nations into a functioning, thriving whole. Having expended its native vitality, Europe had disintegrated into a cluster of squabbling nation-states, each of which sought to compensate for its spiritual losses through the acquisition of colonial possessions. Each nation-state in turn had identified itself (rather than Europe as a whole) as the central unit of political organization. According to Nietzsche, however, the frenzy of imperial expansion could never provide a viable substitute for the pulsating vitality of an integrated European culture. He thus exposed European imperialism as a quick, desperate fix for a horrible systemic affliction. The scramble for exotic colonies could serve at best to distract Europeans, and then only temporarily, from having lost their common center of gravity. Rather than signal the cultural superiority of the nations of Europe, imperial expansion had simply exported the self-contempt and dissolution that drove these nations apart from one another in the first place. Misery loves company, and the European imperial powers were bent on remaking the world in their own miserable image.

Despite his grim diagnosis of European imperial expansion, Nietzsche, too, was immersed in the business of founding an empire. Rather than scour the globe for territories ripe for colonial conquest, however, he turned his attention inward, to the disintegrating culture of Europe itself. Deeply suspicious of the modern model of empire, whereby European nation-states acquired inexpensive labor and natural resources through aggressive exploitation, he instead embraced the ancient model of empire, especially as it was perfected by the Romans toward the beginning of the Common Era. He praised the Roman Empire as an example of "grand architecture," for "its construction was designed to prove itself through thousands of years" (*A*, 58). He detected in the Empire an expression of "the will to tradition, to authority, to responsibility for centuries to come, to the solidarity of chains of generations, forward and backward *ad infinitum*" (*TI*, 9:39). He consequently regarded the Empire, "this most admirable work of art in the grand style," as neither a historical relic nor an antiquarian curiosity, but as "a beginning" (*A*, 58).

To Nietzsche, the Roman Empire was not simply the last great European triumph of concentrated strength and unity of purpose. He also believed that the imperial legacy in Europe was still both viable and generative. He consequently saw in the Roman Empire the promise of

Europe's future. In particular, he described the "good Europeans," whom he hoped to rally to his imperial cause, as "the rich, oversupplied, but also overly obligated heirs of thousands of years of European spirit" (GS, 377). He consequently intended to counter the decadent trend toward nationalism by reviving contemporary Europe's faded linkages to the Roman Empire. Indeed, it was only with reference to the viable imperial legacy of contemporary Europe that he could describe the outbreak of nationalism as a historical aberration. Whatever degree of unity or integrity he intended to claim for a rejuvenated Europe would derive from a living inheritance of the grandeur of imperial Rome. If, despite all appearances, "*Europe wants to become one*" (BGE, 256), this is possible only because Europe has "*been one*" once before.

Nietzsche does not use the word "empire" (*Reich*) to convey the intended aim of his political aspirations. He writes instead of his wish to contribute to "the cultivation of a new caste that will rule Europe [*an die Züchtung einer neuen über Europa regierenden Kaste*]" (BGE, 251). This terminological preference has less to do with the nature of his political aims than with his opposition to Bismarck, whose celebrated Reich he openly criticized.[8] He certainly did not want his grandiose vision of European reintegration to be confused with the petty, militaristic nationalism that was the pride of Germany in the late 1880s. Whatever Bismarck's Reich might have been, it was not an empire in the grand, unified sense that Nietzsche associates with Rome.

Bismarck's triumph may have tainted the word Reich, but it also fueled Nietzsche's enthusiasm for the founding of a *real* European empire, one that would exceed in cultural influence the military might of Bismarck's Germany. "Culture and the state," he explains, "are antagonists. . . . One lives off the other, one thrives at the expense of the other" (TI, 8:4). He consequently hoped to contribute to a reversal of Bismarck's victory, so that culture might once again thrive at the expense of the state. He thus conceived of empire on a much grander scale, as comprising a comprehensive, integrated program of pan-European acculturation.[9] The goal of this program was nothing less than the organized production of those great human beings who alone warrant the future of humankind. Only Europe itself, revived and reintegrated, could realistically stage the production of exemplary human beings. The resources of any single nation-state, including Germany, were simply too meager and dispersed to undertake the grand program of acculturation that he envisioned.[10]

The cultivation of a new European ruling caste was made both possible and desirable by the recent decay of the political authority of Western Christianity. Viewed from the epic perspective that Nietzsche presumed to command, the history of European civilization appeared as a staccato succession of empires and counter-empires, each of which in turn had bent the whole of Europe to its will. So it was that the counter-empire of Christianity originally supplanted the Roman Empire. So it was, too, that Christianity most recently reasserted its dominance by dispatching the Reformation to squash the Renaissance (GM, I:16). Over the course of its long reign, however, these retaliatory expenditures had exacted a heavy cumulative toll from the counter-empire of Western Christianity. Nietzsche sensed that the time was ripe once again for a shift in the balance of imperial power. He settled on Germany as the new center of the empire in part because the former center — Rome — had been corrupted by its extended association with the Church.[11]

But the widespread decay that made possible this proposed shift in the balance of imperial power also rendered most Europeans unfit for the business of founding a new empire. If Nietzsche was to fashion an empire from the anemic peoples and nations of late nineteenth-century Europe, then he would need to introduce a powerful leavening agent into the inert, indiscriminate mass that Europe had become. To procure this leavening agent, he reached beyond both Europe and modernity, to the Jews. Indeed, the most surprising detail of his blueprint for empire is his apparent change of heart toward the Jews. He not only recruited them to participate in the founding of the new empire, but also reserved for them an honored place in his new European order. The Jews were central to his designs on empire, for he counted on them to supply the enervated nation-states of Europe with a transfusion of spirit and strength. In light of the decadence that gripped Europe, he simply could not proceed without the cooperation of the Jews.

The importance of the Jews to Nietzsche's imperial aspirations explains in large part the gestures of conciliation that punctuate his post-Zarathustran writings. In a book chapter provocatively entitled "Peoples and Fatherlands," he boldly maintains that "[a] thinker who has the development of Europe on his conscience will, in all his projects for this future, take into account the Jews" (BGE, 251). A consideration of the Jews is necessary, he explains, because "[t]he Jews . . . are beyond any doubt the strongest, toughest, and purest race now living in Europe; they know how to prevail even under the worst conditions (even better than under favorable conditions)" (ibid. 251). Borrowing a compliment from his beloved Horace, he even describes the Jewish people as "*aere perennius*" — more enduring than bronze (ibid. 251).

He is consequently "certain" that "the Jews, if they wanted it — or if they were forced into it, which seems to be what the anti-Semites want — *could* even now have preponderance, indeed quite literally mastery, over Europe" (BGE, 251). Hoping to accommodate the Jews' supposed "wish . . . to be absorbed and assimilated," he provocatively recommends that "it might be useful and fair to expel the anti-Semitic screamers from the country [i.e., Germany]" (ibid.). In a "joking" conclusion to his "serious" consideration of the "future of Europe," he goes so far as to recommend a program of "cautious" and "selective" intermarriage between Jews and Germans (ibid.). Taken together with the pro-Jewish and anti-anti-Semitic sentiments expressed in other books from the late 1880s, these passages convey his regard for the Jews as the potential saviors of European civilization.

Nietzsche's conciliatory gestures toward the Jews are surprising for (at least) two reasons. First of all, his general attitude toward the peoples and nations that his empire would comprise expressed a fairly uniform measure of contempt. He fancied himself an amoral lawgiver, and he regularly presented himself as fully prepared to treat all European peoples as anonymous, interchangeable, raw materials.[12] Owing to the rampant miscegenation and social leveling that characterized the late modern epoch, his contemporaries had become remarkably homogeneous, pliable, adaptable, docile, confused, aimless, and anemic—which means that they were unusually receptive to the imposition of a single order of law. They may not have been the stuff of free spirits and *Übermenschen*, but they were certainly the stuff of imperial rule.

The new empire, Nietzsche promised, would both accommodate and exploit the adaptability of this new, "mishmash" type of European. The utilitarian disposition of his imperial aspirations thus reduced *all* European peoples to the status of standing reserve. They had value only insofar as they contributed to the greater glory of Europe and its refurbished empire. No people, race, or nation—except the Germans, for whom he chauvinistically reserved the command center of his empire—could realistically expect its concerns to be taken seriously by his empire. Although he does not say so explicitly, Nietzsche apparently believes that the goal of pan-European renewal would justify *any* means necessary, including, as he says, "slavery" and the deliberate "cultivation of tyrants" (*BGE*, 242).

In light of Nietzsche's undisguised contempt for all other peoples and nations of modern Europe, is there any reason to believe that his conciliatory gestures toward the Jews are sincere? To be sure, he did not explicitly refer to the Jews as anonymous, interchangeable resources. In fact, he located in their possession the spirit and strength that would resuscitate European culture. At the same time, however, he acknowledged no moral scruple that would have prevented him from treating the Jews (or anyone else) as disposable means to a glorious end. He crudely refers to "the quantum of 'Jew'" that various European nations were able (or not) to "digest" (*BGE*, 251), which indicates that he thought of the Jews as reducible in principle to measurable "quanta" of power and utility. Even if the Jews would initially receive preferential treatment in exchange for their unique contribution to the founding of the new empire, this treatment would presumably be contingent upon their continued usefulness to the empire. What was to stop him from using them and then eventually using them up?

Second, Nietzsche elsewhere volunteers that he is extremely suspicious of the Jews. He regarded them as inveterate enemies of empire, and he blamed them for preventing the cultural ascendancy of "noble" values. As he sees it, the Jews have repeatedly avenged their native weakness by ensuring that no one else is able for long to wield imperial power:

> All that has been done on earth against "the noble," "the powerful," "the masters," "the rulers," fades into nothing compared with what the *Jews* have done against them; the Jews, that priestly people, who in opposing their enemies and conquerors were ultimately satisfied with nothing less than a radical revaluation of their enemies' values, that is to say, an act of the *most spiritual revenge* (*GM*, I:7).

He thus figured the Jews as exemplary practitioners of the kind of non-negotiable tribalism that bedevils the architects of empire. On this point, he stood in agreement with the anti-Semites of his day, who also feared the Jews (although for very different reasons) as a destabilizing force in the mix of European politics. Unlike the anti-Semites, however, he did not fear the Jews because their presence in Europe imperiled the purity of the Aryan race. Rather, he feared the Jews because he believed that they had historically (and successfully) resisted the trends toward assimilation that are involved in any consolidation of imperial power. He feared the Jewish people as the rock upon which entire empires had foundered and crumbled.

According to the sweeping narrative that underwrites his "genealogy of morals," the Jews are ultimately responsible for such world historical calamities as the "slave revolt in morality," the birth of Christianity, the fall of the Roman Empire, the decline of the Renaissance, the rise of the Protestant Reformation, and the outbreak of the French Revolution (*GM*, I:16). He goes so far as to propose "Rome against Judea, Judea against Rome" as his preferred "symbol" for the historical struggles that have collectively defined the identity and destiny of European civilization (ibid.). Although he employs "Judea" as a shorthand designation for any macropolitical expression of resentment, especially those of Christian lineage, he also traces all such expressions to their origins in Jewish hatred. Turning the familiar, arboreal imagery of genealogy to his own ends, he depicts the family tree of Western morality as sickly and diseased, as a "tree of vengefulness and hatred" (GM, I:8). The "trunk" of this tree, he explains, is "Jewish hatred," "the profoundest and sublimest kind of hatred," from which Christian love emerged as an early, enduring, and bitter fruit (ibid.). His arboreal imagery has grave implications for his political thinking in general, and his imperial aspirations in particular.[13] In order for "Rome" finally to triumph over "Judea," the poisonous outgrowth of Christianity must be eliminated at its root. In his mind, this meant that the Jews must no longer be suffered to pose a toxic threat to the flowering of "noble" systems of evaluation.

In light of these two concerns, what are we to make of Nietzsche's political overtures to the Jews? Some scholars are inclined to downplay the anti-Jewish sentiments expressed in *On the Genealogy of Morals*.[14] His references to "Judea," it is often proposed, were usually meant to designate Christianity. His enmity for "Judea" thus need not betray a blanket anti-Jewish sentiment, for it targets only, or primarily, the "priestly" Jews of the Second Temple period, from whom Christianity was directly descended.[15] Other scholars point to the complex rhetorical aims of Nietzsche's writings, including his likely intention to reproduce (and thereby mock) the vulgar passions of anti-Semitic agitators.[16] He candidly advertises *On the Genealogy of Morals* as "a polemic" (*eine Streitschrift*), which perhaps suggests that his anti-Jewish remarks are to be taken (by select readers) as largely or exclusively rhetorical. Still other scholars note that he may have felt obliged to attempt in strategic fashion to accommodate the anti-Jewish predilections of his likely readers.[17] If he could draw them in with his apparently anti-Jewish invective, then he might have been able to educate them about the evils of anti-Semitism.[18]

All of these interpretations are plausible, but they collectively suggest a Nietzsche who enjoyed nearly full control of the anti-Jewish sentiments expressed in his writings.[19] This suggestion in turn betrays the presence of a distinctly un-Nietzschean piety with respect to the sanctity of rhetorical mastery and authorial intention. If "all philosophers" are either unwitting "advocates . . . for their prejudices" (*BGE*, 5), "author[s] of a kind of involuntary and unconscious memoir" (*BGE*, 6), or "flatterers" (*BGE*, 7), then why should Nietzsche be any different?[20] Why should we accord him full control over sentiments, passions, and prejudices that he convincingly revealed to be profoundly out of control in the decadent epoch of late modernity? Would it not be more plausible to assume that he (like Zarathustra) was *both* a critic of these vulgar prejudices *and* an (involuntary) mouthpiece for them? If, as he allowed, these anti-Jewish sentiments were partially definitive of the character of the late modern epoch, then we should fully expect that they have claimed him, too—even (or especially) as he exposed their barbarity.

"One Jew More or Less—What Does It Matter?"

The most illuminating evidence of Nietzsche's imperial aspirations is found in the context of his lavish praise for the Roman Empire. The (idealized) figure of the empire came to exert an increasingly formative influence on his post-Zarathustran writings. He regarded the Roman Empire not merely as the zenith of European culture on a grand scale, but also as the source of European renewals to come. He thus appropriated the empire as a model for his own political adventures. But his fascination with the Roman Empire also affords us a glimpse of the darker reaches of his imperial aspirations. If, as he claimed, the course of European civilization was determined by the polar opposition between "Rome" and "Judea," then he could not realistically have hoped to renew the cause of "Rome" without vanquishing "Judea" in the process. In this light, his overtures toward the Jews take on a distinctly sinister cast. He welcomed them into his new European order, but only on the condition that they would no longer pose a threat to his planned consolidation of imperial power.

Nietzsche's designs on empire were informed by his perception of the amoral disposition of the Roman Empire toward its constituent peoples and nations. In particular, he modeled his imperial aspirations on the steely indifference displayed by Pontius Pilate, the Roman governor who delivered Jesus to an angry mob (and, in so doing, furnished Nietzsche with the title of his autobiography).[21] According to Nietzsche, Pilate alone redeems the New Testament that Christians have crudely appended to the venerable Hebrew Bible. Indeed, Nietzsche credits Pilate with the succinct, compact (that is, Roman) expression of two insights that convey his own appreciation for the nobility of empire:

> In the whole New Testament there is only a *single* figure who commands respect[:] Pilate, the Roman governor. To take a Jewish affair *seriously* — he does not persuade himself to do that. One Jew more or less — what does it matter? The noble scorn of a Roman, confronted with an impudent abuse of the word "truth," has enriched the New Testament with the only saying *that has value* — one which is its criticism, even its *annihilation*: "What is truth?" (*A*, 46).[22]

It is no coincidence that Nietzsche admired Pilate above all other imperial figures (except, of course, for Julius Caesar, whom he regarded as the inspiration for the empire). Pilate, the "Roman governor" of a remote Middle Eastern outpost, possessed an imperial sense of perspective, which issued from his unflinching appraisal of the real weight of human affairs. As a representative of the grand expansionist ambitions of the empire, Pilate refused to lower his hyperopic gaze to consider seriously the local struggles of the Jews. He was unsentimental, "nobly scornful," indifferent, and loyal only to the empire. In fact, he was like the Roman Empire itself, for he cared only about the maintenance and expansion of imperial power. He was only minimally—and therefore optimally—human, and he thus resembled those embodied forces of nature whom Nietzsche extols as the apotheoses of human flourishing.

On this retelling of the story, Pilate was the first to confront the imperial dilemma that Nietzsche now faced—namely, what is to be done about the Jews? By merit of his alleged show of indifference, moreover, Pilate responded to this dilemma in a way that Nietzsche deemed admirable. He consequently honors Pilate not only for his self-less service to the empire, but also for his resolve in *giving the Jews their due*. As Nietzsche explains, Pilate does not persuade himself "[t]o take a Jewish affair *seriously*. One Jew more or less—what does it matter?" (*A*, 46).[23] This declaration of indifference is chillingly amoral, and we should certainly wonder about Nietzsche's admiration for its putative wisdom. But the matter is even more complicated, for this declaration of indifference cannot be traced reliably to Pilate. Neither the declaration itself, nor the (anti-Jewish) sentiment it expresses, is to be found in any of the depictions of Pilate in the Gospels. If anything, Pilate is portrayed in the Gospels as attentive to the Jews and mindful of their customs.[24] It is highly unlikely, moreover, that this sentiment *could* have been expressed by Pilate, for it betrays a retrospective standpoint that he did not command. Pilate simply could not have known about the Jews what Nietzsche, writing with the benefit (or curse) of hindsight, claimed to know about them.

In fact, it was not Pilate who targeted the Jews for indifference and noble scorn, but Nietzsche. *He* regarded the Jews as the most potent enemies of the Roman Empire. Perhaps the case could be made that Pilate displayed an indiscriminate indifference to the affairs of the Jews and all other peoples living under his jurisdiction. But it was Nietzsche who singled out the Jews as *the* people whom imperial aspirants cannot afford to ignore. He consequently placed in the mouth of Pilate a teaching that was his alone—namely, that the pursuit of empire requires a "noble scorn" for the Jews. His *homage* to Pilate thus involves a bit of creative ventriloquy and more than a bit of indirect self-congratulation.

Nietzsche's portrayal of Pilate thus affords us a productive insight into his own designs on empire. Here we see, in fact, that his admiration for the Roman Empire was inextricably linked to his reservations about the Jews—precisely as he insisted in the "polemical" passages cited above from *On the Genealogy of Morals*. He imagined himself to have inherited Pilate's problem, for he, too, wished to pursue the greater glory of empire while granting the Jews their due. Yet he was not in a position to avail himself of Pilate's supposed solution to this problem. Part of his concern was historical in nature. The advanced decay of European culture had amplified the comparative advantage of the Jews in strength and spirit. Whereas Pilate is applauded for not "tak[ing] a Jewish affair *seriously*," Nietzsche allows that he *must* "take into account the Jews" (*BGE*, 251). Giving the Jews their due thus required him to bestow upon them the (comparative) honors they deserved.

Another part of his concern was strategic in nature. As we have seen, Pilate is reported by Nietzsche to have subscribed to the principle "one Jew more or less." This means that Pilate feared neither the Jews nor the fledgling Christ cult as threats to the mighty empire. According to Nietzsche, however, this was a strategic mistake, for the Jews were ultimately responsible for the demise of the empire (*GM*, I:16). Pilate's underestimation of the Jews and early Christians, compounded by similar miscalculations by other imperial functionaries, thus rendered the empire vulnerable to those "cunning, stealthy, invisible, anemic vampires" who eventually "drained" the empire of its vitality (*A*, 59). Pilate's stolid indifference toward the Jews may have been an expression of Roman "nobility," but it was also a strategic blunder. Champions of empire, Nietzsche has learned, cannot afford the luxury of indifference toward the Jews.

Nietzsche did not take lightly the repeated failures of "Rome" in its struggles with "Judea." With Europe plunged into the throes of pandemic decay, the relative strength of the Jews was greater and more obvious than ever before. Active measures needed to be taken to ensure their smooth assimilation into the new empire. In fact, if their strength and spirit could be productively transfused into the new empire, then he could claim for himself an impressive double victory. He would have succeeded not only in neutralizing the most formidable opponent to the consolidation of imperial power in the history of Western civilization, but also in harnessing the spirit of the Jews for the task of rejuvenating European culture. Rather than wage yet another losing skirmish in the ongoing battle between "Rome" and "Judea," he consequently proposed what appears to be a truce of sorts, whereby Jews and Europeans might collaborate toward mutually beneficial cultural goals. After all, he surmised, Europe needed an infusion of spirit and the Jews needed a home.[25] He thus offered to broker a deal that would satisfy the needs of both parties.

But Nietzsche admired Pilate not only for his indifference to matters of infra-imperial import. He also endorsed Pilate's skeptical position vis-à-vis truth. As we recall, he commends Pilate for contributing to the

New Testament the "only saying *that has value* — one which is its criticism, even its *annihilation*: 'What is truth?'" (*A*, 46). In this light, we should hardly expect Nietzsche to have been overly concerned to convey the literal or complete truth about his plans for the Jews. He reaches out to the Jews, moreover, in a book whose title — *Beyond Good and Evil* — leaves little to the imagination. It seems to me, in fact, that he attempted to solve the problem he inherited from Pilate by joining the latter's two key insights. That is, Nietzsche lies to his readers (and perhaps to himself) about his plans to give the Jews their due. His proposal of a truce between "Rome" and "Judea" masks a veiled wish to energize "Rome" and neutralize "Judea" by means of European assimilation. His overtures to the Jews are therefore strategic, although not exclusively so, and they are consistent with his more enduring suspicions of the Jews as the enemies of empire.

By attributing to Nietzsche the dissemination of a strategic lie, I do not mean to portray him as an amoral, Machiavellian schemer. Truth be told, he was nowhere near as cold and calculating as he pretended; his legendary bravado was mostly false. In fact, his admiration for the Jews, and his offer to them of a central place in his new European order, were almost certainly genuine.[26] But he does not tell the whole story about what *he* stood to gain from the European homecoming he promised to arrange for them. In particular, he does not disclose that he feared the Jews at least as much as he needed them. Nor does he reveal that he anticipated their political neutralization at least as eagerly as he welcomed their contribution to the spiritual renewal of Europe. Nor does he share with them his belief that they would finally be purged of their "priestly" taint only when fully assimilated into his new empire. Against the backdrop of his designs on empire, his fundamental ambivalence toward the Jews appears in much sharper relief. His admiration for the Jews of modern Europe is mitigated by his suspicions of their aversion to empire, which they have inherited, he believes, from their "priestly" forebears. He consequently resorts to a subterfuge, which was designed to assimilate the Jews while simultaneously neutralizing the threat they posed to his empire. He needed the Jews to cooperate with him, but he needed even more for them not to oppose him.[27] He consequently arranged what one scholar has called "a gentle final solution."[28]

The Noble Scorn of a Roman?

On the face of it, Nietzsche's plans for the Jews may seem harmless, and perhaps even humane. He devised what appears to be an ingenious so-

lution to a vexing political problem. He did so, moreover, not by deni-
grating the Jews and consigning them to a ghettoized existence, but by
reserving for them a place of honor in the new European order.²⁹ As
"the strongest, toughest, and purest race now living in Europe" (*BGE*,
251), the Jews could reasonably be expected to distribute their excess
spirit to the enervated nation-states of late modern Europe. In exchange
for this donation, they would acquire a permanent home amid grateful
European neighbors.

Nietzsche is justly praised by scholars for his appreciation of the Jews
and his (relatively) sensitive attunement to their political plight in late
nineteenth-century Europe.³⁰ He is also justly applauded for his untimely criticisms of the destructive, decadent instincts at work in the
parallel careers of anti-Semitism and European nationalism. Let us
grant, then, that the intentions that informed his plans for the Jews
were more or less charitable. But on what factual basis were these intentions formed? Whence his *understanding* of the modern Jews whose
cause he presumed to champion? This question is important, for a credible promise of homecoming on his part would necessarily presuppose
his intimate knowledge of the Jews. Indeed, the difference between the
successful *assimilation* of the Jews into the new empire and the *elimination* of the Jews as an identifiable people or nation would have rested in
large part on the depth and acuity of Nietzsche's understanding of
them. In order to serve effectively as their patron in the new European
order, he would have needed to possess a firm grasp of their needs and
interests. That he vaunted his own understanding of the Jews is clear,
for he claimed to know, even better than they, what they wanted. How,
then, did he come to place his finger on the pulse of European Jewry?

Here it becomes clear that Nietzsche's claims to an enlightened cosmopolitanism were often exaggerated. In many respects, in fact, his understanding of the Jews differed little from those of the anti-Semites,
whom he meant to oppose. For his understanding of the Jews, he drew
liberally from a familiar repertoire of stock prejudices. He described the
Jews as asocial wanderers, cheaters in the grand game of cultural advancement, falsifiers of nature, resentful spoilers of empire, cunning
necromancers, blazers of dark paths, histrionic illusionists, and so on.³¹
While it is true that he fastened many of these epithets to the "priestly"
Jews of the Second Temple period, it is also true that he apportioned a
derivative, residual measure of "priestliness" to modern Jews. Although
he praised the Jews of modern Europe for their resiliency, pluck, inge-
nuity, and perseverance, he also traced the habituation of these virtues
to the extraordinary conditions engendered by the original "slave revolt
in morality," which he associates with the "falsification of nature" perpetrated by the "priestly" Jews (*A*, 24).

Modern Jews have traveled an impressive distance (both literally and figuratively) from their ancestors, but they remain implicated nonetheless in the subversive legacy of hatred and resentment.[32] As evidence of the "priestly" inheritance of modern Jews, Nietzsche cites their otherwise inexplicable weakness of will. They could master Europe, but they choose not to do so. They want to assimilate, but they cling to their exclusionary customs. They long to cease their wandering, but they remain nomadic. They wish to prevail "under favorable conditions," but they are accustomed to prevailing "even better" "under the worst conditions" (*BGE*, 251). They seek to denounce the "decadent instincts" that they have pretended to serve, but they remain reliant on the "power" they have "divined" in (and harvested from) these "instincts" (*A*, 24). They have become strong *not* as a consequence of their own direct volition, but as a consequence of their reaction to the conditions of crisis created by their "priestly" apostasy from nature. They have secured for themselves an elite status among modern nations and peoples, but only by observing an alternative standard of nobility. Precisely what made them attractive to him was attained by means that he categorically abhorred. Hence Nietzsche's inevitable caveat when complimenting the Jews of modern Europe: They have made themselves strong, *but only at the expense of arresting the advance of European civilization as a whole*.

Despite his lingering suspicions of their counter-imperial tendencies, Nietzsche did not hate the Jews. As we have seen, in fact, he candidly acknowledged his dependence on the Jews to infuse his empire with its animating spirit and strength. And although his plans for their homecoming might have spelled disaster for the Jews, it would be facile to conclude that he simply wished for them to dissolve without a trace into the mix of his new empire. No one was more cognizant than he of the continued need in Europe for the strength and spirit embodied by the Jews. What he *really* wanted was for the Jews to assimilate, quietly and enthusiastically, *and* to continue to observe those fructifying cultural practices that had endowed them with their superlative strength and spirit. Nietzsche did not hate the Jews, but he *did* fear them. And he feared them, in large part, because he did not understand them.

Nietzsche's ignorance of the Jews was no accident, moreover, for it also sustained the avowed "immoralism" of his imperial enterprise. To see modern Jews as fellow Europeans, who have borne unmistakably human costs for their endurance as a people, was impossible for him. To do so would have not only placed greater responsibility on the "good Europeans" to match the spirit and strength of the Jews, but also complicated his plan to use the Jews to secure the cultural foundation of his empire. Here, in fact, we encounter the limits of his celebrated "immoralism." Nietzsche may have possessed the imagination for empire, but he altogether lacked the stomach for it. If he were as cold and calculating as he insisted, then he presumably would have had no need to mythologize (and thus depersonalize) the Jews. Were he the imperial lawgiver he pretended to be, he would have been able to assess the potential contributions to his empire of the *real* Jews. But Nietzsche was no Pilate. He could not muster the "noble scorn of a Roman." He may have admired the Roman Empire, but he could not sustain in himself its enabling indifference to human suffering. He consequently figured the Jews as a mythic people, strangers to both Europe and modernity, for whom loss was either unthinkable (owing to their superfluous reserves of spirit) or fairly compensated by their new home in Europe. His ignorance of the Jews was therefore a *willed* ignorance, without which he could not have attempted to execute his plan for pan-European integration.

Nietzsche's willed ignorance of the Jews also reveals the limits of his commitment to empire. Had he acknowledged the Jews not as a mythic people, but as recognizably human and inextricably enmeshed in the complexities of the modern world, they immediately would have commanded his allegiance. Had he not fixed the Jews against a mythic, "orientalizing" backdrop, he might have concluded (or at least considered) that they have resisted European assimilation *for good reasons* — perhaps for the very reasons that he summons in conjunction with his diagnosis of late modern Europe. He might have determined that the Jews made themselves strong by refusing the blandishments of imperial consolidation, thereby inoculating themselves against the decay that must invariably follow. He might have realized, in short, that he had misreckoned the European legacy of the Roman Empire and overestimated the spiritual resiliency of European culture. He might then have been obliged to acknowledge the Jews, and not the "good Europeans," as the modern people best suited to birth the kind of cultural empire that he hopefully envisioned. A true champion of empire would have unflinchingly appraised the peoples and nations at hand and cast his lot with the strongest amongst them. Indeed, a true champion of empire would not have been blinded by nostalgic attachments to nations, peoples, or cultures in decline. But in the end, Nietzsche was not a champion of empire. He was a champion of Europe, of *his* Europe, the Europe inspired by Caesar and periodically refreshed by the fortuitous appearances of Cesare Borgia, Napoleon, Goethe, Mozart, and Beethoven — a Europe in which the Jews were still regarded as strangers. It is only because this Europe (supposedly) flourished under imperial rule that he pins his current hopes on a renewal of empire.

By all rights, Nietzsche should have admired the Jews above all other peoples, races, nations, and cultures. According to his own interpretation, the Jews experimented on themselves with no concern for public opinion, conventional morality, natural law, or established thresholds for the tolerance of pain. They consequently made themselves strong through self-imposed disciplines, and they ventured well beyond good and evil in the process. They affirmed their fate and turned an unhappy destiny to their advantage. They wrought health from decadence. They steadfastly refused the fads and fashions of modernity. Everything that did not kill them made them stronger. Their achievement as a people was strikingly familiar, in fact, to the triumph that Nietzsche claims for himself in *Ecce Homo*. Like him, the Jews *became what they are*, which is the only reliable proof of strength and health.[33]

In short, the Jews have fulfilled every prescription that Nietzsche issued in association with his advocacy of "great politics" and the restoration of "noble" ideals. Every prescription, that is, save one. The Jews have not acknowledged "Europe" as the proper site of cultural advancement, which means that they have not endorsed his imperial plan for the renascence of noble values. He consequently feels obliged to malign the cultural achievements of the Jews, blaming them for initiating the malaise that has finally crippled Europe in the nineteenth century. In fact, he suggests, they have pursued their own advantage at the expense of a rebirth of European civilization. Rather than directly promote the ascendancy of "noble" values, they have indirectly secured nobility for themselves, by pretending to promote values of decadence and servility (*GS*, 361).

Here Nietzsche reaches the internal limits of his own political thinking. Ideally, he might have learned from the Jews and their alternative, extra-imperial pursuit of cultural advancement. Although they did not succeed in constituting themselves as an imperial power, they also never succumbed to the decadence that Nietzsche's own analysis indicates must invariably follow in the wake of imperial demise. They also outlasted the various empires that have been raised and razed over the erratic course of Western civilization. Indeed, their failure to experience either imperial grandeur or post-imperial devastation suggests that they have learned to operate productively outside the boom-and-bust cycle of European cultural advancement. But this was an opportunity squandered. Nietzsche's allegiance to a distinctly European culture, unified under the banner of empire, turned out to be non-negotiable. He was prepared to face the uncertain future only if fortified by the comfort he derived from the distant past. There he stood; he could do no other.

Nietzsche's ambivalence toward the Jews thus strikes to the very heart of his imperial aspirations. Despite his bold, Europhilic swagger, he feared that *they* may have succeeded in formulating the optimal strategy for promoting cultural advancement in late modernity. Perhaps their preference for the consolidated vitality of a well-defined people expressed an extra-imperial wisdom to which Europe still aspired. Perhaps, as their epic history suggests, the Jews are simply more mature than their European (i.e., Christian) counterparts, closer to nature and more intimately familiar with those non-negotiable realities that Nietzsche claimed to honor. Simply by virtue of their presence in Europe, and the basis they provided for cultural comparison, the Jews stood as painful reminders of the depths of European decay.

In the end, Nietzsche's imperial aspirations turn out to be as anachronistic and nostalgic as they initially appeared. The Europe he revered had passed, and it would not be revived by even the most extreme or inventive of measures. More to the point, his fascination with empire, especially on the model of Rome, reveals the distinctly retrospective orientation of his political thinking. Notwithstanding his familiar rhetoric of novelty, creation, revaluation, and rebirth, he is essentially a reactive political thinker, responding to the new challenges of the late modern epoch with proposals recycled from premodern Europe. Here again, he appears as a largely impotent transitional figure, born either too early or too late to place his stamp on a Europe in which he might finally feel at home.[34]

Notes

1. For an illuminating account of Hitler's relationship with Elisabeth Förster-Nietzsche, see Ben Macintyre, *Forgotten Fatherland: The Search for Elisabeth Nietzsche* (New York: Farrar, Straus, Giroux, 1992), chap. 8.

2. I am indebted here to Steven E. Aschheim's excellent study *The Nietzsche Legacy in Germany 1890–1990* (Berkeley: University of California Press, 1992), esp. chaps. 8–9.

3. Ibid. 232–55.

4. I take my bearings here from an observation by Jacques Derrida: "Even if the intention of one of the signatories or shareholders in the huge 'Nietzsche Corporation' had nothing to do with it, it cannot be entirely fortuitous that the discourse bearing his name in society, in accordance with civil laws and editorial norms, has served as a legitimating reference for ideologues. There is nothing absolutely contingent about the fact that the only political regime to have *effectively* brandished his name as a major and official banner was Nazi." "Otobiographies: The Teaching of Nietzsche and the Politics of the Proper Name," in *The Ear of the Other: Otobiography, Transference, Translation*, ed. Christie V. MacDonald, trans. Peggy Kamuf and Avital Ronell (New York: Schocken Books, 1985), 30–31.

5. For a fine account of Nietzsche's shifting attitudes about the foreign policy of Bismarck's Reich, see Peter Bergmann, *Nietzsche, "The Last Antipolitical*

German" (Bloomington: Indiana University Press, 1987), chap. 6. Bergmann suggests that it is "no coincidence" that "Nietzsche embraced the concept of *grosse Politik* precisely at the moment when Germany was suddenly creating her colonial empire" (163).

6. See Macintyre, *Forgotten Fatherland*, 114–18.

7. With the exception of occasional emendations, I rely throughout this essay on Walter Kaufmann's translations/editions of Nietzsche's writings for Viking Press/Random House (see Bibliography for full citations).

8. In his staging of a "conversation between two old 'patriots,'" Nietzsche places into the mouth of one "patriot" a thinly veiled criticism of Bismarck's Reich: "This is the age of the masses: they grovel on their bellies before anything massive. *In politicis*, too. A statesman who piles up for them another tower of Babel, they call 'great'; what does it matter that we, more cautious and reserved, do not yet abandon the old faith that only a great thought can give a deed or cause greatness?" (*BGE*, 241).

9. For an account of the historical events that led Nietzsche to focus on Europe as the site of his empire, see Bergmann, *Nietzsche*, 162–66.

10. Here I am in agreement with and indebted to Yirmayahu Yovel, who explains that "[i]n place of nationalism in its various guises, Nietzsche favored Europeanism as an ideal—not in today's basically economic form but as the product of 'a grand politics' that would overcome all petty, aggressive nationalisms and set forth a supranational culture fused with a 'Dionysian' quality and a 'revaluated' sense of life." *Dark Riddle: Hegel, Nietzsche, and the Jews* (University Park: Penn State Press, 1998), 133.

11. In explaining his disgust with "the 'final Wagner' and his *Parsifal* music," Nietzsche alludes to Rome in a distinctly disapproving tone: "Is this still German?—You still stand at the gate, perplexed? Think! What you hear is *Rome—Rome's faith without the text*" (*BGE*, 256). More pointedly, he bids his reader to "consider to whom one bows down in Rome itself today, as if they were the epitome of all the highest values—and not only in Rome but over almost half the earth, everywhere that man has become tame or desires to become tame: *three Jews*, as is known, and *one Jewess*" (*GM*, I:16).

12. He remarks on one occasion that "All of us are no longer material [*Material*] for a society" (*GS*, 356).

13. Nietzsche reprises this arboreal imagery in *The Antichrist*, where he identifies "the Jewish instinct" as the "soil out of which [Christianity] grew" (*A*, 24). His explicit appeal to the arboreal imagery of genealogy complicates any attempt to limit his anti-Jewish animus to the "priestly" period in the history of the Jews (see Yovel, *Dark Riddle*, 152–58). If the "trunk" of this "tree" is "Jewish hatred," then presumably all of its fruits and outgrowths will be tainted to some extent by this hatred. This would mean that Nietzsche's enmity for "Judea" extends not only to Christians (ibid., 151–52), but also to those modern Jews who fall in the lineage of the "priestly" betrayal of the "kingly" people of Israel.

14. According to Weaver Santaniello, "[Nietzsche's] ambivalent views toward priestly-prophetic Judaism, especially the bitter and shrill tone in the *Genealogy* (1887) . . . are neither . . . unequivocal, careless, unguarded, [nor] irre-

sponsible" (*Nietzsche, God, and the Jews: His Critique of Judeo-Christianity in Relation to the Nazi Myth* [Albany: State University of New York Press, 1994], 140). See also Walter Kaufmann, *Nietzsche: Philosopher, Psychologist, Anti-christ*, 4th ed. (Princeton: Princeton University Press, 1974), 298–300.

15. Yovel maintains that Nietzsche's enmity is directed only at the "priestly" Jews of the Second Temple period. His anti-Jewish sentiments, Yovel believes, therefore do not touch the Diaspora Jews or the Jews of modern Europe: "He distinguished three different modes or phases in Judaism, and expressed admiration for two of them: for biblical Judaism and for the Jews of the later Diaspora. His harsh critique targets exclusively the middle phase, the Second Temple 'priestly' Judaism (as he calls it) which began the 'slave revolution' in morality—namely, Christianity. Nietzsche's true target is Christianity: so much so, that often he reads the ideas and even the phrases of the New Testament directly into what he derogates under the name of Judaism" (*Dark Riddle*, xiii). Similar (and similarly restrictive) interpretations of Nietzsche's anti-Jewish invective are advanced by Michael Duffy and Willard Mittelman in "Nietzsche's Attitudes Toward the Jews," *Journal of the History of Ideas* 49 (1988): 302–3; and Santaniello, *Nietzsche, God, and the Jews*, 140. As I attempt to show, however, this influential distinction between "priestly" Jews and modern Jews is a good bit neater than Nietzsche's own distinction. In fact, his reservations about modern Jews derive from his suspicion that they continue in some attenuated form the signature resentment of their "priestly" ancestors.

16. Yovel thus suggests that "Nietzsche sometimes exploits an anti-Semitic image in order to derogate his opponents by attributing a 'Jewish' quality to them" (*Dark Riddle*, 150).

17. Santaniello in *Nietasche, God, and the Jews* thus maintains that "Nietzsche's views were formed by, and should be interpreted within, the theological and political categories that preexisted in Germany. . . . As a minority who was an obscure author, Nietzsche was essentially a powerless voice opposing very prominent leaders" (140). Santaniello mitigates the force of this claim, however, by immediately noting that some anti-Semites in fact "regarded Nietzsche as an 'insolent' enemy and attacked his later works" (140).

18. With respect to Nietzsche's allusion to the possible mastery of Europe by the Jews, Yovel remarks, "His strategy, here again, is to play with his readers' expectations and prejudices, producing a surprise effect that reverses the anti-Semitic stereotype's intention and unsettles its owner" (*Dark Riddle*, 175).

19. Yovel thus attributes to Nietzsche a seemingly superhuman capacity for psychological compartmentalization: "Nietzsche avoids carrying over his negative analysis of ancient Judaism into his attitude toward contemporary Jews. This methodological *epoché*, a self-disciplinary move (and a hallmark of his uncommon psychology), allows Nietzsche to be—at the same time, and with the same passionate ardor—both an anti anti-Semite and a critic of ancient Judaism as the cradle of Christianity" (ibid., 118). By dint of a successful act of "self-overcoming," Nietzsche has gained control of his anti-Jewish sentiments and may now turn them to his own rhetorical advantage. Yovel thus explains that although Nietzsche "has overcome his youthful anti-Semitic 'disease,' he has not erased its traces from memory, but uses them in the war he now wages against

Christianity" (ibid., 152). Almost immediately, however, Yovel qualifies his account, thereby suggesting that Nietzsche may not have gained full control over his anti-Semitism after all: "Possibly his self-overcoming enabled Nietzsche to use the traces of his conquered anti-Semitism without allowing them to repoison his mind. Yet this is a dangerous game. Nietzsche is playing with fire here, both with himself and with his audience" (ibid., 152).

20. Registering his apparent agreement with Nietzsche on this point, Yovel concludes that Nietzsche's enmity for the "priestly" Jews of the Second Temple period actually confirms the success of his campaign to "overcome" the anti-Semitic prejudices of his day: "Nietzsche has freed himself of anti-Semitism. . . . His scorn for one period of Judaism and admiration for another testify to a certain maturity and/or freedom of mind gained in dealing with the Jews. A person who has not overcome anti-Semitism will often hesitate to express even fair criticism of the Jews" (ibid., 163).

21. Although Pilate appears in all four Gospels, the extended account that Nietzsche cites here appears only in the Gospel of John. The "*ecce homo*" passage is found in John 19:5.

22. Pilate poses this "redeeming" question in John 18:38.

23. Nietzsche's admiration for the slogan "One Jew more or less" thus recalls his nostalgia for "a freer, more generous, *more Roman* conception of law when the Twelve Tables of Rome decreed it a matter of indifference how much or how little the creditor cut off in such cases: '*si plus minusve secuerunt, ne fraude esto*'" (*GM*, II:6).

24. For example, all four Gospels attest to Pilate's disputation of the guilt of Jesus (Matthew 27:23; Mark 15:14; Luke 23:13–16; John 18:38). In the Gospel of John, Pilate volunteers to honor (what he takes to be) the Jewish custom of releasing one prisoner to commemorate the Passover (John 18:39). Despite his belief in the innocence of Jesus, he honors the crowd's request that he instead release Barabbas (John 18:40). My point here is not to exonerate Pilate, but to reveal the extent to which Nietzsche's portrayal of him deviates from that which is found in the Gospels.

25. Yovel captures the gist of Nietzsche's solution to the problem of the Jews in Europe when he describes it as a "*creative assimilation*, whereby the Jews are secularized, excel in all European matters, and serve as catalysts in a new revolution, this time a curative, Dionysian revolution—that will overcome Christian culture and the 'modern ideas' born of it" (*Dark Riddle*, 129). As I explain later in this essay, this description of Nietzsche's plan does not account for the lingering influence of his anti-Jewish sentiments. His plan for "creative assimilation" is ultimately faulted by his belief that he must neutralize at all costs the political opposition that he attributes to the Jews—lest "Judea" triumph once again over "Rome." Nietzsche's plan for "creative assimilation," I believe, places the Jews at risk of disapppearing as a distinct people, race, or nation. On this point, it is instructive to compare Yovel's remarks on "creative assimilation" with Hubert Cancik's account of the "gentle final solution," in "'Mongols, Semites and the Pure-Bred Greeks': Nietzsche's Handling of the Racial Doctrines of his Time," in *Nietzsche and Jewish Culture*, ed. Jacob Golomb (London and New York: Routledge, 1997), 65–67.

26. I say "almost certainly" because it is not clear to what extent Nietzsche is reliant on the Jews for the spirit that will animate his empire. Perhaps their role is far more catalytic—and therefore transient—than he cares to admit. He may need the Jews only for the founding of the empire, at which point the "good Europeans" will take over and rule.

27. I am indebted here to Josef Simon, who deftly exposes the operation of Nietzsche's resentment (or "counter-resentment") of the Jews: "Anyone who attempts to experience this particularity as an outsider inevitably finds that he has no access to this intellectual spirit. Rather, the experience that one has here is of the *other*, of an alienating way of behaving that calls forth a counterresentment" ("Nietzsche on Judaism and Europe," in *Nietzsche and Jewish Culture*, ed. Jacob Golomb [London and New York: Routledge, 1997], 107).

28. Cancik, "'Mongols, Semites," 65–67. Cancik describes Nietzsche's "solution to the problem" as "tasteful," as "precisely that solution acceptable to an intellectual aristocracy" (66). Cancik later remarks, "In this elevated, fine, tasteful, gentle anti-Semitism, a thematic communality between Wagner and Nietzsche reveals itself, one going deeper than any disagreement in other areas, whether personal, musical, or religious" (67).

29. Yovel offers the following charitable interpretation of the "creative assimilation" that Nietzsche has in mind for the Jews of modern Europe: "The Jews are thereby called to give up their peculiar, separate historical identity and contribute their value-creating power to a common European effort, *no longer as members of the Jewish religion, but as graduates of the Jewish existential and historical experience*" (*Dark Riddle* 176–77).

30. Santaniello goes so far as to claim that "Nietzsche was fighting against the social persecution that was being launched against the Jews in the latter third of the nineteenth century" (*Nietzsche, God, and the Jews*, 144).

31. Yovel furnishes a somewhat different list of the "negative images of Judaism" that "continue to reside in Nietzsche's mind" (*Dark Riddle*, 151–52). As we have seen, Yovel also believes that Nietzsche has "overcome" these "negative images," thereby gaining (nearly) full control of these stereotypes, such that "he radically reverses their course and subjects them to his own rhetorical needs" (150).

32. Notwithstanding his optimistic appraisal of Nietzsche's labors of "self-overcoming," Yovel concedes that Nietzsche continues to link modern Jews to their "priestly" forebears: "Diaspora Jews . . . arrived on the doorstep of the modern world *mostly* recovered from their ancestors' *ressentiment*" (*Dark Riddle*, 188, emphasis added). Obviously, a great deal rests on what Yovel means by describing Diaspora Jews as "mostly recovered from their ancestors' *ressentiment*." However, his implication that their "recovery" is not yet complete is sufficient to warrant my emphasis on Nietzsche's lingering reservations about modern Jews. If European Jewry inherits even the smallest quantum of priestly resentment, then Nietzsche is bound by his own account of Jewish history to extend his suspicions to modern Jews, even as he extends to them a welcoming hand. My hunch here is that Nietzsche was willing to view their "recovery" as complete only as a result (and not as a condition) of their assimilation into his pan-European empire.

33. I am indebted here to Sander Gilman's fascinating thesis that Nietzsche gradually came to identify himself with the Jews, in "Heine, Nietzsche, and the Idea of the Jew," in *Nietzsche and Jewish Culture*, ed. Jacob Golomb (London and New York: Routledge, 1997), 76–100. According to Gilman, "The function of the 'Jews' in all of their stereotypical representation within Nietzsche's world was to externalize many of the qualities associated with Nietzsche's psychic life" (80).

34. I wish to thank the editors of this volume for their instructive comments on earlier drafts of this essay.

9

A Question of Responsibility: Nietzsche with Hölderlin at War, 1914–1946

Stanley Corngold and Geoffrey Waite

Nietzsche, Zeppelins, and poisoned-gas go ill together.
But Great Indra! One may envy Nietzsche a little; think of
being so illusive, so mercurial, as to be first swallowed
whole, then coughed up, and still remain a mystery!
—Hart Crane, 1918

What to do with someone who says
Hölderlin, and means Himmler?
—Hans Magnus Enzensberger, 1960

1.

For every person who reads Friedrich Nietzsche as "the step-grand-father of fascism" (Leo Strauss)[1] or German National Socialism's "indirect apologist" (Georg Lukács),[2] at least two others embrace him as a man of the Left: whether allegedly for having "*made himself* fascist in order better to fight fascism" (François Laruelle)[3] or for his deconstruction and rejection of the moral and conceptual preconditions of fascism or, of a different thing, national socialism. The theoretical question of Nietzsche's "responsibility" for this apparently contradictory range of opinions subtends every possible historical question about his "influence" on, or "responsibility" for, all or any imaginable states of affairs that were or are to come, including Italian Fascism or German National Socialism *inter alia inter pares*. No local application of "what Nietzsche means" (George Morgan)[4] should ignore this point, which turns on Nietzsche's hidden but programmatic interest in producing such variability. His program may be something we will always be in the dark about; nevertheless, it is clear that the range of opinions that he produces cannot be structured as a contradiction—e.g., Left versus Right. It presents itself as a single unacknowledged consensus founded on the readiness to avoid the question of Nietzsche's responsibility for this general misreading. He appears to have anticipated it, programming it into his illocutions to have surreptitious perlocutionary effect in whatever historical conjuncture it might reemerge. But to what specific end?

As a post- or pre-Enlightenment thinker, Nietzsche designed the imagined "free" and "plural" range of opinions about his work so that deeper, never explicitly stated, esoteric doctrines would be incorporated by readers sub rosa, beneath the faculties of reason ever to perceive or to know them. It is likely that these are then marked out by the more or less exoteric categories such as "will to power" (*Wille zur Macht*) and intellectual and social "order of rank" (*Rangordnung*) yet in a sense so drastic as to elude understanding by the current hegemony of pluralist ideology and humanism. This very impossibility is partly an effect of Nietzsche's commitment to a rhetorical and stylistic esotericism. On the one hand, he wrote openly that the exoteric-esoteric distinction has existed in every historical society grounded (to his mind, very properly so) on order of rank. Esotericism, he continued, is well known to virtually all major philosophers globally, giving the following as examples: "Indians as well as Greeks, Persians, and Muslims, in short, wherever one believed in an order of rank, *not* in equality and equal rights."[5] On the other hand, what he never said was how he intended to implement "order of rank" esoterically, with his own German prose. In his programmatic but unpublished early essay "The Greek State" (1872), he explicitly promoted not merely the modern version of what he called "slavery" (*Sklaverei*) but the necessity for its "conscious or unconscious" acceptance by "slaves" or "workers" in their expropriated "surplus labor" (*Mehrarbeit*). At the same time, he recognized the necessity for an "esoteric writing" appropriate to "the esoteric doctrine of the relation between the State and genius [*Geheimlehre vom Zusammenhang zwischen Staat und Genius*]."[6] And by "State" he had any state in his sights.

Nietzsche's deep tripartite knowledge — of classical rhetoric, Schopenhauer's doctrine of unconscious Will, and Wagner's translation of that doctrine into music and cultural politics — was never merely thematic. He meant to put this knowledge to work as an effect of style with delayed effect, his *actio in distans*. Like Machiavelli, Nietzsche was "a captain without an army," who had to "recruit it only by means of books."[7] This means he wrote not for his own times but only to have maximum possible and subcutaneous effect in the future, under the sign, as he put it, "*sub specie trecentorum annorum*."[8] "To be ignited in 300 years — that is my desire for fame."[9] He also spoke (in quasi-Darwinian terms) of millennia, producing his own version of a thousand-year Reich: "The age of experiments! The claims of Darwin are to be tested — through experiments [*Versuche*]! As is the evolution of higher organisms out of the lowest. Experiments must be conducted for millennia! Raise apes into men!"[10] Hence, historical questions posed in the form "Nietzsche, godfather of fascism?" cannot fully embrace Nietzsche's transhistorical adherence to order of rank and its subliminal persistence qua will to power.

Unlike most of his many readers ("Nietzschean" or not), Nietzsche was willing to take responsibility. *For everything*: *carte blanche* (so why not also Hitler?). He believed that he had covered his transhistorical esoteric tracks well enough to avoid historical exoteric detection. So in his 1883 notebooks he wrote, for his eyes only, "Wie leicht nimmt man die Last einer Entschuldig[ung] auf sich, so lange man nichts zu verantworten hat. *Aber ich bin verantwortlich* [How lightly one takes the burden of an ex[cuse] upon oneself, so long as one has to be responsible for nothing. *But I am responsible*]."[11] And *verantwortlich* means not merely "responsible" but "accountable." This obviously would include what would have been for him—logically, and personal scruples and matters of "taste" apart, and given that he wrote "beyond good and evil," and from the perspective of the "eternal return of the same"—the merely second-order and epiphenomenal matter of, say, "Nietzsche and fascism."

2.

Nonetheless, we will attempt the assigned task—one less theoretical than historical. The question "Nietzsche: Godfather of Fascism?" (understood as his influence on, or responsibility for, fascism or national socialism, their antecedents and their still continuing legacy) can be profiled by comparing the function of the philosopher Nietzsche in Hitlerian Germany with another figure: the poet Hölderlin. Nietzsche's reception in Nazi Germany has been meticulously detailed.[12] In spite of many "reception histories" of Hölderlin, there is no comparable analysis of his reception in the same period.[13] But to date unrecognized is the extent to which Nietzsche was continually viewed in association with Hölderlin—a manner of national and polemical thinking that began with Nietzsche himself in boarding school days and found its definitive culmination in Heidegger's political ontology. To the very end, this nexus remained a basic resource of the Nazi cultural and exegetic idiom.

The depth of German commitment to the Heraclitian notion that "war is the father of all things" ought not to be over- or underestimated.[14] It certainly extended from the experience of the trenches in World War I deep into academic, scholarly discourse thereafter. The "war to end all wars," for example, not only killed and maimed millions, and intensified animosities at home and abroad, it also brought people together, often in strange, previously unknown alliances. Links of solidarity were forged that otherwise would have taken decades of historical experience and intermittent struggles to form. Within four years, in the mud and blood of the trenches, a spiritual world emerged that was avid to form itself into permanent and dynamic social structures and institutions.[15]

Literary critics, many of whom continued to publish and have distinguished careers at German universities after World War II (East and West), bought lock-stock-and barrel into the notion of war as the greatest single factor determining the destiny of all nations, but especially Germany.[16] Hölderlin, for example, was continually read through the lens of Zarathustra's indeed memorable, proto-Schmittian thesis in *On War and a Nation at War* [*Vom Krieg und Kriegsvolke*] that "the good war makes every issue holy" and of his numerous rhetorical questions: "What good is a long life?" "What warrior wants to be spared!"[17]

The topic "Hölderlin and Nietzsche" — to state this with a provisional generality — involved a constellation of themes of longing, rage, and struggle for a purer, divinized Germany, in which Hölderlin's yearning figures as the precursor to Nietzsche's praxis, Hölderlin's "Thought" is father to Nietzsche's/Hitler's "Deed."[18] In saying this, we want to stress that at different historical conjunctures and in different Nazi political camps every single one of these terms would be differently accented. Nevertheless, a remark made from the sanctuary of retrospection after the war by Ernst Barthel, the former Nazi and friend of Elisabeth Förster-Nietzsche, secures a central thematic strand:

> There is probably no more tragic drama of intellectual development than Nietzsche's trajectory from the yearning of Hölderlin to the Machiavellian philosophy of Italian leaders of mercenaries, Bismarckian power of the fist, and mass interest in so-called "great" politics.[19]

"Tragic," perhaps, but many writers writing during the Third Reich did not fail to see this development as exemplary. And in this dual-mirror relation, conversely, Hölderlin was always to some extent "Nietzscheanized" (to employ an ugly word for an uglier thing).

The topic of Hölderlin-Nietzsche attracted academics and other intellectuals immediately after World War I, as university life to some extent normalized. Outspoken nationalists (including especially nationalist students) readopted the old theme as their own.[20] In 1920, a journalist by the name of Georg Mönius, in an article entitled simply "Höderlin-Nietzsche," felt it necessary to attack the "*Hakenkreuzler*" who were in the process of desecrating what he considered to be a "noble" topic.[21] Symptomatically for the temper of the times, Mönius did not make clear which "swastikers" he meant—those of Stefan George or Nazism.

Mönius's warning was needed, but was in vain. Even after turning themselves into Nazi Party intellectuals, comparatively neutral academics continued to muse on the Nietzsche-Hölderlin nexus as they had for so long, as if nothing were going on outside their own heads. They did so right through the Nazi seizure of power, the *Gleichschaltung*, the Röhm purge, the camps, *Kristallnacht*, the war, the "final solution," Stalingrad, and the capitulation—and they did not stop after the war ended. During the war the Nietzsche-Hölderlin nexus was also addressed explicitly in the larger public sphere; much of this work was done by teachers and journalists, and it is impossible to ascertain exactly what audience they reached. But all more or less neutral and conscientious scholarship was swamped by essays written by men of the type of one Richard Groeper, who wrote in 1940 in the leading Nazi journal of pedagogy, the *Nationalsozialistisches Bildungswesen*, on "Hölderlin and Nietzsche as Prophets of the Twentieth Century":

> Hölderlin and Nietzsche, astral siblings like Castor and Pollux, casting their luminescence toward the German earth! By their Being and their work they belong together, each dominating and commanding in his own sphere of greatness, invincible and purely German in their completion. With and through them have the eighteenth and the nineteenth centuries given birth to the twentieth, the century that history will one day only be allowed to call German.[22]

The intense interest granted both Nietzsche and Hölderlin for explicitly ideological purposes in the Third Reich probably ought to be considered less the result of a disastrous intellectual drought than the foul usufruct of previous interest, less a travesty than a drift and exacerbation of the way the nexus had already been appropriated by the George Circle among others. In any case, the major elements in the thinking of the nexus recur with variations that respond to the political requirements of the moment: one can recall Alfred Bäumler's appeal in the late thirties to "Nordic Germany, the Germany of Hölderlin and Nietzsche," and Hans Reeder's assertion at the same time that Hölderlin and Nietzsche shared a common "passion for the Empire" and that Hitler was their necessary, "racial fulfillment." Such notions may seem "ironic" (if such a word is allowed) in light of the fact that both Hölderlin and Nietzsche would have been legally sterilized, if not actually killed, during the Third Reich, were they considered to have fallen within the retroactively binding euthanasia laws (July 14, 1933) applicable to the disabled.[23]

3.

It is significant that, with the partial exception of the more sporadic work on a "National" edition of Friedrich Schiller's works,[24] only two major philological projects in philosophy and literature received substantial financial support from the Nazi Party. These were collected editions of Nietzsche and Hölderlin. And while both, though never completed, were produced under relatively little ideological pressure, one very striking distinction between them exists. Work on Nietzsche's first historical-critical edition ceased in 1942. The reasons ranged from methodological and petty personal squabbles among the editors, and financial and personnel shortages caused by the Russian campaign, to high-level dissatisfaction with Nietzsche's views on the Jews, especially after the "final solution" was put into gear. Yet, under the same conditions, work on Hölderlin's first historical-critical edition was begun just a year after Nietzsche's went defunct, in 1943. One rumor about the reasons behind the abandonning of the Nietzsche edition was that Hitler had personally ordered all positive references to the Jews to be omitted.[25] It can be tempting to see symbolism in dates — a temptation to which many in the Third Reich succumbed. Hölderlin died in 1843, Nietzsche was born months later in 1844. In 1943 the centenary of Hölderlin's death was celebrated by countless publications and eulogies and by some three hundred public activities of various kinds spread throughout the greater German Reich. It is important to stress that these activities were officially sanctioned by the National Socialists and were also genuinely popular, independent manifestations of public sentiment. Men like Hanns Johst, who was known to have read passsages from Hölderlin to Hitler on the Führer's birthday, took part. Goebbels presided over the founding of the Hölderlin Society, at which time a wreath in Hitler's name was the first laid on Hölderlin's grave. On the same occasion, Karl Cerff, then director of the so-called *Hauptkulturamt*, reactivated a theme that had been passed down from George to Heidegger. Cerff stressed that it was the soldier-philologist von Hellingrath who had discovered the most German of poets, Friedrich Hölderlin. According to Cerff's laconic and timely formula, "German soldiers have saved Hölderlin's work" and hence the work of "the poet of preparedness for the ultimate sacrifice."[26] It was in this spirit, presumably, that the *Hauptkulturamt* of the Party gave its substantial financial support to Beissner's new critical edition for the occasion.

On the other hand, 1944 was the centenary of Nietzsche's birth. We will be noting Alfred Rosenberg's address at the Nietzsche archives in Weimar at that event, but this was a kind of exception that proves a rule. Nothing even remotely comparable to the excitement surrounding Hölderlin's death was undertaken in Nazi Germany for Nietzsche's birth — neither by the Nazi Party nor by popular demand. In short, Hölderlin's death was more important to all of Germany than Nietzsche's birth. What was behind this?

Nietzsche was undoubtedly more problematic to the Nazis than Hölderlin. If there was any single culture industry in the Third Reich that served a legitimating and hegemonic function unproblematically, it was the poet's work, not that of the philosopher. In Nietzsche's case, no such consensus prevailed. In the recurrent discussion about Nietzsche as the alleged "precursor of Hitler," the assumption persists that the Nietzsche Industry was one of the main, if not the most important, intellectual underpinnings of the Third Reich. Interestingly enough, however, the most monochromatic version of this notion was not propagated by the Nazis themselves. Their view of Nietzsche was in fact deeply divided.

It is relatively easy to show how some Nazis ostensibly "manhandled" Nietzsche. All that is required is to appeal to "the original contexts" that they elided or to other, exoteric texts Nietzsche had written that they suppressed or to more complex readings of the ones they liked. But what is seldom realized is that many of these same, supposedly more differentiated texts and readings had already been used by other Nietzsche scholars inside Nazi Germany — rabid Nazis among them — precisely to discredit Nietzsche. The National Socialist appropriation of Nietzsche was deeply ambivalent and internally contested (much more so than that of Italian Fascism)[27] — conflicted from before the Nazi seizure of power to the bitter cyanide end. Contrary to the assumptions of many Anglo-American and French writers on Nietzsche, Bäumler's was hardly the only game in town. His work, alongside that of other Nazis like Joachim Günther, did indeed try to mediate positively between Nietzsche and National Socialism, though even they occasionally freely admitted the difficulties in doing so.[28] Bäumler's general position can even be characterized, as strange as this may seem, as having tried to "represent a Hitlerism without anti-Semitic racism," using Nietzsche as his main exhibit.[29] Yet other Nazis — Curt von Westernhagen, Christoph Steding, and Heinrich Härtle among them — argued that Nietzsche was not serviceable for Nazi ideology, because he was too pro-French, too anti-German, and even too "philo-Semitic."[30] And often these views — unlike Bäumler's — were published in the official Nazi Party publishing house, as in the case of Härtle, for instance. Westernhagen wrote in his book, *Nietzsche, Jews, Anti-Jews* (1936), that "in the passage-at-arms [*Waffengang*] between the Jewish and the German essence, Nietzsche stood in the ranks of the Jews, out of inclination and calculation, with his heart and his head."[31] According to Steding's massive, 772-page tome, *The Reich and the Disease of European Culture* (1942), which went through four editions in the Third Reich, the problem with Nietzsche was not only his philo-Semitism but also his antistatism and anti-imperialism: Nietzsche belonged in the Second Empire, not the Third.

4.

The substantial uncertainty about Nietzsche in the remarkably heterogeneous state that was Nazi Germany is crucial to remember in light of Heidegger's often repeated claim that his lectures on Nietzsche (and Hölderlin) in the late 1930s and early to mid-forties were somehow forms of "opposition" to the Nazi regime. The widespread fantasy that Nietzsche was the "official" Nazi philosopher—a notion to a great extent accepted today even by Derrida, among others—misconstrues the role actually played by Nietzsche in the 1930s and 40s and the complexity of Fascist and National Socialist hegemony. This oversight may also say quite a lot about the level of insight into political philosophy that has been attained today by the philosophical discourse of poststructuralist and postmodernist Nietzscheanism or Heideggerianism. The accounts of both Derrida and Lacoue-Labarthe, sophisticated and philosophically intriguing at they are, are also simplistic historically and politically. Both philosophers seem to know very little about National Socialism or Fascism as a problem of social history or political praxis, and they rarely if ever cite the major books on the subject by historians or political theorists.[32] Not to understand the contradictory nature of the Nazi appropriation of Nietzsche runs the risk of unwittingly repeating parts of it.

For the Nazis it was not only possible but even desirable to allow apparent "debate" on subjects like "Nietzsche" so as to conceal or control much deeper levels of common interest and ideology. "Divide and conquer" or "annex and rule" was one very basic principle of power in the Third Reich, the hegemonic structure of which is characterized by an inherent potential for instability.[33] Hitler himself knew Nietzsche and Hölderlin pretty much by name only, although he certainly knew them that way. But Hitler was happy to use any name or issue that served his

ends. (That he knew Schopenhauer somewhat better should not be interpreted as any real "influence" on the Führer, given the overdeter-
mined nature of his sources, the most important of which were racist
pamphlets, and so on.) At the same time, however, throughout the
Third Reich and especially as time began to run out on it, Nietzsche's
importance came to be shunted aside by Hölderlin, to the point where it
was not possible to argue between 1933 and 1945 (at least to our
knowledge, it never happened) that Hölderlin was anything but a crucial pillar of support for the entire Nazi project. This is not to say, of
course, that Hölderlin scholarship, too, could not be self-critical (Heidegger's exceedingly intricate vision of Hölderlin remains by far the
most important exhibit). But Nazi scholarship on Hölderlin did not,
could not, and more importantly never sought to critique Hölderlin in
the way that Nietzsche scholarship could, and sometimes openly did,
attack Nietzsche. Certain books written on Hölderlin were criticized for
a variety of reasons. For example, Hildebrandt's major book *Hölderlin:
Philosophy and Poetry*, including its thesis on Hölderlin's yearning for
a "German" god, was taken to task by several critics further to the
Right.[34] And (to his credit, we suppose) a Nietzschean-like Paul Böckmann could even suggest in public that Hölderlin's "Death for the Fatherland" ought to be read in the context of the Napoleonic wars. This
was something very rare at the time (not to say before or after it), and
something for which some Nazis, like Heidegger, never forgave him.[35]

But Hölderlin's writing itself and the necessity to read it were never
seriously challenged in intellectual circles. To interpret such allegiance
to Hölderlin as "evidence that science was possible even in the National
Socialist era," as has been done recently,[36] will lead eventually to a misunderstanding and obfuscation of the complexity of Nazi hegemony
and its politics of appropriating the past. The use of a contradictory
politics was, after all, part of the very meaning signaled by Hitler's
purge of Ernst Röhm's SA at the end of June 1934, and by the other
subsequent (initially so successful) attempts by Hitler not to destroy but
to appeal to and appropriate for his own ends established institutions
like the military, the churches, and the educational system.[37] It was
therefore under specific circumstances that apparent disagreement was
not only "possible" but also absolutely desirable — on the obvious condition that it could help insure Hitler's power and its corporativist economic base. It was the circumstances and the conditions that were significant, not some imaged "scientificity" or lack thereof with regard to
Hölderlin — and Nietzsche — scholarship. In 1935, many books, "even"
those like Böckmann's *Hölderlin and his Gods*, proclaimed Hölderlin
as one of the "*Führer* in German life" (vii), and those who considered
the book risible, like Heidegger, never stopped admiring the Leader-

principle itself. Beissner, who admired Böckmann's work, produced a painstaking mode of philological Hölderlin scholarship that—because of the historical context in which it was produced, even more than his own intention, perhaps—ended up doing more to legitimate Nazi cultural politics than to deconstruct them. As for the officials, the relevant Nazi censorship apparently considered anything written about Hölderlin to be at least acceptable and at best the closest thing to cultural legitimation they ever needed.

Thus the Nietzsche-Hölderlin nexus illustrates some significant aspects of Nazi hegemony, or what Gramsci once called "non-coercive coercion." Hölderlin "worked," via the Nazis' *a priori* assumption about his positive value, Nietzsche through an *a posteriori* debate about what his true value was. Their *nexus* itself, however, remained absolutely intact and absolutely untouchable.

5.

The Nazi branch of the Hölderlin industry took on incredible proportions after news of the defeat at Stalingrad in February 1943, when "rumors" increased about the implementation of "the final solution." By this time most Germans had recognized that the tide had finally, irreversibly turned against them. Even by the bleak winters of 1941–42 and especially 1942–43, many writers (from hacks to Heidegger) were drawn explicitly to celebrate death as the necessarily tragic and appropriately German destiny. Their service to Thanatos was in some ways a quite "logical" fulfillment of antirationalist Nazi ideology, extending retroactively from Hitler's final days to the psychological and sociopsychological roots of the movement. It apparently did not seem at all unusual, for example, in 1943 for an academic to link Hölderlin's "Death of Empedocles" to the "destiny" of Germany after Stalingrad.[38] It was to be in this context (and we do not understand either fascism or political ontology if this sounds incredible to us) that in June 1943 Heidegger would use his centennial talk on Hölderlin's poem "Homecoming" (*"Heimkunft"*) as the occasion to welcome home the defeated *Wehrmacht* from the eastern front, much as, in his lecture course on Parmenides in the winter just ended, Heidegger had spoken, with explicit reference to current events, of personal and national death as the most authentic confrontation with the truth of Being.[39] It was at such "textual" points, in addition to the larger historical ones, that Hölderlin's "Death for the Fatherland" became the tragically "legitimate" death not only for "German" but also now for "European" values in the final battle against "Bolshevism."

This poem became, very probably, the most cited single literary text in Nazi Germany. It was reprinted as part of the frontispiece to the new Stuttgart edition of Hölderlin's work (*Stuttgart in the War Year 1943*) as the "consolation and proud, binding imperative over the graves of our dead.[40] But even much earlier, nearer the beginning of the Thousand Year Reich, Jesse Owens and the other athletes of the world had marched into the *Reichssportsfeld* in Berlin for the 1936 Summer Olympics under the following inscription, engraved in stone: "*Lebe droben, o Vaterland, / Und zähle nicht die Toten! Dir ist, / Liebes! nicht Einer zuviel gefallen* [Live on up there, O Fatherland, / And do not count the dead! For you, / My Beloved, not One Man too many has fallen]."[41] Presumably these lines had sounded different then, or when written, at least to Germans — better, to Swabian Jacobins — than they would during the Blitzkrieg against France or in the rubble of Minsk, Stalingrad, and finally Berlin. But the signifiers were the same — to the embarrassment of the too few readers of Hölderlin, who have always been able to find some other passage in his work to read. Hölderlin had already provided at least some retractions or sublimations of this kind of chauvinist stance, as had Nietzsche. Paradoxically, however, this particular "Nietzschean" Hölderlin was quickly forgotten or forgiven after the war, whereas Nietzsche's case went on somewhat longer. Hölderlin's largely unblemished reputation continued without much of a hitch after the war, with many of the same scholars resurfacing to work on Hölderlin in a way that was much less possible in the case of Nietzsche.[42]

In the cultural climate of 1943, over a dozen "Hölderlin readers" were published for civilian consumption by presses directly under Nazi Party control and by those relatively independent of it (although the latter were of course not free from the various Party censorship instances). At least four different such readers appeared in 1944 alone; that is, even as paper and human resources for such projects were becoming increasingly scarce and as the German economy belatedly headed toward a total-war economy and *Götterdämmerungsstimmung*. Many editions of Nietzsche's works were also reprinted at about this time, including a complete *Volksausgabe* and the scholarly critical-historical edition (which had ceased publication in 1942). (A *Volksausgabe* of his selected works had already been published in the early forties). In addition, there were the field-gray military editions not only of Nietzsche's *Thus Spoke Zarathustra* but a collection of his aphorisms; and, strange to say, a field edition of his juvenilia was begun.[43] The old George-intimate Kurt Hildebrandt edited Nietzsche's poems for the popular Reclam edition.[44] But all this publication of Nietzsche was outstripped by that of Hölderlin.

There continued to be, of course, a corresponding outpouring of secondary literature on both Nietzsche and on Hölderlin. But to under-score the point, work on Nietzsche increasingly tended to circle around the question of his usefulness to Nazi ideology, whereas work on Hölderlin was always evenly divided into more or less neutral interpretations and explicitly ideological manipulations (with Heidegger's "elucidations" oscillating somewhere in between). The differing Nazi appropriations of Nietzsche and Hölderlin were, in the larger context of the Third Reich, ultimately less a matter of substance than degree. The point, in the last analysis, would not be that Hitler was a sometime visitor at the Nietzsche archives in Weimar but merely sent a wreath to Hölderlin's grave in Tübingen *in absentia*.[45] The point is that Hitler ultimately did not give a sweet damn about either of them, individually or qua nexus. But Hitler cared a great deal in general about the interactions between points of cultural hegemony and raw power that each of them differently represented, along with their various constituencies. Hitler did not have to invent the possibility for these interactions; for years they had been prepared by brilliant and not so brilliant intellectuals (virtually all of whom Hitler privately held in incandescent contempt). And this prior work was systematic and powerful enough for the Nietzsche-Hölderlin nexus to do extraordinarily well throughout the Third Reich, notwithstanding the occasional, controlled resistances to Nietzsche.

6.

One of the very last texts produced by the inner circle of the Nazi intellectual elite on Nietzsche was also one of the last philosophical texts it had time to produce on any subject: Alfred Rosenberg's too often ignored pamphlet, *Friedrich Nietzsche*. Rosenberg (1893–1946) was the leading Nazi ideologist and Minister of Culture.[46] An architect by training, he was — along with Goebbels, Albert Speer, and Hitler himself — part of what Manfred Frank has called the "crypto-aesthetic base" that was such a substantial part of the deformed post-Romantic legacy of the National Socialist "movement."[47] Rosenberg's last academic lecture was delivered on October 15, 1944, at the Nietzsche archives in Weimar on the occasion of the centenary of Nietzsche's birth. The fact that this event would be hardly marked at all throughout Germany, and yet commemorated in Weimar by a man near the top of the Nazi Party hierarchy, is significant, since the Nazis had pretty much given up "officially" on Nietzsche by 1942. For Rosenberg, however, Nietzsche was once more hot stuff as twilight fell again on an imperialist Germany. In 1944, on the basis of a fairly explicit "tragic" admission that the military situation was very grave — indeed that a disastrous outcome was a foregone conclusion — Rosenberg in his pamphlet seized the occasion to pose once more the question that he took to be Nietzsche's essential one: "Is human greatness still possible today?" (3). Confronting head on and at some length the apparent fact that Nietzsche himself had been ambivalent about German nationalism (and, by extension, German National Socialism) as a possible answer to this overriding question, Rosenberg reverted back to a major interpretive strategy used by George, Bertram, Bäumler, and even Heidegger: in a significant sense, Nietzsche (like Hölderlin) had never really *meant* his attacks on Germany, based, as they were, on his isolation and the impossibility of politically fulfilling his search for cultural renewal. Bäumler's original version of this argument, first made implicit by George and explicit by Ernst Bertram, had been that although Nietzsche may have sometimes appeared "anti-German," this was due only to the contingent linkage of superficial "Roman," "Christian," or "Mediterranean" influences on his thought with the political situation of Germany in the late nineteenth century. Like Hölderlin's own vision, Nietzsche's desire to lay the foundations for a radically new state based on "will to power" and the cultivation of human greatness was never "anti-Germanic" at root.[48] This move lies at the core of Rosenberg's argument.

He suggests that whoever asks how such a battle for the fatal transvaluation of values could ever be won, does not understand that the question answers itself. The tragic beauty of the question, for Rosenberg, lies in the fact that the battle cannot be won, at least not for the time being. Hölderlin's and Nietzsche's attacks on Germany must be understood in their "original" historical and political context. Nietzsche's claims to be a "good European" have now become the claims of Nazi Germany in its fight against international Bolshevism and for a postwar capitalism. Here, at the end of the war and the Third Reich, the Hölderlin of "Death for the Fatherland" was once again being fused with the more "cosmopolitan" and "non-Heraclitian" Nietzsche in a single nexus. Citing at length Nietzsche's own lament in the *Untimely Meditations* that Hölderlin was unable to "hold out" in the political and cultural climate of Germany, Rosenberg evoked, finally, the need for comradeship among bearers of "the German spirit." What he meant by "German spirit" was now something that he and many other Nazis had been calling "*greater* German" (*Grossdeutsch*). Germany itself remains what Hölderlin had named it in "Song of the Fatherland": "The holy heart of peoples," though now transformed into "Fortress Europe" against the Allies closing in from two sides — the "pincers" of Americanism and Bolshevism (still alluded to by Heidegger long after the war). As such, however, Germany was also beginning the process of returning to what Thomas Mann, back in Weimar in the early twenties, had called "the nation of the middle, and of cosmopolitan, bourgeois values," "the last outpost of Western civilization" against the "Bolshevik menace."[49] Late in 1944, in the context of post-Stalingrad, post-D-Day Germany, however, this meant more than merely the struggle to maintain the geographical territories annexed as part of the earlier drive for German *Lebensraum*. The long-term future of fascist ideology was at stake, as was how to continue its fraternal relationship to capitalism.

To stress this point: Rosenberg intimated strongly (pretty much in synchrony with Hitler's own view, it seems) that the geopolitical war looked very grim; indeed the outcome was a *fait accompli*. The present war of physical "maneuver" (whatever its result, but especially if it were lost) had to be continued as a "war of position" so that psychological war could continue far into the future — yet another Nietzschean *actio in distans*. And it would be a war in the name not of Germany alone, but of the Germany that was once again the vanguard defending Europe against its worst enemy. In his pamphlet, Rosenberg commemorates Nietzsche's legacy in these terms:

> When we proudly declare that National Socialist Germany is the only defender of old Europe, when we, perhaps in a somewhat different sense than Nietzsche in the nineteenth century, but speaking from out of an even greater depth of experience, say that we today are the "good Europeans" — then this is a right that we have wrested honorably from history. At the same time, however, we want in all modesty to state, in order not to fall prey to that Tartuffery that Nietzsche so rightly censured, that many phenomena of that age are still perceptible in us today (21).

The trick of appropriating Nietzsche for the Right, prepared for in general by the tradition of German literary history after Gervinus and in detail by Dilthey and the George Circle, had now reached a point of ultimate drift. The enemy was no longer merely internal cultural decadence in Germany, or even in Europe, but something international and belonging to the future. To put it most bluntly and brutally, not even the capitalist Jews are, now for National Socialism at the moment of its defeat (not to mention its inception), the most lethal and undefeatable enemies of fascism and of capitalism, but something else: communism. The real reason that Nietzsche can be thought to be "our near relative, our spiritual brother in the battle for the rebirth of greater German spirituality" (23) is that he was the earliest critic of Marxism (14). By late 1944, then, as is shown in the "textual" moment of Rosenberg's talk, the hot war had ended for Nietzsche and Hölderlin, and a new use for the Nietzsche-Hölderlin nexus was being conceived.

7.

We can now return from the historical problem of the Nietzsche-Hölderlin nexus in German wartime to the theoretical problem posed at the outset. If the question "Nietzsche, godfather of fascism?" is asked in terms of Nietzsche's influence on Hitlerian Germany or of his responsibility and accountability for it, we can debate this question endlessly. The answer is going to depend on how we define "influence," "responsibility," and "accountability," how we view a bundle of hardly coherent facts, and how we can ever come to grips with Nietzsche's esoteric subtext. Obviously, it did not require Nietzsche or the Nietzsche-Hölderlin nexus for Hitlerian Germany to be what it was — they were, at the very most, one of its many necessary but not sufficient historical preconditions. The theoretical question, however, of Nietzsche's responsibility and accountability for the "order of rank" that preceded fascism and German National Socialism — including Nietzsche's responsibility and accountability for implementing that "order of rank" subliminally, beneath our capacity to register and combat it — can be answered in the words Nietzsche himself proclaimed, considerably before his own twilight: "*Ich bin verantwortlich.*"

Notes

The sources quoted in the opening epigraphs are, respectively, Hart Crane, "The Case against Nietzsche," *The Pagan* 2, no. 3 (April/May 1918): 34–35; here, 35.

Hans Magnus Enzensberger, "Schaum," *Landessprache* (Frankfurt am Main: Suhrkamp 1960), 41.

1. Leo Strauss, "Liberal Education and Responsibility," in *Liberalism Ancient and Modern* with a new foreword by Allan Bloom (1968, Ithaca and London: Cornell University Press, 1989), 9–25; here 24. The essay was originally published elsewhere in 1962.

2. See Georg Lukács, *The Destruction of Reason*, trans. Peter Palmer (Atlantic Highlands, N.J.: Humanities Press, 1981), esp. 202–3, 309–99.

3. François Laruelle, *Nietzsche contre Heidegger: Thèses pour une politique nietzschéene* (Paris: Payot, 1977), 9.

4. See George Morgan, Jr., *What Nietzsche Means* (Cambridge: Harvard University Press), 1941.

5. Friedrich Nietzsche, *Jenseits von Gut und Böse: Vorspiel einer Philosophie der Zukunft* (1886), *Kritische Gesamtausgabe, Werke*, ed. Giorgio Colli and Mazzino Montinari (Berlin: de Gruyter, 1967ff), VI 2:44–45 [Part II, Aph-

orism 30]. This edition will be cited as *KGA*, with appropriate volume, section, and page numbers. Nietzsche's unpublished notebooks will be cited from this edition as *NF*, with the dates assigned by the editors.

6. See Nietzsche, "Der griechische Staat" [1872]; *KGA* III 2:258–71, here 261, 270, 271.

7. Compare Leo Strauss's thesis about the Machiavelli who "has discovered new modes and orders which he opposes to the old and established modes and orders. He has discovered and explored territory hitherto inaccessible to men of his kind. He begins a war against the established order—a new war in a new land against a new enemy of the highest possible reputation. But he is a captain without an army. He must recruit his army. He can recruit it only by means of books" (*Thoughts on Machiavelli* [1958; Chicago: University of Chicago Press, 1978], 153–54).

8. "*NF*, Juli–August 1882,"; *KGA*, VII 1:9.

9. "*NF*, November 1882–Februar 1883," *KGA*, VII 1:195.

10. "*NF*, Frühjahr–Herbst 1881"; *KGA*, V 2:406.

11. "*NF*, Juni–Juli 1883"; *KGA*, VII 1:383.

12. See Martha Zapata Galindo, *Triumph des Willens: Zur Nietzsche-Rezeption im NS-Staat* (Hamburg: Argument, 1995). Especially good on the case of Italian fascism is Bernhard H. F. Taureck, *Nietzsche und der Faschismus: Eine Studie über Nietzsches politische Philosophie und ihre Folgen* (Hamburg: Junius, 1989). Rich in empirical detail but without sustained interest in theoretical issues or in the question of Nietzsche's "responsibility" for his reception (the author generally ignores Nietzsche's own writings), is Steven E. Aschheim, *The Nietzsche Legacy in Germany 1890–1990* (Berkeley: University of California Press, 1992); on Nietzsche and Nazi Germany, see esp. chaps. 8 and 9.

13. The evidence of Hölderlin's reception in the Third Reich is assembled in Werner Volke, "Hölderlin-Forschung," in *Klassiker in finsteren Zeiten 1933–1945: Eine Ausstellung des Deutschen Literaturarchivs im Schiller-Nationalmuseum, Marbach am Neckar*, 2 vols., ed. Bernhard Zeller (Stuttgart: Ernst Klett, 1983), 1:325–26, and, in the same work, Reinhard Tgaht's documentary essay, "Hölderlin im Tornister," 2:300–335.

14. Especially as Heraclitus's fragment continues, "and some he shows as gods, others as men; some he makes slaves, others free." Heraclitus (Diels, no. 53), *The Presocratic Philosophers: A Critical History*, ed. and trans. G. S. Kirk and J. E. Raven (Cambridge: Cambridge University Press, 1969), 195.

15. Anonymous [Antonio Gramsci], "Workers and Peasants," in Antonio Gramsci, *Selections from the Political Writings (1910–1920): With Additional Texts by Bordiga and Tasca*, ed. Quintin Hoare, trans. John Mathews (New York: International Publishers, 1977), 83–87; here, 85.

16. Hermann Pongs, for example—one of many such ideologue-scholars—had argued in 1934 that the standard of literature and thought was "the extent to which it keeps alive in the nation the memory of war as the way of sacrifice for millions," and so on. See Hermann Pongs, "Krieg als Volksschicksal im deutschen Schrifttum," *Dichtung und Volkstum* 35 (1934): 40–86, 182–219. See also his "Neue Kriegs- und Nachkriegsbücher," *Dichtung und Volkstum* 37

(1936): 219–35; and "Weltkrieg und Dichtung," *Dichtung und Volkstum* 39 (1938): 193–212. For a still very readable and informative account of the influence of war in general and World War I on German intellectuals (written in the early stage of World War II), see William K. Pfeiler, *War and the German Mind: The Testimony of Men of Fiction Who Fought at the Front*, foreword by George N. Shuster (New York: Columbia University Press, 1941). Pfeiler has a good discussion of Pong's theories on 313–18.

17. Nietzsche, *Also sprach Zarathustra* [1883–85], KGA VI 1:55–56.

18. In February and March 1944, the German papers in Croatia and in the Ukraine carried front-page feuilletons by Hans Hartmann, entitled "Seers and Creators: Hölderlin and Nietzsche as the Shapers of the New Occidental Image of Humanity." "The thought," Hartmann concluded one version of his hastily proof-read essay, "may and ought to fulfill itself as deed [*Der Gedanke darf und sol[l] sich auch in der Tat erfüllen*]." See Hans Hartmann, "Seher und Schöpfer: Hölderlin und Nietzsche als Gestalter des neuen abendländischen Menschenbildes," *Deutsche Ukraine-Zeitung* [Luzk], March 25, 1944, p. 1.

19. Barthel's remark is found in his *Nietzsche als Verführer* (Baden-Baden: Hans Bühler Junior, 1947), 49. On Barthel's activities in the Third Reich, see George Leamon, *Heidegger im Kontext: Gesamtüberblick zum NS-Engagement der Universitätsphilosophen*, trans. by Rainer Alisch and Thomas Laugstien (Hamburg: Argument, 1993), 30.

20. See the anonymous article, "Hölderlin und Nietzsche: Vorträge zweier Münchner Studenten in der Aula des Barmer Gymnasiums," *Elberfeld-Barmer-Zeitung*, April 22, 1921, p. 1.

21. Georg Mönius, "Hölderlin-Nietzsche," *Das heilige Feuer* 7 (1919/1920): 274–76.

22. Richard Groeper, "Hölderlin und Nietzsche als Künder des 20. Jahrhunderts," *Nationalsozialistisches Bildungswesen* 5 (1940): 406–12; here, 412.

23. See Benno Müller-Hill, *Murderous Science: Elimination by Scientific Selection of Jews, Gypsies, and Others, Germany 1933–1945*, trans. George R. Fraser (Oxford: Oxford University Press, 1988), 94–95.

24. See Benno von Wiese, "Schiller-Forschung und Schiller-Deutung von 1937–1953," *Deutsche Vierteljahrsschrift für Literaturwissenschaft und Geistesgeschichte* 27, no. 3 (1953): 452–83.

25. See Günther Neske, "Nachwort des Mitherausgebers," *Antwort: Martin Heidegger im Gespräch*, ed. Günther Neske and Emil Kettering (Pfullingen: Günther Neske, 1988), 284.

26. Karl Cerff, speech at Hölderlin's grave, June 6, 1943; cited in *Klassiker in finsteren Zeiten*, 2:98.

27. See again Taureck, *Nietzsche und der Faschismus*.

28. See Joachim Günther, "Nietzsche und der Nationalsozialismus," *Nationalsozialistische Monatshefte* 2 (1931): 560–63.

29. Taureck, *Nietzsche und der Faschismus*, 101.

30. For a sharp Nazi distinction between Nazism and Nietzsche on important matters, see Heinrich Härtle, *Nietzsche und der Nationalsozialismus* (Munich: Zentralverlag der NSDAP, 1937). This book was reprinted three

times, in 1939, 1942, and 1944. For other, equally energetic attempts by Nazis to de-Nazify Nietzsche, see Curt von Westernhagen, *Nietzsche, Juden, Antijuden* (Weimar: A. Duncker, 1936); and Christoph Steding, *Das Reich und die Krankheit der europäischen Kultur*, with a foreword by Walter Frank (Hamburg: Hanseatische Verlagsanstalt, 1938), esp. 159–60, 215–16. Westernhagen (born 1905), a leading Wagnerian, has continued to publish on Wagner almost up to the present time. Steding (1903–38) wrote his dissertation in 1932 on "Politics and Science in Max Weber"; *Das Reich und die Krankheit*, his magnum opus, was reprinted twice in 1942.

31. Westernhagen, *Nietzsche, Juden, Antijuden*, 73.

32. We are thinking primarily of Derrida, *Otobiographies: L'enseignement de Nietzsche et la politique du nom propre* (Paris: Galilée, 1984). But as naive in this regard is Philippe Lacoue-Labarthe's Derridian-inflected account of Nazism in his *La fiction du politique: Heidegger, l'art et la politique* (Paris: Christian Bourgois, 1988). We should add that the most explicit critique to date of this problem is overly polemical and is itself insufficiently grounded in research into Nazism and fascism qua historical phenomena: Luc Ferry and Alain Renaut, *Heidegger et les modernes* (Paris: Bernard Grasset, 1988).

33. See Nikos Poulantzas, *Fascism and Dictatorship: The Third International and the Problem of Fascism*, trans. Judith White (1970; London: New Left Books, 1974), 71–88.

34. See Johannes Hoffmeister, *Hölderlin und die Philosophie* (Leipzig: Felix Meiner, 1942); and Ernst Müller, *Hölderlin: Studien zur Geschichte seines Geistes* (Stuttgart and Berlin: Kohlhammer, 1944), esp. 6–7. Müller was also the author of a political tract entitled *Hitler, wie er wirklich ist* (Luxembourg: Moselfränkischer Zeitungsverlag, 1941).

35. See Böckmann, *Hölderlin und seine Götter* (Munich: C. H. Beck, 1935), 179. More or less veiled allusions to Böckmann (who for his part was by no means ill disposed toward Heidegger at the time) are scattered throughout Heidegger's work on Hölderlin. For a representative reference, see Heidegger, *Hölderlins Hymne "Der Ister"* [Freiburg, Summer Semester 1942], *Gesamtausgabe* (Frankfurt am Main: Vittorio Klostermann, 1984), II 53: 38.

36. Compare the commentary on the otherwise useful compilation of evidence in Volke, "Hölderlin-Forschung," in *Klassiker in finsteren Zeiten*, 1:340.

37. For a classic version in English of these contested issues, see Alan Bullock, *Hitler: A Study in Tyranny* (New York and Evanston: Harper & Row, 1962), esp. 280–311, in the chapter "Revolution after Power"; as well as *Der "Führerstaat": Mythos und Realität: Studien zur Struktur und Politik des Dritten Reiches*, with an introduction by Wolfgang J. Mommsen, ed. Gerhard Hirschfeld and Lothar Kettenacker (Stuttgart: Klett-Cotta, 1981), esp. the essay by Tim Mason, "Intention and Explanation: A Current Controversy about the Interpretation of National Socialism," 23–42.

38. See Heinz Kindermann, *Hölderlin und das deutsche Theater* (Vienna: Frick Verlag, 1943), esp. 6 and 46–47.

39. See Heidegger "Vorbemerkung zur Wiederholung der Rede (am 21. Juni 1943 in der Aula der Universität)," *Erläuterungen zur Hölderlins Dichtung*,

Gesamtausgabe (Frankfurt am Main: Vittorio Klostermann, 1981), I 4:193; and *Parmenides* (Winter Semester 1942–43), *Gesamtausgabe* (Frankfurt am Main: Vittorio Klostermann, 1982), II 54: 250.

40. The unpaginated frontispiece of the first edition of 1943 was elided from printings after the war.

41. Hölderlin, *Sämtliche Werke, Grosse Stuttgarter Ausgabe*, ed. Friedrich Beißner (Stuttgart: J. G. Cottasche Buchhandlung, 1943ff), 1/1:299.

42. The existence of Bäumler's postwar introductions to Nietzsche's works, suitably sanitized, represents something of an exception to this rule. And so does Heidegger, though his case is far more complex, not least because, as in the writings of both Hölderlin and Nietzsche, there is a powerful current of esotericism in his work.

43. The Deutsches Litaraturarchiv in Marbach am Neckar has the manuscript draft of this aborted project, edited by Kläre Buchmann, an editor at J. G. Cotta.

44. See *Gedichte von Friedrich Nietzsche*, ed. Kurt Hildebrandt (Leipzig: Reclam, n.d. [circa 1943]).

45. On Hitler in the Nietzsche archives, see H. F. Peters, *Zarathustra's Sister: The Case of Elisabeth and Friedrich Nietzsche* (New York: Crown, 1977), 215–24.

46. See Alfred Rosenberg, *Friedrich Nietzsche: Ansprache bei einer Gedenkstunde anläßlich des 100. Geburtstages Friedrich Nietzsches am 15. October 1944 in Weimar* (Munich: Zentralverlag der NSDAP, 1944).

47. And this despite the fact that Rosenberg's magnum opus, *Der Mythos des 20. Jahrhunderts*, was ridiculed in the innermost circle, by Goebbels, as a "metaphysical belch." On the "crypto-aesthetic base," see Manfred Frank, "*Der Mythos des 20. Jahrhunderts* (Alfred Rosenberg, Alfred Baeumler)," *Gott im Exil: Vorlesung über die neue Mythologie*, II. *Teil* (Frankfurt am Main: Suhrkamp Verlag, 1988), 105–130; here, 105.

48. See Alfred Bäumler, *Nietzsche der Philosoph und Politiker* (Leipzig: Reclam, 1931), esp. 88–90.

49. See Thomas Mann, "Goethe und Tolstoy," *Gesammelte Werke in dreizehn Bänden* (Frankfurtam Main: S. Fischer Verlag, 1974), 9:58–173; here, 9:171.

10

The Elisabeth Legend: The Cleansing of Nietzsche and the Sullying of His Sister

Robert C. Holub

At the close of the World War II it was common knowledge in the Western world that Nietzsche was a precursor of fascism. Although in the Third Reich there were several voices who sought to disclaim his philosophical legacy, or who at least believed that significant portions of his writings were useless for National Socialism,[1] most German writers and propagandists embraced Nietzsche as one of their own. Steven Aschheim points out the extent of Nietzsche's assimilation into Nazi thought and institutions, "the dense and broad diffusion through which suitably adapted Nietzschean notions became a differentiated and integral part of Nazi self-definition."[2] Not only was he a favorite of chief National Socialist ideologues and academics like Alfred Rosenberg and Alfred Bäumler; Nietzschean themes and thoughts pervaded almost every aspect of daily life, from education and law, to policies on eugenics and race, to simple life wisdom. Once the war started, military propaganda also found it easy to adapt Nietzsche for bellicose purposes. During World War I, when Nietzsche was hardly considered the official spokesperson for the Second Empire, *Zarathustra* had been distributed to 150,000 soldiers in a special, durable edition. In World War II, when Nietzsche was considered the prophet of the Nazi revolution, his works became indispensable for the military. Typical in this regard was a 1941 Kröner Pocketbook edition entitled "Sword of the Spirit" ("*Schwert des Geistes*"), which contained excerpts from Nietzsche's work and which was written for "German fighters and soldiers." The editor Joachim Schondorff, in his brief introduction, compares Nietzsche to the fresh breeze [*Tauwind*] — an allusion to a passage from *Zarathustra* — since Nietzsche was "a young, revolutionary, clarifying spring storm" who, like Adolf Hitler in his day, swept away the rotten construction of traditional prejudices and false ideals.[3]

Most foreign observers as well were ready to believe that Nietzsche was implicated in National Socialism. During World War I, when Nietzsche reached the zenith of his initial period of popularity, French and British intellectuals indicted him for the nationalist and imperialist interpretations of his work. The West was thus already predisposed to regard Nietzsche as a forerunner of Hitler when hostilities broke out in 1939. Writing in the series "Makers of Modern Europe," Crane Brinton captured well the reputation Nietzsche had even in academic circles during the early forties. Brinton concedes that there are many ways in which Nietzsche can be and had been interpreted. He dissects Nietzsche devotees into two groups: the "gentle Nietzscheans," who tend to downplay the more belligerent and reprehensible passages in Nietzsche's writings, and the "tough Nietzscheans," who revel in the rhetorical flourishes about the superman, war, struggle, and overcoming. Although Brinton recognizes that much in Nietzsche's works does not suit Nazi purposes, he concludes that there is a great deal more that corresponds nicely to their propaganda:

> Nietzsche, then, fits into National Socialist needs both in what he damned and in what he praised. He damned democracy, pacifism, individualism, Christianity, humanitarianism, both as abstract ideals and as, in some vague way, actual descriptions of modern European society. He praised authority, racial purity, the warrior spirit and practice, and the stern life and the great health, and urged upon his fellow-citizens a complete break with their old bad habits and ideas.[4]

There were, of course, still many "gentle Nietzscheans" in the 1930s and 1940s; but from 1933–45 the image propagated by the "tough Nietzscheans" appears to have held the upper hand in Germany and increasingly throughout the world.

During the postwar period Nietzsche's reputation was thus in desperate need of repair, and it was not long before supporters inside and outside of Germany rushed to his defense. Nietzsche had had many antifascist adherents, of course, even during the period when he was generally accepted by the Western intellectual world as a proto-Nazi. Thomas Mann, Theodor Adorno, Karl Löwith, and a host of other German émigrés actively combated the image propagated by tough Nietzscheans of the fascist and antifascist camps. But if Nietzsche was going to be purged of his fascistoid image, there had to be some explanation for how he had been recruited so readily for such nefarious purposes. Above all, scholars would have to provide plausible arguments for the falsity of Nietzsche's appropriation during the Third Reich, and possibly in the period before Hitler came to power, in order to justify their own more scholarly, more accurate, or more faithful approach to the philosopher and his thought.

They were aided enormously in their efforts by being able to point to the existence of a person closely connected with Nietzsche and his writings, a person who came to exercise a domineering influence over his works and reception, and who had also tampered with manuscripts, fabricated evidence about Nietzsche and his life, and defied the accepted traditions and voices of the scholarly community. This person was Nietzsche's sister, Elisabeth Förster-Nietzsche, who, after her return from a failed colonial venture in Paraguay in 1893, took charge of her brother, his writings, and his literary remains. Through cunning, deceit, and perseverance, she allegedly made Nietzsche into a cult figure of the early twentieth century, and turned the archives that housed Nietzsche himself until his death in 1900, and his manuscripts thereafter, into a cultural center of German life.

In several ways Elisabeth was an easy scapegoat for Nietzsche's fascist appropriation. Married to a known anti-Semite and political agitator, Bernhard Förster, who committed suicide in 1889, when his mismanaged colony of Nueva Germania was on the verge of collapse, Elisabeth at times appeared to share the views of her husband, which were closer to those of the Wagner circle than to the ideas of her brother. Soon after her return to Europe she began to scheme about how she could obtain the rights to her brother's writings, and by the close of the decade she was in sole possession of almost all Nietzscheana of any importance. She took charge of publishing his complete works, dismissing one editor after another when they disagreed with her or countered her wishes, and allowed portions of her brother's writings to remain unpublished for many years, while publishing other parts under titles or arranged in collections that were neither authorized by Nietzsche nor philologically sound. From early on, persons working with her in the Nietzsche archives discovered that she was suppressing certain letters penned by her beloved "Fritz" that portrayed her in an unfavorable light, and even before her death in 1935 there was either suspicion of, or evidence for, numerous forgeries, distortions, or deceptions. Politically Elisabeth, like her brother, was hostile to democracy: before 1918 she leaned toward monarchism; during the Weimar Republic she made no secret of her conservative proclivities and of her animosity toward the parliamentary order. She admired Mussolini and spoke favorably of his fascist regime when it came to power in Italy. And she was flattered by the attention Hitler showered on her and the archives in the early 1930s, speaking admiringly of him when he was appointed Chancellor in January of 1933. When she died on 9 November 1935 the official organs of National Socialism sung her praises, and Hitler himself attended her funeral.[5]

Because of a life trajectory that saw her move from the petty-bourgeois mentality of the German provinces to a liaison with a notorious anti-Semite and ultranationalist to an admiration for fascism and its "heroic" leaders, Elisabeth Förster-Nietzsche was a perfect target for postwar scholars wishing to explain away Nietzsche's unfortunate reception. It is therefore not surprising that the chief postwar rehabilitators frequently attack her in their publications. Karl Schlechta, best known for his three-volume Nietzsche edition of 1956, is perhaps the chief German representative of this trend. Schlechta had worked in the Nietzsche archives since the early 1930s, and he knew Förster-Nietzsche personally, discovering quite early on that she was responsible for falsifications in her brother's correspondence. In the "Philological Postscript" to his edition, Schlechta produces the usual litany of complaints about Nietzsche's sister: she had no understanding for her brother's philosophy; she was interested only in producing volumes quickly and in spreading Nietzsche's fame; she illicitly published *The Will to Power* from notes in Nietzsche's literary remains that were not meant for publication, or at least not in that form or under that title. He is able to establish, moreover, that Förster-Nietzsche falsified a significant number of letters, making it appear that correspondence destined for others was actually written to her.[6]

In talks and in essays written shortly after the publication of his edition, Schlechta was more explicit about the consequences of Elisabeth's malicious deeds. Speaking of the German catastrophe, he argued that the reason Nietzsche was made coresponsible for it was primarily due to his obsessively ambitious sister hitching her wagon to the fate of the Third Reich, producing simplified editions and portrayals of her brother. Here the connection between philological shenanigans and political responsibility is more or less explicit. As an extra bonus, in the process of repudiating Elisabeth, Schlechta's own archival discoveries become tantamount to antifascist resistance. Reporting about his exposé in 1937 to the committee charged with oversight of the scholarly work of the archives, Schlechta writes, "Here Frau Förster-Nietzsche, who had been honored only two-and-a-half years before by a state funeral which the Führer himself attended, was exposed as a swindler."[7] The reader of Schlechta's explanations should have no trouble drawing the appropriate conclusion: by concocting the Nietzsche legend, Elisabeth perpetrated a political act that besmirched her brother's reputation by entwining his fate with National Socialism.

In the United States and throughout the English-speaking world, Walter Kaufmann was the rehabilitator who played the most important role through his translations and editions of Nietzsche and his seminal study (which went through four printings), in domesticating the politically suspect philosopher for a liberal postwar Anglophone audience. Nietzsche was not a protofascist, argued Kaufmann; he was an existentialist concerned with the creativity of the human spirit and with a strengthening of individualism. With regard to Elisabeth, Kaufmann, like Schlechta, often cites faulty philology rather than pernicious ideology. He complains at length about her editorial practices, in particular her withholding of texts like *Ecce Homo* from publication. And he is especially outraged at the publication of *The Will to Power* as Nietzsche's magnum opus, although in a strange turnabout he himself published an English edition of the same work in 1967 and even followed the arrangement of the previously published German editions.[8] He, too, agrees that Elisabeth was unsuited to be her brother's interpreter and apostle. Although Kaufmann does not focus on her falsifications, he makes it clear to the reader that she is not to be trusted. His ideological assault is similar to Schlechta's. Elisabeth is responsible for propagating a "Nietzsche legend" that eventually became the property of National Socialism. Kaufmann claims that she never accepted his break with Wagner, that she "doggedly persuaded the Nazis to accept her brother as their philosopher, and that it was in response to her insistent invitations that Hitler eventually visited the *Nietzsche-Archiv* — on a trip to Bayreuth."[9] Clearly Kaufmann, despite philological differences with Schlechta, also places the blame for Nietzsche's Nazi appropriation squarely at the feet of his sister.

The French rehabilitation of Nietzsche was not as arduous as the German or the Anglophone rehabilitation, largely because, as the example of Martin Heidegger demonstrates, France has been traditionally less sensitive to the fascist affiliations of German philosophers. Nonetheless among the postwar rehabilitators of Nietzsche and scapegoaters of Elisabeth we also find a French scholar, Richard Roos, whose articles echo in smaller format the proclivities we have already witnessed in the writings of Schlechta and Kaufmann. Roos is centrally concerned with Elisabeth's editorial practices in the last works, which are difficult anyway to disentangle because of Nietzsche's less than stable mental condition and of the plethora of plans and projects he sketched in his notebooks during the last years of his sane life.[10] In an essay dealing with Elisabeth as "the abusive sister," however, he is more explicit about her purportedly fascist proclivities. Her influence, we are told, has been "sometimes baneful, often embarrassing, and almost always contrary to the ideas and interests of her brother."[11] Roos leaves no doubt that Elisabeth's influence is primarily responsible for bringing Nietzsche into the proximity of the Nazis, whose assumption of power was "opportune" for her: "In effect, the Nietzsche that Bäumler and Rosenberg made the prophet of the party coincides perfectly with her portrayal of him. Henceforth [after Hitler's assumption of power] any attack on the tradition of the Nietzsche archives was able to be considered a manifestation hostile to Nazi doctrine."[12] In reproducing damaging documents that demonstrate Elisabeth's enthusiasm for Hitler and the National Socialist regime, Roos, at the close of his essay, makes it clear by innuendo how Nietzschean philosophy became associated with a political regime Neitzsche himself would have detested.

The Elisabeth legend has become so widespread and powerful that it is hardly ever questioned, even by researchers who are otherwise skeptical and assiduous in their scholarship. In the Nietzsche literature over the past few years alone, examples of the propagation of unfounded assertions about Elisabeth abound. Janet Lungstrum, for example, writing from a feminist perspective, condemns the "uniquely masculinist ideology on Nietzsche, spawned as the protofascist Nietzsche myth by Elisabeth Förster-Nietzsche."[13] In the *Cambridge Companion to Nietzsche*, the volumes' editors refer to "Elisabeth Förster-Nietzsche, and her fascistic and racist compatriots," claiming Elisabeth's edition of *The Will to Power* was arranged in a fashion emphasizing themes that appeared "friendly to the ideals of National Socialism."[14] Later in the same volume, R. J. Hollingdale, repeating the canards of earlier scholarship, abuses Elisabeth for her commercialism (although he himself enjoyed obvious commercial success with his various Nietzsche translations), and contends that "as far as she could she imposed Förster's values," that is, anti-Semitism and proto-Nazism, on the Nietzsche archives "and adapted Nietzsche in accordance with them."[15] The foremost historian of the Nietzsche archives, David Marc Hoffmann, wrote that Elisabeth propagated "the image of an authoritarian and racist Nietzsche, which ultimately could be used by Mussolini and Hitler for their purposes."[16]

The editors of a volume on "Jewish Nietzscheanism" also label Elisabeth an anti-Semite and place her next to the notorious anti-Jewish preacher Adolf Stöcker and the Gobineau enthusiast Richard Wagner.[17] Perhaps the most virulent recent assault on Elisabeth, however, occurs in an essay by Weaver Santaniello, who labels Elisabeth a "protofascist," "a virulent Christian anti-Semite," and "a staunch supporter of Hitler and the Nazis."[18] According to Santaniello there is a direct line

from Wagner and Elisabeth to the Third Reich; the "process of manipu-
lating Nietzsche . . . began with Elisabeth and culminated with Hitler."[19]
The extent to which Elisabeth's Nietzsche is equated with the most pernicious parts of Nazism in the mind of the general public is perhaps
shown best in Paul Strathern's *Nietzsche in 90 Minutes*, when he asserts
that after Nietzsche's mental collapse, Förster-Nietzsche began "doctor-
ing her brother's unpublished notebooks, inserting anti-Semitic ideas and
flattering remarks about herself."[20] Only rarely in the commentary on
Nietzsche do we find a more differentiated — or an informed — opinion
concerning "Zarathustra's sister"; since the 1950s, when Schlechta, Kaufmann, and Roos launched their apologetic offensives, Nietzsche has
been consistently extricated from his Nazi entanglements by regarding
Elisabeth as the chief architect of his fascist reputation.

The legend that currently circulates is as spurious as the one that the
postwar scholars destroyed, and as false as the Nietzsche legend that
Elisabeth propagated. Like all legends, however, it is based on truths
and half-truths, and because it does not consist of outright falsehoods,
it is more pernicious, and more impervious to attack. Elisabeth did manipulate texts, especially in Nietzsche's correspondence; she appears to
have produced fraudulent letters, mostly written to herself. She certainly
did try to obtain sole rights to her brother's writings, and to all of
his correspondence, sometimes using somewhat unprincipled means to
achieve her ultimate goal. It is also apparent that she suppressed certain
documents and texts, and that she carefully controlled what was produced by the scholars hired to edit critical editions. From the records we
have available she also appears to have been a headstrong and sometimes pugnacious woman, jealously protecting what she perceived as
items in her domain and not hesitating to heap abuse on those with
whom she disagreed. She had redeeming features, of course, which are
rarely mentioned today in discussions. She was fiercely loyal to her
brother, doing what she believed was in his best interests. She was entre-
preneurial, succeeding in establishing the Nietzsche archives as a center
of culture in Weimar and in making her brother the most widely read
philosopher of the nineteenth century. She could also be charming and
captivating, and she impressed many intelligent men and women who
knew her, even if they sometimes became disillusioned with her in time.
But Elisabeth, for all her good and bad qualities, did not bias her
brother's work in a way that made him acceptable to fascism. She did
not distort his thought on issues essential to National Socialism, and she
cannot be held responsible — and certainly not to the degree that she has
been held responsible since the fifties — for the fact that Nietzsche was
widely identified with the Nazi political regime.

To understand why Elisabeth is innocent of fashioning the protofascist image of her brother, we need to look at a few of her misdeeds and find out why she perpetrated them. Let us begin with the falsifications, perhaps the most heinous crime to the philologically minded rehabilitators of the postwar era. Schlechta produced the most evidence against Elisabeth in the epilogue to his edition. In his commentary he reproduces a document that he and Wilhelm Hoppe sent to the academic committee of the Nietzsche archives in 1937 detailing irregularities in the correspondence between Nietzsche and his family. After going through the manuscripts and papers the two young editorial assistants found that there existed no original manuscripts for thirty-two letters that Elisabeth had included in the fifth volume of Nietzsche's collected letters, which appeared in 1909. All of these letters were addressed to the sister except for two, which were written to the mother. In 1937 Schlechta and Hoppe merely expressed their suspicion that these letters were forgeries: they claimed that they were "of very limited value" and noted further that their list may not have been complete.[21] In 1956 Schlechta explained what had occurred. The letters were falsifications, but not entirely fiction. It seems that Elisabeth took letters or drafts of letters and doctored them to make them appear that Nietzsche had sent them to her. In addition, and Schlechta does not mention this in his epilogue, Elisabeth also added and subtracted phrases or entire paragraphs from these letters.

Schlechta's philology is slightly lacking in accuracy, due perhaps to his inability to examine again originals and documents in the Nietzsche archives after the war. As it turns out, several letters that Schlechta deems forgeries are real and were taken verbatim into the critical edition of Nietzsche's correspondence edited by Giorgio Colli and Mazzino Montinari. Several other letters are based on existing drafts and are credible at least as actual correspondence from Nietzsche's pen. Others have such mundane and innocuous content that it is difficult to understand why they would be included by Elisabeth if they were not authentic. And some letters that appear to have been "edited" by Elisabeth may even be genuine.

Still there are undoubtedly numerous falsifications, and these distortions, omissions, and outright forgeries, combined with Elisabeth's later praise for fascism and Hitler have fueled the suspicion that she is indeed responsible for making her brother's thought appear to be the intellectual property of the far Right. In fact, however, Elisabeth's falsifications, when examined for their content, add little or nothing to the Nazi image of Nietzsche. Most of the suspicious letters focus on personal matters, on his loneliness, on the weather, on his need for someone to care for him (a wife or a housekeeper), on his feeling of betrayal by the German public, or on his need for a new publisher. If there is any consistency in the letters that Schlechta lists as doctored, it involves the almost constant avowal of affection for Elisabeth and occasional remarks in some letters directed against persons whom Elisabeth had come to dislike, in particular Ida Overbeck and Lou Salomé. In their document from 1937 Schlechta and Hoppe claimed that the tendency in the questionable letters was to present a more intimate relationship between brother and sister, and a less favorable view of the mother;[22] in 1956 Schlechta notes that the letters also present evidence for Elisabeth's version of the Lou Salomé affair, presenting Salomé, Paul Rée, and Franz and Ida Overbeck as the malicious parties.[23] We should note, however, that genuine letters also and often contain fond sentiments, as well as words of kindness, concern, and gratitude that Nietzsche directed toward his sister, and that during specific periods of time Nietzsche also wrote critically and harshly about Frau Overbeck, Lou Salomé, and Paul Rée. In addition, the suspect letters also contain passages that are highly unflattering for Förster and Elisabeth.

In one such missive Nietzsche rebukes Förster for mixing his "highly moralistic Wagner veneration and his anti-Semitism in the Rée-Lou-affair." He further accuses Förster of complaining to Elisabeth about her brother's inconsiderateness, and takes her to task for her engagement: she has demonstrated only too clearly that she is going to sacrifice herself not "for his highest goals, but for those 'ideals' that I have already overcome and that I now have to combat (Christianity, Wagner, Schopenhauerian compassion)." He closes by adding, "Now I will not conceal that I regard this engagement as an insult—or as a stupidity that will harm you as much as it will me." A footnote to this purportedly falsified letter makes its status even more mysterious. With regard to Wagner's perfidious cohorts, Elisabeth includes an editorial comment explaining that the letter was written in anger and is full of errors.[24] It is difficult to understand what Elisabeth was trying to accomplish with this letter if it was indeed a falsification, but certainly by including a letter in which Nietzsche distances himself from Wagner and from the ideology of her husband, she does not make her brother more appealing for the extreme Right of a later era.

In fact it is difficult to find anything in these thirty-two letters that would have changed the ideological profile of Nietzsche toward the Right, or made him more susceptible to Nazi appropriation. There are a few strange moments. In the last letter that Schlechta suspects is doctored, Nietzsche writes of his admiration for the young Kaiser (Nietzsche is referring to Wilhelm II) for opposing anti-Semitism and the conservative *Kreuzzeitung*, remarking that his sister should emulate him, and that the Kaiser would certainly understand the principle of the will to power.[25] By contrast, in *Ecce Homo*, which would have been composed at about the same time as the letter, Nietzsche writes that he would not give the young Kaiser "the honor of being his coachman."[26] However, in a letter to Franz Overbeck from September 14, 1888, Nietzsche writes in a similar vein to the purportedly falsified letter: "[T]his young Kaiser is gradually presenting himself more advantageously than one could expect, — recently he came out strongly against anti-Semitism."[27] Again it is difficult to assess the degree of falsification. In another letter he accuses Elisabeth of hiding the anti-Semitic nature of her colony Nueva Germania, but adds that perhaps the Party is supporting it in words and not deeds.[28] In yet another letter Nietzsche rails against anti-Semitism and anti-Semites, but concedes that among the anti-Semites there are "respectable, diligent, and strong-willed characters."[29] What is striking, however, is the consistency of the ideological position: in these letters Nietzsche is never overtly nationalistic and always opposed to anti-Semitism, perhaps the central ideologeme that Elisabeth is accused of infusing into his writings, and of course a central tenet of National Socialism.[30] Occasionally Nietzsche is even critical of his sister for allowing herself to become involved with the anti-Semitic movement: "You have committed one of the greatest stupidities, my dear llama — for yourself and for me! Your connection with the chief anti-Semite is totally foreign to my nature and fills me again and again with anger and melancholy. You have said that you married the colonizer Förster and not the anti-Semite, and this is true; but in the eyes of the world Förster will remain until his death the head anti-Semite."[31] Elisabeth's motives for misrepresenting Nietzsche's letters is not entirely clear, but we can be certain that she did not do so to make her brother appear to be a more fervent supporter of German chauvinism, or to make him appear to be an anti-Semite.

Another area in which Elisabeth allegedly did preparatory tasks for the Nazi appropriation of Nietzsche was in her own writings on her brother. Indeed, during her lifetime her opinions on Nietzsche were not uninfluential; they carried the air of authority because of her unique access to documents in her possession and in the Nietzsche archives, and because she could justifiably claim a long and intimate relationship with her brother. In the haste to disqualify Elisabeth and make her responsible for any blemishes on Nietzsche's ideological surface, it is often forgotten how truly close the siblings really were. Growing up in the same household and being only two years his junior, Elisabeth had insights into areas of Nietzsche's upbringing and personality that no one else had, with the possible exception of Nietzsche's mother or his closest childhood friends. When he went to Pforta and then to the University of Bonn and Leipzig, Elisabeth and Fritz remained in frequent contact through correspondence and visits.

After he had received his professorship in Basel, Elisabeth became perhaps even more important for her brother since she spent a good deal of time living with him, running his household, and taking care of day-to-day business for him. Although her extended visits were not quite as long as she claimed they were, she still lived with him in Basel about half of the time he spent there. At times she functioned in a manner more similar to wife than to a sister; only in the summer of 1878 did they abandon for good their common household.[32] In the 1880s, when Nietzsche led his itinerant existence and Elisabeth married and moved to Paraguay, the ties between the two loosened to an extent. But even in this period, and despite Nietzsche's occasional outbreaks of frustration and anger toward Elisabeth, especially for her interference in the Lou Salomé affair, the siblings demonstrated obvious affection for one another. Nietzsche was concerned about his sister's welfare, in particular when she and her husband undertook their colonialist adventure in South America; she in turn was always solicitous of his health and his work. There were obvious strains in their relationship in the 1880s; but it is simply false to believe that these strains destroyed the intimacy that had existed between them for three decades.

It is not difficult to understand why Elisabeth's critics claim that in her writings she originated a Nietzsche legend, although almost every feature of this legend has its basis in Nietzsche's own writings or self-image.[33] But it is more difficult to understand why anyone would believe that this "legend" made him any more easily exploited by National Socialism. Elisabeth does not portray her brother as political in the usual sense of the word; she does not make him into a nationalist or a backer of the German Reich; nor does she associate him more closely with Wagner and the Wagnerians than he actually was. In particular, she takes pains to dissociate him from any sympathy toward anti-Semitism. Those who are acquainted with Nietzsche's life and works know that there are various moments when anti-Jewish sentiments played a role in his life. Nietzsche's letters are not entirely free from derogatory remarks about Jews, and there are scattered references that one could interpret as anti-Semitic, in particular in the writings on the history of religious thought. Furthermore, even a good friend such as Franz Overbeck regarded Nietzsche as anti-Semitic in some sense of the word.[34]

Elisabeth, however, who along with her mother was the recipient of many of these casual Judeophobic slurs, does not include these passages in her biography and does not mention them in any of her writings. Another missed opportunity came with the discussion of the aftermath of the publication of *The Birth of Tragedy*. The pamphlet written against Nietzsche's book by Ulrich von Wilamowitz-Moellendorff was understood by several of Nietzsche's friends, probably under the influence of Wagnerian anti-Semitic attitudes, as a product of Jewish culture. Upon hearing of Wilamowitz's assault on Nietzsche, Carl von Gersdorff wrote that the former had already sunk to the level of "Berlin literary Jewishness."[35] Erwin Rohde responded, "That is really a scandal in all its repugnant Jewish opulence."[36] Nietzsche never mentions the Jewish connection in his correspondence, although he too may have seen a nefarious Berlin influence in Wilamowitz's attack. The point, however, is that Elisabeth, who was not only in possession of documents associating Wilamowitz with a Jewish milieu, but also living with her brother at the time, never brings the Jewish factor into play. Nor does she mention Jewishness later in her biography in connection with Paul Rée, although the Wagners attributed Nietzsche's wayward path to the "Semitic" influence of his new friend.[37] If Elisabeth had wanted to produce an anti-Semitic Nietzsche, she had occasions and evidence, but obviously did not use them.

Elisabeth did not slant her depiction of Nietzsche toward anti-Semitism because she knew that he was virulently opposed to it; with regard to his view on Jews and anti-Semites there is absolutely no evidence that she attempted to falsify the record. Indeed, on numerous occasions in her biography[38] and in other writings she informs her readers of Nietzsche's antipathy to any form of anti-Jewish sentiment. In contrast to Wagner, Elisabeth writes, "my brother was never an anti-Semite; in addition, he was never completely convinced that Germany should be placed above everything; he always recognized that the Jews had done a great service for the intellectual movement in Germany, especially at the beginning of the century."[39] According to Elisabeth, the aggressive anti-Jewish remarks her brother wrote during the early 1870s were due to his attempt to conform to Wagner and his milieu. Later in her biography she again relates a criticism that her brother leveled at Wagner for his negative views of Jews;[40] she mentions in the second part of the second volume that the "unfortunate anti-Semitic movement" delayed the publication of *Zarathustra*;[41] and she reports that Nietzsche opposed the colonial enterprise of Förster because he suspected it had anti-Semitic tendencies.[42]

In other works, for example the book *Wagner and Nietzsche at the Time of Their Friendship* (1915), Elisabeth does not hesitate to quote occurrences of anti-Jewish statements in Nietzsche's letters, but she does not emphasize them and gives no indication that Nietzsche himself harbored ill feelings toward Jews. To the contrary, in this book she again argues that Nietzsche's anti-Jewish statements were meant to please Wagner: "In his letters there are attacks on the Jews that were an expression of Wagner's views, and not his own."[43] So consistent and accurate was Elisabeth in her presentation of Nietzsche's attitude toward the

Jews and toward the anti-Semitic movement her husband had helped found that no reader of her writings can conclude with any justification that she misrepresents her brother's views. If Nietzsche was going to be recruited for the anti-Jewish campaigns of National Socialism, racists could not depend on the writings of Elisabeth for any support.

Perhaps the last resort of those critics who would make Elisabeth responsible for Nietzsche's Nazi reputation is Elisabeth's own views and associates. As a member of the Wagner circle, she shared many Wagnerian values and beliefs, including those that were protofascist. Her marriage to Förster brought her into close proximity to the anti-Semitic movement; many of her Wagnerian acquaintances were convinced racists. During the Wilhelmine period she seems to have been a faithful and patriotic subject of the Prussian king, and like most of her compatriots, she was an enthusiastic supporter of German participation in World War I. She remained an ardent nationalist until the end of her life, despising the Weimar Republic and blaming treachery for the German defeat. Like her brother, she hated socialism, social democracy, and all democratic forces. We have already seen that she admired Mussolini and Italian fascism in the 1920s, and that she was not averse to the tributes paid to her and Nietzsche by right-wing parties and persons, including the National Socialists.

When Hitler came to power Elisabeth wrote,

> We are drunk with enthusiasm, because at the head of our government stands such a wonderful, indeed phenomenal, personality like our magnificent chancellor Adolf Hitler. That is why the tremendous upheaval in Germany probably appears quite different to us than to people abroad. They cannot understand how we endure these fast transformations so cheerfully. Well, the reason is that we have suddenly achieved the *one* Germany which for centuries our poets have depicted longingly in their poems and which we have all been waiting for: *Ein Volk, Ein Reich, Ein Führer.*[44]

This sort of endorsement might have been typical and expected if she were simply representing the Nietzsche archives, but it appears in a private letter. There is at least a body of evidence, then, to link Elisabeth with the political views that were associated with Nietzsche during the Third Reich, and from which the postwar rehabilitation sought to liberate him.

But Elisabeth's case is not quite so simple. In some ways she fits the mold into which her critics want to force her, but in some respects she does not. It is true that she was inclined toward nationalism, but she certainly shared these feelings with the vast majority of Germans, Europeans, and Americans during the decades prior to and following 1900.

Only occasionally did she try to make her brother into a supporter or potential supporter of Germany; in most instances she recognized that he remained critical of Germany and touted his own Europeanism as an alternative. She opposed the Weimar Republic, but again the antipathy to the parliamentary system forced onto Germany after the war was felt by millions of her compatriots on the left and the right. Her antidemocratic views were not significantly different from the views of many German conservatives prior to 1945, both those who would have shared Nietzsche's vehement rejection of the notion of equality itself, and those who stubbornly advocated a continuation of traditional privilege. Elisabeth's enthusiasm for Mussolini is repugnant, but understandable: here was a recognized world leader who had declared his enthusiasm and monetary support for her brother's philosophy. Elisabeth's main function since her return from South America had been to popularize Nietzsche's philosophy, to gain for him the reputation that he was denied during his sane life. In this context the backing of Mussolini must have seemed a great honor.

Her reactions to Hitler's homage and the patronage of the National Socialists has a similar rationale. Elisabeth was courted in 1929 by the Socialist minister in Berlin, Karl Severing, as well as the Nazi minister in Weimar, Dr. Wilhelm Frick,[45] and if Herbert Hoover or other world leaders had declared allegiance to Nietzsche, she would have no doubt responded favorably to their declarations as well. Indeed, in contrast to many other members of the archives, Elisabeth was not a member of the National Socialist Party. After World War I she joined the conservative German Fatherland Party; in the 1932 election for president of the Weimar Republic she declared her support for Hindenburg, not Hitler.[46] Although she quite obviously leaned toward the Right, she maintained for the archives an outward independence in terms of political affiliation.[47] Only with the advent of National Socialism did the archives become a more or less official institute of Nazi ideology.

Above all, Elisabeth was not an anti-Semite, despite her marriage to Förster, and despite her later adulation of Hitler and the Nazis. Her acceptance of Jewish support for Nietzsche and the archives was not based on hypocrisy or dishonesty, but rather on the one principle that really mattered to her in the final four decades of her life: the promotion of her brother and his works. It is in this context that we can understand her friendship with Ernest Thiel, a Swedish banker and industrialist brought up as an orthodox Jew. They may have differed on certain political issues, especially as the Weimar period drew to a close, but both were determined to make the Nietzsche archives a cultural centerpiece in Germany. Elisabeth did her part through tireless efforts at organization and relentless activity on behalf of her brother; Thiel contributed large sums of money, for which Elisabeth always expressed her sincerest gratitude.[48] Elisabeth also supported Jewish scholarship on Nietzsche, especially when it concurred with her views. A case in point is Paul Cohn's book *Concerning Nietzsche's Demise (Um Nietzsches Untergang)*, which appeared in 1931 and to which Elisabeth contributed an appendix with letters she wrote to Cohn.[49] Cohn himself was a physician from Breslau and an active member of the Jewish community; his work argued in part that Nietzsche's illness was due to hashish, and not to syphilis, an interpretation that Elisabeth greatly appreciated, especially since it came from a medical expert. And finally, there is much evidence that Elisabeth, if she had ever supported anti-Semitism, had disavowed her former convictions long before she began dealing seriously with her brother's writings and the archives.

In her Nietzsche biography she claims that she temporarily adopted anti-Semitic positions out of respect for her husband, while he was away in South America and needed someone to defend him in Germany. But she adds that anti-Semitism "was always unpleasant" for her and that she "did not have the slightest reason" to be an anti-Semite.[50] Hitler's rise to power evidently did not alter this conviction. In April of 1933 she wrote to Andreas Heusler, "Only the persecution of the Jews that Minister Goebbels wrenched from our excellent Chancellor seems to me a bad blunder and is very unpleasant for me. I am certain that it has not been pleasant for our splendid Chancellor Adolf Hitler, and that he will do everything to ameliorate this mistake of his fellow party members." And a few days later she reiterates these feelings: "I am not entirely in agreement with the anti-Jewish movement, even though I would have reason to approve of it, since as widow of the first leader of the anti-Semites I have been treated very badly by the Jewish press."[51]

Indeed, Erich F. Podach, who was anything but an apologist for Elisabeth, notes that she was critical of Max Öhler for suppressing the name of a Jewish author, Albert Levy, who wrote on Nietzsche and Stirner. She had no patience with such opportunism: "To be sure at no time did she ignore the political tendencies that might be favorable for her, but when push came to shove, she not only demonstrated a civil courage that was seldom seen in those times and supported her friends, but also she, the widow of Bernhard Förster, wrote anti-anti-Semitic petitions."[52] It is admittedly difficult to admire Elisabeth Förster-Nietzsche's political opinions. She obviously held positions that are loathsome to postwar supporters of democracy, equality, and cosmopolitanism, and some of her views coincided with those of avowed National Socialists. But with regard to anti-Semitism, that central feature of Nazi doctrine, she not only did not try to fashion her brother as a Judeophobe; she herself was free from overt, biologically based notions of racism.

Erich Podach, whose preoccupation with the life and works of Nietzsche had begun in the 1930s, saw rather clearly what had happened by 1961, at a time when the initial postwar rehabilitation had been almost completely achieved. By then Elisabeth Förster-Nietzsche had been successfully recast in the role of scapegoat for the Nazi Nietzsche appropriation. In his introduction to Nietzsche's last works, he points out that before 1933 practically the entire academic world paid tribute to Elisabeth and supported the efforts of the archives. Only after the war did Elisabeth become the object of scorn for Nietzsche scholars and enthusiasts: "Today, since no one stands up for her any longer, people have made it easy for themselves: The honorary doctor Elisabeth Förster-Nietzsche and she alone bears the guilt for everything."[53] The situation that Podach described has indeed persisted in the postwar years: the blanket condemnation of Förster-Nietzsche has been uncritically adopted by subsequent generations of Nietzscheans. Their knowledge of Elisabeth's activities is based more on conjecture and rumors than actual facts, more on unquestioned acceptance of traditional shibboleths than the results of research, more on wishful thinking than archival findings. Occasionally she is grudgingly given credit for the yeoman-like service she performed for over four decades in making her brother's work known to a broader public; at times, especially in recent years, even her critics will note that Elisabeth was exemplary as an independent, single woman, making her way in a male-dominated society, among academics and philosophers who traditionally showed little respect for women.[54] In general, however, she has been unjustly branded as an ardent Nazi, who from the very beginning connived to obtain the rights to Nietzsche's works and exercised an absolute hegemony over publications and manuscripts, subsequently distorting his thought through fraud and forgery in order to make him acceptable to a pernicious right-wing, jingoistic, racist clique. This image, manufactured in the 1950s in order to rehabilitate Nietzsche from his National Socialist admirers, is false. It is a legend that provides an easy explanation for a historical state of affairs that scholars have not wished to investigate.

If Elisabeth was not primarily responsible for Nietzsche's Nazi reputation, then who was? Like all matters of historical reception, there are no easy answers to this question. But after we are finished blaming Nietzsche's family, the workers in the Nietzsche archives, German right-wing philosophers such as Rosenberg and Bäumler, Mussolini, and Hitler, we ought to look to Nietzsche himself. We should not treat the issue ahistorically, as has too often been the case in the past. We can only speculate about how Nietzsche himself would have responded to the rise of National Socialism, and what exactly he himself would have done or written in the face of the Third Reich. If we examine Nietzsche's views in their historical context, however, we can more easily determine what kinds of ideologemes in his writings might have appealed or contributed to a fascist reception. We can note, first of all, that Nietzsche was certainly not an anti-Semite, and that there are relatively few disparaging remarks about Jews in his works.[55] At the same time, Nietzsche like most other thinkers in the nineteenth century, harbored certain racial, if not racist, prejudices, some of which at least appear to have been based on a popularized view of biology. He read Galton, showed an interest in what we would today call eugenics, and even sketched out plans for an engineered society in some of his notebooks.[56] By now it is generally known that after the early 1870s Nietzsche was not a nationalist, and that there are frequent and virulent comments against Germany, German patriotism, and the German people scattered throughout his writings.

But Nietzsche also wrote often about war and cruelty in an extremely positive and troubling fashion, praising the warrior ethos and promulgating a European hegemony over the entire earth. Finally, Nietzsche was against all movements of his time that promoted equality in the social, political, or economic realm. He railed against democracy, parliamentary systems, the feminist movement, and socialism; he incessantly lauded hierarchy and declared himself, if necessary, in favor of slavery.[57] His views on these issues were often out of touch with reality, and they appeared radical even for a German conservatism that abhorred the political changes brought by the liberal nineteenth century. Not all of Nietzsche's positions, therefore, could be appropriated by National Socialism, and some of his views certainly conflicted with Nazi doctrine, as some Nazis themselves noticed. But others were quite susceptible to exploitation by the Third Reich. We should also not forget that Nietzsche's style, his radical sensibility and rhetorical hyperbole, as well as the apocalyptic imaginings and exhortatory visions contributed to a general atmosphere that made the Third Reich possible.[58] Thinkers, of course, cannot be held responsible for the misrepresentation of their thoughts; but neither are they completely innocent of future appropriations of their ideas. Nietzsche's sister, in making her brother's works available to a broad public, certainly contributed to his reputation. But it is time that we ceased scapegoating her for the National Socialist version of Nietzsche and understand this unfortunate chapter in his reception as an effort to which Nietzsche himself and a host of his perhaps unwanted disciples made the most seminal contributions.

Notes

1. Chief among these voices were a variety of anti-Semites, who found in his writings too many positive images of Jews and too many diatribes against Judeophobia. See Steven E. Aschheim, "Nietzsche, Anti-Semitism and the Holocaust," in *Nietzsche and Jewish Culture*, ed. Jacob Golomb (London: Routledge, 1997), 3–20; here 7.

2. Steven E. Aschheim, *The Nietzsche Legacy in Germany 1890–1990* (Berkeley: University of California Press, 1992), 240.

3. Friedrich Nietzsche, *Schwert des Geistes: Worte für den deutschen Kämpfer und Soldaten*, ed. Joachim Schondorff (Stuttgart: Kröner, 1941), viii.

4. Crane Brinton, *Nietzsche* (Cambridge: Harvard University Press, 1941), 216.

5. The story of Elisabeth Förster-Nietzsche has been told on several occasions, but never with much sympathy. The most extensive study is H. F. Peters, *Zarathustra's Sister: The Case of Elisabeth and Friedrich Nietzsche* (New York: Crown, 1977). Erich F. Podach's sketch of "Bernhard and Eli Förster" (in his *Gestalten um Nietzsche* [Weimar: Erich Lichtenstein Verlag, 1932], 125–76) focuses mostly on the colonial enterprise in Paraguay. See also Klaus Goch, "Elisabeth Förster-Nietzsche 1846–1935: Ein biographisches Portrait," in *Schwestern berühmter Manner*, ed. Luise F. Pusch (Frankfurt: Inscl, 1985), 361–413; and Karl S. Guthke: "Zarathustras Tante," *Neue Deutsche Hefte* 29, no. 3 (1982): 470–83.

6. Karl Schlechta, "Philologischer Nachbericht," in vol. 3 of Friedrich Nietzsche, *Werke in drei Bänden* (Munich: Hanser, 1956), 1383–432, esp. 1390–1417.

7. Karl Schlechta, *Der Fall Nietzsche* (Munich: Hanser, 1959), 78.

8. Friedrich Nietzsche, *The Will to Power*, trans. Walter Kaufmann and R. J. Hollingdale, ed. Walter Kaufmann (New York: Random House, Vintage, 1967).

9. Walter Kaufmann, *Nietzsche: Philosopher, Psychologist, Antichrist*, 4th ed. (Princeton: Princeton University Press, 1974), 46. Kaufmann provides no evidence or documentation for his claims here. Elisabeth did not seem to mind that the Nazis regarded her brother highly, but she generally supported anyone who praised her brother provided that they did not oppose her.

10. Richard Roos, "Les derniers écrits de Nietzsche et leur publication," *Revue philosophique* 146 (1956): 262–87.

11. Richard Roos, "Elisabeth Förster-Nietzsche ou la sœur abusive," *Etudes Germanique* 11, no. 4 (1956): 321–41; here, 322.

12. Ibid., 339.

13. Janet Lungstrum, "Nietzsche Writing Woman / Woman Writing Nietzsche: The Sexual Dialectic of Palingenesis," in *Nietzsche and the Feminine*, ed. Peter J. Burgard (Charlottesville: University Press of Virginia, 1994), 135–57; here 150.

14. Bernd Magnus and Kathleen M. Higgins, "Nietzsche's Works and Their Themes," in *The Cambridge Companion to Nietzsche*, ed. Bernd Magnus and

Kathleen M. Higgins (Cambridge: Cambridge University Press, 1996), 21–68; here 57.

15. R. J. Hollingdale, "The Hero as Outsider," in *The Cambridge Companion to Nietzsche*, ed. Bernd Magnus and Kathleen M. Higgins (Cambridge: Cambridge University Press, 1996), 71–89; here 86–87.

16. David Marc Hoffmann, "Vorbemerkung," *Rudolf Steiner und das Nietzsche-Archiv: Briefe und Dokumente 1894–1900*, ed. David Marc Hoffmann, Veröffentlichungen des Archivs der Rudolf Steiner-Nachlaßverwaltung, vol. 6 (Dornach: Rudolf Steiner Verlag, 1993), 7.

17. Werner Stegmaier and Daniel Krochmalnik, "Einleitung," in *Jüdischer Nietzscheanismus, Monographien und Texte zur Nietzsche-Forschung* 36 (Berlin: de Gruyter, 1997), xiv.

18. Weaver Santaniello, "A Post-Holocaust Re-Examination of Nietzsche and the Jews: Vis-à-vis Christendom and Nazism," in *Nietzsche and Jewish Culture*, 21–54; here, 21.

19. Ibid., 23, 43.

20. Paul Strathern, *Nietzsche in 90 Minutes* (Chicago: Ivan R. Dee, 1996), 42.

21. Schlechta, "Philologischer Nachbericht," 3: 1417.

22. Ibid.

23. Ibid., 1412.

24. Friedrich Nietzsche, *Friedrich Nietzsches Gesammelte Briefe*, vol. 5, *Friedrich Nietzsches Briefe an Mutter und Schwester*, ed. Elisabeth Förster-Nietzsche (Leipzig: Insel, 1909), 557–59.

25. Ibid., 801–802.

26. *KSA*, 6:268. For the remainder of this essay all citations from Nietzsche's works and notebooks will be taken from Friedrich Nietzsche, *Sämtliche Werke, Kritische Studienausgabe*.

27. *KGB*, 8:433.

28. *Friedrich Nietzsches Gesammelte Briefe*, 5:726.

29. Ibid., 5:776.

30. Indeed, Elisabeth did not include material she had in her possession that could have made Nietzsche appear more anti-Semitic.

31. *Friedrich Nietzsches Gesammelte Briefe*, 5:733–34.

32. See Goch, "Elisabeth Förster-Nietzsche," 373.

33. See Erich F. Podach, "Anhang," *Friedrich Nietzsches Werke des Zusammenbruchs* (Heidelberg: Wolfgang Rothe Verlag, 1961), 407.

34. See *Begegnungen mit Nietzsche*, ed. Sander L. Gilman, 2nd exp. ed. (Bonn: Bouvier, 1985), 471–73. After carefully explaining Nietzsche's views on Jews in the academic circles he frequented, Overbeck turns to his religious thought and concludes that "his anti-Christianity was chiefly founded on anti-Semitism."

35. *Nietzsche Briefwechsel*, *KGA*, II 4:9.

36. Ibid., II 4:11.

37. Cosima Wagner's remarks probably express feelings that were common among Wagnerians in the late 1870s. Discussing Nietzsche's turn from the Wagnerian cause, Cosima attributes his waywardness to the intervention of Israel

"in the form of a Dr. Rée, very sleek, very cool, at the same time as being wrapped up in Nietzsche and dominated by him, though actually outwitting him—the relationship between Judaea and Germany in miniature." Cited in Ronald Hayman, *Nietzsche: A Critical Life* (New York: Oxford University Press, 1980), 204.

38. Elisabeth Förster-Nietzsche, *Das Leben Friedrich Nietzsche's* (Leipzig: Naumann, 1895–1904). Volume one appeared in 1895; the first part of volume two appeared in 1897; the second part in 1904.

39. Ibid., II 1:208.

40. Ibid., 232.

41. Förster-Nietzsche, *Das Leben Friedrich Nietzsche's*, II 2:431.

42. Ibid., II 2:501.

43. Elisabeth Förster-Nietzsche, *Wagner und Nietzsche zur Zeit ihrer Freundschaft* (Munich: Georg Müller, 1915), 211.

44. Cited in Peters, *Zarathustra's Sister*, 220.

45. Ibid., 217.

46. Ibid., 205, 216.

47. See Karl-Heinz Hahn, "Das Nietzsche-Archiv," *Nietzsche Studien* 18 (1989): 1–19; here, 17.

48. Thiel seems not to have balked in his support for Elisabeth, nor in his friendship with her, even when she wrote enthusiastically about Hitler (Peters, *Zarathustra's Sister*, 220–21). Elisabeth evidently led him to believe—and she may have believed this herself—that the persecution of the Jews by Nazis was the result of a few misguided party members, and that when things settled down, the Nazis would obviously allow the best of the "alien race" to remain in Germany.

49. Paul Cohn, *Um Nietzsches Untergang: Beiträge zum Verständnis des Genies*, mit einem Anhang von Elisabeth Förster-Nietzsche, Die Zeit von Nietzsches Erkrankung bis zu seinem Tode (Hanover: Morris-Verlag, 1931).

50. Förster-Nietzsche, *Das Leben Friedrich Nietzsche's*, II 2:469.

51. Both citations are taken from Roos, "Elisabeth Förster-Nietzsche," 340.

52. Podach, "Anhang," 414. Podach claims that there is documentary evidence for his assertions, but cites nothing specifically.

53. Podach, "Vorwort," *Friedrich Nietzsches Werke des Zusammenbruchs*, 11.

54. The "feminist" angle is a leitmotif in the biographical essay by Goch.

55. See Robert C. Holub, "Nietzsche and the Jewish Question," *New German Critique* 22, no.3 (1995): 94–121.

56. For example, *KSA*, 9:189–90.

57. See chap. 5 in Robert C. Holub, *Friedrich Nietzsche* (New York: Twayne Publishers, 1995), 79–101.

58. See Aschheim, "Nietzsche, Anti-Semitism and the Holocaust," esp. 14–16.

11

Nietzsche, Mussolini, and Italian Fascism
Mario Sznajder

Most of the writings dealing with the intellectual origins of fascism mention the name of Friedrich Nietzsche as one of the philosophers whose work influenced Nazism.[1] However, when examining the central sources of Italian Fascism as a political regime and movement, little or no mention is made of Nietzsche's influence. Here we will try to assess the relationship between Nietzsche's work and Italian Fascism through an examination of Gabriele D'Annunzio, the warrior poet who interpreted and introduced Nietzsche into Italy and was one of the main figures of Italian culture between the 1890s and the advent of fascism; and we shall also look at Mussolini's uses of Nietzsche during his transition from socialism to fascism and subsequently as *Duce* of Italy.

In the 1930s, at the zenith of fascist power, Mussolini had pronounced D'Annunzio as Italy's greatest living writer, yet the poet never held any official position in Fascist Italy except that of President of the Royal Academy. Still, D'Annunzio's influence on Fascism was considerable. He was, for example, seen as one of its cultural precursors, having co-authored with Alceste De Ambris (a national syndicalist leader closely related to Mussolini and the "fascism of the first hour" in 1919) the *Carta del Carnaro*. The constitution of the Regency of Fiume in 1920, was seen as a model for Italy. Fascism even claimed that its corporative model and ideas were inspired by it. D'Annunzio also invented the political style later adopted by Mussolini and fascism, stressing the

,ide of politics, the mise en scène of political rallies, and direct between the leader and the masses. D'Annunzio later sup- ascism in the critical year of its ascent to power and saw in ₁. ₁ni a modern Italian hero. In this context, it is interesting that Nietzsche's ideas not only played a central role in shaping D'Annunzio's views, but also, through the poet's literary and political activities, they became a vehicle for the dissemination of a distinctive brand of Nietz- scheanism in Italy and in the fascist movement.

Mussolini's views on Nietzsche also became at a very early stage im- portant in the shaping of his political vision and leadership style. Al- ready as a revolutionary socialist, Mussolini began using concepts and a terminology drawn from Nietzsche and relating to the German philoso- pher as one of his main sources of inspiration. With varying levels of intensity, the future *Duce* of Italian Fascism kept relying on or referring to Nietzsche throughout his political career, in different contexts. Al- though Mussolini did not place Nietzsche among the intellectual ances- tors of Italian fascism, there is little doubt about the strong influence that the German philosopher's thought had on his views, however ma- nipulative Mussolini's use of them may have been.

An examination of how these two bridging figures dealt with Nietz- sche demonstrates a striking paradox—namely his ideological influence on fascism despite the highly individualistic views and aristocratic ethos that he espoused. Yet leaders like D'Annunzio and Mussolini could per- sonally identify with major themes of Nietzsche's thought—such as life as art, the "Overman," or "living dangerously," while translating these ideas into a political movement, oblivious to the highly distorting effect of "Nietzschean" mass politics.

Nietzsche on Politics

The political dimension in Friedrich Nietzsche's thought is inseparable from his general philosophical approach in all its logical, ontological, and aesthetic manifestations. There has been a marked tendency to see Nietzsche's political thought only in terms of his philosophy of power. Yet Nietzsche argued that social habit and custom were the elements that keep society together, that functional hierarchies were superior to social and economic equality. The ideal historical model of society for Nietzsche was the one that governed the ancient Greek *polis* and the European aristocracy of the Renaissance. In modern terms, his political preferences could be characterized as neo-aristocratic conservatism, hostile to democratic rule but also to the state and the German nation- alism that developed in the Second Reich, as well as to anti-Semitism.[2]

In *Thus Spoke Zarathustra*, the state is depicted as "the coldest of all monsters" that likes to surround itself with heroes and honorable men (Z, I: "On the New Idol"). According to Nietzsche's view, the politics of domination would eventually give way to a society without government or administration—essentially a free entity, metapolitical in its nature.[3] There is, moreover, a kind of irrationalism in Nietzsche's thought whereby action becomes a value in itself, regardless of its results. This serves as a differential criteria between "vulgar people" and heroes, defining the great individual who was able to transcend himself. Nietzsche could only show contempt for people who felt satisfied with their own selves—who were unable to act or to conduct an affirmative struggle. Equally, he deplored the critical rationalist spirit that had destroyed Greek culture and had become the enemy of instinctive life, creation, and all the noble virtues. This Socratic-Platonic rationalist tradition had become the guiding light of Western civilisation, leading it to decadence and destruction. Such trends were even more manifest in Christianity, which embodied a kind of popular Platonism or mass rationalism of the weak-minded, the lifeless, and the passively suffering.[4] All these elements become the core of nihilism—the devaluation of all values or the negation of life—exemplified by egalitarianism, the herd or slave morality, misplaced compassion, and the repression of healthy instinct. This is sharply contrasted to the aristocratic ideal of social distance and hierarchy, the value of genius and solitude. Similarly a rejection of guilt was preferred by Nietzsche to the spirit of resentment, which acted in oblique ways to favor preservation of the weak against the strong and powerful. Nietzsche equally deplored all efforts to escape to a timeless world of eternal ideals, values, and truths. He linked this to the attempt by Christianity to erase all differences and institutionalize a "slave morality," a gospel of and for the weak. Christianity, following the path of Judaism, had inverted the morality of the "masters" and sublimated the instincts. Asceticism thereby turned into the ultimate revenge of the powerless against strength and instinctive life. This negation of natural values had been transmitted through the Christian heritage to secular political modernity and transmuted into egalitarianism, democracy, and socialism, all abhorred by Nietzsche.

Nietzsche perceived the crisis of modernity as being related to impersonalization, loss of individuality, lack of ideals, banal materialism, and an outlook that preferred the truth to life itself. The "last man," as Nietzsche called this prototype "is the result of a political culture that had mediated power relations between individuals through external identities such as those of God and country. . . . The existence of the "last men" leaves a fertile ground for invasion of the self by the state or any other institutionalized power."[5] This invasion of the self, or total

237

...al identity and rights, climaxed in modern political terms
...olishment of totalitarianism, an event that in Nietzschean
...have to be seen as deplorable. Unlike most liberal thinkers,
...ad always feared that democracies would become the tool of
...   majority, used by it in order to impose herd values on the
whole ... society. Deeply preoccupied with culture, he saw in the modern state a clear antagonist along with egalitarianism and the loss of individual identity implicit in modern nationalism: "Culture and the state — one should not deceive oneself about it — are antagonists. . . . All great ages of culture are ages of political decline: what is great culturally has always been unpolitical, even *antipolitical*."[6] It is in this sense that we see in Nietzsche's thought an antagonism between the individual and the state. It should be clear that his preoccupation with individuality, creativity, and personal authenticity could not find a political solution in the strengthening of the state, least of all one that appropriated these terms and used them to stress collective results.[7]

The crisis of modernity is epitomised by Nietzsche with the dramatic affirmation: God is dead. Historically this statement means at the same time that our faith in God existed previously and that a cultural situation has evolved in which it is impossible to keep believing in his existence. Here, Nietzsche was following the path of Feuerbach, Schopenhauer, and Marx, but elaborating their critique of religion into an atheism of the Right. He attacked Christianity and democracy as moralities of the weak herd, as decadent forms of human life, contrary to the need for an aristocracy of powerful and heroic values, personified by his ideal superman. The superior being must have the courage to live dangerously and to use his passion and vital energy in a creative way. This will to power is, however, *antipolitical* in the sense that it works against any attempt to formalize or institutionalize historical development. Life as art, or as a manifestation of the will to power, is dynamic and impossible to capture in a functional structure or systemic philosophy. Nietzsche's thought escapes any teleological historical direction since no ultimate reality or historic law was discerned by the author. The essence of life lay in action not in the social, political, or historical links that may exist among the actors. No utopia or any ultimate aim or state could be established in advance. The creative will, the deed itself, was for Nietzsche everything.

The will to power did not, of course, represent the whole scope of Nietzsche's political thought though it still remained central to it. But the exercise of the will to power symbolized reaching a higher stage of humanity by the elimination of value contradictions between human behavior and human nature. According to Nietzsche, the forms of decadence that evolved as nihilism represented antivalues (or negative values)

as they appeared in Christianity, and even more so, in modern life. St.
tegically nihilism may be overcome by transvaluation, a reversal o.
moral standards similar to the one he attributes to the Jews of ancient
times.

Nietzsche presents the qualities of the Overman, essential for revaluation: individualism, integrity, and authenticity; delicacy, culture,
and nobility—as opposed to the qualities of the mass man. This is not a
definite formula or a precise description but a set of qualities that could
promote revaluation through the acts of their possessors, all of them
superior men. Politically, it may be interpreted in terms of the qualities
needed by national leaders. From Nietzsche's point of view, these qualities would not only enable revaluation to take place but also have a
profound revolutionary character, as they would help destroy the social
and political order based on the "slave morality." As a result, the
masses—socialist, nationalist, or simply individual consumers reordered
by the forces of the market—would be subject to the domination of
superior men. Thus, we return to the aristocratic conservatism of Nietzsche, which, coupled with his lack of system in the area of political
thought, opened his influence in many possible directions. Nietzsche's
fate was for his writings to be quoted selectively and to be interpreted
and misinterpreted many times according to the will, the needs, or the
(mis)understanding of the interpreter.

D'Annunzio and Nietzsche

Nietzsche toured Italy frequently between 1876 and 1889, and the
places he visited there were related to and reflected in his work. Still, his
influence in Italy would not be felt until the 1890s, first in restricted
cultural and philosophical circles and then, above all, through the work
of Gabriele D'Annunzio.[8] It could be claimed that the lack of diffusion
of Nietzsche in Italy was not exceptional. At the beginning of the 1890s
he was little known in Germany and in France, except through the polemics around the publication of *The Birth of Tragedy* in 1872 and *The
Case of Wagner*, in 1888.[9]

It was Gabriele D'Annunzio who relocated Nietzsche from the philosophical terrain into the realm of literature, so central in the culture of
Italian *Risorgimento*, providing the elements of diffusion and success.
By creating a literary "case" that turned him into a myth, D'Annunzio
was getting a wider audience for Nietzsche and, simultaneously, with-
drawing him from the philological sifting of the philosophers and
critics, from the rigor of specialists "to prepare for himself the superhuman reading [of Nietzsche], its use in an aristocratic key."[10]

Guy Tosi claims that the discovery of Nietzsche by D'Annunzio took place in 1892, the same year in which the philosopher became famous and was widely discussed in France. It seems that in D'Annunzio's poem "*La nave,*" there is a reminiscence for those who want to distance themselves from the rabble, as described in *Thus Spoke Zarathustra.*[11] Later in the same year, D'Annunzio published a strongly antidemocratic article "*La bestia elettiva*" in which, along the same lines previously used by Nietzsche, the Italian poet attacked the political principles of the French Revolution ("*il dogma dell'ottantanove*" — ["the dogma of eighty nine"]) for eliminating natural differences among human beings. D'Annunzio also rejected the idea of creating a state able to produce "public happiness," which, in his opinion, would lead nowhere. D'Annunzio quoted Nietzsche's analysis of the relationship between European decadence and slave morality, imposed by Christianity and modernization, turning to the aristocratic view that equated *noble* with *good*; he concluded that since nobility had clear class implications, it had to be recognized that the aristocracy created the concept of *good*. This was seen by scholars as the beginning of the development of an aristocratic aesthetics by D'Annunzio, who used motives already expressed by Nietzsche, which led to the publication of *Le vergini delle rocce*. This work, first published in episodes in *Il Convito* (D'Annunzio's own review) beginning in January 1895, can be seen as his own political manifesto on the "Overman." Since no Italian translations of Nietzsche were yet available, D'Annunzio, well versed in the French cultural developments of the period, read Nietzsche's writings as they were being published in Paris. Nietzschean and D'Annunzian ideas found a special echo in Naples, where Parisian intellectual life was frequently discussed and referred to by the academic and intellectual elites.[12]

By mid-1893 D'Annunzio was presenting Nietzsche to Italian readers in highly complimentary terms, adopting the idea of the will to power to the point of claiming that humanity should be divided into a superior race, "heightened by the pure energy of its will," and an inferior one, devoid of this quality. Well-being, according to D'Annunzio, would be for the privileged since "their personal nobility will make them worthy of all the privileges." But a note of discord already appears since D'Annunzio was more "a Wagnerian than a Nietzschean" (a fact clearly seen in D'Annunzio's *Il trionfo della morte* [*The Triumph of Death*]), one who rejected the accusations and ironies of the kind expressed by Nietzsche in 1888 in *The Case of Wagner*. D'Annunzio did not deem this worthy of a philosopher, even if Nietzsche avoided *decadence* by placing himself outside of his own time.[13] Adopting a "realistic" aesthetic, D'Annunzio was distancing himself from Nietzsche in favor of Wagner. But even more, he was making a statement about the lack of responsibility of the artist for the impact of his own work.[14] In other words, D'Annunzio was claiming that neither Wagner's art nor his own oeuvre could be judged from a moral point of view. All this, in spite of the fact that the preface of *Il trionfo della morte* finished in a strikingly Nietz-schean spirit, stating, "We open the heart to the voice of the magnani-mous Zarathustra or Cenobiarca; and we prepare in art with sure faith the advent of the *Übermensch*, of the Overman."[15] D'Annunzio's work was a powerful vehicle for the literary entrance of Nietzsche's ideas into the Italian cultural realm and even beyond, since his novels were read by a wide public and his articles published in the most prestigious intel-lectual publications of the time. D'Annunzio became a leading actor in the intellectual revolution of the late nineteenth century that rejected the cultural tradition of the Enlightenment and the political legacy of the French Revolution. This intellectual revolution in which modern nation-alists and anti-Marxist socialists came together to elaborate the basis of fascist ideology before the First World War, was also the context in which Nietzsche's ideas found their widest echo.[16]

Having adopted the idea of the "Overman" in *Il trionfo della morte*, D'Annunzio, deeply embedded in Italian nationalism, went one step fur-ther. In *Le vergine delle rocce*, he tried to describe the age of the Italian Renaissance as a time where "supermen" lived and acted. This ap-peared as a counterpoint to the decadence of the Italian nobility at the end of the nineteenth century, an aristocracy awaiting extinction.[17] The rebellion against modernization, the need for an aristocracy of intellec-tuals (which D'Annunzio saw himself as leading) as well as sensuality and eroticism as marks of "real" life, the depiction of popular masses as a rabble, the cult of strength, and strong antidemocratic biases were all featured in his writings. They reflected Nietzsche's rejection of Enlight-enment values and served as a rallying point for new antidemocratic forces of all kinds. Christianity, the bourgeoisie, and sociopolitical deca-dence were linked together by these antidemocratic forces and depicted in highly negative terms. Those who found inspiration in Nietzsche or in D'Annunzio's interpretation of his ideas would become increasingly critical of Italian liberal parliamentarism and its main leader, Giovanni Giolitti. They would pose revolutionary alternatives to the political es-tablishment and the timid attempts made by reformists to gradually change the situation. The cataclysm of the First World War acted as a catalyst in two directions: it would seriously weaken the capacity of the establishment to satisfy the demands of all those Italians who directly or indirectly had made huge contributions to the war effort; and it would lead to a large crisis—the *bienno rosso* of 1919–20—a failed socialist revolution that provided the momentum for an imminent fascist acces-sion to power. Here again, D'Annunzio made good use of Nietzschean thought and motives when he moved from artistic life to the battlefield to become a war hero, seeking political leadership through the occupation of Fiume in 1919. For D'Annunzio, war brought the desire to apply the will to power and its results turned this need into a political imperative.

D'Annunzio had first entered politics in the 1890s and in September 1897 had been elected to parliament on an extreme Right platform. But some months later the poet announced that he had undergone a political conversion. Henceforth he proclaimed that he was a man of the Left, having moved "from death to life, from Right to Left."[18] D'Annunzio's politics was in fact closely linked to his personal life and philosophical views. He became a nationalist primarily out of aesthetic considerations. For him, Italy's past and present represented the artistic centre of Western culture and individuals like himself were to carry out the revival of what had been glorious traditions. Politics were a vehicle for the imposition of noble and beautiful life ideals. The aesthetization of politics—to use Walter Benjamin's concept—could serve as a means to bring the masses to support a new aristocracy of supermen by arousing their passions. It was the task of the exceptional individual to set the pace, to channel popular energies and guide the masses in order to achieve national greatness. D'Annunzio was now moving from explicitly Nietzschean influences into what would become one of the main characteristics of the fascist style in politics. He was convinced that the masses could be inspired and led to higher stages of achievement and culture.

The entrance of the masses into politics was an undeniable reality and the Italian poet confronted it in his own terms. D'Annunzio, in a clear antipositivistic and antimaterialistic way, still opposed cold rationalism, devising a new role for the "Overman" as Artist and Savior of society. This was to be done by a combination of artistic and political entrepreneurship, by aestheticizing politics, by making it the domain of the artist. Nationalism was the proper venue for what D'Annunzio believed to be the true aggressive nature of human beings and especially of Italians, as inheritors of the Roman Empire and its habitat, the shores of the Mediterranean (*Mare Nostrum*). This had brought him to support Italian colonial aspirations and to volunteer, at the age of fifty-two to serve at the front in the First World War.

D'Annunzio was an interventionist, pushing for Italy to enter the Great War. It is in this context that he wrote an oration where he exalted youth, which was closely associated with change and the noble, heroic values of the new elite. Vitality, vigor, and virility were the components meant to complete the *Risorgimento* in an ultranationalist and warrior-like fashion by cultivating the heroic values of the Romans for the greatness of the Kingdom of Italy. At the beginning of the war, D'Annunzio was in Paris, where he would develop a new life-style and begin to transmute his concept of the Nietzschean superman into practice. Describing his feelings in Paris at the beginning of the war, D'Annunzio wrote, "Every night I went to the gloomy stations to greet the wounded, to adore the splendor of blood, to breathe the strength and power of the people, to feel the heroic quiver deify the undernourished mass. All the centuries of the race became intermingled in the waves of my constant emotion. The nearer the danger was, the more beautiful and strong the city appeared to me."[19]

The role of the hero as deeply involved, in spite of age and circumstances, in the workings of war, was surfacing, but in a different way from that imagined by Nietzsche. The new heroes were struggling at the head of nations and empires that had mobilized masses of men and technology in the gigantic bureaucratic machinery of modern armies. The "Overman" was still needed, perhaps more than ever, not as a lone hero of superior morality but rather as a leader of the enrolled masses, trying to instill them with his own values, which were symbolically entangled with those of the nation or empire. It is in this sense that D'Annunzio and other forerunners of fascism understood, interpreted, and practiced Nietzsche's ideals, in a time of the engulfing tragedy of the Great War. Failure to participate in it, for people like D'Annunzio or Mussolini (and many other interventionists) would have been the greatest of crimes.

After Italy entered the war, on May 24, 1915, D'Annunzio volunteered at the age of fifty-two. A celebrity and a well-educated man, he was commissioned as a lieutenant in the Light Horse of Novara regiment but began flying and sailing, simultaneously addressing soldiers and sailors and becoming a propaganda asset highly appreciated by the General Staff and the government. Famous as a great lover before the war, D'Annunzio discovered that comradeship was the dominant emotion in war and that "the most secret quiver of unspoken love is nothing in comparison with certain looks, exchanged by two companions in times of danger, which confirm their fidelity to the idea, the silent sacrifice of the morrow."[20] In February 1916 he was seriously wounded in the eye and was obligated to convalesce for a period of six months.

After he returned to active duty in September 1916, D'Annunzio served mostly with the infantry and elite units, being promoted to captain and receiving the Croix de Guerre from the French government. D'Annunzio was truly a hero, being promoted for bravery and collecting awards and medals for heroic acts and exemplary conduct under fire. He was acting out his own version of the Overman, presenting the world with another version of the "master morality." If before the war he did this in writing and speeches, it was now his deeds that made him a hero, primarily in the eyes of his comrades and all those who knew of his exploits. The crowning act of D'Annunzio's participation in the Italian war effort took place in August 1918 when he flew over Vienna, leading the Serenissima squadron — the historic name of Venice — bombing the city with leaflets in which the Viennese were called to abandon their Prussian allies and surrender.[21]

At the end of the war, D'Annunzio was a self-created Italian legend in which literary fantasy and reality mixed freely. Deeds and words had, through the D'Annunzian act, become a mixture of the poet's interpretation of the Nietzschean superman, heavily daubed with the colors of Italian nationalism. After the war, when international politics brought everyone down to reality, this image would be difficult to live with. For Italy, the political results of three-and-a-half years of supreme sacrifice with heavy human and material losses, were extremely sparse and frustrating. D'Annunzio faced once more the dilemma of action constrained by political reality. He had to live up to his heroic reputation and nationalist creed. Still, the political reality was closing all avenues.

In early 1919, D'Annunzio published in Paris a small book, *Aveux de l'Ingrat*, in which he reflected on the political destiny of Italy after the war. Recalling the Italian sacrifice in the war, he compared the French wish for the Rhineland with the Italian demand for Dalmatia, which had been rejected by the Allies.[22] President Wilson became his bête noire. In April–May 1919, D'Annunzio revived the radiant spirit of May 1915 (*Maggio Radioso*) with speeches about Dalmatia and Italy and later met Mussolini in Rome. *Il popolo d'Italia*, (the recently founded newspaper of the *Fasci di combattimento* movement) was already supporting D'Annunzio's irredentist position toward the coast of Dalmatia. D'Annunzio, like Mussolini, was attacking pacifism, the former neutralism of many Italian politicians, parliamentary democracy, socialism, and materialism, and was calling on the Italians to act heroically again.

Supported by a large number of armed followers, D'Annunzio occupied the city of Fiume, in the name of Italy, on September 12, 1919. This act was against the orders sent by the Italian government to all of its army units in the area, and it stood in direct contradiction to the political decisions contemplated in the peace settlements elaborated in France that year. Although France and Great Britain were implicated in Fiume, they decided to stand aside and let the Italian government deal with the crisis. D'Annunzio entered Fiume and assumed the title of *Commandante*. Rome responded by blockading the port. For D'Annunzio, Fiume was a dramatic scene in which he served both as director and leading actor, as well as a political laboratory where all kind of "revolutionary" social and political ideas could be presented — some were even put into practice. Among the followers of D'Annunzio and the legionaries of Fiume one could find a wide spectrum of supporters ranging from ex-revolutionary syndicalists and interventionists on the Left to fascists, futurists and extreme nationalists on the Right, as well as many adventurers and professional soldiers locking for action. The Italian inhabitants of Fiume also became active participants in the experiment.

The most lasting product of Fiume was the Carta del Carnaro, an extraordinary political document whose theoretical framework was prepared by Alceste De Ambris, a former revolutionary syndicalist who became an interventionist in 1914 and an ideological guide to Benito Mussolini and the fascists immediately after the war.[23] Although the basic political framework (actually the constitution of the self-proclaimed Regency of Fiume) was De Ambris's work, D'Annunzio imprinted his views on the final version of the document. Italian Fascism would later claim the Carta del Carnaro as a source of inspiration and even as a basic document of the movement and regime, though profound differences existed between the Fiume constitution and the practice of fascism. Nevertheless, one could claim that fascism did learn a way of conducting mass politics from D'Annunzio's Fiume experiment.[24]

Many of the elements that appear in the Carta del Carnaro such as productionism and corporativism were internalized by the fascists, though in Fiume the spirit had been more libertarian and mystic rather than authoritarian or statist. D'Annunzio's contribution not only reflected Nietzsche's influence on his beliefs but was also passed on to fascism, though in a rather distorted way. For example, he adopted the medieval Florentine motto *Fatica senza fatica* (work without weariness) in order to ensure that "in the new city, man would regain the joy of living." This vision of the "new man" included such elements of life as art as well as the dream of eliminating alienation through creative work. The departure from Nietzsche lay in the belief in "constructivism" and the possibility of creating a new man by educating people into a new set of values. Labor, in order to become an element of freedom and a way to overcome alienation, had to be spiritualized.[25] The aestheticism of D'Annunzio comes to fullest expression in the last articles of the Carta del Carnaro, where he deals with architecture, sanitation, urban planning, and even ecological issues. These sections also deal with the role of music as a religious and social institution and the possibility of creating a "lyric" way of life accessible to the people of Fiume without cost, through the staging of major performances in a special amphitheater, all financed by the city.[26] As defined in the Carta del Carnaro, these articles relating to the lyric lifestyle with their Nietzschean echoes, were part of the "content" of D'Annunzio's proposed order for Fiume — and eventually for Italy. Of course, D'Annunzio's understanding and interpretation of Nietzsche was peculiar, since he somehow saw himself (and other great thinkers, writers, and artists of the time) as incarnations of the Overman, as part of an extremely select elite embodying the real values of humanity. The application of these aesthetic concepts, first to a lifestyle and then to the public sphere of politics, had been influenced by Nietzsche but at the same time took D'Annunzio far from the original source.

Art, music, the choreography of public gatherings, the rhetorical dialogue between the Commandante and his legionaries, the gatherings in front of Fiume's Municipal Palace, various symbolic acts of political sacralization, were all part of a new style of politics. The strong antiparliamentarian character of the dialogue between the charismatic leader and the crowd; the tendency toward violence; the vulgar and direct exercise of the will to power against all norms, laws and written agreements; the imposition of the will of the few or of the leader over the mass, not only by theatrical means but by force; the use of symbols to produce mass emotion and even catharsis—all pointed in the direction of fascism. Fiume indeed became the scene of a collective psychodrama.[27] A certain element of theatricality exists everywhere in politics, especially in relation with public appearances. In D'Annunzio's Fiume, this dimension became mixed with a political content determined by the will of the leader, whose charisma and capabilities became the central element that would migrate from Fiume to Italian Fascism. Fascism in practice totally abandoned D'Annunzio's spiritual-aesthetic and even mystical-religious appeal, retaining only the political style related to it. It also distanced itself from the libertarian and socially redeeming aspects of the Carta del Carnaro while declaring it a foundational document for the Italian Fascist State.[28] D'Annunzio's aesthetic politics, which reflected Nietzsche's thought, undoubtedly influenced fascism in these sometimes tortuous and complex ways. For D'Annunzio, Nietzsche was "the Messiah of super-humanity," and in the German philosopher's obituary, the poet called his madness a "preposterous act of presumption on the part of a philistine Providence!"[29] Fearing for his own future, yet overcoming fear, D'Annunzio proceeded to write his Hymn to Nietzsche.[30]

Mussolini on Nietzsche

The relationship between Mussolini and Nietzsche was of a rather different character. This was partly due to the fact that Mussolini, born in 1883, was twenty years younger than D'Annunzio. Moreover, Mussolini's coming of age began in a period when Nietzsche's fame and influence were already established in Italy (as elsewhere in Europe), whereas D'Annunzio still had to struggle to introduce Nietzscheanism into Italy. The other factor that must be taken into account is that in spite of his prolific writing, mostly of a polemical nature, Mussolini never reached a central position in the realm of Italian culture. D'Annunzio, on the other hand, was one of the most prominent cultural celebrities of his time.

Still, Benito Mussolini himself read Nietzsche, discussed him, reacted to his ideas while recognizing his greatness, and was deeply influenced by the philosopher's thought, specially in the formative years of his life. His reading of Nietzsche exercised an influence on the future Duce of Italian Fascism, which, though reshaped by his own selection and interpretation, would last to the end of his life.

In October 1924, in an interview for the *New York Times* with Oscar Levy (the English translator of Nietzsche's oeuvre) Mussolini recalled that he read Nietzsche as a young man at the time he was being expelled from one canton to another in Switzerland. It seems that it was in this period that Mussolini learned German and read both *Beyond Good and Evil* and *Toward a Genealogy of Morals*[31] It was also in this formative period, from 1902 to 1904, that Mussolini became acquainted with the work of Sorel, Le Bon, and Pareto. As a publicist, Mussolini first referred to Nietzsche in writing a long three-part article that appeared in the Republican journal of Forli, *Il pensiero romagnolo*, on November 29, December 6 and 13, 1908. The fact that he was a member of the revolutionary wing of the Italian Socialist Party when he published this article on Nietzsche in a Republican paper points to a certain "revolutionary openness" and lack of Marxist dogmatism in the young politician. At this time, Mussolini admiringly reviewed Claudio Treves's lecture *La filosofia della forza* (*Wille zur Macht*) as a "clear, brilliant and synthetic presentation of the theories of Friedrich Nietzsche."[32] Attacking the idea of a "philosophical system," Mussolini reminded his readers about the Mediterranean character of Nietzsche, so far removed from the heavy scholastic traditions of philosophy. No wonder that artists from Ibsen to D'Annunzio had followed in his footsteps.

Following Treves's analysis, Mussolini dealt at greater length with the problem of the state in Nietzsche. After quoting from *On the Genealogy of Morals* about the "blond beasts . . . unleashing their primordial instinct of cruelty" Mussolini qualified the strong individualism and personal strength of this "race of lords and conquerors" by the principle of solidarity that governs the relations among these beasts, as a first limitation of individual will. He cited the discipline of warriors as a proof of a "preexisting solidarity of interests" and also the need to preserve the means of production, including slaves, because in order to live one needs not only "new tables of moral values, but [there is a need] to humbly produce bread."[33] Here, relying on the human social instinct as explained by Darwin, Mussolini claimed that the Nietzschean hero, constrained by the need for internal solidarity, released his will to power externally, through war and conquest. He could thereby combine positive solidarity within his own group and "domination," or negative solidarity, toward the conquered.

This reading of Nietzsche recognized the existence of basic social organizing principles that are not contradictory to the instincts of conquest and the cruelty characteristic of warriors. Mussolini felt that war and external conquest strengthened the links of solidarity among warriors. Here the issue of the "uniqueness" of the Nietzschean superman first appears. Is he above any law or are there any limits to his individual judgment? This produces an unbearable tension that, according to Mussolini's interpretation of *Beyond Good and Evil* is only relieved in "the orgy of the final palingenesis in which the one dares to be 'unique' against everything and everybody. As a result of the unlimited clash of wills and egoism, the social organization of the aristocratic castes sinks. The alternatives are suicide or mediocrity of a humanitarian and altruist kind: "It is then that the table of values "inverts" and the ascetic ideals of the Buddhist and Christian religions rise. The slave morality finishes by poisoning the joy of the downfall of the old castes—and the weak triumph over the strong and the pale Jews unmake Rome—What was good becomes bad."[34] If the Jewish spirit of asceticism and weakness (in Mussolini's interpretation of Nietzsche) represents the slave morality, it will reach its personification and zenith in the figure of Jesus Christ. By posing an alternative to priestly Judaism, Jesus allowed all the adversaries of the people of the Book to engage in the slave revolt in morals that finally destroyed Rome, which for Mussolini was the last society of true rulers.

As a young socialist in 1908, Mussolini stressed the positive side of Nietzsche's anti-Christianity, which he linked in his interpretation with anti-Germanism. Mussolini observed that Nietzsche imagined that he had Polish noble ancestors. He hated both Teutonic gravity and English mercantilism. His anti-Christian position could be seen as a reaction against semi-feudal Protestant and pedant Germany: "Facing a people who drink with the same unsated avidity both beer and the Bible—in the face of the milky theologists of the North—Nietzsche proclaims divine bankruptcy and intones a hymn for who will be enough [of a] "man" to become "the assassin of God."[35]

Slave morals, as represented by Christianity were a denial of life in Mussolini's interpretation of Nietzsche. Therefore, the assumption of an anti-Christian position could be equated with an abandonment of the valley of tears in favor of the joy of life. The corollary of the slave mentality, the modern European of the troubled conscience, and the egalitarian theories derived from Christian teaching had to be abandoned. In his acceptance of this kind of elitist principle, Mussolini was turning into an extremely unorthodox socialist, whose sympathetic interpretation of Nietzsche — especially of the revolutionary potential of transvaluation and the role of the Overman — seemed to mark him as a left-wing Nietzschean. Mussolini dealt with the question of Nietzsche's Overman in terms of a return to the realm of the ideal, of free spirits strengthened by war, solitude, and great dangers, able to overcome both God and nothingness. Under the premise "Nothing is true, everything is allowed!" truly free spirits would seek to bring about an apotheosis of egoism and conquest as human beings in revolt, ready to enjoy life in a Dionysian way, and intent on developing their own will to power. Mussolini saw in Nietzsche a spiritual brother of Jean-Marie Guyau, whose motto was "*Vivre ce n'est pas calculer, c'est agir.*" Beyond any abstract philosophical questions, the young Italian socialist rebel found in Nietzsche a philosophy of action or rather another path toward revolution. Perhaps, as De Felice suggests, Nietzscheanism was a way to inject virility into a socialism that had become paralyzed by social-democratic reformism and orthodox Marxist determinism.[36]

Mussolini, in his review of Treves (which was the first of his articles on Nietzsche) rejected the interpretation of the Overman as a symbolic representation of youth. He insisted that the Overman as a symbol proved both the weakness of European civilization and the possibility of a revolutionary and non-Christian redemption, a formula that could break the tedium of bourgeois existence. It represented a hymn to life, a rejection of equality in favor of uniqueness, a breaking of the existing structures, and an opening to a different future. Politically militant conclusions could easily be drawn from Nietzsche's teachings by a person such as Mussolini, who was looking for a real and practical way to revolution in which his personal potential and character could find expression. Nietzsche provided an outlook on life that Mussolini would transform into direct action. The relationship between revolution, the will to power, and the superhuman actor was seen by the young socialist as the confirmation of his own dreams and ideas. This was facilitated by the fact that since 1908 Mussolini had already absorbed the ideas of revolutionary syndicalism, the influence of Georges Sorel, and a non-Marxist socialism as well as the antipositivist cultural revolution of the 1890s, in which Nietzsche's thought was a central force.

The original lecture of Claudio Treves on Nietzsche, presented at Forli in November 1908, which sparked Mussolini's articles was more significant than Ernst Nolte implies.[37] This becomes clear from the examination of a few details. Mussolini wrote a full fledged analysis of considerable length — ten pages in the *Opera Omnia* — consequently published in three different issues of the *Pensiero Romagnolo*. He mentioned Treves three times, at the beginning of sections I, II and VI. The first reference describes the lecture as "clear, synthetic, brilliant." On the second occasion, Mussolini adds to Treves's presentation the point about the state. The third time, Mussolini offers an alternative interpretation of the concept of Superman, to the one proposed by Treves. The rest of Mussolini's text is dedicated to his own view of Nietzsche's philosophy and what he sees as its main points. Undoubtedly, as Nolte constantly repeats, Mussolini was looking for the revolutionary "echoes" of Nietzsche's philosophy, but were those necessarly Marxist? The answer is negative. Mussolini's identification with the superhuman, the will to power, and anti-egalitarianism (central concepts in Nietzsche's thought), implied his acceptance of ideas that were clearly anti-Marxist. It is difficult to see any compatibility between them and Marxist egalitarianism, collectivism, determinism, or historical materialism.

The only points in common are the total opposition to the current state of European civilization at the end of the nineteenth century and the possibility of radical change. Contrary to what Nolte claims, the main point of Mussolini's article was not to defend Nietzsche against the "grossly psychologizing criticism of Nietzsche by Treves."[38] On the contrary, Mussolini praises Treves for his presentation of the philosophy of power as the axis of Nietzsche's thought, adapting this analysis as an activist revolutionary formula. Certainly Mussolini was following here in the footsteps of anarcho-syndicalism, seeking a new theory of revolution to be carried out by an activist elite in opposition to bourgeois tendencies towards passivity and compromise. But even if we could sustain a degree of compatibility between Nietzsche and Marx's negation of Christianity (as Nolte does) it would be unconvincing to argue that in this article Mussolini tried to reconcile Marx and Nietzsche. It would be more plausible to suggest that by reevaluating Nietzsche's central concept in such a personal way, Mussolini was moving toward an original theory of revolution, distancing himself from Marxism in order to emerge finally as an anti-Marxist fascist.

Margherita Sarfatti, the mistress and biographer of Mussolini, quotes most of the article on Treves and distinguishes between D'Annunzio and Mussolini in terms of their interpretations of the Nietzschean superhuman figure. Sarfatti asserted that while the aristocratic ideal of D'Annunzio was hedonistic, voluptuous, and cruel, reviving the image of the Renaissance princes, Mussolini relied more on images of the lean and passionate *Trecento*, or fourteenth century. "He is not a disciple of the

Hellenistic Caryatids, he is one of the original tough-skinned Romans, to whom all which is gay and soft seems effeminate; and unworthy of the race of conquerors, of the *virtu* of the lords. Austere and rough, in spite of his sporadic attempts to rebel, he is finally an ascetic-warrior Catholic, for whom conquest is a satisfaction in itself; and [one] that recognizes in renunciation after conquest the privilege of the supreme aristocracies, as they were, are and will be — *gens* and barons, *ras* and *samurai* — as long as they remain uncorrupt in their vital principles." This is a rather different interpretation of Mussolini's Nietzsche, in which Treves is not even mentioned — leaving all the originality to the future *Duce* himself. Sarfatti claimed that Mussolini absorbed much from Nietzsche while rejecting the Lutheran Protestant and Slav background that produced Germanic mysticism, iconoclastic sadism, and even Satanism. All the while Mussolini adapted Nietzsche to traditions and values akin to his own Italian culture and changing political circumstances.[39]

The interpretation of Mussolini as looking to Nietzsche for the clues and keys to revolution is greatly strengthened in an interview of the Duce with Yvon De Begnac in the 1930s. Recalling the Treves lecture at Forli, Mussolini stated that it was from Treves that he learned that Nietzsche was far from being an an irrationalist since reason was reconstructed by revolution — which entailed the transformation of the habits of a people and a radical change in the culture. Mussolini recalled that Nietzsche had shown him how man could be made aware of the mysteries of philosophy while Treves taught him to reject the commonplace idea that Nietzsche was an apostle of violence. Violence had no place in the process of historical renewal, it was simply a means and not an end.[40] Mussolini made it clear that from his standpoint, Nietzsche had universal validity, evoking his discussions with Giovanni Gentile and Ugo Spirito on the nature of revolution to emphasize the point. "I, more down to earth [than the above mentioned philosophers], stated that Nietzsche is valid for everyone; everybody understands him; the deluded recover courage by reading him; the revolutionaries conquer again a faith by experiencing him."[41] Mussolini, already the Duce of fascism and of Italy, was here redefining the nature of revolution in the realm of culture and downplaying violence from the role it had assumed in Sorel's thinking and in earlier interpretations both of the will to power and the "superhuman" as it had been borrowed from Nietzsche.

In August 1912, after the triumph of the revolutionary wing in the regional congress of the Italian Socialist Party a month earlier, Mussolini became a member of the directorate of his party. The following month he published in *Avanti!* a review of the Italian translation of Daniel Halévy's French-language biography of Nietzsche. Praising

Halévy's work, Mussolini pointed out that while Nietzsche did not establish a philosophical system, there was method in the philosopher's own life: "To know the life of Nietzsche is to live it again, it means to penetrate and live again the philosophy of the Superman. Halévy's book is an initiation. When you have read it and meditated [on it], when you are familiar with Nietzsche [the] man, confront Nietzsche [the] philosopher and poet: the gates of his ivory tower will no longer be closed for you."[42]

Mussolini, already a prominent socialist leader, now saw in Nietzsche a tragic personality with a misanthropic nature who had suffered terribly as a result of his contemporaries' indifference to his work and the intensity of his friendships, which always finished in quarrels or abandonment. Mussolini repeatedly observed that no one discussed or reviewed most of the great works of Nietzsche when they appeared, while the philosopher was obliged to finance his own small editions, which hardly anyone bought. Only in his last three years of sanity, there arose the first winds of hope: "Three noble and great spirits, from three diverse horizons, [who] came in the crepuscular hour to comfort him [Nietzsche]: Taine from France, Brandes from Denmark, Strindberg from the Scandinavian mists. But it was already too late. The 'saint' had already drunk all the bitter cup and concluded his sacrifice in unmindful and therefore divine madness."[43] Mussolini expresses admiration here for Nietzsche's life, for his philosophy, and for the quality of the biography written by Daniel Halévy, who, like Treves and Sarfatti, was of Jewish origin.

In this context it is interesting to see how Margherita Sarfatti recalled the birth of fascism as a political movement and Mussolini's discourse: "It is then that on his lips begins to appear frequently and insistently the word "aristocracy." The constitution of the first *fasci*, and the political discourse with which they were founded, is wholly a call to the new aristocracies that came out of the war, the aristocracy of combatants, the *"aristocrazia trinceista"* (aristocracy of the trenches) in which he [Mussolini] finds again a reflection of those castes, of supreme sacerdotal and warrior virtue, already longed for by Nietzsche."[44]

As the leader of fascism, Mussolini addressed Nietzsche's writings again in order to obtain philosophical legitimization for the new movement. In 1921 he wrote an article for *Il popolo d'Italia* (the official journal of Fascism), *"Nel solco delle grandi filosofie. Relativismo e fascismo"* (On the track of the great philosophies. Relativism and Fascism). Commenting on Adriano Tilgher's book about contemporary relativism, he agreed with the statement that fascism was a form of absolute activism transplanted to the terrain of politics.[45] This comment was made in relation to the relative character of the (Italian) state, which, according to Tilgher "is" not—and does not exist in itself as an autonomous entity—neither by itself or as an autonomous institution. On the contrary, it is "made" and remade by those that believe in it and want it to exist and function. In Mussolini's view, the relationship between a relativistic philosophical view and fascist activism, made the fascist movement a manifestation of practical relativism. This was related to the nonprogrammatic nature of fascism, which resembled a kind of intuitive relativism.

Examining fascism as the derivative of a philosophy of action, Mussolini stated, "The Italian Fascist phenomenon must seem to Tilgher as the highest and most interesting manifestation of relativist philosophy; and if, as Vaihinger states, relativism is linked to Nietzsche and also to his *Wille zur Macht*, Italian Fascism has been and is the most formidable creation of an individual and national 'will to power.' "[46] It is interesting to note that Mussolini published this article at the end of November 1921, when the first stage in the institutionalization of fascism pointed in a direction opposed to the spirit of the article. Thus during the last stage of the Fiume crisis at the end of 1920, Mussolini undertook steps of tactical collaboration with Giolitti's government and in 1921 the Fasci di Combattimento even took part in Giolitti's "national bloc." Most of the leftist elements within fascism left the movement while the *squadri* became more violently antisocialist in their actions. These actions were part of the background behind the signing of the Pacification Pact between the Fascist Movement, the Italian Socialist Party (PSI), and the Confederation of Labour (controlled by the Socialists) on 3 August 1921, which created strong tensions within fascism, specially since the agrarian *squadri* proved unwilling to disarm and align with the "parliamentarian" policies of Mussolini. Tensions within the movement brought about the resignation of Mussolini from the central committee of the Fasci di Combattimento, as the Pacification Pact was not being implemented, mainly by Agrarian Fascism. In November 1921, at the Rome Congress, Mussolini regained control over the movement and transformed it into a political party, the *Partito Nazionale Fascista*—PNF (National Fascist Party). On November 15, 1921, the Pacification Pact was denounced in *Il popolo d'Italia*. It was against this backdrop that Mussolini stressed the relativist and activist nature of fascism as well as its close links with Nietzsche's philosophy. Beyond his personal beliefs and philosophy, Mussolini was writing here for a political audience, and the article on relativism could also be read as a justification of the acrobatic maneuvering that had characterized fascism and Mussolini's tactics in 1920 and 1921.

Before the March on Rome, as part of his antidemocratic rhetoric, Mussolini fiercely attacked what he sarcastically called "His Holiness,

the mass." Recalling Nietzsche again, he quoted his dictum that all material well-being should be provided to the masses to prevent them from
disturbing the higher transcendent manifestations of the spirit. Mussolini claimed that fascism was not opposed to the prosperity of the
masses where it was compatible with other needs; but he rejected the
religion of the masses, which democrats and socialists since 1789 had
inflated to grotesque proportions. Echoing Nietzsche, he favored those
who represented the spirit against the masses and quality over numbers,
as the basis for Fascism's elitist syndicalism.[47]

In August 1924, Mussolini experienced a major crisis after Giacomo
Matteotti's assassination. He addressed the inaugural session of the National Council of the Fascist Party at Palazzo Venezia in Rome. On this
occasion, the Duce sharply attacked the opposition and specially those
fascists who were faltering in their loyalty when confronted by the political storm. Once more Mussolini quoted Nietzsche as his guide to life
and politics: "A German philosopher has said: 'Live dangerously.' I
would like this to be the *motto* of the passionate, young Italian Fascism:
'Live dangerously.' This must mean to be ready for everything, any sacrifice, any danger, any action, when it comes to defending the fatherland
and fascism."[48]

Reviewing Guido de Pourtales's book *Nietzsche en Italie*, the Duce
took advantage of the occasion to stress the fact that most of the German philosopher's work was written in Italy. He also pointed out that
Nietzsche considered the Italian genius to be superior to that of the
French, the Germans, or the English:

> It was only in the land where this genius was established through
> the centuries and in multiple universal expressions that Nietzsche
> could give freedom to the course of his philosophy. . . . Some ele-
> ments of the Nietzschean philosophy, also because of the winged
> form of their tradition, became the nourishment of a minority of
> youth before and after the war. . . . Today the "will to power" in
> Europe is represented solely by fascism.[49]

It is interesting to note, however, that in the official definitions of
fascism in the 1930s and 40s, Nietzsche was not credited as a source of
inspiration for Fascism or its antecedents. The entry on "fascism" in the
Enciclopedia Italiana was written by Mussolini in close cooperation
with Giovanni Gentile, and it includes the names of Sorel, Péguy, and
Lagardelle from the *Mouvement Socialiste*, and it includes also the Italian revolutionary syndicalists Olivetti from *Pagine libere*, Orano from
La Lupa, and even Enrico Leone from *Il Divenire sociale*, who opposed
fascism in 1921. But no mention at all is made of Nietzsche or any of
his works.[50]

In March-April 1932, Emil Ludwig conducted several interviews with Mussolini, later published as a book. When mentioning the subject of race, Mussolini defined it as a belief, an illusion, a feeling, something that a man could choose for himself:

> "Well, I have chosen the Mediterranean, and here I have a formidable ally in Nietzsche." The name aroused an association in his mind and, speaking in German, he quoted the proudest of Nietzsche's utterances "Do I seem to strive for happiness? I strive on behalf of my work!"[51]

Stressing the importance of the German philosopher in a different sense, Mussolini also recalled his admiration for and friendship with Oswald Spengler, whose work he perceived as a continuation of Nietzsche. Mussolini suggested that Spengler had found in Nietzsche the vision with which to counter scientific laws and the predictions of Marxism as they were acted out in contemporary reality and to propose a Caesarian alternative. The Duce went further and claimed that overcoming Spengler's prophecy of the downfall of the West was now a miraculous possibility—in Nietzschean "Superhuman" terms—one currently being carried out by Mussolini and his followers as the creators of a new Europe.

Years later Mussolini would mention Nietzsche again in two different contexts. He gratefully remembered that Hitler had sent him "a really monumental" edition of Nietzsche's complete works with an autographed dedication. It was a "marvel of German publishing. . . . The admiral [Brivonesi] brought me a great box with Nietzsche's complete works marvellously bound. There [were] twenty-four volumes sent to me by the Führer for my sixtieth birthday through Marshal Kesserling." It is on this occasion that Mussolini confirmed having read the first four volumes containing Nietzsche's youthful poetry and the "first philosophy [philology?] works on the Latin and Greek languages, which the German thinker knew as well as his mother tongue."[52]

The final mention of Nietzsche occurred in the context of the Salo Republic, during which Mussolini returned once more to the revolutionary sources of fascism. Here, the German philosopher served Mussolini as a legitimation for antimonarchic sentiment. Monarchies had lost, according to the Duce, what Nietzsche once called the "plastic force," the capacity "to grow from the intimacy of the individual, to remodel and re-create the past and what is external to us, healing the wounds, replacing what has been lost, reconstructing destroyed forms [and] bringing them out of themselves."[53] This article of September 1944 exuded the sense of betrayal felt by Mussolini when confronting the pro-Allied attitude of the king of Italy, Vittorio Emanuele III, more than it reflected republicanism. Still, the terms of the accusation were not those of betrayal but rather of decadence and a lack of vitality, of fortitude, and of heroism when confronting difficulties. In other words, Mussolini employed a Nietzschean vocabulary when settling his accounts with the Italian monarchy.

Conclusion

Nietzsche undoubtedly played a central cultural role in twentieth-century Europe by providing forceful arguments against and alternatives to the heritage of the Enlightenment and the political thought and practice of the French Revolution. Furthermore, both D'Annunzio and Mussolini, as well as many other intellectuals, politicians, activists, and readers of Nietzsche, found in him a rich and varied source for polemics about what was wrong with fin de siècle European civilization. The Nietzschean arguments also provided the basis for revolutionary attitudes since his philosophy spoke of transvaluation and even of a new kind of man, who, through his creative impetus and imposition of values on reality, would destroy the existing structures of a decadent society.

Nietzsche was one of the fiercest critics of the political culture and heritage on which both liberalism and socialism, democratic republicanism, and Christian democracy were based. His assault did not present any systematic or alternative model, let alone a clear political direction. The diffuseness and openness of his writings was such that they could inspire conservatives and revolutionaries as well as a wide range of opinion in between them. But they contained implicitly (and sometimes in an overt and manifest way) many of the elements that would later be found in fascism. Nietzsche's teachings and writings pointed to the causes of decadence and evoked the feeling of crisis and loss of social identity that affected many individuals and social groups following the accelerated processes of modernization in Europe, at the end of the nineteenth century.

At the same time Nietzsche also posed serious questions for those aspects of fascism related to *étatisme* and totalitarianism. In this area the contradictions between Nietzsche's individualism and fascist collectivism were difficult, if not impossible, to bridge. This perhaps explains why both D'Annunzio and Mussolini manifested their interest in and adherence to Nietzsche's thought with much more emphasis in the "revolutionary" period of fascism, when the movement had not fully crystallized, rather than after the seizure of power or during the period of attempted totalitarian institutionalization.

It is significant that Nietzsche was not seen by official fascism in power as a forerunner or as a direct intellectual godfather, although his name was evoked in different contexts. Armando Carlini, writing in 1934, tried to establish the true relationship between Nietzsche and Mussolini. He insisted that the concept of the Overman or Superhuman (in the sense of man overcoming his own limits and becoming a bridge to higher spheres) stayed with the Duce. He also mentioned freedom from prejudice, anti-philistinism, hostility to democracy, and the warrior instinct as guidelines that Mussolini learned from Nietzsche. But Carlini also noted what was rejected by the Duce, including the anti-Christian animus and the contempt that Nietzsche showed for any religious or moral tradition, something that was alien to Mussolini. Mussolini remained faithful to Christian beliefs even though as a young man, he had absorbed Nietzsche's activist concept of life as the creation of new spiritual values.[54]

Carlini's views were published as part of a larger group of publications under the fascist regime, which tried to place Mussolini above and beyond Nietzsche (or any other personality) while adapting to the political line pursued by fascism at the time. A careful reading of young Mussolini's writings would prove beyond any doubt that in the first decades of the twentieth century he did express anti-Christian thoughts no less strong than those of Nietzsche, as well as many other ideas that later became unfashionable. The ascent to power, the stabilization of the regime, and the series of political compromises that fascism made with the monarchy, the army, and the Catholic Church rendered earlier experimental or revolutionary thinking increasingly redundant.

There were apologists of the Duce who claimed that parts of the cultural theory and political ethics of fascism were related to Nietzsche — for example, the historic mission embodied in the Overman and incarnated in Mussolini himself who had opened a new era for Italy. At the same time, Nietzsche's admiration for classical Greece conflicted with the fascist model of ancient Rome, which had imposed Law as the foundation of empire. This cult of Imperial Fascist Rome still awarded a high place and value to Christianity.[55] A similar analysis was elaborated by Mario Ferrara, an expert in modern history, literature, and corporativism. He saw similarities between Nietzsche and Italian Fascism in the cult of realism, the acceptance of inequality and the need for hierarchies; the high value given to danger, risk, and activism; the admiration for the ancient Roman state; the acceptance of the need for war and the respect for institutions and traditions. In reality, of course, Nietzsche did not claim that states should be respected, any more than institutions, traditions, or religions, but Ferrara, in his *Machiavelli, Nietzsche and Mussolini*, (published in 1939 in Florence), paid little attention to such details. He did find a clear difference in that Mussolini — like Machiavelli — applied "superhuman" energies and capacities to the cause of the *patria*, while the Nietzschean Overman, concerned himself with abstractions, thus becoming an illusion, a piece of poetry. Hence, Ferrara could conclude that the application of the will to power led, in Nietzsche's case, to a superhuman exasperation ending in madness, while in Mussolini, it acquired a living and human content achieving its full political realization.[56]

Officially, Nietzsche did not enter the list of fascist godfathers. In the entry on Nietzsche in the *Enciclopedia Italiana* published during the fascist period, Giuseppe Gabetti, an expert in Nietzsche and Søren Kierkegaard, presented the German philosopher at quite another level of analysis and sophistication. For Gabetti, Nietzsche was the last great exponent of romanticism. He centerd his analysis on the idea of the eternal return, the negation of all values so that "man becomes again a creator of eternal values and appears, in reality as 'absolute master'; only with the idea of the 'eternal return' man was given a measure which could serve as counterweight to the absolute freedom he had been granted."[57]

Gabetti also touched on Nietzsche's social and political views, arguing,

> In [his] social and political criticism, the reaction against the dominant democratic, liberal, socialist, communist tendencies anticipated coming historical developments that have [since] taken place — with an intuition of future political historical situations that sometimes seems stupefying; and as in his theoretical thought and his ethical conceptions N[ietzsche] interprets, in a climate of high spiritual passion, the so often forgotten revolutionary demand which is immanently implicit in the eternal renewal in which life is generated, in such a way that his thought has been largely influential — from pragmatism to intuitionism, to relativism, to irrationalism — over many of the latest developments of modern philosophy."[58]

It is perhaps through these words that we can best find a clearer insight into Nietzsche's role in fascism. Nietzsche was the prophet of an imminent crisis of values whose causes he was determined to elucidate and for which he sought to present a prognosis. His field of thought was, however, so wide and all-encompassing that many individuals from different backgrounds and points of view could find anchoring points for their own ideas. Nietzsche's lack of elaboration and precision in those areas directly related to political thought or theory opened his work up to selective "political" readings by all those convinced by his analysis of the crisis of Western modernity. Such readings did not directly produce coherent political doctrines, but they were influential since Nietzsche's attack against the tradition of the Enlightenment and the heritage of the French Revolution could not be ignored. The result was to make him appear complicit with the fascist forces that assaulted democracy out of hatred for the liberal, rationalist, and universalist traditions of the West.

Notes

I am indebted to Robert Wistrich for his expert editing of this article and his helpful comments.

1. On the influences shaping fascism, especially the Italian variety, see, Renzo De Felice, *Mussolini il rivoluzionario* (Turin: Einaudi, 1965), 59–61; Hugh R. Trevor-Roper, "The Phenomenon of Fascism," in *Fascism in Europe*, ed. Stuart J. Woolf, (London and New York: Methuen, 1983), 28; Ernst Nolte, *Three Faces of Fascism* (New York: Holt, Rinehart and Winston, 1966), 7, 26, 35, 43, 47, 62–3, 126, 149–56, 244; Enzo Santarelli, *Storia del Fascismo* (Rome: Riuniti, 1981), 2:504, 538; Peter H. Merkl, "Comparing Fascist Movements," in *Who Were the Fascists*, ed. Stein Ugelvik Larsen, Bernt Hagtvet, Jan Peter Myklebust (Bergen, Oslo, Tromso: Universitetsvorlaget, 1980), 753; Stanley G. Payne, *Historia del Fascismo* (Barcelona: Planeta, 1995), 39; Roger Eatwell, *Fascism: A History* (London: Chatto & Windus, 1995), 8, 34–36, 38, 56; Roger Griffin, *The Nature of Fascism* (London and New York: Routledge, 1993), 6, 42, 59, 60; Emilio Gentile, *Le origini dell'ideologia fascista (1918–1925)* (Bologna: Il Mulino, 1996) 24, 32, 65–6, 113–14, 296, 307, 344, 476, 481, 500; Noel O' Sullivan, *Fascism* (London and Melbourne: J.M. Dent & Sons, 1983), 139; Dennis Mack Smith, *Mussolini. A Biography* (New York: Vintage, 1983), 7, 12; and Zeev Sternhell, Mario Sznajder, Maia Asheri, *Naissance de l'idéologie fasciste* (Paris: Fayard, 1989), 41, 54, 207, 224, 270, 282, 314.

2. Mark Warren, *Nietzsche and Political Thought* (Cambridge and London: MIT Press, 1988), 212–13.

3. Michel Haar, "Institution et destitution du politique selon Nietzsche," *Epokhe* 6 (1996): 232–33.

4. Nietzsche, "Beyond Good and Evil," in *Basic Writings of Nietzsche*, trans. Walter Kaufman (New York: Random House, 1968), 193.

5. Warren, *Nietzsche and Political Thought*, 220–21

6. Ibid., 222

7. Here I follow Warren's analysis (ibid., 222–23) and concur with his thesis about the parallelism between nihilism and totalitarianism.

8. The first articles on Nietzsche that reached the educated audience in Italy were published by Pasquale Villari in 1891. They described a part of Nietzsche's *On the Use and Disadvantage of History for Life*, published in its first German edition in 1873. See P. Villari, "La storia e una scienza?" *Nuova Antologia*, February 1, April 16, and July 16, 1891.

9. Apparently, the first mention of the publication of *The Birth of Tragedy* appeared as a short review in *Rivista Europea* (April 1872). Here, Nietzsche is presented as an admirer of Wagner who interprets the relationship between music and Greek tragedy in Apollonian and Dionysian terms.

10. Domenico M. Fazio, *Il caso Nietzsche. La cultura italiana di fronte a Nietzsche. 1872–1940* (Settimo Milanese: Marzotti Editore, 1988), 26.

11. Guy Tosi, "D'Annunzio découvre Nietzsche," *Italianistica* (September–December 1973). The quotation from Nietzsche reads, "And some who turned away from life only turned away from the rabble: they did not want to share well and flame and fruit with the rabble." Nietzsche, *Z*, II: 209.

12. Fazio, *Il caso Nietzsche*, 28–30. See also, Gabriele D'Annunzio, "La bestia elettiva," *Il Mattino*, September 25, 1892.

13. Gabriele D'Annunzio, *Il trionfo della morte* (1894; Milano: Treves, 1921). It should be noted that the 1921 edition begins with a quotation from Nietzsche's *BGE*.

14. Fazio, *Il caso Nietzsche*, 33–34.

15. D'Annunzio, *Il trionfo della morte*, xi.

16. On this subject see, Zeev Sternhell, Mario Sznajder, and Maia Asheri, *Naissance de l'idéologie fasciste*, 11–51.

17. Delio Cantimori, *Storia e storici* (Turin: Einaudi, 1971) 431–36. See also Philippe Jullian, *D'Annunzio* (London: Pall Mall Press, 1972), 98–99.

18. Michael Ledeen, *The First Duce: D'Annunzio at Fiume* (Baltimore and London: Johns Hopkins University Press, 1977), 6. Ledeen quotes Nino Valeri, *Da Giolitti a Mussolini*, on the subject of D'Annunzio's political shift.

19. Ibid., 249–50; quotation from D'Annunzio's *Envoi de la France*.

20. Ibid., 263.

21. On D'Annunzio's participation in the Great War see Ledeen, *The First Duce*, 9–11; Jullian, *D'Annunzio*, 258–67, 272–76; and Gerald Griffin, *Gabriele D'Annunzio: The Warrior Bard* (Port Washington, N.Y. and London: Kennikat Press 1970), 113–26.

22. Gabrielle D'Annunzio, *Les Aveux de l'Ingrat* (Paris: Bernard Grasset, 1919).

23. On the ideological evolution of De Ambris and his influence on Mussolini see Mario Sznajder, "Social Revolution and national Integration: Alceste De Ambris and Italian Fascism," *Canadian Review of Studies on Nationalism* 20, no. 1–2 (1993): 57–66.

24. Emilio Gentile, *Le origini della ideologia fascista*, 241–44.

25. Angelo O. Olivetti, "La gioia di vivere," *Pagine libere*, December 1922, p. 403.

26. Renzo De Felice, *Sindacalismo rivoluzionario e fiumanesimo nel carteggio De Ambris-D'Annunzio* (Brescia: Morcelliana, 1966), 71–75; and De Felice, ed., *La Carta del carnaro nei testi di Alceste de Ambris and Gabriele D'Annunzio* (Bologna: Il Mulino, 1972), articles LXIII, LXIV, and LXV (the articles of the *Carta del Carnaro* written by De Ambris were numbered with Arabic numerals and those written by D'Annunzio, with Roman numerals).

27. George L. Mosse, "The Poet and the Exercise of Political Power," *Yearbook of Comparative and General Literature* 22 (1973): 40.

28. Mario Sznajder, "The 'Carta del Carnaro' and Modernization," *Tel Aviver Jahrbuch fur deutsche Geschichte* 23 (1979): 459–61.

29. Griffin, *Gabriele D'Annunzio*, 35–36.

30. Gabriele D'Annunzio, "Per la morte di un distruttore. F. N. XXV Agosto MCM," in *Laudi del cielo—del mare—della terra de degli eroi* (Verona: Arnoldo Mondadori Editore, 1947): 465–82. Partially translated into German as *In memoriam Friedrich Nietzsche* (Leipzig: Insilverlag, 1904). This elegy to Nietzsche was translated by Otto Freiher von Taube and published in Leipzig in a limited numbered edition of 400 copies of which the first twenty-five were printed in pergament paper.

31. Renzo De Felice, *Mussolini il rivoluzionario*, 59. See also, Alessandro Roveri, *Mussolini. La carriera di un dittatore attraverso I suoi scritti e discorsi* (Milan: Mondandori, 1994) 20–21.

32. Benito Mussolini, "La filosofia della forza *Opera Omnia di Benito Mussolini*, a cura di Edoardo e Duilio Susmel (Florence: La Fenice, 1972), 1:174.

33. Ibid., 1:175.

34. Ibid., 1:177.

35. Ibid., 1:179.

36. De Felice, *Mussolini il rivoluzionario*, 60.

37. Ernst Nolte, *Il giovane Mussolini. Marx e Nietzsche in Mussolini socialista* (Carnago, Varesse: Sugarco, 1993), 66–89.

38. Nolte, *Il giovane Mussolini*, 70–71.

39. Margherita G. Sarfatti, *Dux* (Milan: Mondadori, 1930) 105. We must remember that at the end of the 1920s the Duce solved the historical tension between the Italian state and the Catholic Church by signing the Lateran Pacts (February 11, 1929) after two-and-a-half years of secret negotiations. In the text of Mussolini's article "La filosofia della forza," as quoted by Sarfatti, the biographer, according to the spirit of the time, eliminates the strongest anti-Christian expressions of both Nietzsche—as quoted by Mussolini—and of Mussolini himself. See ibid., 102–103.

40. Yvon De Begnac, *Taccuini mussoliniani*, (a cura de Francesco Perfetti) (Bologna: Il Mulino, 1990) 383–84.

41. Ibid., 384.

42. Mussolini, "La vita di Frederico Nietzsche," in *Opera Omnia*, 4:184.

43. Ibid., 190. In a letter sent from Forli prison on November 3, 1911, while serving a sentence for his role in the antiwar general strike of September 1911, Mussolini wrote to Cesare Berti that lately he had ascended the highest mountains of thought called "Stirner, Nietzsche, Goethe, Schiller, Montaigne, Cervantes," and, submerged again in the German language, had become *ein echter deutscher* (a real German). See Mussolini, "Lettere," *Opera Omnia*, 4:257–258. This expressed not only Mussolini's admiration for German culture but also a continuous link with and reading of Nietzsche's writings in the various circumstances of his life.

44. Sarfatti, *Dux*, 217.

45. Mussolini, "Nel solco delle grandi filosofie. Relativismo e fascismo," *Opera Omnia*, 17:267.

46. Ibid., 269. See also Sarfatti, *Dux*, 247.

47. Mussolini, "Adagio," *Opera Omnia*, 18:409–10.

48. Mussolini, "'Vivere pericolosamente,'" *Opera Omnia*, 21:40. In relation to Mussolini's adoption of Nietzsche's teachings about living dangerously, Sarfatti recalls the flying accident Mussolini suffered before the above-mentioned speech. Injured after a jump from a height of forty meters, in which the airplane suffered great damage but the engine was saved, Mussolini was quoted as saying, "Still life is beautiful. . . . It merits to be risked, it needs to be risked every now and then—in order to feel how much it is worth" (cited in Sarfatti, *Dux*, 233).

49. Benito Mussolini, "Itinerario Nietzschiano in Italia," *Opera Omnia*, 25:91.

50. Mussolini, *La Dottrina del Fascismo* (Milan and Rome: Treves-Treccani-Tumminelli, 1932) 8–9, 15; Mussolini, "Fascismo," in *Enciclopedia Italiana* (Roma: Istituto dell'Enciclopedia Italiana, 1929–36), 14:848.

51. Emil Ludwig, *Talks with Mussolini* (Boston: Little Brown, 1933), 228. This is a translation from the original German version, *Mussolini. Gespräche mit Emil Ludwig* (Berlin, Wien, Leipzig: Paul Zsolnay, 1932).

52. Mussolini, "Il primo discorso dopo la liberazione," *Opera Omnia*, 32:2; and, in the same work, "Pensieri pontini e sardi," 34:299 and "Da Ponza alla Maddalena al Gran Sasso," 34:363–64. See also Mussolini, *Corrispondenza inedita*, a cura di Duilio Susmel (Milan: Edizioni del Borghese, 1972) 249–50.

53. Mussolini, "Parola di Re," *Opera Omnia*, 32:405–6.

54. Armando Carlini, *Filosofia e religione nel pensiero di Mussolini* (Brescia: Il settimo sigillo, 1983), 25–26, 43. This is a new edition of the original, published in 1934 under the same title, in Rome, by the Istitituo Nazionale Fascista di Cultura.

55. Salvatore Lombardo Restivo, *Riflessi di Nietzsche nelle dottrine sociali-politiche contemporane* (Rome: Universalitá fascista, 1935), 101.

56. Fazio, *Il caso Nietzsche*, 207–9.

57. Giusepe Gabetti, "Nietzsche, Friedrich Wilhelm," in *Enciclopedia Italiana* (Rome: Istituto della Enciclopedia Italiana, 1934), 24:807.

58. Ibid., 809.

12

Nietzsche and the Fascist Dimension: The Case of Ernst Jünger

David Ohana

The Nietzschean Revolution: From Ethics to Aesthetics

What was the nature of the intellectual revolution instigated by Friedrich Nietzsche in the late nineteenth century? Why were both left-wing and right-wing groups inspired by this revolution? Why does it still continue to disturb so many people? It is impossible to separate out any one element of Nietzsche's thought as the answer to these questions — the death of God, the critique of morality and religion, the "Overman" or the will to power. It is rather the revolutionary combination of the consciousness of nihilism and the will to power that brings Nietzsche so close to us at the beginning of a new century: When the "new Man" rebelled against the burden of the past and rejected the contents of Western history, he became the midwife of his own world. Thus the nihilistic revolution is necessarily linked with the aesthetic one: Nietzschean nihilism[1] — having gone beyond the traditional criteria of good and evil, truth and falsity — led to the new creative principle of the will to power. Traditional ethics was replaced by a new aesthetics.

Nietzsche made use of a philosophy of unmasking that attempted to dig down to the root of things and eliminate the disguises worn by Western culture throughout history. But his critique itself led to a historicism that examines concepts along the continuum of time. This method became a nihilistic unmasking that undermined the origins of traditional values. Even the basic notions behind what is generally considered Nietzsche's positive philosophy—self-overcoming, eternal recurrence, the "Overman," the will to power—expose the Janus-faced aspect of Nietzsche's method: on the one hand, the compulsory nihilism of the notion of "the eternal recurrence of things," yet on the other, the love of fate (*amor fati*) and the total affirmation of life as the implication of the Overman's will to power. The primacy of nothingness and the primacy of life are mutually linked.

Walter Kaufmann's *Nietzsche: Philosopher, Psychologist, Antichrist* played a vital part in the essential task of clearly separating Nietzsche from Nazism.[2] Yet this influential book left Nietzsche without teeth and deprived him of his philosophical hammer. He was given a place of honor among other humanist thinkers. But we must not ignore the fact that in the twentieth century fascist thinkers seized upon different aspects of Nietzsche's nihilism, painting it with their own political colors. Nietzsche's philosophical radicalism presaged various forms of *political radicalism*.[3]

Those thinkers, culture critics, and artists who were close to fascism seized upon various elements in the existentialist approach of the Nietzschean school, but added a political dimension. This approach repudiated historical and romantic assumptions just as it rejected the philosophy of progress and Enlightenment. While historicism was guided by the past, the Enlightenment stressed the openness of the future, from which it derived the concept of progress. In contrast, the fascist intellectuals ignored both the guidance of the past and the open future in favor of the dynamic present. This led to the rejection of the concept of progress, since historical continuity, in either the open rationalist sense or the rigid determinist one, was broken, and the dynamic present was detached from the cultural context with its centuries of accretions.

The existentialist approach is centered around the Nietzschean assumption that the enhanced concept of humanity can be given a variety of interpretations, and is continually developing and self-creating. The historical, romantic, determinist and progress-minded approaches described the individual as a culture-dependent and tradition-dependent historical entity; Nietzsche, however, created an original, unique anthropological image of the individual as affirming his fate (*amor fati*), yet also shaping it with his own hands by using the will to power as a creative principle.[4] No longer must the individual blindly follow the heritage of the past; from now on the continually evolving world is identified with the continually evolving self, as the essence of the existentialist idea. Since the world is dynamic and self-creating, the individual must not remain fixed, but rather identify with the world's rhythm.

The existentialist approach to history thus served as a revolutionary turning-point by rebelling against the Judeo-Christian ethic and the classical tradition, and adopting the notion that the (nonrational) self must shape aesthetically the (nonrational) reality. This aesthetic view of reality is not subject to the domination of reason and goes beyond the accepted ethical distinctions of good and evil to adopt new distinctions based on creativity, stagnation, or degeneration. The implications of this view are far-reaching: sanctifying the here and now, affirming activism, and adopting a clear modernist approach that is neither teleological nor ethical, and that does not constitute a necessary link in the chain of progress or an accretion to the achievements of humanity that are passed on through cultural experience. This view thus disqualifies the concept of culture as the consolidation of historical continuity, consciously annihilates the continuity of time, and affirms the dynamic moment in the present.

Nietzsche was also the prophet of modern secularism—not the kind that claims, with Spinoza, that the sacred is within us, but the sort that reveals the secular without the sacred, a new humanity sovereign over the world.[5] This world has no universalist pretensions, whether sacred, rational, or moral. Perspectivist philosophy thus reached nihilist conclusions. It is not searching for the truth as the primary ambition of philosophy, but instead seeks to create the world as a new myth. At the same time, there arises a dynamic and creative conception of time. This modern concept, which creates myth, is not a reactionary call to return to our mythical roots in the past, but a claim that only the future will permit the rise of myth.[6]

Underlying this modern mythology was Nietzsche's genealogical approach and philosophy of unmasking, which were intended to remove all moral, utilitarian, and directional camouflage from culture—whether this disguise took the form of a messianic paradise in the secular progressive vision, or a golden age in the religious version. Nietzsche was committed to a cyclical concept of a nonteleological history, and Zarathustra is the personification of the myth of eternal recurrence.[7]

The revival of myth paradoxically constituted the conclusion of philosophical inquiry. In place of the philosophy of reason Nietzsche sets up the myth of the will to power; in place of the search for objective truth, he extols subjective creativity; in place of universal rationalism he urges creative aesthetics. The traditional philosophers had hitherto offered interpretations of the world or attempted to justify its existence; in contrast, the new philosophers—including those of fascism—were trying to create a world ex nihilo in their own image. This style of mythical creation, which has profoundly shaped modern civilization, is a product of the kind of aesthetic imagination first embraced by Nietzsche.

The "new Man" is the crown jewel of the myth-creating fascist ideol-

ιs an individual who identifies with the rhythm of the modern
who is tested in action rather than contemplation, through ini-
:ather than continuity, and creativity rather than the preservation
of cuιιure. Such a person considers the reality of conflict to be the natural arena and the necessary condition for the creation of authenticity.
Nietzsche's "new Man" is a source of inspiration for the future, while
the "old Man" is a historical type who has been defeated by the past.
Out of the mass society of "old persons" Nietzsche hoped to create an
"Overman" who would look soberly at the world with a modern awareness of nihilism, and would activate and enhance the will to power.[8]

It was this Janus-face of nihilism and the Overman's will to power
that attracted radicals like Ernst Jünger, who created the "totalitarian
nihilistic syndrome."[9] They considered nihilism the litmus test for distinguishing between the weak and the powerful, while the will to power
distinguished between the degenerate and the authentic. Nihilism of the
negative-type pattern — to use Nietzsche's language — frightens the weak
and makes them flee to their refuge of passivity and paralysis; while
nihilism of the positive or active variety — again in Nietzsche's terms —
provides a challenge for the powerful, who create a new reality ex nihilo in the process of coping with it.[10] Similarly, there is a degenerate
will to power that is the province of the weak, while the will to power
of the powerful is an authentic one.

The Overman is the challenge of the intellectual revolution which
Nietzsche instigated in Western civilization — destroying the classical
heritage, historical culture, the Judeo-Christian ethic — and at the same
time strengthening the will to power as an existential, aesthetic, and
metaphysical principle. Destruction and rebuilding are the methods of
the "new Man," who is continually creating and destroying his own
world. He is destroying super-illusions and striving for comprehensive-
ness. He is not interested in categorizing or defining his values, but only
in creating them and continually overcoming them. He does not sanctify
permanent values as such, and contradictions do not frighten him. He is
therefore considered a master of deceit and a legislator-king. Since the
authentic individual — the crown of existential thought — emerged from
the Nietzschean school, the will to power is his human and cosmological principle. The individual as will to power is characterized by self-
overcoming, while the world as will to power is characterized by the
eternal recurrence; neither has any ethical aspect, both are lawless and
meaningless. Therefore neither the existence of the individual nor the
world — both of which have been revealed as nihilistic — requires any
particular content or meaning, and they can be actualized and bestowed
with meaning only in an aesthetic context.[11]

The world's eternal recurrence and humanity's self-overcoming con-

sist of development without any goal, which implies a
that continually annihilates itself, or by the same to
itself. Either way the result is the same: there is nei
goal.[12] Nietzsche affirms energy for its own sake, and so the
aspect of the "Overman" — who annihilates all values and affirms c.
tence as it is — has no force. After all, the "Overman," who strives to be
a sovereign individual and attempts to enhance the will to power, lives
with "empty energy" — energy that consumes itself. Nietzsche calls this
energy "the world" and demands that we accept it as it is. The change
in values therefore consists of replacing the value of the goal by that of
the process, the value of reason by authenticity, and ethics by the principle of the will to power; moreover, ethics is no longer a social issue but
an issue between the individual and his world. The concepts of good,
rational, and true are abandoned in favor of the concept of the authentic identity of the individual and the world (that is, the will to power) as
a new unified conception.

Nietzsche's concept of the new Man is totally subjectivist and thus
open to various interpretations. If there are no universal, objective criteria, then the whole basis of Western civilization is called into question.
Each human being is a force of separate will to power, which means
that he exists for his own sake and is validated by his own power. Thus
all the foundation stones of Western civilization topple one after another; Judeo-Christian morality, rationalist philosophy, historical tradition. In legitimizing all interpretations, Nietzschean perspectivism also
includes its own weak points, since objective explanations, moral norms,
and rational validity are no longer possible. Nietzsche uses history as a
point of departure for reconstructing Western philosophy:[13] After rejecting whatever has become redundant in history, what is left is the affirmation of existence — not out of historical conditioning or inherited custom, but out of a *heroic* existential approach, which embodies the
exaltation of freedom and power in its "Yes." The will to power — as
the central manifestation of the subject, and an existential, intuitive cognitive assumption — replaces the old criteria with new distinctions that
affirm the authentic rather than the degenerate, the strong rather than
the weak, the individual rather than the collective. Nietzsche's radicality
stems from the fact that he rejected the traditional criteria of Western
thought and placed a new philosophical principle at the helm to drive
the "new Man": the will to power.[14]

The will to power displaced reason from its central position. If Kant
is the outstanding representative of the "classical aesthetics" of the eigh-
teenth century, then Nietzsche is the exact opposite: In his view aesthetics, as the "critique of judgment," is not parallel to morality, as the
"critique of practical reason," but rather replaces it. This is indeed

8

_ne's great revolution — substituting the will to power, as a partic-
Arist aesthetic principle, for the universal moral imperative. Separating
aesthetics from morality, which means raising creativity from a normative to a metaphysical level, was the central axis of the revolt against
bourgeois norms in the late nineteenth century. The Nietzscheanism of
the radical Right led in the end to the aestheticization of philosophical
thought and moral principles: Although the concept of "the aesthetic
education of humanity" had already been formulated by Schiller, Kant,
Schelling, and Schopenhauer, the principal innovation of the intellectual
trend under discussion was the interweaving of the political dimension,
existential experience, and the aesthetic conception as complementary
manifestations of the new Man.

The Burden of Responsibility

Half a century after the vanquishing of European fascism, as we gained
an increasingly clear insight into the causes of fascism's rise and success,
we can identify that nihilism is hidden at the core of fascism — in its
essence, its nature, its genes. The roots of the fascist mentality lie in its
utopian view of the "community of experience" and the quest for the
new man. As a cultural phenomenon, fascism accords pride of place to
action rather than to thinking, to experience rather than to awareness,
to style rather than to content. Its political acts are performed for the
sake of the action itself, divorced from the social context. Fascism is not
interested in social change, but in a *perpetuum mobile* that creates the
illusion of change on the road to some utopian destination.

The importance of the European thinkers, cultural critics, and writers
like Ernst Jünger who were informed by Nietzsche's existential credo,
lies in their fabrication of a modern political mythology that inspired
politicians and leaders of mass movements.[15] They created a new terminology and political dictionary of modernism, based on such key
concepts as the "new man," "political myth," "dynamism," "will to
power," and "community of experience." This new style signified a
transition from the centrality of ideology to that of myth. The modern
political style of "anti-intellectual" intellectuals, who gave myth prece-
dence over reason, became the heart of a dynamic political culture that
created the "generation of 1914" and shaped the fascist mentality that
arose in its wake.

What is the intellectual mainspring of the *bellicose* enthusiasm of the
1914 generation? In a chapter entitled "The Impulse of Nietzsche," in
The Heritage of Our Times, Ernst Bloch answers that it is "Dionysus as
a symbol of abstractly fantastic escape into anarchy: only here do we
grasp Nietzsche's serious impact on the age."[16] The danger, as Bloch sees

it, is inherent in the Nietzschean theory of the "eternal recurrence of the same," which he qualifies as "a strange doctrine," "banal," and so on. This cyclical notion, when added to Nietzsche's "boundless willpower," is an explosive mixture. "That is why," Bloch writes, "super-fascist Nietzsche interpreters, such as Bäumler, for instance, seek to eliminate Dionysus."[17]

Even if Nietzsche is not directly responsible for fascism, he certainly had an intellectual influence on the 1914 generation that metamorphosed into fascism. As Ernst Bloch wrote,

> The struggle for existence rages on endlessly . . . with the "eternal natural right of the stronger" as its sense and content. This kind of activism, evil activism of course, obviously derives from Sorel and also from Nietzsche. . . . Yet neither Sorel nor Nietzsche consciously intended their use by fascism: to this extent their wishful images of power are still ante rem. . . . Nonetheless, both philosophers were usable by fascism.[18]

The utopian visions of German Nietzscheans such as Alfred Rosenberg, Möller van der Bruck, and Ernst Jünger contributed to the myths that helped shape fascism as "community of experience." The demagoguery of Ernst Jünger's imagined unity of workers and soldiers ultimately comes down to something comparable to the blood and flames of Rosenberg. Fascism utopized the dynamism anchored in the myths that stimulate experience.[19] This syndrome first appeared in the intellectual climate of the fin de siècle and the 1914 generation, in the cultural milieu of the interwar decades, and in the fascist movements and regimes that constituted its political zenith.

A Man for All Seasons

Ernst Jünger, born in Heidelberg in 1895, was the eldest of four sons in a typical German bourgeois family.[20] In his early years, his family moved to Hanover, following the decision of his father, the owner of a chemical factory, who was concerned for his children's economic welfare. However, dissatisfaction with a comfortable bourgeois existence caused the seventeen-year-old Jünger to seek out a life of danger and adventure. He crossed the French frontier at Metz and burnt all the money in his possession in order to sever his connection to the past. He then made his way to Africa where, like Marinetti, the founder of the Italian Futurist movement, he discovered what he called "the promise of happiness."[21] After he had stayed a few weeks at Sidi-Bal-Abbas in North Africa, his father brought him home, but he did not remain there for long. Later, Jünger described the reasons for his frequent flights from home: "We grew up in the atmosphere of a materialistic epoch, and we all consequently had a taste for something out of the ordinary, for situations of great danger."[22]

In 1914, before the outbreak of war, he volunteered for the 73rd Hanover Fusilier Regiment, in which he served for four years. He began as a private, and a year later was appointed a junior officer. He did not volunteer for ideological or nationalistic reasons, but in the hope of finding in the army what he had sought in Africa: a life of existential significance, of danger, of spontaneity and vitality. He finally found his Africa in the fields of Flanders. The primitivism he longed for changed in content but not in essence, and his myth of Africa was now replaced by the myth of the war. In those years in which he dwelt in the trenches of northern France, Jünger was in charge of platoons of commandos and was wounded seven times. Like Rommel, he received the highest decoration for valor in the German army. After the war, he returned to his defeated country, and began to take his first steps in civilian life. His sojourn in the trenches had given birth to an exhaustive battle diary documenting his experience in the war. The diary, which appeared in 1920 under the title *Stahlgewittern* (*The Storm of Steel*), won its author immediate fame and was an instant best-seller. Jünger became the spokesman of the generation of the trenches that had sacrificed all without receiving anything in return.[23]

From 1927 onward, Jünger lived in Berlin and imbibed the atmosphere of intrigue and machinations, clubs that spawned utopias, subversive agitation in beer cellars, violence in the streets, and corruption in high places. Jünger declared in the spirit of that time (as Thomas Mann had done a dozen years previously) that all democratic regimes were in contradiction to the essentially tragic nature of the human destiny. His interest in botany and zoology was not scientific but metaphorical: he wished to study the sphere of animals and vegetation as a language of symbols for an understanding of the metaphysical essence of the world. In the 1930s, he traveled a great deal in Brazil, Morocco, Scandinavia, and France, and in his travel notes there was still a sense of nostalgia for the primitive and a feeling of hostility to the compromises and adjustments of the world in which he lived. In 1932, Jünger published *Der Arbeiter* (*The Worker*), a technological utopia of the modern world that was the high point of his intellectual achievement.[24]

Jünger took the "nihilistic-totalitarian syndrome" to its ultimate conclusions. He used the myth of the "masculine community" of the trenches and the public memory of the first mechanized war in order to construct a utopia in which technology directed, guided, and molded man and his role in the new hierarchical society. Indeed, the Jüngerian technological utopia would be prophetic of a new political form of totalitarian nihilism.

13

A Godfather Too:
Nazism as a Nietzschean "Experiment"
Kurt Rudolf Fischer

It is important to keep in mind that the "real Nietzsche" was not the historically effective Nietzsche. My interest turns to the Nietzsche we knew *before* Giorgio Colli and Mazzimo Montinari prepared their critical edition.[1] The historically effective texts allowed Nazi as well as anti-Nazi readings from a Nazi standpoint as well as from an anti-Nazi standpoint! Thus from two opposite ideological points of view two opposite results were possible, and indeed existed.

In approached the problem of Nietzsche's relation to fascism, I find it necessary first to raise the question of the meaning of "fascism." There have been at least two uses of this expression: a narrower use that refers especially, and sometimes exclusively, to the movement, party, and worldview initiated by Benito Mussolini. Mussolini indeed referred explicitly to Nietzsche in a well-known speech of May 21, 1934. And there is a second use of the expression, which points to a wider meaning—mainly employed by the Left—which not only includes but especially refers to the Hitler movement. I am familiar with this use of the expression since my adolescence in Austria and Czechoslovakia. At that time, among others, the Austrian *Christlich Soziale Partei* (and later the *Vaterländische Front*) as well as many radical Right movements were considered to be fascist in this wider sense of the term.[2]

It may be of interest to remark on the similarities and differences of the two main fascist movements, the German and the Italian.[3] The dif-

For Jünger, the Second World War was a completely different experience from the first one. If the First World War was a hell in the trenches, the second was for Jünger a pleasurable experience in the streets of Paris. As an officer of the German occupation, he spent his time in the French capital in the company of "collaborationist" authors and cultural critics, visiting artists like Picasso and Braque and in frequenting literary clubs and cafés on the boulevards. All this is described in his wartime notes, the first part of which was published in 1942 under the title *Gärten und Strassen* (*Gardens and Streets*).²⁵ Toward the end of the war (1943), his book *Der Friede* (*The Peace*) appeared and was popular among the young German soldiers on the western front. When the war ended, his books were banned in the British zone of occupation in Germany, but at the same time were freely available in London. In November 1944, when he lost his eighteen-year-old son Ernestal on the Italian front, he wrote that "the only true community of the war" was the community of the bereaved. His stay in Paris was interrupted by a six-week journey to the Caucasian front, but the quiet places he visited there in no way recalled his experiences in Flanders. These landscapes were later described in his utopia *Heliopolis* (1949), which developed the theme of *Auf den Marmorklippen* in which the representatives of anarchy and the representatives of nihilism confront each other in the person of the hero, Lucio de Gir.²⁶ After his commander General Heinrich von Stülpfnagel was executed, Jünger was sent back to Germany, and in October 1944 he was discharged from the army. His diary (1949), which covers the period of the Second World War in detail, ends with the entry of American tanks into a village near Hanover in April 1945.²⁷

After the war, there was talk of him being placed on trial in Nuremberg. Seeking to preserve his honor, Jünger refused to be tried by the de-Nazification court, although clearance would have enabled him to publish his books freely. However, Jünger lived on to become the most important cultural figure in Germany after Heidegger. His long life and his many books, which appeared in successive editions, caused the character of his youthful writings to be forgotten. In 1982, he received a dramatic rehabilitation when he was awarded the prestigious Goethe prize in a splendid ceremony in Frankfurt. Three years later, the chancellor Helmuth Kohl made a pilgrimage to the village of Wilflingen, where Jünger lived, to congratulate him on his ninetieth birthday. He died in 1998, at the age of a hundred and three.

The Aesthetics of War

In the writings of his youth, Jünger seized on the war as an "existential moment" in terms derived from Nietzsche. Unlike many thinkers who betrayed Nietzsche when they took Zarathustra into the trenches, he had a profound understanding of the Nietzschean *Lebensphilosophie* and an intense sympathy for the progenitor of the "will to power." When Jünger fused his interpretation of Nietzsche with his sense of the aesthetic attraction of the war and the experience of the trenches, he was no longer one more author writing about the war but had become its most enthusiastic advocate. Jünger saw the First World War as the most concrete manifestation of Nietzsche's existential, aesthetic, and nihilistic vision. He did not look for the most "exalted" moment but for *the* moment. One cannot prepare oneself for a mystical moment of this kind, for such a moment is like an earthquake that overtakes a man unawares. According to Jünger, the experience of the war was not relative but absolute, enabling a man to discover himself and finally understand the meaning of life.[28]

Stahlgewittern is a realistic description of the soldiers in the trenches. Jünger strikes an admirable balance between the perspective of the soldier who feels horror when going into battle and that of the detached observer who tries to perceive the real meaning of the scenes of the war. In his battle diary, the private and later the officer Jünger noted everything that took place and "what he thought about it at the time it happened."[29] The war was depicted soberly: columns of soldiers filled with their bodies a battlefield that was like a desert of the insane; the dugouts, trenches, and holes that served as shelters and homes for millions of soldiers were a sort of microcosm of Dante's *Inferno*. The war changed its character after the Somme offensive of 1916, and it was now clear to many young people that it would not be a temporary affair and a joyous youthful adventure, but was something with which they would be burdened for weeks, months, and years. What was the value of men's lives when the eye became accustomed to the daily sight of thousands of exploding bodies flying in the air? Nothing existed except a frenzied crescendo of mutual slaughter. Noble feelings ceased having any significance at a time when the machine dominated humanity. Men were hardened and became atoms, and their outward appearance reflected this: this was the first time that German soldiers wore steel helmets. In the shadow of death, stiffness and rigidity became a way of life. The soldiers became a laboratory for the production of death on a massive scale and for the exploitation of means of destruction.

Jünger's description of the war reached its climax in his account of the great German offensive of March 1918. The moment approached for the last supreme effort. The fate of nations was to be sealed in blood and steel, and the destiny of the world hung in the balance. Jünger was aware of the historical significance of this moment and was convinced that each man felt that his individual existence was rendered insignificant by the weight of the historic responsibility placed on his shoulders. Such moments made him feel that in the final analysis, the history of nations and the fate of the individual were decided in battles. On the eve of the battle, the tension in the air could be cut with a knife. The officers gathered in a circle exchanged nervous jokes and were unable to preserve their clarity of mind as the artillery bombardment proceeded. Nerves were paralyzed, and people were no longer even frightened. Death lost its meaning because "the will-to-live passed collectively to the nation." This made everyone indifferent to his personal fate. This jumble of feelings mixed with alcohol as the army advanced toward the enemy aroused both the bestial and the godlike in man. The army was infused with a blood-lust.

In *Der Kampf also inneres Erlebnis*, the war was also described as an aesthetic and existential phenomenon:

> All goals are past, only movement is eternal, and it brings forth unceasingly magnificent and merciless spectacles. To sink into their lofty goallessness as into an artwork or as into the starry sky, that is granted only to the few. But who experiences in this war only negation, only inherent suffering and not affirmation, the higher movement, he has experienced it as a slave. He has no inner, but only an external experience.[30]

Jünger experienced the reality as a mysterious movement of spirit: "We are confronted with a riddle: the mystery of the spirit that pours out now and then across the world, seizing whole multitudes of men together. No one knows where it originates."[31] Ernst von Salomon also wrote of the thread binding together the loyalties of a single race, in which each person shares the same sufferings and is subject to the same penetrating vibrations.[32] Jünger described the riddle and at the same time provided the interpretation: he was a barometer who experienced the present within himself but who also discerned the significance of his era and his place in it. Men of action like Salomon and Jünger described themselves in their books as reflecting the things that were taking place in their time.

The Vanguard that Precedes the Reich

According to Josef Goebbels, the overriding aim of the radical national-ists in the time of the Weimar Republic was to transform the masses into a people. In the war, order had been universally imposed: the masses disappeared overnight, and an exultant, enthusiastic mob had been transformed into a people marching into battle. Jünger describes how this mob became a people and an army:

> New gods were raised to the throne of the day: strength, the fist, and virile courage. The long columns of armed youth thundering along the asphalt embodied all of these qualities: the crowd was suffused with jubilation and reverential awe.[33]

This was the vanguard that preceded the Reich. The mob was organized into a fighting formation, and the moral Jünger drew from it was, "This is how things should be!" The anarchic nature of existence should be molded by the will into strength, audacity, and courage. After the war, with the defeat of Germany, the people had split apart into a disorganized mass as it had been before. According to Jünger, the subculture of the Weimar Republic now raised up the masses from the dunghill and made them the arbiter of cultural norms in place of the elite. Jünger expressed his patrician disdain for this phenomenon in language reminiscent of the Nietzschean contempt for the "herd":

> Since the mass is unable to emulate the few, the few are being called upon to emulate the mass. Politics, drama, artists, cafés, patent-leather shoes, posters, newspapers, morality, tomorrow's Europe, the world of the day after tomorrow: all this is to become thundering mass. The mass is a beast of a thousand heads, it obstructs all movement, crushes anything it cannot swallow or engulf; it is envious, parvenu, common. The individual has once again been defeated, betrayed most savagely by men born to represent him.[34]

Jünger advocated a nationalism of a new kind — one based on the individual rather than social beliefs or traditions. The existential outlook that connected the individual with his universe automatically identified nationhood with the individual.

> It [nationalism] is more than just one idea among others. It does not seek out the measurable, but the measure. It is the surest route to the maternal being that gives birth to new forms in every century. And we have seen that there are still men who can create after the fashion of the warrior.[35]

Jünger's existential nationalism was based on an affirmation of the instincts, a merging with the cosmos and the creation of a new man, ex nihilo, entranced by the rhythms and "bestiality" of war.

The subject of Jünger's article "On Pain" was this man of steel or "new man." According to this article, bourgeois culture tries to disregard poverty and servitude by creating a whole world of political and technical "comfort." This was exemplified by Nietzsche's "last man," who was bourgeois, hedonistic, and comfortable. The meritorious man, on the other hand, is the one who is full of contempt toward the world of bourgeois mediocrity, and who is able to bear the pain of the technological era. An elite group or an artist or hero knows the value of self-discipline and realizes that it is pain that directly creates the power of life. The body is not regarded as having any value in itself, but is an object or tool for the attainment of higher values that are achieved through the technological impulse. Man must therefore be transformed into a machine. Discipline is "the means by which man connects himself to pain."[36] For the bourgeoisie, a "good" man is one who can be influenced, who is changeable, mobile, somewhat restless. By contrast, "the disciplined man is closed up: he has a stern mentality — one-sided, objective, hard." Above all, a man must learn the value of self-sacrifice. From this aesthetic starting point, man can achieve a complete objectivization of his own body. This self-objectivization can take place only in a world in which the concepts of space and time have radically changed.[37]

The battlefield was the progenitor of the "new man." Jünger's patrician Nietzscheanism led him to the conclusion that the masses who invaded the battlefield destroyed the image of an organized army of select individuals. In his opinion, the bourgeoisie had opened up the trenches to the masses and made a business out of the war, which is the only place where a man can be truly a man: "Only one mass-phenomenon is not ridiculous: the army. But the bourgeoisie has made even the army ridiculous."[38] According to Jünger, the man who was not militaristic was "bourgeois." Jünger attacked Marxism at a sensitive point by depicting its mentality as bourgeois and antimilitaristic, or, in other words, as degenerate. The answer to degeneracy was dynamism. The "new man" paved the way for a society, culture, and nation that existed on a permanent war-footing. This model had been forged in the trenches.

The mentality of the soldiers at the front was exemplified not only by Jünger but in the *Freikorps*, private armies that sprang up after the First World War. Klaus Theweleit's study *Male Fantasies* (1978) seeks to examine their psychology.[39] These "white troops" — hence the name "white terror" — were used by the socialist government of Friedrich Ebert to suppress the communist insurrection of the years 1919–20. They saw the radical German working-class movement as the greatest threat to their image of the German nation. Theweleit's study, which covers about 250 novels and memoirs by the members of the Freikorps, investigates their hopes and fears as well as their glorification of war and violence. A literature of recollection was popular in the 1920s, and there were hundreds and thousands of books giving an obsessive description of feelings of violence, male fantasies, and experiences of the war. This mass phenomenon paralleled the flowering of a protofascist literature in France and Italy in the 1920s reflecting the rise of militarism and a longing for male comradeship and nostalgia for one's lost heroic youth.

The writers of the Freikorps were also drawn to an existential rather than to the National Socialist ideology. Their aim was not to communicate but to totally uproot and destroy. In their writings, the self became machine-like through what Foucault once called "techniques of the self." Theweleit analyzed the discourse of the Freikorps, and *Male Fantasies* is undoubtedly a work of political symbolism. It is not an ideological survey of the subject but a study of the symbolic construction of the "other" as a mechanism for consolidating the self. Fascism, according to Theweleit, was not "a form of domination, a general ideology or a system at all"[40] but a sexual language, an "epistemological code," an anti-Eros in the service of nihilism. Underlying fascist propaganda, there is a constant war against anything that contains enjoyment and pleasure.[41] War is not regarded as a process of maturation in which the fighter passes through an initiation ceremony on the path to maturity, an event that sharpens his perception of the world. War is an experience one chooses, a mirror that reflects one's identity. War is neither an initiation ceremony nor a confrontation with the beast within us. Theweleit effects a deconstruction of these myths concerning war, which describe it as an initiation to manhood or to bestiality.

In 1925, Jünger joined the staff of the journal Stahlhelm, whose principles were similar to those of the '*Croix de feu*' in France: namely, opposition to the treaty of Versailles, to the republican regime and to universal franchise. In 1926, Jünger described war as the mother of modern nationalism: "Modern nationalism . . . needs that which is out of the ordinary. . . . The mother of the nation is war. . . . War is our mother, it infuses us with soul . . . so that our values will be heroic values, values of fighters and not of shopkeepers. . . . We do not want the useful, the private, and the pleasurable, but what is necessary and what is required by destiny."[42] By 1927, he was disappointed with the leagues of the *Bund* (association) of front-line soldiers (and especially with the *Stahlhelm*), which he had ceased to see as suitable models for a future society since they had become party-like structures. Jünger now conceived his "new man" in the image of the soldier-worker of the trenches of the First World War. The anonymous soldier of the war was a fitting symbol of the hero of the industrial-military process: "His positive feature is that he is replaceable, and for each one that falls there is another to take his place."[43] The community of "new men" came into being with the new modes of existence and new industrial forms that grew out of the war era: "This war is not the end but the beginning of violence . . . a breaking of new frontiers. . . . The war is a great school and the new man will spring forth from our race."[44] The war, which produced the new communal masculine relationship, was not seen by Jünger as an experience of the past, a trauma, or something unrepeatable, but as an ever-valid model and a creative phenomenon: "Battle is not only destruction but also the masculine form of recuperation from sickness."[45]

Total Mobilization

According to Jünger, the choice that faced the ordinary worker in the new era of technological nihilism was to participate of his own volition as a cog in the vast machinery or to stand aside. Only the loftier natures, the heroic worker-warriors, were fit to experience the modern work-war process. With the concept "total mobilization," Jünger meant to express the full scope of technology. In the war of the future, the country that produced the most material would win. War was a "storm of steel" because of the massive mobilization of material—an enormous work-process involving continual production and consumption.[46]

In his article "Total Mobilization" ("*Die totale Mobilmachung*"), published in 1930, Jünger argued that Germany was defeated in the war because it had failed to achieve total mobilization. Too many sections of the German bourgeoisie cherished ideas like safety, pleasure, comfort, individuality, private freedom, rationality, investment, and progress. The Germans did not want to risk everything for the sake of some noble ideal. In the wars of the future, however, no one would be safe. Anticipating the aerial battles of the Second World War, Jünger saw that the age of directed fire had already passed. The commander of the squadron could no longer differentiate between combatants and noncombatants, and a cloud of deadly gas would hover henceforth over every living creature. The prospect of a threat of this kind permitted neither partial nor general mobilization, only a total mobilization that would include even a baby in the cradle.

Jünger expanded his experience in the trenches into the more general conception of a work-state. From his appreciation of mechanized warfare he progressed to the vision of a society based on perpetual mobilization for total war. Total mobilization operated in the same way in a world war as in a world revolution, and it had infused the First World War with the "genius of warfare" and the "spirit of progress."

But Jünger was also one of the last representatives of the aesthetic tradition that began with Edgar Allan Poe and was developed by decadent aesthetes of the nineteenth century like Baudelaire, Wilde, and

Beardsley.[47] Poe's aestheticization of horror was intended to have a definite emotional effect on the bored readers of Victorian society. Wilde believed that art reveals the dark mystery of the soul, its dormant lusts and secret desires. It permitted one to see beyond the veil of everyday existence into the realm of the mysterious, the irrational. Many artists and thinkers in Germany such as Tillich and Heidegger had spoken of a revelatory experience, a "moment of truth" in which the banality of everyday life is transformed through some event that disrupts routine. A radical change of form takes place that requires a "decision" outside the sphere of normal social or political discourse. Jünger went further than his predecessors by aestheticizing war and modern technology through a kind of "heroic realism" that sought to objectivize the trauma of daily life in the modern era.

In Jünger we can find "a separation of aesthetics from morality, a raising of beauty from a normative level to a metaphysical level."[48] The aestheticization of political irrationalism is expressed by Jünger as follows:

> Today we are writing poetry out of steel and struggle for power in battles in which events mesh together with the precision of machines. In these battles on land, on water and in the air there lies a beauty that we are able to anticipate. There the hot will of the blood restrains and then expresses itself through the dominance of technical wonder-works of power.[49]

Since the aesthetics of war are unconnected with its purpose or moral validity, one is left with a total aestheticism. Jüngerism as a fusion of aestheticism and militarism does not distinguish between categories of "what" but between categories of "how," between

> the restoration front and the other camp determined to carry on the war by any means, and not only by means of war. We have to know where our true allies are to be found. They are not to be found in a place where people wish to be protected, but in a place where people want to attack; we are close to a situation in which any conflict that erupts anywhere in the world will strengthen our position.[50]

Conflict is the anvil on which the new moral dichotomy between "people who wish to be protected" and "people who want to attack" is forged.

The First World War, in which the lethal weapons of modern technology were used for the first time, was the crucible of the "new man." What motivated the "new man" was "the attraction of the machine" and the challenge of "existing without feelings." Here, Jünger's observation, "Technology is our uniform," was apt. The machine, which had formerly been seen as functional and utilitarian, was now viewed as expressing the true essence of the modern man:

> Yes, the machine is beautiful. It must be beautiful for him who loves life in all life's fullness and power. The machine must also be incorporated into what Nietzsche (*who, in his Renaissance landscape, still had no place for the machine* [emphasis added]) meant when he attacked Darwinism. Nietzsche insisted that life is not only a merciless struggle for survival but also possesses a will to higher and deeper goals. The machine cannot only be a means of production, serving to satisfy our paltry material necessities. Rather, it ought to bestow on us higher and deeper satisfactions. . . . The artistic individual, who suddenly sees in technology the totality [*Ganzheit*] instead of a functional assembly of iron parts and thus grasps a strategy that seeks to break off from the path of production by seeing that totality and that strategy in war, this artistic individual is as involved in finding the solution, that is, finding the deeper and more elevated satisfactions in the machine, as the engineer or the socialist is![51]

This "aestheticization of technological form," with its invocation of Nietzsche, is indicative of the direction in which Jünger's critique of modernism was moving. As Jeffrey Herf pointed out, Jünger became the most prominent spokesman of "reactionary modernism," a cultural trend "which reconciled the anti-modern, romantic and irrational ideas present in German nationalism with the clear, rational functionalism of modern technology." They (the reactionary modernists) combined political reaction with technological progress. At a time when German conservatives spoke of technology *or* culture, the reactionary modernists taught the German Right to speak of both technology *and* culture." This school of thought included thinkers like Oswald Spengler, Martin Heidegger, Carl Schmitt, Hans Freyer, and Werner Sombart, many of whom had been influenced by Nietzsche.

Unlike the reactionaries of the *Volksgemeinschaft* who rejected industrialization and technology as harmful to the spirit of the people, these thinkers of the "conservative revolution" came to the conclusion that Germany had to adopt modern technology and at the same time create a socio-economic system that was capable of mastering it. The aim was to consolidate German national power through the embrace of modern industrialization, to create an authoritative national socialism that would constitute a "third way" between capitalism and communism. They hoped to encourage a spirit of self-sacrifice and a love of danger in place of the Enlightenment spirit of calculated rationality.

This outlook cultivated the qualities of masculinity, bravery, hardness, discipline, and honor. The reactionary modernists sought to embrace technology within the framework of culture—which they identified with community, blood, will, independence, form, creativity, and race—while rejecting the characteristics of urban civilization—reason, intellect, internationalism, and materialism. These ideologues of the new radical nationalism wished to create order out of the chaos that existed in Germany after the First World War.[52]

The Work-State

The Jüngerian view of man and the world is modeled on a Nietzschean vision of "will to power" overcoming the chaos. Existence had to be not only accepted, but also intensified. The will did not perform any actions and had no intentions. It was a blind Dionysian force, a phenomenon without a purpose, something irrational, without a consciousness. Unlike Schopenhauer, who wanted the will to be denied, Nietzsche wished it to be intensified. In the conditions of the universe, everything that existed was an obstacle and a stumbling block for everything else, with the result that there was no harmony. The basis of power was really the disharmonious nature of the universe. Nietzsche placed the emphasis on *existence* itself and not on relationships. In this Heraclitean situation, all beings sought power, tried to expand, and came into conflict with other beings. The principle of adaptation for survival gave way to the Nietzschean princple of the will to power. The Nietzschean revolution was that of abandoning the idea of purpose in favor of the idea of a process for its own sake.

> Our technological world is not an area of unlimited possibilities; rather, it possesses an embryonic character that drives toward a predetermined maturity. So it is that our world resembles a monstrous foundry. . . . Its means have a provisionary, workshop character, designed for temporary use.[53]

Der Arbeiter hovers somewhere between dream and nightmare—an impression that is enhanced by a radio broadcast of the period, in which Jünger said, "I wanted to avoid using general unifying terms such as are used by all the political parties: terms like culture, soul, ideal, personality, psychology, Goethe, Hegel, Shakespeare. . . . I wanted to describe our reality as it would be described to a man from the moon who had never seen a motor car and had never read a page of modern literature."[54] After the Second World War, Jünger persistently claimed that his book had been intended as a diagnosis rather than a prognosis. He had merely been a seismograph or barometer of his time.

In *Der Arbeiter*, Jünger takes the Nietzschean will to power to its ultimate fascist conclusion in formulating a technological vision of the modern world. Where Jünger had once emphasized the "existential moment" of war, he now envisaged a "total mobilization" in which labor had no limits and individuals could be sacrificed to the requirements of society. The "worker" was neither a nationalist nor a socialist, neither a democrat nor a revolutionary, but a technician, a member of the "ranked state," the "new order," or the "work-state." The "worker" achieved personal satisfaction not through pursuing any external goal but through manifesting energy in production, transportation, and management. These three activities gave rise to a new phenomenon, the "*Gestalt* of the worker." Originally, Jünger saw the Gestalt of the frontline soldier as the model for the "worker." In the modern battlefield and in the modern work-process, the individual was a standardized phenomenon wearing a uniform, not a private person but a type.[55]

Jünger distinguished between the bourgeois era, which he identified with modernism, and the age of the worker, which was more modern than modernism, even postmodernist.[56] His starting point is the Nietzschean belief that the death of God and consequently the decline of Christianity and its secular counterpart, the bourgeoisie, were decisive events of the modern period. As Jürgen Habermas has stated, modernism was the project of the Enlightenment and the equality of man. Jünger sought to subvert this program and developed an anti-Enlightenment dialectic. According to him, there was no possibility of liberation, only the a deterministic assumption implicit in his concept of "forms" (*Gestalten*) — the behavioral patterns of history — as against free will. Jünger therefore wished to "inform his time from the viewpoint of an archaeologist." In this, he foreshadowed major manifestations of postmodernist thought like Michel Foucault's "archaeology," Jacques Derridas's "traces," and the "metanarrative" (myth) of Jean-François Lyotard.

In the metaphor of "archaeology," which has become a synonym for Foucault's subversive thought, one may discern the fingerprints of Nietzsche, the ultimate source both for Jünger and postmodernism. "Archaeology" meant that history was not a continuous narrative but a series of layers, of different organic cultures. This view, which conformed to Oswald Spengler's concept of history as a succession of different cultures, posits a cultural relativity in which there are neither eternal truths nor suprahistorical values. Values change with historical circumstances. The archaeological approach meant a total historicism whose political implications could be embraced by thinkers like Heidegger and Spengler or historians like Ernst Nolte.

It is also not surprising that ideologists of the Third Reich like Alfred Bäumler and E. Krieck employed a similar vitalistic and mythical language to Jünger in attacking the bourgeoisie. Bäumler, the author of *Nietzsche, der Philosoph und Politiker* (1931), suggested that intellectuals should train to live "the life of political soldiers." The life of the soldier was regarded as an ideal and the "political soldier," the man of the SS or the SA, represented the ultimate fulfillment. In *Der Mythos vom Orient und Occident* (1926), the Nietzschean Bäumler considered the relationship between myth and history: "Myth is definitely unhistorical. Myth not only reaches prehistory, but also attains the ultimate foundations of the human soul."[57] An illustration of Bäumler's thesis was the Jüngerian "worker," a myth of the modern world—a world that is a workshop, as opposed to the museum-like character of bourgeois life. The workshop, comparable to a battlefield, was perceived in terms of a myth of belligerence for its own sake. In his attack on bourgeois culture, Jünger fused creative vitalism with irrational nihilism to create a new mythical language. With Jünger, this mythical language became the very heart of a doctrine of vitalist consciousness.

Heidegger: The Will to Will

Martin Heidegger's attraction to Jünger's writings, especially to *Der Arbeiter*, no less than his friendship with the author himself, is also deserving of our attention. Heidegger wrote,

> Ernst Jünger's work *Der Arbeiter* is important because it, in another way than Spengler, achieves what all the Nietzsche literature was up to now unable to achieve, namely, to communicate an experience of the entity and of how it is, in the light of Nietzsche's project of the entity as Will to Power. To be sure, Nietzsche's metaphysics is by no means conceived in a thoughtful way [*denkerisch begriffen*]; on the contrary, instead of being questionable, in the true sense, this metaphysics becomes self-evident and apparently superfluous.[58]

In 1938–39, Heidegger gave a university course entitled "Beyond Metaphysics," and in the winter 1939–40, he gave a private seminar at the University of Freiburg on the work of Jünger, and especially *Der Arbeiter*. The seminar aroused opposition in the National Socialist Party, and he was finally prevented from giving it. Jünger was the only writer or thinker with whom Heidegger corresponded on a regular basis and with whom he had a close relationship. Their first meeting, which occurred only after the Second World War, took place in the heart of the Black Forest. There, Heidegger suggested to the writer of *Der Arbeiter* that he should bring out a new edition of his book. Jünger refused, and that was the end of the conversation concerning *Der Arbeiter*. Nevertheless the two thinkers shared a common desire to understand the modern world and the universal domination of technology. In 1955, Heidegger showed Jünger his article "The Front Line," which was first published in the *Festschrift* for Jünger's sixtieth birthday; in 1959, the article appeared as a book under the title *Zur Seinsfrage* (*On the Question of Being*).

Throughout the 1930s, according to Michael E. Zimmerman, Heidegger's reflections on technology involved a constant exploratory movement back and forth — from Jünger to Nietzsche and to Hölderlin. Jünger described modern technology better than anyone else, but took his ideas about technology as an aesthetic phenomenon from Nietzsche. Nietzsche's doctrine of art as form-giving activity that restores weight and meaning to life resonated with Heidegger's conviction that art could save Germany from the leveling effects of the one-dimensional technological mode of "working and producing."[59]

Heidegger was fascinated by Jünger's criticism of bourgeois decadence, his elitist conceptions, and his desire for an authoritarian community. At the same time, Heidegger welcomed the National Socialist revolution as a means of preventing the realization of precisely the technological utopia envisioned by Jünger.[60] Heidegger viewed the advent of the new Reich as an opportunity to revitalize the German *Volk*, in contrast to Jünger's vision of making the entire world into a single technological planet. In formulating this vision, Jünger was not only speaking to all Germans, but to all Europeans. Heidegger was convinced that Hitler's National Socialism made possible a "third way," an alternative to a technological conception of reality such as that which had gained acceptance in the United States and Russia. *Der Arbeiter* represented for him the best description of this new technological understanding of reality. Jünger's Nietzsche-inspired aestheticism made an impression on Heidegger, and many of his works could be seen as a confrontation with Jünger's thought. In this connection, it is worth mentioning Heidegger's series of seminars on Nietzsche given from 1936 to 1940 and from 1940 to 1946. Heidegger did not compare Nietzsche to Kierkegaard, and unlike Jaspers he did not see him as an existentialist thinker, but regarded him as the last of the metaphysicians of the West.

In their contempt for mass culture, Jünger and Heidegger were influenced by Nietzsche's analysis of the dialectic between master and slave. Mass culture was identified with the bourgeois world that aimed at comfort, mediocrity, and security. Moreover, Jünger and Heidegger both believed that the technological era could reach fulfillment only under the leadership of an elite that would reject the shallow optimism of the masses. Both of them awaited the Nietzschean Overman who would complete the nihilistic process.[61]

In *On the Question of Being*, Heidegger explained the relationship between the Nietzschean metaphysics of nihilism and the will to power as well as the conclusions Jünger drew from them in *Der Arbeiter*. For him, the conclusion was clear: "Jünger's interpretation of nihilism is entirely expressed in terms of Nietzschean categories."[62] Total mobilization is the large-scale realization of man's domination of the world by means of technology. Total mobilization is the process whereby the type of the "worker" mobilizes the entire world, so that work, identified with Being, becomes the very style of existence and of man's domination of Being. Total mobilization is a form of active nihilism, in that it is an expression of the nihilistic will to power since man's mastery of technique has no significance, direction, value, purpose, or content. It is will to power for its own sake, mobilization for its own sake, man's way of preserving his own vitality, or, as Heidegger expressed it, the "will to will." Nihilism is no longer European or Western but metaphysical; it becomes the fate of the whole world as a normative condition: "The metaphysical character of the type of the 'worker' corresponds to the intentions of the type of Zarathustra with regard to the metaphysics of the will to power." Believing that the technological era that Jünger envisaged was the climax of Western metaphysics, Heidegger not only hoped for a new beginning for Germany but saw Hitler's revolution as a new dawn for Europe as a whole.

Heidegger believed that for Nietzsche the essence of modernism lay in the dominance of nihilism, which had three manifestations: the supremacy of science and technology, work as a universal style, and the recognition of existential nihilism as a normal condition. Nietzsche had already declared in the early 1880s that the age of barbarism had begun and that the scientists would serve it. The question that Jünger and Carl Schmitt would subsequently ask was the question of Zarathustra, which appears in the fourth and last part of the book: "Who will have the courage to be lord of the earth?" Nietzsche did not identify the lord of the earth, but in 1881–82 he had prophesied, "The time will come when the struggle over the rule of the earth will be decided, and it will be decided in the name of essential philosophical doctrines." In 1883, he again asked, "How can one rule the earth?" and a year later he added, "I am writing for a race of men who do not yet exist, for the rulers of the earth." Although Zarathustra was the prototype that personified the metaphysics that made the Overman possible, he was not yet the Overman but rather his spokesman. Only after 1918 would Jünger and other thinkers emerge — each one fashioning his hero — Spengler's barbarians, Sorel's syndicalists, Russian Bolsheviks, and Italian futurists — each in accordance with a metaphysical model containing residues of Nietzsche's Zarathustra.

The Jüngerian Order

By the end of the 1920s, Jünger feared that the Nazis would betray the purity of their original national-revolutionary ideals. J. P. Stern believes that Jünger's teachings had initially served as an "intellectual superstructure" for the Nazi political program and indeed, after 1933, he was the most important writer to remain in Germany.[63] Significantly, he hardly made any attempt to oppose or to protest against Nazi exploitation of his name as a soldier and a patriot in order to glorify their aims.

Jünger never joined the Nazi party, but, to say the least, he did not regret the fall of the Weimar Republic. On the contrary, he felt that the Nazis' rise to power was the "metaphysical solution" that would put into practice the scheme of total mobilization in its pure form.[64] The many explanations that have been given as to why Jünger did not join the Nazi party all agree on one point. Jünger, with aristocratic disdain, fundamentally rejected the *plebeian* aspects of Nazism. Jünger's aloofness toward the Nazis from 1930 onward, despite his closeness to them in the previous decade, was due to his wish to preserve the idealistic purity of the new nationalism. He feared that the Nazi party was open to the same "party egoism" as he found in the other parties, and he rejected its legalistic tactics and compromises with the Weimar Republic. He believed that Nazism was only a temporary phenomenon.[65] Nor did his ideas really correspond to Nazi ideology, since he did not believe in a biological racism. The rejection by the Nazis of his intellectual and aesthetic criteria should also be noted.

However, the Jüngerian "new man" did foreshadow and pave the way for the men of the SS. Indeed, his ideal was not so different from the Nazi stormtrooper of the period — part ex-serviceman, part delinquent, displaying an attitude of 'heroic realism,' which meant 'fighting for its own sake.' "[66] Stanley Rosen saw a connection between Heidegger's *Being and Time* and Jünger's views in *Der Arbeiter*, and their respective attraction to Nazism. Nihilism and fascism were linked by an umbilical cord: "Jünger is of interest because his career provides us with a series of steps similar to those traversed by Heidegger: at first, an active encouragement of the contemporary nihilistic motives; then, disillusion with the political mobilization of what was supposed to be a spiritual purification; last, . . . waiting for new, anti nihilistic revelations of Being."[67] In Rosen's opinion, the nihilization of Western civilization proceeded in a straight line from *Der Arbeiter* to Nazism. In 1934, one year after Hitler came to power, one Nazi writer expressed appreciation of Jünger's contribution to the outlook of German youth in the following terms: "German youth is first of all indebted to Ernst Jünger for the fact that technology is no longer a problem for us. They have accepted the admirable views about technology expressed in *Feuer und Blut*; they live in harmony with them. They no longer need an ideology with which to overcome [technology]. Jünger has liberated us from that nightmare."[68] The "nightmare" in question was the hostility to the automobile, to technology, to industrialization, and to urbanism that had characterized *völkisch* antimodernism, the cultural despair of Möller Van den Bruck, and Spengler's pessimism.

Augier, a myth-maker in the service of the Third Reich, would write in 1950 that the French SS groups "were the most perfect expression of the nihilistic world order"[69] — a historical development he traced back to Nietzsche: in Nietzschean perspectivism, one interpretation is no better than another, and the nihilistic revolution initiated by Nietzsche left behind it ruins where wild growths flourished. If Nietzsche had been asked, he would undoubtedly have disowned his political interpreters, but that is not the point. The problem is the possible implications of Nietzschean nihilism in the absence of the universal rule of reason. The starting point laid down by Albert Camus is relevant here: "Let us recognize first of all that we will never be able to speak in the same breath of Nietzsche and Rosenberg."[70] But can we disregard the nihilistic inner logic that Nietzsche explicated, thus facilitating its development in the twentieth century? Can we avert our eyes from the laying of a path of directionless dynamism from Nietzsche toward the politics of Rosenberg, who wrote, "Let our style be that of a marching column, and it doesn't matter in which direction the column marches, or for what reason"?[71] The question continually recurs (especially with regard to Nietzsche) as to how a philosophical system comes to be distorted, perverted, and emasculated by the ideologists who speak in its name? How is it that certain "necessary" conclusions come to be drawn? Camus acutely observed, "Philosophy profanes the ideal, and tyrants come and immediately profane the philosophy that gives them the right to do so." It was the political factor that became all-dominant in the twentieth century, and when fused with nihilist and aesthetic elements, it ultimately made possible a totalitarian interpretation of the Nietzschean philosophy. Perhaps it is symbolically significant that in the year in which Hitler and Heidegger were born, Nietzsche went insane.

Notes

The author gratefully acknowledges the assistance and advice of Robert Wistrich in editing this essay.

1. Hereby I follow Richard Schacht's definition of nihilism as "the doctrine that there is and can be no such thing as 'truth' where reality is concerned . . . [or] the doctrine that axiological principles have no objective basis in reality." See his "Nietzsche and Nihilism," in *Nietzsche: A Collection of Critical Essays*, ed. Robert C. Solomon (Notre Dame: University of Notre Dame Press, 1980), 30. See also Arthur Danto's definition: "An essentially chaotic reality . . . (there) is neither order nor purpose, things nor facts, nothing there whatever to which our beliefs can correpond," in his *Nietzsche as Philosopher* (New York: Macmillan, 1965), 33. Compare other interpretations: Elizabeth Kuhn, *Friedrich Nietzsches Philosophie des europäischen Nihilismus* (Berlin: de Gruyter, 1992); Michael Allen Gillespie, *Nihilism before Nietzsche* (Chicago: University of Chicago Press, 1995), chaps. 6–7.

2. Walter Kaufmann, *Nietzsche; Philosopher, Psychologist, Antichrist* (Princeton: Princeton University Press, 1950); and compare Walter H. Sokel, "Political Uses and Abuses of Nietzsche in Walter Kaufmann's Image of Nietzsche," *Nietzsche-Studien* 12 (1983): 429–35.

3. Tracy B. Strong, *Friedrich Nietzsche and the Politics of Transfiguration* (Berkeley: University of California Press, 1975); Bruce Detwiler, *Nietzsche and the Politics of Aristocratic Radicalism* (Chicago: University of Chicago Press, 1990).

4. Martin Heidegger, *Nietzsche*, 2 vols. (Pfullingen: Gunther Neske, 1961); Jacques Derrida, *Spurs: Nietzsche's Styles*, trans. Barbara Harlow (Chicago: University of Chicago Press, 1979).

5. Gianni Vattimo, *La sécularisation de la pensée*, trans. Charles Alunni (Paris: Seuil, 1986).

6. David Ohana, "The Role of Myth in History: Nietzsche and Georges Sorel," in *Religion, Ideology and Nationalism in Europe and America* (Jerusalem: Historical Society of Israel and the Zalman Shazar Center for Jewish History, 1986), 119–140.

7. For other interpretations, see also Ivan Soll, "Reflections on Recurrence: A Re-Examination of Nietzsche's Doctrine, *die Ewige Wiederkehr Des Gleichen*," *Nietzsche: A Collection of Critical Essays*, 322–42; Arnold Zuboff, "Nietzsche and Eternal Recurrence," In ibid., 343–57; Bernd Magnus, *Nietzsche's Existential Imperative* (Bloomington and Indianapolis: Indiana University Press, 1978).

8. Compare with Robert C. Solomon's assumption that "the themes of nihilism and the will to power . . . function together as the key poles of Nietzsche's thought." See his "Nietzsche, Nihilism, and Morality," in *Nietzsche: A Collection of Critical Essays*, 203. See also Gilles Deleuze's argument: "Nihil in 'nihilism' means negation as quality of the will to power," in *Nietzsche and Philosophy*, trans. Hugh Tomlinson (NewYork: Columbia University Press, 1983), 143.

9. David Ohana, "Nietzsche and Ernst Jünger: From Nihilism to Totalitarianism," *History of European Ideas*, 11 (1989): 751–58; for another interpretation, see Philippe Barthelet, "Sur deux vertus nietzschéennes," *Ernst Jünger, L'Oeil-De-Boeuf* (Special Issue), nos. 5–6 (Decembre 1994): 45–46.

10. Stanley Rosen, *Nihilism: A Philosophical Essay* (New Haven: Yale University Press, 1969), 1–27; Gillian Rose, *Dialectic of Nihilism: Post-Structuralism and Law* (Oxford: Basil Blackwell, 1984), 131–207; Keith Ansell-Pearson, "Nietzsche's Overcoming of Kant and Metaphysics: From Tragedy to Nihilism," *Nietzsche-Studien*, 16 (1987): 310–39.

11. Allan Megill, *Prophets of Extremity: Nietzsche, Heidegger, Foucault, Derrida* (Berkeley: University of California Press, 1987), 30.

12. Ofelia Schutte, *Beyond Nihilism: Nietzsche without Masks* (Chicago: University of Chicago Press, 1984), 50.

13. For the psychological dimension of the will to power, see Jacob Golomb, *Nietzsche's Psychology of Power* (Ames: Iowa State University Press, 1989).

14. David Ohana, *Misdar Ha-Nihilistim (The Order of the Nihilists): Leidata shel Tarbut politit be-Europa 1870–1930* (Jerusalem: Bialik Institute, 1993), in Hebrew.

15. David Ohana, "The 'Anti-Intellectual' Intellectuals as Political Mythmakers," in *The Intellectual Revolt Against Liberal Democracy 1870–1945* ed. Z. Sternhell (Jerusalem: Israel Academy of Sciences and Humanities, 1996), 87–104.

16. Ernst Bloch, "The Impulse of Nietzsche," in *Heritage of Our Times*, trans. by Neville and Stephan Plaice (Berkeley: University of California Press), 325.

17. Ibid., 330; See especially, Anson Rabinbach in his "Unclaimed Heritage: Ernst Bloch's Heritage of Our Times and the Theory of Fascism," *New German Critique* (Spring 1977).

18. Quoted in David Ohana, "Georges Sorel and the Rise of Political Myth," *History of European Ideas* 13, no. 6 (1991): 733–46.

19. Ansgar Hillach, "The Aesthetics of Politics: Walter Benjamin's Theories of German Fascism," *New German Critique* 17 (Spring 1979): 120–28.

20. J. P. Stern, *Ernst Jünger — A Writer of Our Time* (Cambridge, UK: Bowes and Bowes, 1953), 8–17; H. Becher, *Ernst Jünger — Mensch und Werk* (Warendorf, 1949); M. Meyer, *Ernst Jünger* (Munich: Carl Hanser, 1990).

21. E. Jünger, *Afrikanische Spiele* (Hamburg: Hanseatische Verlags-Anstalt, 1936), 46–47.

22. Jünger, *In Stahlgewittern* (Hanover: Selbstverlag des Verfassers, 1920), 1.

23. Jünger, *Der Kampf als inneres Erlebnis* (Berlin: Mittler, 1922); *Das Wäldchen 125 — Eine Chronik aus den Grabenkampfen 1918* (Berlin: Mittler, 1925), 154; *Feuer und Blut — Ein kleiner Ausschnitt aus der grossen Schlacht* (Magdeburg: Stahlhelm,1925).

24. Jünger, *Der Arbeiter — Herrschaft und Gestalt* (Hamburg: Hanseatische Verlags-Anstalt, 1932).

25. Jünger, *Gärten und Strassen* (Berlin: Mittler, 1942).

26. Jünger, *Heliopolis — Rückblick auf eine Stadt* (Tübingen: Heliopolis, 1949).

27. Jünger, *Strahlungen* (Tübingen: Heliopolis, 1949).

28. P. Fussel, *The Great War and Modern Memory* (New York: Oxford University Press, 1975); W. Struve, *Elites Against Democracy — Leadership Ideals in Bourgeois Political Thought in Germany, 1890–1933* (Princeton: Princeton University Press, 1973), 378; W.M.K. Pfeiler, *War and the German Mind — The Testimony of Men of Fiction Who Fought at the Front* (New York, 1941).

29. Jünger, *In Stahlgewittern*, ix.

30. Jünger, *Der Kampf als inneres Erlebnis*, 107.

31. Ibid., 82.

32. Ernst von Salomon, *Die Geächteten* (Berlin, 1930).

33. Jünger, *Der Kampf als inneres Erlebnis*, 30.

34. Ibid., 54.

35. Jünger, ed., *Der Kampf um das Reich* (Essen, 1929), 9.

36. Jünger, "Über den Schmerz," in *Werke* (Stuttgart: Klett-Cotta, 1978–83), vol. 5, Essays, pt. 1, 171.

37. See Michael E. Zimmerman, *Heidegger's Confrontation with Modernity — Technology, Politics, Art* (Bloomington: Indiana University Press, 1990), 57.

38. Jünger, *Der Kampf als inneres Erlebnis*, 63.

39. R.G.L. Waite, *Vanguard of Nazism: The Free Corps Movement in Postwar Germany, 1918–1923* (New York: Norton, 1969).

40. K. Theweleit, *Male Fantasies, Vol. I: Male Bodies — Psychoanalysing the White Terror*, trans. E. Carter and C. Turner (Cambridge: Polity Press, 1989), 221.

41. Ibid., 2:8.

42. Ernst Jünger, "Vorwort," in Friedrich Georg Jünger, *Der Aufmarsch des Nationalismus* (Leipzig, 1926), 11.

43. *Die Standarte*, May 20, 1925.

44. Jünger, *Der Kampf als inneres Erlebnis*, 77.

45. Ibid., 53–54.

46. Jünger, "Die totale Mobilmachung," in *Werke*, vol. 5, Essays, pt. 1, 130.

47. K. H. Bohrer, *Die Ästhetik des Schreckens — Die pessimistische Romantik und Ernst Jüngers Frühwerk* (Munich: Carl Hanser, 1978), 325–35.

48. J. Herf, *Reactionary Modernism: Technology, Culture, and Politics in Weimar and the Third Reich* (Cambridge: Cambridge University Press, 1984), 77.

49. Jünger, *Kampf als inneres Erlebnis*, 107.

50. Jünger, *Der Arbeiter*, 157–58.

51. Jünger, *Feuer und Blut* (Magdeburg: Stahlhelm, 1925), 81; trans. by J. Herf, in *Reactionary Modernism*, 79.

52. See Thomas Nevin, *Ernst Jünger and Germany: Into the Abyss, 1914–1945* (Durham: Duke University Press, 1996), 122.

53. Jünger, *Der Arbeiter*, 181–82; trans. by M. E. Zimmerman, *Heidegger's Confrontation with Modernity*, 60.

54. K. O. Paetel, ed., *Ernst Jünger in Selbstzeugnissen und Bilddokumenten* (Hamburg: Reinbek, 1962), 51.

55. Jünger, *Der Arbeiter*, 119.

56. Walter H. Sokel, "The 'Postmodernism' of Ernst Jünger in His Proto-Fascist Stage," *New German Critique* 59 (Spring–Summer 1993): 33–40.

57. A. Bäumler, *Der Mythos vom Orient und Occident* (Munich, 1926), xc.

58. M. Heidegger, *Zur Seinsfrage* (Frankfurt: Klostermann, 1956), 42–45; J. M. Palmier, *Les Écrits Politiques de Heidegger* (Paris: L'Herne, 1968), 196; my translation.

59. M. E. Zimmerman, *Heidegger's Confrontation with Modernity*, 188–90.

60. Cf. J.-P. Faye, "Heidegger et la Révolution," *Médiations* 3 (Autumn 1961): 151–59; P. Bourdieu, *L'ontologie Politique de Martin Heidegger* (Paris: Minuit, 1988); K. Löwith, "Les implications politiques de la philosophie de l'existence chez Heidegger," *Les temps modernes* 2 (November 1946): 343–60; Richard Rorty, "Taking Philosophy Seriously," *The New Republic*, April 11, 1988; R. Wolin, "Recherches récentes sur la relation de Martin Heidegger au National Socialisme," *Les Temps Modernes* 42 (October 1987): 45–85; V. Farias, *Heidegger et le Nazisme*, trans. M. Benarroch and J. B. Grasset (Paris: Verdier, 1987); Wolfgang Matz, "Nach der Katastrophe: Jünger und Heidegger," *Text + Kritik*, 105/106, (January 1990): 74–81.

61. Heidegger, "The Rectorate 1933–1934 — Facts and Thoughts," trans. K. Harries, *The Review of Metaphysics* 38, no. 3 (March 1985), 484; G. Nicholson, "The Politics of Heidegger's Rectoral Address," *Man and World* 20 (1987): 171–87.

62. M. Heidegger, *Zur Seinsfrage*, 10–11.

63. Compare J. P. Stern, *Ernst Jünger — A Writer of Our Time*, 11.

64. Ibid., 12.

65. H.-P. Schwarz, *Die Konservative Anarchist: Politik und Zeitkritik Ernst Jüngers* (Freiburg-im-Breisgau: Rombach, Freiburger Studien zu Politik und Soziologie, 1962), 111–15, 120–21.

66. J. Orr, "German Social Theory and the Hidden Face of Technology," *European Journal of Sociology* 15 (1974): 315.

67. Rosen, *Nihilism*, 118.

68. Herf, *Reactionary Modernism*, 189–216.

69. M. Augier, *Götter Dammerung. Wende und Ende einer Zeit* (Buenos Aires, 1950), 79.

70. Cited by Albert Camus, in his *L'Homme Révolté* (Paris: Gallimard, 1951), 101.

71. Ibid., 224.

ference between them can hardly be overstressed. It stands out in the genocidal racism of German National Socialism that we do not find in the Italian variety of fascism, nor in Austrian or Spanish fascism. The second difference between these fascisms is perhaps of lesser significance: the difference between the unlimited power of the Führer, and the power of the Duce that was limited by the king of Italy. Some of these differences can also be explained by the objective contrast in conditions under which the two nations found themselves, and under which they actually existed. The Italians, a Mediterranean people, had only 50,000 Jews in their territory; and these Jews moreover did not have to serve as scapegoats for defeat in World War I because Italy was one of the victorious powers. But there were also significant similarities, and Hitler knew about them. He admired the Duce for his merciless brutality toward his political enemies. A most important point of similarity was that both the German and the Italian fascist parties tried and succeeded in attracting workers even while fighting the trade unions, the communists, and the socialists. Both detested parliamentary democracy and desired a strong state. Both worried about the condition of Western culture, which they wished to save by the use of propaganda and terror. One is also reminded that Mussolini began his career as a socialist journalist, and that Hitler admired Social Democratic techniques of organization and their propaganda. Both Hitler and Mussolini aimed at expansion of their territory—the former wanted more *Lebensraum* in the East, while the latter wished to expand in the Mediterranean area and the Danube basin. Moreover, although both Nazi Germany and fascist Italy were deadly enemies of communism and of the Soviet Union—there are strong similarities between the Third Reich and Stalinist Russia. But that similarity is not relevant to the topic of this chapter.[4] Both the genuine and the forged Nietzsche were opposed to communism and socialism.

I am concerned here with Nietzsche and National Socialism, and thus with one particular branch of fascism in the wider sense of the term. At the same time, I believe that the historically effective Nietzsche can be read from two opposite perspectives with two opposite results, both as a proponent and as an opponent of National Socialism. In this endeavor, I think that I am close to Nietzsche's own methodological view as expressed in the *Genealogy of Morals*:

> There is *only* a perspective seeing, only a perspective "knowing"; and the *more* affects we allow to speak about one thing, the *more* eyes, different eyes, we can use to observe one thing, the more complete will our "concept" of this thing, our "objectivity," be.[5]

The "real" Nietzsche was not too different from the contaminated and forged Nietzsche, had no historical effect, and played no role in the pro-

or anti-Nazi interpretations of the respective camps. A pivotal role in those readings was played by Nietzsche's concept of the will to power. Nietzsche was first read as a radical egoist, then as someone concerned with a thorough critique of the bourgeois mind, and later still as a philosopher, through the efforts of his sister Elisabeth. She produced an edition of his posthumous writings—irresponsibly, to be sure—under the title *Der Wille zur Macht*. In addition, it is she who was responsible for an adulteration of Nietzsche's letters. Still later there were controversies over whether Nietzsche had or did not have a system. It was surmised that his illness prevented him from developing one. And there were speculations as to how to remedy the contradiction that seemed to prevail between Nietzsche's two main ideas of will to power and "eternal recurrence." It was Alfred Bäumler who played down the conflict between them and degraded, so to speak, the doctrine of eternal recurrence into merely being Nietzsche's private religion. To Heidegger, on the other hand, the conflict between the two ideas seemed to be necessary, and was to be expected.

But let me return to the different perspectives with respect to Nietzsche as a "godfather" of fascism. The following assertions have become commonplace over the years:

(1) Anti-Nazis have claimed Nietzsche as part of a distinctive German intellectual tradition responsible for Nazism and two world wars. This viewpoint was expressed in the books by the liberal-minded William McGovern and the Marxist George Lukács.[6]

(2) Nazis, too, claimed Nietzsche as their forerunner, notably the previously mentioned Alfred Bäumler. Bäumler, incidentally, was not—as has been assumed by Hollingdale—merely an agent of the Nazis. He was a real, convinced and committed Nazi. Nor was he an "ersatz scholar," or, as Kaufmann put it, a "philosophical nobody."[7] In this context it suffices to point out the Bäumler occupied a chair of philosophy at Dresden *before* the Nazis came to power and that he wrote a book that, in the words of the historian of German philosophy Lewis White Beck, "provides all the needed background for study of Kant's *Third Critique*."[8] This was no mean accomplishment in philosophical scholarship! Bäumler's work counts as an important contribution to the history of aesthetics and as an indispensable aid in the study of Kant's aesthetics. Although there is no reason to believe that he manipulated Nietzsche's texts, Kaufmann is, however, right in pointing out that posthumously published notes have been used in Bäumler's interpretation. Bäumler's special claim, that the real Nietzsche can be found above all in his *Nachlass*, may be controversial but is certainly not absurd. In any case, the real Nietzsche is *also* in the *Nachlass*, properly or improperly edited.

(3) There were also Nazi scholars who also denied a connection be-

tween Nazism and Nietzsche. Christoph Steding, for instance, in his monumental work of 1938, entitled *Das Reich und die Krankheit der europäischen Kultur*, made no attempt à la Bäumler to reinterpret Nietzsche's animosity to Bismarck's Reich.[9] He rather perceived in that animosity, and in Nietzsche's preoccupation with intellectual or cultural rather than with political and military history, a dangerous tendency inimical to the establishment of any state. Even though Hitler and the Nazis were less concerned with the state as such than with a *Weltanschauung* that was to be actualized in a political community of Aryan-German racial origin and national stock, they did reject the Nietzschean concern with states of mind and feelings — the insistent preoccupation with higher culture and inwardness.

(4) Walter Kaufmann and some other anti-Nazi intellectuals have therefore denied that there is any connection between Nietzsche and the Nazis.[10] Their view has prevailed in the educated public, certainly in the United States, where many who followed Kaufmann's example neglected to notice Nietzsche's passion and ferocity, or turned to those aspects of his work in which the question of fascism plays no role at all.

Nietzsche has in fact been de-Nazified. Of course, if we see — as retrospectively we must — in the physical destruction of the Jews and in the aggressive urge to obtain *Lebensraum* in the East the essential features of Hitler and Nazism, then there is no connection with Nietzsche. He desired neither the one nor the other.[11] But more is involved here than simple misinterpretation or willful falsification. Nietzsche was not *that* unrelated to Hitler and Nazism, contrary to what the Kaufmann school has implied.

The situation is not dissimilar to defining the relationship between Nietzsche and twentieth-century philosophical trends such as existentialism or logical positivism. If Nietzsche is claimed as a most important and influential thinker, from that perspective he may appear as the precursor of much that we find in the twentieth century — including modernistic trends in art, literature, philosophy, and psychology, as well as ideologies such as fascism or Nazism. From this viewpoint Nazism can be understood as a phenomenon of post-Nietzschean culture, more specifically as a Nietzschean "experiment."[12] In Nietzsche's posthumously published notes we find the exclamation "*Wir machen einen Versuch mit der Wahrheit! Vielleicht geht die Menschheit daran zugrunde! Wohlan!*"

Indeed, if one sees modernist culture as beginning with Nietzsche, then one is entitled to write — as R. J. Hollingdale did — that the twentieth century was born in the 1880s.[13] And if one sees in Hitler and Nazism a Nietzschean experiment — as Alfred Bäumler did — one may write half a century later, in the 1930s, that the twentieth century was only just beginning.[14] In finding features of Nazism in Nietzsche, one is not claiming that Nietzsche was an incomplete Nazi. No more so, in any case, than one could claim him as an incomplete existentialist or logical positivist because some of his ideas might constitute the meta-philosophy (as it were) of existentialism, logical positivism, or even psychoanalysis. Similarly one may concede that Nietzsche is a godfather or forerunner of Nazism as he is of so much else in this century without having to maintain that he would have been a Nazi, had he lived in the *Third* rather than in the *Second* Reich. That he would have been a Nazi had he lived in the Third Reich has been argued by Bäumler.[15] But that Nietzsche would have been a Nazi is no more likely than the claim that he would have been a logical positivist, an analytical philosopher, or a psychoanalyst had he been instructed in the appropriate methods and techniques. In Nietzsche's time none of the paths traced back to his influence had yet been taken. If the historical logic of his thought led him into nihilism — as has been maintained — such an interpretation is quite compatible with the many thought experiments that he carried out and that led in so many unforeseeable directions.

Under these circumstances, it seems proper and useful to reassert the connection between Nietzsche and Nazism in order to gain a more comprehensive view of the recent history of the human mind. A godfather need not be someone from whom only one path leads to that phenomenon of which he is said to be an originator. It is sufficient that he presents such a possibility. As Crane Brinton once put it, "Nietzsche was half a Nazi and half an anti-Nazi."[16] The intricateness of the relationship between Nietzsche and Nazism was also acknowledged many years ago, in George H. Sabine's old standard work, *A History of Political Theory*.[17] What Gerhard Masur called "the insoluble contradictions which Nietzsche presents to the reader," rather than the "two Nietzsches" (Crane Brinton oversimplified the matter), were ultimately responsible for "why he was claimed by power-drunk totalitarians and good Europeans alike."[18]

Nietzsche can in fact be seen as a precursor or indeed a godfather in various ways. The following familiar consideration is proposed: If God is dead and if there are no accepted values, all possibilities are open and must consequently be explored whether as an antidote to, or as an attack on, nihilism. We may and indeed we must experiment! Experimenting is not confined nor is it confining. As Walter Kaufmann himself has pointed out, Nietzsche's experimentalism includes not only thought experiments or scientific experiments but has an "'existential' quality; it is an experimenting that involves testing an answer by trying to live according to it."[19] This experimenting may take the form of an existential heroism that is to last for centuries and unambiguously points to action.

In *The Gay Science*, in an aphorism entitled "Something for the industrious," Nietzsche recommends all kinds of new historical investigations for the "study of moral matters," histories "of love, of avarice, of envy, of conscience, of pious respect for tradition, or of cruelty." Then, after recommending investigations "of the moral effects of different foods" and of many other matters, he concludes,

> If all these jobs were done, the most insidious question of all would emerge into the foreground: whether science can further goals of action after it has proved that it can take such goals away and annihilate them; and then experimentation would be in order that would allow any kind of heroism to find satisfaction — centuries of experimentation that might eclipse all the great projects and sacrifices of history to date. So far, science has not yet built its cyclopic buildings, but the time for that, too, will come.[20]

Nietzsche specifically connected experimenting with attacks on democracy, liberalism, and the "herd animal morality." "The *democratic* movement is the heir of the Christian movement," he writes in *Beyond Good and Evil*, leading to a "diminution of man, making him mediocre and lowering his value" (*BGE*, 202, 203).[21] In aphorism 477 from *Human, All Too Human*, entitled "War indispensable," it is asserted that the contemporary Europeans stand in need of the biggest and most terrible wars in order not to lose civilization through its own vehicles and products. Aphorism 208 of *Beyond Good and Evil* reads, "The time for petty politics is over: the very next century will bring the fight for the dominion of the earth — the *compulsion* to large-scale politics."[22] The Nazi experiment is now permissible. In previous times, Nietzsche points out in aphorism 501 of *The Dawn* entitled "Mortal Souls," when we had faith in the immortality of the soul, our salvation depended upon our soul's short life on this earth. But now "we may take on tasks the grandeur of which would have appeared to former times as insanity and as a gamble with heaven and hell."[23] And in *Ecce homo*, in the first section of "Why I Write Such Good Books," it becomes clear that a kind of Nazi-style brutality is at least suggested, and definitely not excluded:

> The word "overman," as the designation of a type of supreme achievement, as opposed to "modern" men, to "good" men, to Christians and [to] other nihilists — a word that in the mouth of a Zarathustra, the annihilator of morality, becomes a very pensive word — has been understood almost everywhere with the utmost innocence in the sense of those very values whose opposite Zarathustra was meant to represent — that is, as an "idealistic"

type of a higher kind of man, half "saint," half "genius." . . .
Those to whom I said in confidence that they should sooner look
even for a Cesare Borgia than for a Parsifal, did not believe their
own ears.[24]

Walter Kaufmann's readings of Nietzsche are invariably "gentle."[25]
Two examples must suffice to show the inadequacy of such a practice.
(1) When interpreting Nietzsche's "what is falling, that one should also
push!" he comments, "Nietzsche is not speaking of 'mercy' killings of
the crippled and insane, but of all the values that have become hollow,
all needs out of which the faith has gone."[26] Yet there is nothing in the
text to suggest that Nietzsche is not, or is not *also*, thinking of mercy
killings. (2) Nietzsche's "all truths are for me soaked in blood" is cited
after Kaufmann has remarked that "science and life are no longer
wholly separate, science and philosophy are a way of life."[27] But if philosophy, according to Nietzsche, is to become a way of life—an interpretation that is surely correct—then life, and lived experience too, will
become philosophy. The conceptualizations of philosophy will be absorbed by, and unified with, life, with the living body.

Nietzsche prepared a consciousness that excluded nothing that anyone might think, feel, or do, including unimaginable atrocities carried
out on a gigantic order. Nor is a reading of Nietzsche as a godfather or
precursor of Nazism confined to interpretations of academic scholars
who have been particularly perverse or corrupt. Many a common man,
many a common Nazi of Weimar Germany, must have said to himself
what one of them proclaimed openly: "In Nietzsche I discovered a bit of
my primal self."[28] There are more identitites and similarities of content
in the writings of Nietzsche and in the writings, speeches, conversations,
and particularly in the actions of Hitler and the Nazis. Many of these
definite parallels have been cataloged by E. Sandvoss in *Hitler and
Nietzsche*.[29] Such a catalog may not make Nietzsche an accessory but it
does make him a kind of precursor to at least some of the ideas of
Nazism—perhaps even a sponsor or a part-time godfather.

Notes

This essay is partly based on a previous publication, "Nazism as a Nietz-
schean 'Experiment'" in: *Nietzsche-Studien. Internationales Jahrbuch für die
Nietzsche-Forschung*, ed. by Mazzimo Montinari, Wolfgang Müller-Lauter, and
Heinz Wenzel, Vol. 6 (Berlin: New York: de Gruyter, 1977), 116–22. All of
Nietzsche's texts cited in this paper are translations by Walter Kaufmann.

1. See Mazzimo Montinari, *Nietzsche lesen* (Berlin and New York: de Gruyter, 1982), "Die neue kritische Gesamtausgabe von Nietzsches Werken" (10–

21), previously published as "Nietzsche" in *Literatur Magazin* 12 (Reinbek bei Hamburg: Rowohlt 1980). All quotations will be from Giorgio Colli and Mazzimo Montinari, eds., *Friedrich Nietzsche, Kritische Studienausgabe*, Verleg, abbreviated *KSA*.

2. See F. L. Carsten, *Fascist Movements in Austria—From Schönerer to Hitler*, Sage Studies in 20th Century History, 7 (London: Sage Publications, 1977).

3. See Kurt Gossweiler, "Italienischer und deutscher Faschismus—Gemeinsamkeiten und Unterschiede," in *Antifaschismus* vol. 31 of *Distel Hefte*, ed. Frank Deppe, Georg Fülberth and Rainer Rilling (Heilbronn: Distel Verlag 1996).

4. The similarities between German National Socialism and Russian Bolshevism were explored in Hannah Arendt's *The Origins of Totalitarianism* (New York and San Diego: Harvest Press, 1979).

5. Third essay, section 12. *KSA* 5:365.

6. See William Montgomery McGovern, *From Luther to Hitler* (Cambridge: Harvard University Press, 1941); and Georg Lukács, *The Destruction of Reason* (London: Merlin Press, 1980), esp. the chapter on Nietzsche.

7. See Walter Kaufmann's "Editor's Introduction" to Friedrich Nietzsche, *The Will to Power* (New York: Vintage Books, 1967), xiii.

8. Lewis White Beck, *Early German Philosophy: Kant and his Predecessors* (Bristol: Thoemmes Press, 1996), 538.

9. Christoph Steding, *Das Reich und die Krankheit der europäischen Kultur* (Hamburg: Hanseatische Verlagsanstalt 1938).

10. See Walter Kaufmann, *Nietzsche: Philosopher, Psychologist amd Antichrist*, 4th ed. (Princeton: Princeton University Press, 1974).

11. See Yirmiyahu Yovel, *Dark Riddle, Hegel, Nietzsche, and the Jews* (Cambridge: Polity Press, 1998), pt. 2: "Nietzsche and the People of Israel"; and his previously published "Nietzsche and the Jews: The Structure of an Ambivalence," chap. 6 in *Nietzsche and Jewish Culture*, ed. Jacob Golomb (London: Routledge 1997), 117–34. It turns out that there was no real ambivalence but that one must distinguish in Nietzsche four different attitudes: toward (1) anti-Semitism, (2) biblical Judaism, (3) Second Temple "priestly" Judaism, and (4) Diaspora and contemporary Jews. Nietzsche attacks fiercely (1) and (3) and admires (2) because it was this-worldly and was built on self affirmation. To (4) he "assigns a major role to the Jews *as Jews* within his new Europe." To Nietzsche, the Jews were much closer to the *Übermensch*, and certainly not—as they were for the Nazis—*Untermenschen*.

12. This passage is best left in the original German. For a translation I propose, "Let us make [an experiment; or rather] experiments to attain [true] knowledge! Perhaps mankind will perish [in the course of these experiments]! All right!" The passage is in Friedrich Nietzsche, *Gesammelte Werke, Musarionausgabe* (Munich: Musarionverlag, 1920–29), 14:188, and in *KSA*, 11:88. It appears in the following context:

"Nichts ist wahr, alles ist erlaubt".
Zarathustra "ich nahm euch Alles, den Gott, die Pflicht—nun müßt ihr die *größte Probe* einer *edlen* Art geben.

Denn hier ist die Bahn den Ruchlosen offen — seht hin!
— das Ringen um die Herrschaft, am Schluß die Heerde mehr Heerde und der Tyrann mehr Tyrann als je.
— kein Geheimbund! Die *Folgen* meiner Lehre müssen fürchterlich wüthen: aber *es sollen an ihr Unzählige zu Grunde gehen.*
— *wir machen einen Versuch mit der Wahrheit!* Vielleicht geht die Menschheit dran zu Grunde! Wohlan!

Another fragment, on p. 338 of KSA, vol. 11 is addressed "*An die höheren Menschen,*" and contains the passages, "*Plan: ich suche und rufe Menschen denen ich diesen Gedanken mitteilen darf, die nicht daran zu Grunde gehen.*" Kurt Dite has drawn my attention to the context in which the citation appears that serves as my main grounds for considering Nietzsche as a possible godfather of fascism. Dite's reference strengthens, I think, my case.

13. See R. J. Hollingdale, introduction to *Nietzsche: Thus Spoke Zarathustra*, 1st ed. (Baltimore: Penguin, 1961), 18; omitted in the new introduction (1969).

14. Alfred Bäumler, *Studien zur deutschen Geistesgeschichte* (Berlin: Junker und Dannhaupt, 1937), 244: "Eben begann das 20. Jahrhundert — das 19. begann vor drei Generationen mit Goethe's Tod — das Jahrhundert, das sich im Angesicht Zarathustras entscheiden muß."

15. See particularly Bäumler's *Nietzsche der Philosoph und Politiker*, 3rd. ed. (Leipzig: Reclam, 1937), and some of the studies included in the collection cited in the previous note.

16. See Crane Brinton's "The National Socialists' Use of Nietzsche," *The Journal of the History of Ideas* (April 1940): 131–50; and his *Nietzsche* (Cambridge: Harvard University Press, 1941). In 1965 that text was published as a Harper Torchbook paperback together with a new preface, epilogue, and bibliography. Deleted, and disowned in the preface, was the chapter on "Nietzsche in Western Thought."

17. George H. Sabine, *A History of Political Thought*, 4th ed., revised by Thomas Landon Thorson (Hinsdale, Ill.: Harcourt, 1973).

18. Gerhard Masur, *Prophets of Yesterday* (New York, 1961), 91.

19. Kaufmann, *Nietzsche*, 89.

20. *GS*, 7; *KSA*, 3:379.

21. *KSA*, 5:124–28.

22. *KSA*, 2:311.

23. *KSA*, 3:294.

24. *KSA*, 6:300.

25. For the use of "gentle," see Brinton's *Nietzsche*, 184. See also William A. Preston, "Nietzsche and the Will to Power," *Edinburgh Encyclopedia of Continental Philosophy* (Edinburgh: Edinburgh University Press, 1999), 137: "[W]hat Kaufmann's Nietzsche lacked was that frenzied, Dionysian dimension that explodes politically as an ecstatic outburst of violence." That holds true for any "gentle" text on Nietzsche. This does not mean that one cannot learn a great deal about Nietzsche from the writings of "gentle" Nietzscheans. For a particularly excellent book of the "gentle" kind, see Alexander Nehamas, *Nietzsche: Life as Literature* (Cambridge: Harvard University Press, 1985).

26. Ibid., 109.

27. Ibid.

28. Theodor Abel's *Why Hitler Came to Power: An Answer Based on the Original Life Stories of Six Hundred of His Followers* (135) cited in J. P. Stern, *The Führer and the People* (Sussex: Harvester Press, 1975), 193.

29. E. Sandvoss, *Hitler and Nietzsche* (Göttingen: Musterschmidt Verlag, 1969). See also his "Nietzsche's Verantwortung," *Studium Generale* (1965), 18:150–54.

14

Critique as Apologetics:
Nolte's Interpretation of Nietzsche
Roderick Stackelberg

In his recent study of the political reception of Nietzsche in Germany, Steven Aschheim has warned (with particular reference to Walter Kaufmann) against the kind of intellectual history that tries to discredit particular interpretations of Nietzsche by constructing an essential Nietzsche from which the interpretation in question deviates. Such an essentialist approach, which renders Nietzsche's legacy "either as a record of deviation from, or as faithful representation of, a prior interpretative construction of the 'real' Nietzsche," cannot do justice to the dynamic diversity of Nietzsche's actual influence, nor does it illuminate the actual processes through which Nietzsche historically has been appropriated.[1] In the postmodernist view, Nietzsche's philosophy cannot yield a single definitive interpretation. Viewed through different lenses, Nietzschean texts will always take on a multiplicity of meanings. The critical issue for Aschheim is not to pin down what Nietzsche "really" means, but rather to map the ways he has been received and used. It does not get us very far, Aschheim warns, to convict the Nazis of misusing Nietzsche (although he does concede the usefulness of exposing deliberate distortions such as Elisabeth Förster-Nietzsche's erasures and forgeries), because Nietzsche did indisputably serve as a source of inspiration for many Nazis. What needs to be explained is why this was the case and why the Nazis were so easily able to exploit Nietzsche's philosophy for their purposes.

Although he acknowledges that no unmediated, causally direct relationship between Nietzsche and Nazism can be demonstrated, Aschheim finds that Nietzsche remains relevant as a

> key to explaining national socialism's attraction to the outmost limits, its arrival at a grotesque *novum* of human experience. . . . The perception . . . persists that its historical significance resided in its unprecedented transvaluations and boundary-breaking extremities and its emphases on destruction and violent regeneration, health and disease. Nazism in this sense continues to be regarded by many as a politics—however debased and selectively mediated—wrought in the "Great" Nietzschean mode.[2]

Aschheim cites with approval the thesis of the controversial German historian Ernst Nolte that Nietzsche was the progenitor of the concept of extermination that the Nazis put into practice. Although he is critical of Nolte's evasive language and apologetic agenda, Aschheim finds Nolte's interpretation useful in explaining the important function that Nietzsche served in Nazi ideology, especially after 1933: "Nietzsche's positive quest for life affirmation is linked to his call for the brutal destruction of those life-denying, emancipatory forms responsible for the prevailing decadence and decline of vitality."[3]

There is no doubt that many Nazis derived inspiration from Nietzsche, no matter how much they might be proven wrong about Nietzsche's intentions. At the same time, it should be noted both that a surprising number of Nazis remained skeptical of Nietzsche's purposes[4] and that many anti-Nazis also drew strength and inspiration from Nietzsche's works. The function of Nietzschean texts is not dissimilar to that of the Bible or other religious scriptures, which have also served throughout history to inspire a great variety of actions and beliefs. Aschheim fails to point out, however, that Nolte's approach is far more essentialist than that of critics like Kaufmann, who deny the legitimacy of linking Nietzsche with the Nazis. Nolte's interpretation of Nietzsche is based on an intuition of Nietzsche's "true" purpose and "world-historical" role, not on a close analysis of his works, nor on empirical investigations of the ways in which his works were mediated and received by the Nazis. Influenced by his former mentor Heidegger, Nolte approaches history as a philosopher, seeking not so much to describe historical events as to discern their "inner truths" or "higher truths." His phenomenological method seeks to understand the internal logic of historical actors and events and frees him from having to provide empirical proofs for his assertions and conjectures.[5]

Nolte's Historical Project

The purpose of Nolte's tetralogy on the history of modern ideologies[6] is to situate German National Socialism in the context of a European and eventually worldwide civil war precipitated by the Bolshevik Revolution in Russia in 1917. The apologetic possibilities inherent in this interpretative scheme emerged clearly in the *Historikerstreit* of 1986, in which Nolte deplored the fact that National Socialism had not yet taken its normal place alongside other past events in the public's historical memory.[7] As a passionate foe of the emancipatory movements of the 1960s and of "multiculturalism," Nolte blamed this lack of normalization on the special interest of feminists, pacifists, anti-imperialists, rebellious youth, and Holocaust victims and survivors in keeping alive the memory of Nazism as a uniquely immoral historical movement. His contention that the Holocaust represented an understandable, if not justifiable, preemptive response to the perceived communist threat evoked a storm of protest among historians in Germany and abroad. Nolte's critics accused him of seeking to rationalize and normalize the German past for conservative political purposes.[8]

In Nolte's version of history, Lenin's Russia was the instigator of the European civil war and the pioneer of mass murder. Hitler's Germany, on the other hand, represented the leading edge of the international fascist countermovement that adopted and refined communist techniques in order to destroy its "world-historical" opponent. Nolte in effect transformed Nazism into a *European* phenomenon. By thus down-playing the specifically German and racist features of National Socialism, Nolte devised an interpretative framework ideally suited to normalizing and even vindicating the Nazi past. Nolte's version of history linked Nazism to the revolutionary tradition in a more plausible and dialectical way than conventional conservative accounts. Conservatives tended to describe fascism as the product of a broad revolutionary movement ("the rise of the masses") that had also produced communism. Nolte gave due emphasis to the fundamental difference and mortal antagonism between Left and Right, but he insisted on the causal (and criminal) priority of the left. This interpretative framework also allowed him to invoke Nietzsche as the intellectual and inspirational guru of the Nazi counterrevolution.

Nolte's Nietzsche Interpretation

The attempt to scapegoat Nietzsche as a way of deflecting responsibility for fascism away from the traditionalist conservative right is not new.

After the Second World War, the German Right frequently denounced Nietzsche's anti-Christian animus as the source of fascism, partly as a way of exculpating their own conservative and Christian values from complicity in the Nazi debacle.[9] Nolte's interpretation of Nietzsche is unusual, however, because his purpose is less to discredit Nietzsche by pinning responsibility for fascism on him than it is to dignify the fascist (or militantly anticommunist) cause by tracing its intellectual lineage to Nietzsche. Nolte's dubious appropriation of Nietzsche thus pays indirect tribute to the rehabilitation of Nietzsche after the war. His penchant for metahistorical symbolism and symmetry had already led Nolte, in the last chapter of *Three Faces of Fascism*, the book that made his reputation in 1963, to juxtapose Nietzsche and Marx as the great ideological antipodes of the nineteenth century. Rejecting both "practical transcendence" (exemplified by Marxism) and "theoretical transcendence" (exemplified by Christianity), Nietzsche had called for the unbridled celebration of life and immanent reality that for Nolte typifies fascism.

According to Nolte, the essence of Nietzsche's philosophy (and the spiritual core of fascism) is contained in his summons, in *Ecce homo*, to form a new "party of life" dedicated to the extermination of the sick and degenerate: "That new party of life which undertakes the greatest of all tasks, the improvement of mankind, including the ruthless destruction of all that is degenerate and parasitical, will make possible again that excess of life on earth from which the Dionysian condition must once more grow."[10] In *Der europäische Bürgerkrieg* Nolte again casts Nietzsche as the progenitor of the concept of extermination (*Vernichtungskonzept*) that was put into practice by the Nazis. This provocative thesis forms the core of his book *Nietzsche und der Nietzscheanismus*, published in 1990.[11]

Just as Nazism and the Holocaust represented reactions to and copies of the "more original" Bolshevik precedents, so Nietzsche's philosophy is interpreted as a reaction to the destructive egalitarianism of Marx, whose works, as Nolte concedes, Nietzsche never read, but whose doctrines furnished (in Nolte's view) the most representative statement of the values Nietzsche most despised. To preserve the symbolic symmetry that relates Nietzsche to Marx in the same way that Nazism is related to Bolshevism (as mirror image and diametrical opposite), Nolte stresses the commonalities as much as the differences between these two great thinkers. Both shared an antipathy to the philistine, commercial, bourgeois society of their day; both developed a this-worldly critique of Christianity; both thought in terms of history and prehistory; both shared the idealist impulse to restore an earlier harmony and totality on a higher level; and both viewed ancient Greece as a paradigm for a regenerated future. Most importantly, for Nolte's purposes, both Nietz-sche and Marx supposedly developed similar but diametrically opposed concepts of extermination, Marx calling for the destruction of the *bour-geoisie* (those who rose above the working masses); Nietzsche, in coun-terattacking mode, calling for the destruction of all who blocked the rise of superior individuals. Typically, Nolte considers the egalitarian imperative more destructive in theory (and ultimately in communist practice) than its elitist counterpart. Furthermore, Nolte presents the Nietzschean-Nazi reaction as at least partly justified by the real and potential threat of egalitarian destructiveness.[12]

Nolte is aware that Nietzsche can hardly be constrained within any dogmatic position, let alone a partisan political one, without slighting the many contradictory and apolitical aspects of his philosophy. Indeed, Nolte anticipated objections to his own interpretation by citing what has become a virtual truism of Nietzsche scholarship: By selective quo-tation Nietzsche can be used to defend a variety of contradictory posi-tions.[13] He devoted a large portion of his book to an analysis of Nietz-sche as a "battleground" (*Schlachtfeld*) of contending ideological forces, which then crystallized into distinct movements in the years that fol-lowed the end of Nietzsche's productive life in 1889.[14] Through selective appropriation a variety of movements could draw on Nietzsche for sup-port. By tracing the impact of his philosophy on both the Right and Left up to 1914, Nolte hoped to show the relevance of Nietzsche's antipoli-tics to contemporary political issues and his appeal to political thinkers.

The prevalence of left-wing Nietzscheanism before 1914 actually strengthens Nolte's argument, not only because it illustrates the formal affinities (despite substantive differences) between Left and Right on which Nolte's analysis of fascism rests, but also because it reinforces his contention that Nietzsche embodied the divisions of German society from which fascism and the "European civil war" evolved. According to Nolte, Nietzsche not only prophesied the coming civil war but also furnished the counterconcept to the more "original" exterminatory con-cept of Marx:

> To this socialist concept Nietzsche wants to juxtapose an equally radical concept also aiming at "extermination" — the concept of a biological and simultaneously historical and philosophical exter-mination that is obviously connected to the former, more original concept of social extermination by a causal nexus but is not en-tirely derived from it.[15]

Nolte thus enlisted Nietzsche in the right-wing cause in almost the exact language he used in the *Historikerstreit* in calling for a revision of the received historiography of Nazism. Nietzsche's assigned role is to dignify the cause of counterrevolution, which, like its original model and mortal adversary, the socialist revolution, can also trace its lineage back to one of the seminal thinkers of the modern age. Nietzsche serves another apologetic function as well for Nolte: the sheer scale of his "exterminatory concept" — the eradication of the weak, the sick, the failures [*missratenen*], and the many-too-many [*vielzuvielen*] — makes the Nazi extermination program pale by comparison.[16]

Can the crucial role assigned to Nietzsche in Nolte's sophisticated apologetic project withstand critical scrutiny? Nolte's task is not an easy one. To succeed in constraining Nietzsche within this apologetic framework Nolte must overcome some formidable objections to the notion of Nietzsche as proto-Nazi.[17] First, he must defuse or reinterpret Nietzsche's unequivocal denunciations of anti-Semitism, nationalism, and the German Reich. Secondly, he must show that in breaking with Wagner Nietzsche was not repudiating the *völkisch* ideology for which Wagner and Wagnerism stood. And thirdly, Nolte must face the contradiction that Nazism was fed by precisely those moralistic and moralizing values that Nietzsche opposed. I will deal with each of these issues in turn.

Nietzsche's Denunciation of Anti-Semitism

Particularly his anti-anti-Semitism seems to put Nietzsche in total opposition to what many historians consider the decisive component of Nazi ideology. How could Nietzsche, who in his late fragments called for the execution of all anti-Semites and identified Jewish bankers (as well as Prussian officers) as optimal recruits for his "party of life," be viewed as the spiritual father of a movement that perpetrated the Holocaust?

Nolte employs three partially contradictory arguments to overcome the objection of Nietzsche's anti-anti-Semitism. First, he attributes to Nietzsche a thoroughgoing anti-Judaism based on the fact that Christian morality grew out of Jewish roots. According to this argument, Nietzsche's hostility to Christianity masks an even more fundamental hostility to Judaism, from which Christianity arose. But because Nietzsche's anti-Christian critique of priestly Judaism can hardly be equated with nineteenth-century *völkisch* anti-Semitism, which generally posited the superiority of "German Christianity" and therefore epitomized the ideology that Nietzsche most vigorously denounced, Nolte must resort to a second, more questionable stratagem. By redefining nineteenth-century anti-Semitism as essentially a left-wing movement, a petty form of socialism (*Schmalspursozialismus*), fed by the economic *ressentiments* of the lower middle classes, Nolte can rationalize Nietzsche's opposition to anti-Semitism as a form of antisocialism.

This argument is reinforced by the fact that already in the nineteenth century anti-Semitism was designated by socialists like August Bebel as "the socialism of fools." In Nolte's interpretation, *völkisch* anti-Semitism is transformed into an emancipatory and egalitarian ideology that Nietzsche opposed on those grounds. Not entirely comfortable with such sophistry, however, Nolte also occasionally resorts to a ploy favored by such Nazis as Alfred Bäumler, who asserted that Nietzsche's opposition to anti-Semitism was merely a practically motivated attitude designed not to alienate a group that exercised a powerful role in the publishing field in Germany. Nietzsche was supposedly worried that any association with anti-Semitism would harm his chances of gaining fame.[18]

Nolte's third major argument in his effort to reconcile the contradiction between Nietzsche's opposition to anti-Semitism and his putative function as the intellectual precursor of a movement that undertook the genocide of Jews is to claim that Nazi anti-Semitism was derivative of and secondary to the antisocialism for which Nietzsche and the Nazis stood. According to Nolte, Nazi anti-Semitism was derived from opposition to the liberal and egalitarian values whose eradication Nietzsche had heralded. Nolte thus blithely advances the paradox that both Nazi anti-Semitism and Nietzschean *opposition* to anti-Semitism were similarly motivated by their shared opposition to socialism. This stunning contradiction is plausible only if it can be shown that the nineteenth-century Jew-hatred that Nietzsche condemned was of a qualitatively different kind than the Nazi variety and did not embody the anti-egalitarian, antidemocratic, anti-Marxist values that were so central to Nazi anti-Semitism.

Nolte resolves the paradox by attributing to Hitler greater originality than the historical record allows. It was Hitler who supposedly first made the close linkage of Jews with socialism that provided the motive for the Holocaust.[19] Hitler conceived the radical notion that the only sure way to eliminate communism and all the other supposedly baneful consequences of modern intellectualism was to eliminate the Jews. Hitler must ultimately absorb the blame for the unwarranted radicalization of what Nolte considers an essentially rational and defensible cause — already anticipated by Nietzsche — the defense of Europe against communism. In tracing the excesses of fascism solely to Hitler's lunacy, Nolte echoes a theme that dominated traditional conservative German apologetics in the immediate postwar period.

Is it correct to imply, as Nolte does, that Nazi anti-Semitism had a different motivation than the nineteenth-century Judeophobia which Nietzsche condemned? Numerous studies have shown the continuities in anti-Semitic stereotypes over the centuries.[20] The theme that links all historical forms of anti-Semitism, whether religious, economic, political, or racial, is the identification of Jewishness with materialism and immorality. For centuries Jews were held to be immoral because they stubbornly refused to accept the "superior" teachings of Christ. Jews supposedly rejected the Christian path to salvation through renunciation of the world in order to be free to pursue worldly gain for selfish ends. According to Christian anti-Semites (the particular targets of Nietzsche's scorn), Jews would not abjure material possessions and worldly power for the higher "kingdom within" or "beyond."

In the anti-Semitic mind, Jewishness stood for worldliness, selfishness, intellectual cunning, and lack of precisely that Christian idealism, asceticism, and self-denial that Nietzsche denounced as inimical to life. Nineteenth-century anti-Semitism in fact epitomized those aspects of Christian "virtue" that Nietzsche most abhorred. The Nazis, to be sure, were no Christians, but though their biological worldview deprived Jews of the previously available options of conversion and assimilation, the Nazi images of Jews perpetuated the same age-old anti-Semitic stereotypes that Nietzsche disdainfully rejected. Clear lines of continuity lead from the racial and political anti-Semitism of ideologues like Eugen Dühring, Adolf Stöcker, or Houston Stewart Chamberlain to National Socialism. The identification of Jews with "materialistic" progressive ideologies like liberalism and socialism was not a Nazi innovation; anti-Semitism and illiberalism were closely linked in conservative and right-wing politics in Nietzsche's lifetime as well.[21]

Nietzsche's Denunciation of Nationalism

Nietzsche's opposition to nationalism is easier for Nolte to deal with, because it can be used to support the latter's contentions that fascism was an international movement and that the Second World War was in its essence a European civil war between defenders of traditional European culture and society and their left-wing egalitarian challengers. According to this view, Nietzsche attacked nationalism because it undercut the larger and more important struggle between the transnational elites and the masses. Petty nationalist loyalties merely reflect the resentments of the herd and obstruct the rule of the strong and the healthy across national boundaries.

But then how could Nietzsche be aligned with the Nazis, for whom nationalism surely represented the highest value? Nolte's predilection for thinking in terms of "ideal types" makes the resolution of this paradox possible, too. For Nolte, anti-Marxism remains the defining characteristic of fascism (as it was, in his view, the ruling passion in Nietzsche's work.) Nationalism, no matter how genuinely felt by its adherents, served the primarily instrumental function of mobilizing mass support for the struggle against a militantly international ideology. Nolte accepts the Nazis' claim of defending European culture against the destructive threat of "Asiatic Bolshevism" as more than mere self-serving propaganda. He even adduces their success in recruiting non-German formations for the SS and the *Wehrmacht* as evidence for the validity of their claim. Hence Nietzsche's "good European" can actually be cited in support of Nolte's contention that Nazism must be understood in the context of what would become a worldwide civil war. Insofar as Hitler personified the (admittedly extreme) reaction of the European bourgeoisie to the even more extreme Marxist world revolution, even Hitler could qualify as a "good European." The implication of Nolte's argumentation is that a war between Germany and the Western powers would not have been necessary, if the West had not sought to obstruct the Nazis' counterrevolutionary crusade.[22] In the cold war that followed the Second World War, according to Nolte, the European civil war spread across the globe.

Nietzsche's Denunciation of the German Reich

But what about Nietzsche's growing disillusionment and exasperation with the recently unified German Reich, as expressed in increasingly vitriolic language in his late works? Nietzsche's denunciations of the Bismarckian Reich, culminating in his declaration of war against the House of Hohenzollern in the last weeks before his mental breakdown, pose little problem for Nolte, because he accepts the interpretation of both Nazis like Bäumler and Marxists like Lukács that Nietzsche's attacks on the Reich came from the right, not the left. According to this view, Nietzsche criticized the German Reich not for abusing power, but for failing to exercise it vigorously enough. Although liberal historians, guided by normative notions of civil liberties and representative government, portray the Second Reich as a quasi-absolutist regime, for Nietzsche (as read by Bäumler or Lukács) the Reich was flawed by its readiness to embrace democratizing trends.

It is indeed hard to say with finality whether Nietzsche despised a man like William II's Court Pastor Adolf Stöcker for his anti-Semitism or for his "socialism," for his bigotry or his humanitarianism, or perhaps both, because Nietzsche provided so few references to concrete social policies. Yet the only full-scale study of Nietzsche's reactions to the political currents and events of his own time, Peter Bergmann's *Nietzsche: The "Last Antipolitical German"* (1987), concludes that the

mature Nietzsche attacked the Bismarckian Reich not for its liberal but
for its illiberal tendencies. "Nietzsche's adult life," Bergmann writes,
"was one long flight from the patriarchal politics of the Reich."[23] The
democracy he attacked was the one he saw embodied in the intolerant
right-wing populism of the Second Reich. Nietzsche's contention that
socialists were inspired by resentment and revenge was provoked by
Eugen Dühring's National Socialism and Stöcker's equally bigoted
brand of Christian socialism, not by the doctrines of Marx. Read
against this background, Nietzsche's elitist strictures appear as indict-
ments more of the religious and nationalist right than of the socialist
left.[24]

Significance of the Break with Wagner

Interpreters who link Nietzsche with Nazism usually do so by ignoring
or downplaying his break with Wagner and all that it signifies. Wagnerian ideology foreshadowed, after all, a good deal of the *völkisch*
tenets of National Socialism, including anti-Semitism, social conservatism, and Germanomania. Hitler referred to Wagner in effusively favorable terms in *Mein Kampf*, whereas Nietzsche's name was never mentioned. The links between Bayreuth and the *völkisch* movement are
direct and uncomplicated.[25] *Völkisch* authors displayed a distinct preference for Nietzsche's Wagnerian phase and frequently viewed his later
works with suspicion and distaste.[26] With little exception they admired
the young Nietzsche's fervent critique of the hated century of progress.
In his early works they could find the themes that formed the stock-in-
trade of *völkisch* ideology: the unique character and mission of the German people; the distrust of foreign influences; the exorcism of Socratic
rationalism (and, by implication, "Jewish" rationalism in the present);
the denunciation of a degenerate society in the thrall of secular, materialistic, and democratic values; the need to shape the masses into a
Volk; and the failure of the Bismarckian state to stem the leveling philistine tide or to promote a unified national culture. Wilhelm Laubenthal, author of an intellectual history of late nineteenth-century Germany from a *völkisch* perspective (1939) and admirer of *The Birth of
Tragedy* and the *Untimely Meditations*, regretfully conceded that nothing of value for National Socialism could be derived from Nietzsche's
later works.[27] Nietzsche himself explicitly repudiated the romantic nationalism of *The Birth of Tragedy* in the self-criticism that accompanied
its reissue in 1886.[28] That same year he also refused to reissue the *Untimely Meditations*.

Surely his uncompromising critique of the Wagnerian worldview, which he had enthusiastically embraced in his youth, must absolve the mature Nietzsche of complicity in Nazism? Nolte employs two main arguments to defuse Nietzsche's critique of Wagner. First, Nolte maintains that Nietzsche opposed Wagner as a representative of the revolutionary tradition he came to despise.[29] Nolte conveniently ignores the fact that by the time he befriended Nietzsche, Wagner had long since repudiated his republican sympathies of 1848. Indeed, in *The Case of Wagner* and *Ecce Homo*, Nietzsche makes it quite clear that his break with Wagner involved a rejection of his *völkisch* ideals as well.[30] If Nietzsche opposed Wagner for his revolutionary sympathies, then it was the *völkisch* revolution that he opposed.

Nolte's second, more plausible, and more problematical argument in respect to Nietzsche's apostasy is to insist that in his late phase Nietzsche reverted back to his first anti-Enlightenment stage.[31] This argument deserves careful consideration, for it is indeed crucial to an evaluation of Nietzsche's relationship to Nazism. From his early phase Nietzsche certainly retained the overwhelming regenerative urge so typical of Wagnerian idealism; but the kind of regeneration he now envisioned had little in common with the nationalism, anti-Semitism, and moralism championed by Wagner and his *völkisch* retinue. In his mature works, Nietzsche ruthlessly pursued the origins of the idealist mind-set in the Western moral and religious tradition. At its source he claimed to find a nihilistic inclination to self-destruction that the human being of the future would have to overcome. A transvaluation of values would achieve the ancient Faustian dream, so important in the German intellectual tradition, of creating a higher type of human being, persons more capable of channeling the sufferings of life into creativity than the timid conformists of the common herd.

Nazism and the Western Moral Tradition

No doubt a variety of movements and individuals committed to the revitalization of culture could derive their inspiration from Nietzsche's regenerative zeal. Many Nazis indisputably derived inspiration from Nietzsche, no matter how much they might have misinterpreted him. Nazism was a multifarious movement that did not draw its inspiration from only a single source. The crucial question, however, is this: Was National Socialism a movement inspired primarily by immoralism and the rejection of traditional values, or is it, as I believe, more properly understood as a movement that grew out of excessive moral zeal, a movement of moral rearmament and idealism, however perverted a form this idealism may have taken? In Nietzschean terms, was Nazism a reaction against slave morality or was it itself a form of slave revolt?

This is not a question that can be answered solely by applying normative criteria to Nazi atrocities, which surely would lead us to the conclusion that Nazism violated all normal and conventional moral principles. It is a question that requires empirical historical investigation based on an analysis of the many kinds of sources that shed light on the Nazi mind-set and the *völkisch* world view. Such an investigation reveals, I believe, that the antecedents of Nazism lie in a reaction against amorality and "permissiveness" more than in their fulfillment. In my view, Nazism represents "the triumph of squeamishness, of resentment, of purism and moral intolerance, of the need for rigid control and total order," the triumph, in other words, of the ascetic ideal that Nietzsche denounced.[32] As George Mosse has written, the Nazis "persecuted all those who stood outside the accepted norms of society," the norms that Nietzsche attacked.[33] The closest relative of Nazism is the kind of religious absolutism, fanaticism, and fundamentalism that has so often legitimated the most heinous crimes in the name of higher ideals in the past.

But what about the urge, so central to Nazism, to purify the Germanic race of any persons (or qualities) viewed as weakening, infecting, or degenerating the racial fabric? It is this urge that Nietzsche appears to be encouraging with his call in *The Antichrist* and *Ecce Homo* for the extermination of the weak and the sick. But what did Nietzsche mean by the "weak" and the "sick"? Clearly it was not the Jews that Nietzsche put into this category. His notion of degeneration was elastic, to be sure, including all values, attitudes, and motive forces (foremost, of course, conventional Christian morality) that he regarded as inimical to life. But he is very explicit on one point: the ultimate sickness of the modern age was embodied in Wagner, his music and his ideas. "Is Wagner a man (*Mensch*) at all?" Nietzsche asks in *The Case of Wagner*; "Is he not rather a sickness?"[34] From 1880 on, at the latest, it is clear that for him the movements of Wagner, Stöcker, and Dühring, precursors of Nazism all, embody the chief contemporary expressions of the slave mentality he so consistently decried in his late works. In its venom and intensity Nietzsche's assault on moralism and nationalism remains unsurpassed.

Nietzsche considered Wagner his great antipode, but Wagner hardly qualifies as a philosopher. If Nietzsche's philosophical antipode is taken to be not Marx, but Plato and the idealist, metaphysical mind-set, the more comprehensive political implications of his philosophy are revealed. In his critique of ideology and religion, and in his atheism,

Nietzsche was in fact far closer to Marx than to idea
such as Kant or Hegel, whom the former both criticize
idealist vantage points. If his critique of idealism is put a
his philosophical project, Nietzsche's undeniable antipathy
can then be seen to extend to all its nineteenth-century fort.
revolutionary, Christian, or national. Read in this way, he be
clairvoyant critic of impending totalitarianism who warned of ⌐ ⌐ ras-
cism and communism. His target is the tyranny of the moral majority,
the reign of the true believer, the dominance of idealists who derive their
fervor and conviction from their perceived possession of absolute moral
truth. In such a reading, Nazism itself represents the slave revolt that
Nolte identifies solely with socialism and communism.

The Uses of Linking Nietzsche to Nazism

Attributing responsibility for fascism to Nietzschean amorality serves
conservative purposes by distracting attention from the role of conventional morality and traditional institutions in the origins of fascism. If
Nietzsche's encouragement of amorality and transvaluation formed the
inspirational core of fascism, how seriously do we need to take his anti-
German strictures — or any of his precepts for that matter? His fulmina-
tions against the German Reich and against Christianity and Western
morality lose their sting. The Imperial German system and its ideology
are effectively rehabilitated by being the target of Nietzsche's protofascist assault.

For conservatives the establishment of a motivational link between
Nietzschean amorality and fascist atrocities has the additional advantage of undercutting the Left's appropriation of Nietzsche over the past
thirty years. In postmodernist interpretations the dogmatic prophet of
the *Übermensch* has been largely supplanted by the perspectivist philosopher of pluralism. His critique of reason is no longer perceived as the
road to absolute tyranny, but rather as a liberation from the tyranny
of the absolute. Contemporary postmodern interpretations present a
Nietzsche no less radical than in the past, but one who no longer poses
a political threat to liberal society. Indeed, in interpretations such as
Richard Rorty's, Nietzsche's way of viewing the world offers the best
guarantee against the dogmatisms of Left and Right.[35] Perhaps because
postmodern interpretations have made Nietzsche at least potentially
useful to the Left as a source of subversive strategies and ideas, he has
come under renewed attack from the Right. Imputing protofascism to
Nietzsche becomes a way of discrediting postmodernist interpretations
and foreclosing their interpretative approach. If Nietzsche can be made

responsible for fascist excesses, his enhanced postwar reputation works to the advantage of revisionist apologetics. For if Nietzsche's anti-egalitarian philosophy can be read as the harbinger of a benign post-modern pluralism, then that other alleged offspring of his thought, modern fascism, cannot be all bad, either. Indeed, in his political biography of Martin Heidegger, Nolte defends Heidegger's option for National Socialism as supposedly the only reasonable alternative to communism from the perspective of well-meaning Germans in 1933.[36]

Nietzsche's Susceptibility to Nazi Appropriation

Nietzsche's significance and continuing relevance throughout the twentieth century is the result of the widespread recognition that his works are perhaps the most representative statement of the late nineteenth-century sense of crisis induced by the "death of God," the perceived collapse of objective meaning and universal truth. His prophetic call for a "transvaluation of values" could appeal to a great variety of alienated individuals and groups by no means restricted to the political right. This was due at least in part to the nature of Nietzsche's philosophy, which is deliberately perspectival and open-ended and therefore subject to a variety of interpretations.[37] Nietzsche made a definitive rendering of his ideas virtually impossible by refusing to foreclose any experimental options in the process of thinking and self-overcoming. His thought cannot be classified as simply destructive and reactionary or emancipatory and progressive.

A great variety of political causes have found inspiration in Nietzschean thought, and even today there is nothing approaching complete consensus on Nietzsche's politics. However, if advocacy or rejection of human equality as a social ideal determines the place of individuals or movements on the political spectrum, Nietzsche clearly belongs well on the Right, perhaps even on the extreme Right. Nietzsche and the Nazis (and their Germanomanic precursors as well as Christian conservatives) shared the same political enemies — the democratic, liberal, and socialist movements that emanated from the Enlightenment and the French Revolution. This is probably the most important reason that Nietzsche's philosophy could be so readily exploited by the Nazis, despite his unequivocal condemnation of nationalism, anti-Semitism, the German Reich, Wagnerian Germanophilia, and romanticism. It is also the main reason Nietzsche has been anathema to the Left, especially the Marxist Left, which has traditionally viewed Nietzsche as one of the major precursors of fascism.[38] As a political thinker Nietzsche has always appealed mostly to political conservatives who value hierarchy and rank, the authority of elites, and the subordination of the masses. His works, as much as Wagner's, reflected the undemocratic tenor of German society in his day. Though he may have thought of his "herd animals" and "last men" as members of oppressive "silent" or "moral" majorities, not excluded or exploited groups, and though he may have opposed democracy at least in part because of his apprehensions of the destructive form that the mobilization of the masses was bound to take in Germany, his approach was too apolitical to make these essential distinctions clear.

Nietzsche's rejection of progress and equality made aspects of his philosophy usable for the Nazis without having to distort them. Though a critic of idealist "self-deception" and national vanity, he shared the idealist disdain for merely political freedoms. True to the idealist heritage, Nietzsche's formula for human salvation was not to change material conditions through reform or revolution, as progressives would have it, but to change human ideals. His precepts aimed not at the creation of a just society, but at the development of a higher type of human being. To him, as to the idealists he criticized, politics (i.e., agitation for social and political reform) was a debased activity.

The field of Nietzsche interpretation will continue to provide the terrain, as it has throughout the twentieth century, on which fundamental issues are symbolically fought out. Diverse movements and schools of thought will continue to appeal to his thought. It is precisely because of his radical denial of ultimate truth that today he is hailed as the philosopher of postmodernism. But the criticisms that have been raised against postmodernism — that its political implications even in its left-wing appropriations are profoundly conservative — can be leveled against Nietzsche himself. Nietzsche's failure to provide any concrete social analysis renders futile all efforts to pin down his substantive political position and leaves concepts like "herd animals," "blond beasts," "supermen," "the will to power," "party of life," and "destruction of all that is degenerate and parasitical" to be filled with substantive meaning by his various interpreters. This lack of political consciousness made his philosophy useful to the Nazis and it makes his thinking serviceable to their apologists today.

Notes

This essay draws on portions of my article, "The Philosopher of Fascism? Nietzsche Through the Eyes of Ernst Nolte," *Platte Valley Review* 22, no. 1 (Winter 1994), 38–47.

1. Steven E. Aschheim, *The Nietzsche Legacy in Germany 1890–1990* (Berkeley: University of California Press, 1992), 4–5.

2. Ibid., 330. See also Aschheim's "Nietzsche, Anti-Semitism, and Mass Murder," in *Culture and Catastrophe: German and Jewish Confrontations with National Socialism and Other Crises* (New York: New York University Press, 1996), esp. 71; and "Nietzsche, Anti-Semitism and the Holocaust," in *Nietzsche and Jewish Culture*, ed. Jacob Golomb (London and New York: Routledge, 1997), 3–20.

3. Aschheim, *Nietzsche Legacy*, 325–26.

4. See the dissertation by Hans Langreder, "Die Auseinandersetzung mit Nietzsche im Dritten Reich: Ein Beitrag zur Wirkungsgeschichte Nietzsches" (Christian-Albrecht-Universität Kiel, 1971), and Roderick Stackelberg, "Nietzsche und der Nationalsozialismus," *Prima Philosophia* 2 (July–September 1989): 425–41. See also Aschheim, *Nietzsche Legacy*, 252.

5. See Wolfgang Schieder, "Der Nationalsozialismus im Fehlurteil philosophischer Geschichtsschreibung, zur Methode von Ernst Noltes *Europäischem Bürgerkrieg*," *Geschichte und Gesellschaft* 15 (1989): 89–114.

6. The four volumes of Nolte's tetralogy (in order of publication) are *Der Faschismus in seiner Epoche, die Action francaise, der italienische Faschismus, der Nationalsozialismus* (Munich: R. Piper, 1963), English version, *Three Faces of Fascism: Action Francaise, Italian Fascism, National Socialism*, trans. Leila Vennewitz (New York: Holt, Rinehart and Winston, 1966); *Deutschland und der Kalte Krieg* (Munich: Piper, 1974); *Marxismus und Industrielle Revolution* (Stuttgart: Klett-Cotta, 1982); and *Der europäische Bürgerkrieg, 1917–1945: Nationalsozialismus und Bolschewismus* (Berlin: Propyläen, 1987).

7. On the *Historikerstreit*, see Charles S. Maier, *The Unmasterable Past: History, Holocaust, and German National Identity* (Cambridge: Harvard University Press, 1988); the collection of documents, *Historikerstreit* (Munich: Piper, 1987), unreliably translated into English by James Knowlton and Truett Cates, *Forever Under the Shadow of Hitler: Original Documents of the Historikerstreit, the Controversy Concerning the Singularity of the Holocaust* (Atlantic Highlands, N.J.: Humanities Press, 1993); and Ernst Nolte, *Das Vergehen der Vergangenheit, Antwort an meine Kritiker im sogenannten Historikerstreit* (Berlin: Ullstein, 1988).

8. Jürgen Habermas, "Ene Art Schadensabwicklung, die apologetischen Tendenzen in der deutschen Zeitgeschichtsschreibung" ("A Kind of Damage Control: Apologetic Tendencies in Current German Historical Writing"), *Die Zeit*, July 18, 1986.

9. For postwar conservative critiques of Nietzsche, see Karl August Götz, *Nietzsche als Ausnahme, zur Zerstörung des Willens zur Macht* (Freiburg: Karl Alber, 1949); Ernst Barthel, *Nietzsche als Verführer* (Baden-Baden: Hans Bühler Junior, 1947); Konrad Algermissen, *Nietzsche und das dritte Reich* (Celle: Joseph Giesel, 1946); Alfred von Martin, *Geistige Wegbereiter des deutschen Zusammenbruchs: Hegel—Nietzsche—Spengler* (Recklinghausen: Bitter, 1948); and E. Sandvoss, *Hitler und Nietzsche* (Göttingen: Muster-Schmidt, 1969).

10. *KSA*, 6:313, as cited in Nolte, *Three Faces of Fascism*, 444. "Jene neue Partei des Lebens, welche die größte aller Aufgaben, die Höherzüchtung der Menschheit in die Hände nimmt, eingerechnet die schonungslose Vernichtung aller Entartenden und Parasitischen, wird jenes Zuviel von Leben auf Erden

wieder möglich machen, aus dem auch der dionysische Zustand wieder er-
wachsen muß" (*Der Faschismus in seiner Epoche*, 533). This passage can be
translated to emphasize the biological aspect of *Züchtung* and the genocidal
implications of *Vernichtung*, as does Aschheim in *The Nietzsche Legacy in Germany*, 326: "That new party of life which would take the greatest of all tasks
into its hands, the higher breeding of humanity, including the merciless extermination of everything degenerating and parasitic, would make possible again
that excess of life on earth from which the Dionysian state will grow again."

11. Nolte, *Der europäische Bürgerkrieg*, 514–15; *Nietzsche und der Nietzscheanismus* (Berlin: Propyläen, 1990).

12. Nolte, *Nietzsche*, 23–27, 54, 75.

13. Ibid., 110.

14. Ibid., 10. The term *"Schlachtfeld"* is from a letter to Heinrich Köselitz
(July 25, 1882), *KGB*, 6:230.

15. Nolte, *Nietzsche*, 80.

16. Ibid., 195.

17. For a convincing refutation of the thesis that Nietzsche's thought gave
rise to Nazism, see Weaver Santaniello, "A Post-Holocaust Re-Examination of
Nietzsche and the Jews: *Vis-à-vis* Christendom and Nazism," in *Nietzsche and
Jewish Culture*, ed. by Jacob Golomb (London & New York: Routledge, 1997),
21–54. Santaniello argues that the Nazis deliberately misinterpreted Nietzsche
in order to silence him. They did not misunderstand Nietzsche; they understood
only too well that he was not on their side. See also her *Nietzsche, God, and the
Jews: His Critique of Judeo-Christianity in Relation to the Nazi Myth* (Albany:
State University of New York, 1994). For a contrary view, see Bernhard H. F.
Taureck, *Nietzsche und der Faschismus, eine Studie über Nietzsches politische
Philosophie und ihre Folgen* (Hamburg: Junius Verlag, 1989). Taureck considers
Nietzsche's destruction of reason and his alleged "racial ontology" to be "proto-
fascist." See also Aschheim, *The Nietzsche Legacy in Germany*, esp. 232–330;
Henning Ottmann, *Philosophie und Politik bei Nietzsche* (Berlin: de Gruyter,
1987), esp. 1–8; Stackelberg, "Nietzsche und der Nationalsozialismus," 425–
41; Giorgio Penzo, "Zur Frage der 'Entnazifizierung' Friedrich Nietzsches,"
Vierteljahrshefte für Zeitgeschichte 34 (January 1986): 105–116; Kurt Rudolf
Fischer, "Nazism as a Nietzschean Experiment," *Nietzsche-Studien* 6 (1977):
121; and Langreder, "Die Auseinandersetzung mit Nietzsche im Dritten Reich."

18. Nolte, *Nietzsche*, 107–108, Alfred Bäumler, *Nietzsche der Philosoph
und Politiker* (Leipzig: Reclam, 1931), 105, 146.

19. Nolte, *Der europäische Bürgerkrieg*, 514–15.

20. See particularly Peter Pulzer, *The Rise of Political Anti-Semitism in Ger-
many and Austria*, rev. ed. (Cambridge: Harvard University Press, 1988);
George L. Mosse, *Toward the Final Solution: A History of European Racism*
(New York: Howard Fertig, 1978); and Leon Poliakov, *The History of Anti-
Semitism*, 3 vols. (New York: Vanguard, 1975).

21. See Aldo Venturelli, "Asketismus und Wille zur Macht, Nietzsches Aus-
einandersetzung mit Eugen Dühring," *Nietzsche-Studien* 15 (1986): 107–39;
Geoffrey G. Field, *Evangelist of Race: The Germanic Vision of Houston Stewart
Chamberlain* (New York: Columbia University Press, 1981), esp. 396–458;

Roderick Stackelberg, *Idealism Debased: From Völkish Thought to National Socialism* (Kent, Ohio: Kent State University Press, 1981), 104–60.

22. See the review of *Der europäische Bürgerkrieg* by Hans Mommsen, "Wissenschaft als Ressentiment," *Geschichte und Gesellschaft* 14 (1988): esp. 498–99, 502.

23. Peter Bergmann, *Nietzsche: The "Last Antipolitical German"* (Bloomington: Indiana, 1987), 175.

24. Venturelli, "Asketismus und Wille zur Macht," esp. 138–39. See also Uschi Nussbaumer-Benz, *Nietzsche, Nadelöhr der Philosophie? Eine Einführung in die Wille-zur-Macht-Thematik* (Cuxhaven: Junghans, 1991), esp. 226–43.

25. See Winfried Schüler, *Der Bayreuther Kreis von seiner Entstehung bis zum Ausgang der wilhelminischen Ära: Wagnerkult und Kulturreform im Geiste völkischer Weltanschauung* (Münster: Aschendorff, 1971), esp. 1–27; and Joachim Köhler, *Wagners Hitler: Der Prophet und sein Vollstrecker* (Munich: Karl Blessing, 1997).

26. Stackelberg, "Nietzsche und der Nationalsozialismus," 428, 435.

27. Wilhelm Laubenthal, *Der Gedanke einer Geistigen Erneuerung Deutschlands im deutschen Schrifttum von 1871 bis zum Weltkrieg* (Frankfurtam Main, 1939), esp. 19–20. There are many other examples of works published before and after 1933 that appeal primarily to the Wagnerian Nietzsche. See Stackelberg, "Nietzsche und der Nationalsozialismus," 428.

28. *KSA*, 1:20.

29. Nolte, *Nietzsche*, 147.

30. *KSA*, 6:36–7, 39, 357–64.

31. Nolte, *Nietzsche*, 56.

32. This is my argument in *Idealism Debased*, 159.

33. The quote is taken from Mosse's review of *Homosexualität in der NS-Zeit*, ed. Günter Grau, in *Central European History* 26, no. 3 (1996): 368. Mosse viewed Nazism as the radicalized and corrupted expression of a bourgeois morality and respectability intent upon cleansing the world of any outsiders who could not be "normalized." See, in particular, his *Respectability and Abnormal Sexuality in Modern Europe* (New York: Howard Fertig, 1985) and *Nazism: A Historical and Comparative Analysis of National Socialism* (New Brunswick, N.J.: Transaction, 1978).

34. *KSA*, 6:21.

35. On Nietzsche's pragmatism and perspectivism see, for instance, Richard Rorty's *Contingency, Irony and Solidarity* (Cambridge: Cambridge University Press, 1989) and *Objectivity, Relativism and Truth* (Cambridge: Cambridge University Press, 1991). See also his articles, "The Contingency of Selfhood" and "The Contingency of Language" in the *London Review of Books*, May 8, 1986 and April 17, 1986.

36. *Heidegger: Politik und Geschichte im Leben und Denken* (Berlin: Propyläen, 1992), esp. 296. See also the review by Thomas Sheehan, *New York Review* (January 14, 1993), 30–35, and the exchange of letters, April 8, 1993. See also the chapter on Heidegger in Nolte's *Geschichtsdenken im 20. Jahrhundert* (Berlin: Propyläen, 1991).

37. Aschheim, *The Nietzsche Legacy*, 8.

38. The leading orthodox Marxist treatments of Nietzsche are Georg Lukács, *Die Zerstörung der Vernunft*, vol. 2, *Irrationalismus und Imperialismus* (1954; reprint, Darmstadt: Luchterhand, 1974), esp. 7–87; English version, *The Destruction of Reason*, trans. Peter Palmer (Atlantic Highlands, N.J.: Humanities Press, 1980); and Franz Mehring and Georg Lukács, *Friedrich Nietzsche* (Berlin: Aufbau, 1957).

WORKS OF NIETZSCHE CITED

Kritische Gesamtausgabe der Werke Nietzsches. Edited by Giorgio Colli and Mazzino Montinari. Berlin: de Gruyter, 1967.

Kritische Studienausgabe. Edited by Giorgio Colli and Mazzino Montinari. Berlin: de Gruyter, 1967.

Sämtliche Briefe: Kritische Studienausgabe. Edited by Giorgio Colli and Mazzino Montinari. Berlin: de Gruyter, 1975–84

Antichrist, The. In *The Portable Nietzsche.* Trans. and ed. Walter Kaufmann. New York: Viking, 1954.

Basic Writings of Nietzsche. Translated by Walter Kaufmann. New York: Random House, 1968.

Beyond Good and Evil. Trans. Walter Kaufmann. New York: Random House, 1966.

Birth of Tragedy, The. Trans. Walter Kaufmann. New York: Random House, 1967. *Case of Wagner, The.* Published together with *The Birth of Tragedy* in one volume.

Daybreak. Trans. R. J. Hollingdale. Cambridge: Cambridge University Press, 1982.

Ecce Homo. Trans. Walter Kaufmann. New York: Vintage, 1967.

Gay Science, The. Trans. Walter Kaufmann. New York: Random House, 1974.

Human, All Too Human. Trans. R. J. Hollingdale. Cambridge: Cambridge University Press, 1986.

Nietzsche contra Wagner. In *The Portable Nietzsche.*

On the Genealogy of Morals. Trans. and ed. Walter Kaufmann. New York: Random House, 1967.

"Schopenhauer as Educator." The third of *Nietzsche's Untimely Meditations.* Trans. R. J. Hollingdale. Cambridge: Cambridge University Press, 1983.

Thus Spoke Zarathustra. In *The Portable Nietzsche.*

Twilight of the Idols. In *The Portable Nietzsche.*

Will to Power, The. Trans. Walter Kaufmann and R. J. Hollingdale. New York: Random House, Vintage, 1967.

SELECT BIBLIOGRAPHY

The editors would like to thank Professor Earl R. Nitschke of The Enigma Library (Michigan) for his help in locating some of the bibliographical items.

Acéphale. Réparation à Nietzsche. Paris, January 1937. Double-issue with contributions by Georges Bataille, Pierre Klossowski, Jean Rollin, and Jean Wahl.

Algermissen, Konrad. *Nietzsche und das dritte Reich*. Celle: Joseph Giesel, 1946.

———. "Did Nietzsche Cause the War?" *Educational Review* 48 (1914): 353–57.

Ansell-Pearson, Keith. *Nietzsche contra Rousseau*. Cambridge: Cambridge University Press, 1991.

———. *An Introduction to Nietzsche as Political Thinker*. Cambridge: Cambridge University Press, 1994.

Appel, Frederick. *Nietzsche contra Democracy*. Ithaca: Cornell University Press, 1999.

Aschheim, Steven E. *The Nietzsche Legacy in Germany, 1890–1990*. Berkeley: University of California Press, 1992.

———. "Nietzsche, Anti-Semitism and Mass Murder." In his *Culture and Catastrophe*, 69–84. London: Macmillan, 1996.

———. 'Nietzsche, Anti-Semitism and the Holocaust." In *Nietzsche and Jewish Culture*, edited by Jacob Golomb, 3–20. London: Routledge, 1997.

Barker, Ernest, "Nietzsche and Treitschke: The Worship of Power in Modern Germany." *Oxford Pamphlets*, no. 20. Oxford: Oxford University Press, 1914.

Barthel, E. *Nietzsche als Verführer*. Baden-Baden: Hans Bähler Junior, 1947.

Bataille, Georges. "Nietzsche et les fascistes (1937), *Œuvres complètes*, 447–465. Paris, 1970.

———. "Nietzsche and the Fascists." In *Visions of Excess: Selected Writings 1927–1939*, edited by A. Stockl, 182–196. Manchester: Manchester University Press, 1985.

Bauer, Martin. "Zur Genealogie von Nietsches Kraftbegriff." *Nietzsche Studien* 13 (1984): 211–227.

Bäumler, Alfred. *Nietzsche der Philosoph und Politiker*. Leipzig: Reclam, 1931.

———. "Nietzsche und der Nationalsozialismus." In *Studien zur deutschen Geistesgeschichte*, 281–94. Berlin: Junker und Dannhaupt, 1937.

Bergmann, Peter. *Nietzsche: The "Last Anti-Political German."* Bloomington: Indiana University Press, 1987.

Berkowitz, Peter. *Nietzsche: The Ethics of an Immoralist*. Cambridge: Harvard University Press, 1995.

Bernhard, H. "Nietzsche und die Juden." In *Finis Germaniae*, 115–16. Stuttgart: Halsteiner, 1947.

Bertram, Martin. "Nietzsche on the State: Paideia and War." *Systematics* 11 (1973).

"Blaming Nietzsche for it All," *The Literary Digest* 49 (1914): 4 pages.

Blitz, Mark. "Nietzsche and Political Science: The Problem of Politics." *Symposium* 28 (1974): 74–85.

Brennecke, Detlef. "Die Blonde Bestie. Vom Mißverständnis eines Schlagworts." *Nietzsche Studien* 5 (1976): 113–45.

Brinton, Crane. "The National Socialists Use of Nietzsche." *Journal of the History of Ideas* (1940): 131–50.

———. *Nietzsche*, Cambridge: Harvard University Press, 1941.

Camus, Albert. "Nietzsche and Nihilism." In *The Rebel*, translated by A. Bower. New York: Vintage Books, 1956.

Cancik, Hubert. "'Mongols, Semites and the Pure-Bred Greeks': Nietzsche's Handling of the Racial Doctrines of His Time." In *Nietzsche and Jewish Culture*, ed. Jacob Golomb, 55–75. London and New York: Routledge, 1997.

Carlini, Armando. *Filosofia e religione nel pensiero di Mussolini*. Rome, 1934.

Conway, Daniel. W. *Nietzsche and the Political*. London and New York: Routledge, 1997.

———. *Nietzsche's Dangerous Game*. Cambridge: Cambridge University Press, 1997.

Copelston, Frederick. *Friedrich Nietzsche: Philosopher of Culture*. New York: Barnes and Noble, 1975.

Crane, Hart. "The Case against Nietzsche." *The Pagan* nos. 2–3 (April/May 1918): 34–35.

Dannhauser, Werner J. "Friedrich Nietzsche." In *History of Political Philosophy*, edited by Leo Strauss and Joseph Cropsey, 783–803. Chicago: Rand McNally College, 1972.

———. *Nietzsche and the Problem of Socrates*. Ithaca: Cornell University Press, 1974.

Darby, Tom, Béla Egyed, and Ben Jones, eds. *Nietzsche and the Rhetoric of Nihilism: Essays on Interpretation, Language, and Politics*. Ottawa: Carleton University Press, 1989.

Derrida, Jacques. *Otobiographies: L'enseignement de Nietzsche et la politique du nom propre*. Paris: Galilée, 1984.

———. "Otobiographies: The Teaching of Nietzsche and the Politics of the Proper Name." In *The Ear of the Other: Otobiography, Transference, Translation*, translated by Peggy Kamuf and Avital Ronell, edited by Christie V. McDonald. New York: Schocken, 1985), 30.

Detwiler, Bruce. *Nietzsche and the Politics of Aristocratic Radicalism*. Chicago: University of Chicago Press, 1990.

Diethe, Carol. "Nietzsche and Nationalism." *History of European Ideas* 14, no. 2 (1992): 227–34.

Drews, Arthur. "Nietzsche als Philosoph des Nationalsozialismus?" *Nordische Stimmen* 4 (1934): 172–79.

Dürr, Volker. "The Young Nietzsche: Historical Philosophizing, Historical Perspectivism, and the Nationa Socialist Past." In: *Nietzsche: Literatur and Values*, edited by Volker Dürr, Reinhold Grimm, Kathy Harms, 29–40. Madison: University of Wisconsin Press, 1988.

Eckstein, Walter. "Friedrich Nietzsche and the Present-Day Germany." *The Standard* 31, no. 2 (1944).

———. "Friedrich Nietzsche in the Judgment of Posterity." *Journal of the History of Ideas* (1945): 310–24.

Farrenkopf, John. "Nietsche, Spengler and the Politics of Cultural Despair." *Interpretations* 20, no. 2 (1992): 165–85.

Fischer, K. R. "Nazism as a Nietzschean 'Experiment.'" *Nietzsche-Studien* 6 (1977): 116–22.

Fogel, Philip. "Nietzsche and the Present War." *Swansea Review* 23 (1915): 449–57.

Foster, George. "Nietsche and the Great War." *Swansea Review* 28 (1920): 139–51.

Foucault, Michel. "Nietzsche, Freud, Marx." *Cahiers de Royaumont* (Paris, 1967): 183–92.

Galindo, Martha, Zapata. *Triumph des Willens zur Macht: Zur Nietzsche-Rezeption im NS-Staat.* Hamburg: Argument, 1995.

Gentile, Emilio. *The Sacralization of Politics in Fascist Italy.* Translated by Keith Botsford. Cambridge: Harvard University Press, 1996.

Gilman, S. L. 'The Nietzsche Murder Case; or What Makes Dangerous Philosophies Dangerous." In *Difference and Pathology: Stereotypes of Sexuality, Race, and Madness,* 59–75. Ithaca: Cornell University Press, 1985.

Golomb, Jacob. "Jaspers, Mann and the Nazis on Nietzsche and Freud." *Israel Journal for Psychiatry* 18 (1981): 311–26.

———. "Nietzsche on Jews and Judaism." *Archiv für Geschichte der Philosophie* 67 (1985): 139–61.

———. "Nietzsche's Enticing Psychology of Power." In *Nietzsche as Affirmative Thinker,* edited by Yirmiyahu Yovel, 160–82. Dordrecht: Martinus Nijhoff, 1986.

———, ed. *Nietzsche and Jewish Culture.* London and New York: Routledge, 1997; German edition: *Nietzsche und die jüdische Kultur.* Vienna: WUV/Universitätsverlag, 1998.

———, ed. *Nietzsche and Hebrew Culture.* Jerusalem: Hebrew University Magnes Press, 2002; in Hebrew.

Götz, August. *Nietzsche als Ausnahme, zur Zerstörung des Willens zur Macht.* Freiburg: Karl Alber, 1949.

Goyard-Fabre, S. *Nietzsche et la question politique.* Paris: Sirey, 1977.

Groeper, Richard. "Hölderlin und Nietzsche als Künder des 20. Jahrhunderts." *Nationalsozialistisches Bildungswesen* 5 (1940): 406–12.

Günther, Joachim. "Nietzsche und der Nationalsozialismus." *Nationalsozialistische Monatshefte* 2 (1931): 560–63.

Habermas, Jürgen. *Die Neue Unübersichtlichkeit, Kleine Politische Schriften.* Vol. 5. Frankfurt am Main, 1985.

———. "The Entry into Postmodernity: Nietzsche as a Turning Point." In *The Philosophical Discourse of Modernity,* Translated by F. Lawrence, 83–105. Oxford: Polity Press, 1987.

———. *Nachmetaphysisches Denken: Philosophische Aufsätze.* Frankfurt: Suhrkamp, 1988.

———, ed. *Friedrich Nietzsches erkenntnistheoretische Schriften.* Frankfurt: Suhrkamp, 1968.

Harrison, Thomas, ed., *Nietzsche in Italy.* Saratoga, Calif.: Stanford University Press, 1988.

Härtle, Heinrich. *Nietzsche und der Nationalsozialismus.* Munich, Eher: Zentralverlag der NSDAP, 1937.

Hatab, Lawrence. J. A. *Nietzschean Defense of Democracy: An Experiment in Postmodern Politics*. Chicago: Open Court, 1995.

Heinz, Marion, and Theodor Kisiel. "Heideggers Beziehungen zum Nietzsche-Archiv im Dritten Reich." In *Annäherungen an Martin Heidegger*, edited by H. Schäfer. Frankfurt: Campus, 1996.

Heller, Peter. "Nietzsches Kampf mit dem romantischen Pessimismus." *Nietzsche-Studien*, 7 (1978): 48.

———. "Concerning the Nietzsche Cult and Literary Cults Generally." In *Nietzsche: Literatur and Values*, edited by Volker Dürr, Reinhold Grimm, and Kathy Harms, 199–218. Madison: University of Wisconsin Press, 1988.

Hitler, A. *Mein Kampf*. 2 vols. Munich, 1941.

Hitler's Table Talk. 2nd. ed. Translated by Norman Cameron and R. H. Stevens. London: Weidenfeld & Nicolson, 1973.

Hollingdale, R. J. "The Hero as Outsider." In *The Cambridge Companion to Nietzsche*, edited by Bernd Magnus & Kathleen M. Higgins, 71–89. Cambridge: Cambridge University Press, 1996:

Holub, R. C. "Nietzsche and the Jewish Question." *New German Critique* 22, no. 3 (1995):94–121.

Hunt, Lester. "Politics and Anti-Politics: Nietzsche's View of the State." *History of Philosophy Quarterly* 2, no. 4 (1985): 453–68.

Ibanez-Noe, Javier. "Heidegger, Nietzsche, Jünger and the Interpretation of the Contemporary Age." *Southern Journal of Philosophy* 33 (1995): 57–81.

Jaspers, Karl. "Jaspers Antwort." In *Philosophen des 20. Jahrhunderts, Karl Jaspers*, edited by P. A. Schilpp, 843. Stuttgart, 1957.

Jay, Martin. "Should Intellectual History Take a Linguistic Turn? Reflections on the Habermas-Gadamer Debate." In *Fin-de-Siècle Socialism*, 33. New York: Routledge, 1988.

Jung, Carl Gustav. *Nietzsche's Zarathustra: Notes of the Seminar Given in 1934–1939*, 2 vols., edited by James L. Jarrett. Princeton: Princeton University Press, 1988.

Jünger, Friedrich Georg. *Nietzsche*. Frankfurt, 1949.

Kariel, H. S. "Nietzsche's Preface to Constitutionalism." *Journal of Politics* 25 (1963): 211–25.

———. *In Search of Authority: Twentieth-Century Political Thought*. New York: Free Press, 1964.

Kassler, Kurt. *Nietzsche und das Recht*. Munich, 1941.

Kaufmann, Walter. *Nietzsche: Philosopher, Psychologist, Antichrist*. Princeton: Princeton University Press, 1950.

Kirchoff, J. *Nietzsche, Hitler und die Deutschen*. Berlin: Dionysos, 1990.

Knodt, E. M. "The Janus Face of Decadence: Nietzsche's Genealogy and the Rhetoric of Anti-Semitism." *German Quarterly* 66 (1993): 160–75.

Kohn, H. *The Mind of Germany*. New York, 1960.

Kubizek, August. *The Young Hitler I Knew*. Translated by E. V. Anderson. Boston, 1955.

Kuenzli, Rudolf E. "The Nazi Appropriation of Nietzsche." *Nietzsche Studien* 12 (1983): 428–35.

Lampert, L. *Leo Strauss and Nietzsche*, Chicago: University of Chicago Press, 1996.

Lang, Berel. *Act and Idea in the Nazi Genocide*. Chicago: University of Chicago Press, 1990.

Larmore, Charles. "Nietzsche's Legacy." In *The Morals of Modernity*. Cambridge: Cambridge University Press, 1996.

Laqueur, Walter, ed. *Fascism: A Reader's Guide*. Berkeley: University of California Press, 1976.

Laruelle, François. *Nietzsche contre Heidegger: Thèses pour une politique nietzschéene*. Paris: Payot, 1977.

Lea, F. A. *The Tragic Philosopher: A Study of Friedrich Nietzsche*. London: Methuen, 1957.

Levi, Primo. "Useless Violence:" In *The Drowned and the Saved*. Translated by Raymond Rosenthal. London, 1988: 84–85.

Lichtheim, George. *Europe in the Twentieth Century*. London, 1974.

Lohmann, Elise. *Nietzsche über Krieg und Frieden in seiner Wirkung auf das In- und Ausland*. Munich, 1918.

Lonsbach, R. M. "War Nietzsche ein Wegbereiter des Dritten Reiches? Texte einer Rundfunksendung vom 26.8.1960." In Richard Maximilian Lonsbach (Cahen), *Friedrich Nietzsche und die Juden: Ein Versuch*, 2nd ed., edited by Heinz Robert Schlette. Bonn: Bouvier, 1985.

Love, F. R. *Young Nietzsche and the Wagnerian Experience*. Chapel Hill: University of North Carolina Press, 1963.

Love, N. S. *Marx, Nietzsche, and Modernity*. New York: Columbia University Press, 1996.

Ludovici, A. "Hitler and Nietzsche." *English Review* 64 (January 1937): 44–52 and (February 1937): 192–202.

Lukács, Georg, *Von Nietzsche bis Hitler oder der Irrationalismus und die deutsche Politik*. Berlin: Fischer Bücherei, 1966.

———. *Die Zerstörung der Vernunft*, vol. 2, *Irrationalismus und Imperialismus*. Berlin, 1954; reprint, Darmstadt: Luchterhand, 1974.

———. *The Destruction of Reason*. Translated by Peter Palmer. Atlantic Highlands, N.J.: Humanities Press, 1980.

MacCarthy, Desmond. "Nietzsche and the War." *Experiences* (1935): 194–98.

Magnus, Bernd. "The Use and Abuse of *The Will to Power*." In *Reading Nietzsche*, edited by Robert Solomon and Kathleen M. Higgins, 218–35, Oxford: Oxford University Press, 1988.

Mann, Thomas, *Nietzsches Philosophie im Lichte unserer Erfahrung*. Berlin, 1948.; English edition: "Nietzsche's Philosophy in the Light of Contemporary Events." In Thomas Mann's Addresses: 1942–1949. Washington, D. C.: Library of Congress, 1963.

Marcuse, Ludwig. "Was Nietzsche a Nazi?" *American Mercury* 59 (1944): 737–40.

Martin, Alfred von. *Geistige Wegbereiter des deutschen Zusammenbruchs: Hegel — Nietzsche — Spengler*. Recklinghausen: Bitter, 1948.

McClure, Edmund. *Germany's War-Inspirers: Nietzsche and Treitschke*. 1915.

McGrath, W. J. "Mahler and the Vienna Nietzsche Society." In *Nietzsche and*

Jewish Culture, edited by Jacob Golomb, 218–32. London and New York: Routledge, 1997.

McIntyre A. " 'Virtuosos of Contempt': An Investigation of Nietzsche's Political Philosophy through Certain Platonic Ideas." Nietzsche Studien 21 (1992): 184–210.

Mehring, Franz, and Georg Lukács. *Friedrich Nietzsche*. Berlin: Aufbau, 1957.

Meinecke, Friedrich. *The German Catastrophe: Reflections and Recollections*. Translated by S. F. Fay. Boston: Beacon, 1963.

Michelini, G. *Nietzsche nell'Italia di D'Annuzio*. Palermo: S. F. Flaccovio, 1978.

Middell, Eike. "Totalität und Dekadenz. Zur Auseinandersetzung von Georg Lukács mit Friedrich Nietzsche." *Weimarer Beiträge* 31 (1985): 559–71.

Mittelman, Willard. 'The Relation between Nietzsche's Theory of the Will to Power and His Earlier Conception of Power." *Nietzsche-Studien* 9 (1980): 122–41.

Montinari, Mazzino. "Nietzsche zwischen Alfred Bäumler und Georg Lukács." In *Nietzsche lesen*, 169–206. Berlin: Walter de Gruyter, 1982.

Morgan, George A. *What Nietzsche Means*. Cambridge: Harvard University Press, 1941.

Mosse, George L. *The Crisis of German Ideology*, New York: Grosset & Dunlap, 1964.

———. *Nazi Culture. Intellectual, Cultural and Social Life in the Third Reich*. New York: Schocken, 1981.

Müller, Georg. *Nietzsche und die deutsche Katastrophe*. Gütersloh, 1946.

Münzer, A. *Nietzsche et le Nazisme*. Paris: Kimé, 1995.

Mussolini Benito. *La filosofia della forza* (1908). In *Omnia Opera*, vol. 1. Florence: La Fenice, 1951.

———. *La Volontá di Potenza*, vol. 35 of *Omnia Opera*. Florence: La Fenice, 1962.

Neske, Günther. "Nachwort des Mitherausgebers." In *Antwort: Martin Heidegger im Gespräch*, edited by Günther Neske and Emil Kettering. Pfullingen: Günther Neske, 1988.

Neumann, H. "The Case Against apolitical Morality: Nietzsche's Interpretation of the Jewish Instinct." In *Studies in Nietzsche and the Judaeo-Christian Tradition*, edited by J. C. O'Flaherty, T. F. Sellner, R. M. Helm, 29–46. Chapel Hill: University of North Carolina Press, 1985.

Nicolas, M. P. *From Nietzsche Down to Hitler* [1938]. Translated by E. G. Echlin. Port Washington: Kennikat, 1970.

Nietzsche und Italien: Ein Weg vom Logos zum Mythos? Akten des deusch-italienischen Nietzsche-Koloquiums, Tübingen, 1987, Stauffenburg Colloquium, vol. 14, Tübingen, 1990.

Nolte, Ernst. "Marx und Nietzsche im Sozialismus des jungen Mussolini." *Historische Zeitschrift* 191 (1960): 249–335.

———. *Der Faschismus in seiner Epoche, die Action francaise, der italianische Faschismus, der Nationalsocialismus*. Munich: R. Piper, 1963.

———. *Three Faces of Fascism: Action Française, Italian Fascism, National Socialism*. Translated by Leila Vennewitz. New York: Holt, Rinehart and Winston, 1966.

————. *Der europäsche Bürgerkrieg, 1917–1945: Nationalsozialismus und Bolschewismus.* Berlin: Propyläen, 1987.

————. "A Past that will not Pass Away." *Yad Vashem Studies* 19 (1988), 65–73.

————. *Nietzsche und der Nietzscheanismus.* Frankfurt am Main: Propyläen Verlag, 1990 (includes "Benito Mussolini als Marxist und Nietzscheaner," 260–67).

Oehler, Richard. *Friedrich Nietzsche und die deutsche Zukunft.* Leipzig: Armanen, 1935.

Okonta, Ike. *Nietzsche: The Politics of Power.* New York: Peter Lang, 1992.

Ottmann, Henning. *Philosophie und Politik bei Nietzsche.* Berlin: de Gruyter, 1987.

Pangle, Thomas L. "The Roots of Contemporary Nihilism and Its Political Consequences according to Nietzsche." *Review of Politics* 75 (January 1983): 45–70.

————. "The 'Warrior Spirit' as an Inlet to the Political Philosophy of Nietzsche's Zarathustra." *Nietzsche-Studien* 15 (1986): 140–79.

Parens, Erik. "From Philosophy to Politics: On Nietzsche's Ironic Metaphysics of Will to Power." *Man and World* 24 (1991): 169–80.

————. "Kundera, Nietzsche and Politics: On the Question of Eternal Return and Responsibility." *Philosophy Today* 37, no. 3 (1993): 285–97.

Patton, Paul. "Politics and the Concept of Power in Hobbes and Nietzsche." In *Nietzsche, Feminism and Political Theory,* edited by P. Patton, 144–61. Routledge: London, 1993.

Penzo, Giorgio. *Der Mythos vom Übermenschen: Nietzsche und der Nationalsozialismus.* Translated by B. Hüssler. Berlin: Lang, 1992.

————. "Zur Frage der 'Entnazifizierung' Friedrich Nietzsches." *Vierteljahrshefte für Zeitgeschichte* 34 (January, 1986): 105–16.

Peters, H. F. *Zarathustra's Sister: The Case of Elisabeth and Friedrich Nietzsche.* New York: Crown, 1977.

Pourtalès, Guy de, *Amor fati: Nietzsche in Italien.* Freiburg, 1930.

Pütz, Peter. "The Problem of Force in Nietzsche and His Critics." In *Nietzsche: Literature and Values,* edited by V. Dürr, R. Grimm, and K. Harms, 14–28. Madison: University of Wisconsin Press, 1997.

Rauschning, Hermann. *The Revolution of Nihilism.* New York, 1939.

Read, James. "Nietzsche: Power as Oppression." *Praxis International* 9 (1989): 72–87.

Reschke, R. "Kritische Aneignung und notwendige Auseindersetzung." *Weimarer Beiträge* 29 (1983): 1190–213.

Rich, N. *Hitler's War Aims: The Establishment of the New Order.* New York, 1965.

Roche, Mark. "National Socialism and the Disintegration of Values: Reflections on Nietzsche, Rosenberg, and Broch." *The Journal of Value Inquiry* 26, no. 3 (1992): 367–80.

Roemer, Heinrich. "Nietzsche und das Rassenproblem." *Rasse: Monatschrift für den Nordischen Gedanken* 7 (1940).

Rosenberg, Alfred. *Friedrich Nietzsche: Ansprache bei einer Gedenkstunde anläßlich des 100. Geburtstages Friedrich Nietzsches am 15. October 1944 in Weimar,* Munich: Zentralverlag der NSDAP, Franz Eher Nachfolger, 1944.

————. *Selected Writings*. London, 1970.

Roth, Cecile. *The Myth of the Master Race: Alfred Rosenberg and Nazi Ideology*. New York, 1972.

Salaquarda, Jörg. *Nietzsche*. Darmstadt: Wissenschaftliche Buchgesellschaft, 1980.

Salter, Walter. "Nietzsche and the War." *International Journal of Ethics* (1917): 357–79.

Sandvoss, E. *Hitler und Nietzsche*. Göttingen: Musterschmidt, 1969.

Santaniello, Weaver. *Nietzsche, God, and the Jews: His Critique of Judeo-Christianity in Relation to the Nazi Myth*. Albany: State University of New York Press, 1994.

————. "A Post-Holocaust Re-examination of Nietzsche and the Jews: Vis-à-vis Christendom and Nazism." In *Nietzsche and Jewish Culture*, edited by Jacob Golomb, 21–54 (London and New York: Routledge, 1997).

Schieder, Theodor. "Nietzsche and Bismarck." *The Historian* (1967): 584–604.

Schlechta Karl. "Der Legende und ihre Freunde," In *Der Fall Nietzsche*. Munich, 1959.

Schnapp, Jeffrey. "Nietzsche's Italian Style: Gabriele D'Annuzio." In *Nietzsche in Italy*.

Schroeder, Hans Eggert. *Nietzsche und das Christentum*. Berlin: Lichterfelde, 1937.

Schroeder, R. *Modern Art in the Third Reich*. Offenburg, 1952.

Schutte, Ofelia. "Nietzsche's Politics." *The Journal of the British Society for Phenomenology* 14, no. 2 (1983): 139–56.

————. *Beyond Nihilism. Nietzsche without Masks*. Chicago: University of Chicago Press, 1984.

Slochower, Harry. "Friedrich Nietzsche: The Last Hindenburg Line of Cultural Individualism." In *No Voice is Wholly Lost*, 19–33. London: Dennis Dobson, 1946.

Sluga, Hans. "Fichte, Nietzsche, and the Nazis." In *Heidegger's Crisis: Philosophy and Politics in Nazi Germany*, 29–52. Cambridge: Harvard University Press, 1993.

Sokel, Walter H. "Political Uses and Abuses of Nietzsche in Walter Kaufmann's Image of Nietzsche." *Nietzsche-Studien* 12 (1983): 429–35.

Stackelberg, Roderick. *Idealism Debased. From völkisch Ideology to National Socalism*. Kent: Ohio State University Press, 1981.

————. "Nietzsche and the Nazis: The Völkisch Reaction to Nietzschean Thought." *Research Studies* 51 (March 1983): 36–46.

————. "Nietzsche und der Nationalsozialismus." *Prima Philosophia* 2 (July–September 1989): 425–41.

————. "The Philosopher of Fascism? Nietzsche Through the Eyes of Ernst Nolte." *Platte Valley Review* 22, no. 1 (Winter 1994): 38–47.

Steding, Christoph. *Das Reich und die Krankheit der europäischen Kultur*. Hamburg: Hanseatische Verlagsanstalt, 1938.

Stefani, M. A. *Nietzsche in Italia: Rassegna bibliografica*. Rome: B. Carucci, 1975.

Steiner, George. *In Bluebeard's Castle: Some Notes towards the Re-definition of Culture*. London, 1971.

Stern, Alfred. "Nietzsche and Judaism." *Contemporary Jewish Record* 8 (1945): 31–42.

Stern, F. *The Politics of Cultural Despair*. Berkeley: University of California Press, 1973.

Sternhell, Zeev. "Fascist Ideology." In *Fascism: A Reader's Guide*, edited by Walter Laqueur, 315–76. Berkeley: University of California Press, 1976.

———. *Neither Right nor Left: Fascist Ideology in France*. Berkeley: University of California Press, 1986.

Sternhell, Zeev, with Mario Sznajder and Maia Asheri. *The Birth of Fascist Ideology: From Cultural Rebellion to Political Revolution*. Translated by David Maisel. Princeton: Princeton University Press, 1994.

Stoekl, Allan. "The Death of *Acéphale* and the Will to Chance: Nietzsche in the Text of Bataille." *Glyph* 6 (1979): 42–67.

Strauss, Leo. "Liberal Education and Responsibility." In *Liberalism Ancient and Modern*. Ithaca : Cornell University Press, 1989.

Strong, Tracy B. *Friedrich Nietzsche and the Politics of Transfiguration*. Berkeley: University of California Press, 1975.

———. "Nietzsche's Political Aesthetics." In *Nietzsche's New Seas: Explorations in Philosophy, Aesthetics, and Politics*, edited by Michael Allen Gillespie and Tracy B. Strong, 153–174. Chicago: University of Chicago Press, 1988.

———. "Nietzsche's Political Misappropriations." In *The Cambridge Companion to Nietzsche*, edited by Bernd Magnus and Kathleen M. Higgins, 119–147. Cambridge: Cambridge University Press, 1996.

Talmon, Jacob L. *The Origins of Totalitarian Democracy*. London: Secker and Warburg, 1952.

Taureck, B. *Nietzsche und der Faschismus: Eine Studie über Nietzsches politische Philosophie und ihre Folgen*. Hamburg: Junius, 1989.

Taylor, Seth. *Left-Wing Nietzscheans: The Politics of German Expressionism 1910–1920*. Berlin: de Gruyter, 1990.

Thomas, R. Hinton. *Nietzsche in German Politics and Society 1890–1918*. Manchester: Manchester University Press, 1983.

Trevor-Roper, Hugh. "The Denazification of Nietzsche." *New Statesman* (1965): 443–44.

Vattimo, Gianini. *Il soggetto e la maschera, Nietzsche e il problema della liberazione*. Milano, 1974.

———. *The End of Modernity: Nihilism and Hermeneutics in Post-Modern Culture*. Cambridge: Polity Press, 1988.

———. *The Adventure of Difference: Philosophy after Nietzsche and Heidegger*. Baltimore: Johns Hopkins University Press, 1993.

Viereck, Peter. *Metapolitics: The Roots of the Nazi Mind*. New York: Capricorn, 1941.

Virtranen, Reino. "Nietzsche and the Action Française: Nietzsche's Significance for French Rightists' Thought." *Journal of the History of Ideas* 11 (1950): 191–214.

Waite, Geoffrey. *Nietzsche's Corpse: Aesthetics, Politics, Prohecy, or the Spectacular Technoculture of Everyday Life*. Durham: Duke University Press, 1996.

Waite, Robert L. Hitler: The Psychopathic God. New York, 1977.

Warren, Mark. *Nietzsche and Political Thought*. Cambridge: MIT Press, 1988.

Weichelt, H. *Nietzsche, der Philosoph des Heroismus*. Leipzig: Baußtein, 1924.

Wein, H. "Nietzsche und der faschismus." *Club Voltaire* 4 (1970): 332–41.

Weinrich, M. *Hitler's Professors*. New York, 1946.

Weiss, D. *The Fascist Tradition*. New York, 1967.

Westernhagen, Curt von. *Nietzsche, Juden, Antijuden*. Weimar: A. Duncker, 1936.

Williams, Howard. "Nietzsche and Fascism." *History of European Ideas* 11 (1989): 893–99.

Wistrich, Robert S., ed. *Theories of Fascism*. London: Sage Publications, 1976.

———. *Hitler's Apocalypse*. London: Weidenfeld & Nicolson, 1985.

———. *Between Redemption and Perdition*. London: Routledge, 1990.

———. *Antisemitism: The Longest Hatred*. New York: Pantheon, 1991.

———. *Who's Who in Nazi Germany*, London: Routledge, 1995.

———. "Fascism and the Jews of Italy." in *Fascist Atisemitism and the Italian Jews*, edited by Robert S. Wistrich and Sergio Della Pergola. Jerusalem, 1995.

———. *Weekend in Munich: Art, Propaganda and Terror*. Pavilion Press, 1995.

———. *Hitler and the Holocaust*. New York: Random House, 2001.

Wundt, Wilhelm. *Die Nationen und ihre Philosophie*. Stuttgart, 1941.

Yack, B. *The Longing for Total Revolution: Philosophical Sources of Social Discontent from Rousseau to Marx and Nietzsche*. Princeton: Princeton University Press, 1986.

Yovel, Yirmiyahu. *Dark Riddle: Hegel, Nietzsche, and the Jews*. Cambridge: Polity Press, 1998.

Zimmerman, Michael E. "National Socialism, Nietzsche, and the Work of Art." In *Heidegger's Confrontation with Modernity*. Bloomington and Indianapolis: Indiana University Press, 1990.

INDEX

Adorno, Theodor, 73, 216
aesthetics: D'Annunzio's politics and, 246;
morality, replacement of by, 267–68; nihilism and, 263–64; reality and, 265;
self-objectivization and, 275; of war
and technology, 277–80
Andreas-Salomé, Lou, 110
Ansell-Pearson, Keith, 15n8, 97
Antichrist, The (Nietzsche): Christianity
and Nietzsche's view of the Jews, 116–
20, 154–58, 162–63, 167n48, 191n13;
extermination of the weak and sick,
312; Jews, views of, 109–11, 113; slave
revolt in morality, 125n5
Antisemitic Correspondence (Fritsch),
147–48
anti-Semitism: Förster-Nietzsche's (*see*
Förster-Nietzsche, Elisabeth); as impetus
for interest in the Jews, 111–14;
Nietzsche's, 7, 60, 118–19, 127–28,
149, 158, 225; Nietzsche's anti-anti-
Semitism, 6, 69, 108, 111–14, 132–34,
137–38, 146–48, 151–53, 164, 179,
224, 226, 306–8; power and, 31; Wagner's (*see* Wagner, Richard). *See also*
Jews; race
Arbeiter, Der (Jünger), 270, 280–86
archaeology, metaphor of, 281–82
aristocracy: advocacy of politics of, 92;
D'Annunzio on, 240–41; Mussolini
and, 252; natural inequality and elitist
rule, 55–57, 153–54; natural order of,
121; order of rank, 102–3, 197–98,
210; others, attitude towards, 97; right
to rule of the, 3. *See also* evil heroes; inequality; nobility
asceticism, 27–29
Aschheim, Steven, 9, 58, 169n74, 215,
301–2, 317n10
Augier, M., 286
autonomy, heteronomy, distinguished
from, 30–31
Aveux de l'Ingrat (D'Annunzio), 244

Barthel, Ernst, 199
Bataille, Georges, 6, 162, 169n72

Bäumler, Alfred: anti-anti-Semitism of
Nietzsche, 307; appropriation of
Nietzsche for Nazis, 5, 42n1, 43–44n14,
147, 215, 293–95; interpretation of
Nietzsche compared to that of Lukács,
84–85; mythical language, use of, 282;
nationalist interpretation of Nietzsche,
59; and the Nietzsche-Hölderlin nexus,
200, 202; Nietzsche's disappointment at
reception in Germany, 69; racial inter-
pretation of Nietzsche, 46n36; the Reich,
Nietzsche's denunciation of, 309; scholarly credentials of, 293; will to power,
ideas of, 293
Bayreuth Festival. *See* Wagner, Richard
Bebel, August, 307
Beck, Lewis White, 293
Benjamin, Walter, 161, 242
Benn, Gottfried, 161–62
Berdyczewski, Micha Josef, 161
Bergmann, Peter, 190–91n5, 309–10
Berkowitz, Peter, 16n8
Bertram, Ernst, 208
Beyond Good and Evil (Nietzsche): aristocracy, 92; caves of the hermit-
philosopher, 82; democracy, 296; free
spirits, affiliation with, 78–79; future
philosophers, commanding and legislating authority of, 80; Germans and Jews,
151; Gods as philosophers, 88n43;
Jews, role in European development,
178; Jews, views of, 108, 156–57, 160;
Mussolini's reading of, 248; nobility, expression of, 94; slave revolt in morality,
125n5, 167n47; types of morality, 36
Birth of Tragedy, The (Nietzsche): aftermath of publication, 225–26; Dionysian, presentation of, 41, 77, 87n33;
nihilism, 112; overcoming of positions
in, 128; romantic nationalism, subsequent repudiation of, 310; the tragic
hero, 92; Wagner in, 69, 128, 137, 150
Bismark, Otto Eduard Leopold von, 11,
175, 177
Bizet, Georges, 130, 150
Blanchot, Maurice, 74